Aging Independently

Living Arrangements and Mobility

K. Warner Schaie, Ph.D., is the Evan Pugh Professor of Human Development and Psychology and Director of the Gerontology Center at Pennsylvania State University. He also holds an appointment as Affiliate Professor of Psychiatry and Behavioral Science at the University of Washington. He received the Kleemeier Award for Distinguished Research Contributions from the Gerontological Society of America and the Distinguished Scientific Contributions award from the American Psychological Association. He is author or editor of 32 books including the textbook *Adult Development and Aging* (with S. L. Willis) and the *Handbook of the Psychology of Aging* (with J. E. Birren), both of which are now in their 5th edition. He has directed the Seattle Longitudinal Study of cognitive aging since 1956. His current research interest is the life course of adult intelligence, its antecedents and modifiability, as well as methodological issues in the developmental sciences.

Hans-Werner Wahl, Dr. Phil., is Professor of Social and Environmental Gerontology and Chair of the Department of Social and Environmental Gerontology at the German Centre for Research on Ageing at the University of Heidelberg. His current research interests cover conceptual and empirical issues of environmental gerontology, the psychosocial consequences of age-related vision loss, and the everyday competence of older adults and appropriate intervention strategies. He is the author or coauthor or the editor or coeditor of 10 books and over 100 journal articles and chapters related to the study of human aging. He was awarded the Max-Bürger-Preis for outstanding research in gerontology from the German Society of Gerontology and Geriatrics.

Heidrun Mollenkopf, Dr. Phil., is Senior Researcher at the German Centre for Research on Ageing (DZFA) at the University of Heidelberg, Department of Social and Environmental Gerontology. Her main research interest is the interplay among personal, societal, technical, and environmental conditions with regard to maintaining autonomy and social participation and, by this, quality of life in old age. She has been in charge of large-scale research projects on the outdoor mobility of older people and on technology and aging, and she has published widely in these fields. She was the German delegate to the European COST A5 program "Ageing and Technology," and she was a member in the European Commission's ETAN (European Technology Assessment Network) Expert working group.

Frank Oswald, Dr. Phil., is Senior Researcher at the German Centre for Research on Ageing at the University of Heidelberg, Department for Social and Environmental Gerontology. His research interests are the context of adult development, person-environment transaction, and housing and relocation in old age. He has completed studies on the subjective experience of home and on relocation from home to home, and he is currently involved in two European studies on mobility and housing in old age. He is coeditor of 3 books and the author/coauthor of several articles and chapters in the area of environmental gerontology. He is a member of the editorial board of the Journal of Housing for the Elderly.

Aging Independently
Living Arrangements and Mobility

K. Warner Schaie ▪ Hans-Werner Wahl
Heidrum Mollenkopf ▪ Frank Oswald

Editors

 Springer Publishing Company

Springer Publishing Company, Inc.
536 Broadway
New York, NY 10012

Acquisitions Editor: Ursula Springer
Production Editor: Sara Yoo/Matt Fenton
Cover design by Joanne Honigman

01 02 03 04 05/5 4 3 2 1

Library of Congress Cataloging-in-Publication Data

Aging independently : living arrangements and mobility / K. Warner
Schaie . . . [et al.].
    p. cm.
    Includes bibliographical references and index.
    ISBN 0-8261-1854-2
    1. Aged—Housing. 2. Aged—Orientation and mobility. 3.
Aging—Environmental aspects. 4. Congregate housing. 5. Living alone.
I. Schaie, K. Warner (Klaus Warner), 1928–
HQ1063.A36 2003
305.26—dc21
                                                      2003042789

Printed in the United States of America by Integrated Book Technology

Contents

PART III: AGING INDEPENDENTLY "INDOORS": LIVING ARRANGEMENTS

PART IV: AGING INDEPENDENTLY "OUTDOORS": MOBILITY

PART V: FUTURE PERSPECTIVES OF AGING
INDEPENDENTLY: COMBINING PERSPECTIVES OF
AGING INSIDE AND OUTSIDE THE HOME

Contributors

Neil Charness is Professor of Psychology in the Psychology Department at Florida State University. He is also an Associate of the Pepper Institute on Aging and Public Policy at Florida State University. He received his Ph.D. from Carnegie Mellon University in Pittsburgh, Pennsylvania, in 1974. His current research interests concern age and human factors in technology use, and age and expert performance. He is the author/coauthor of 3 books and over 70 journal articles and chapters related to aging. He is a Fellow of the Canadian Psychological Association, the American Psychological Association (Division 20: Adult Development and Aging), the American Psychological Society, and the Gerontological Society of America.

Berthold Färber is Professor for Human Factors at the University of the Bundeswehr, Munich. He holds a diploma in psychology, received his Ph.D. from the University of Regensburg, and received his habilitation for general and applied psychology from the University of Tübingen. His research interests cover traffic safety, human-centered interfaces for new technologies, and telerobotics. He has been involved in European projects for the enhancement of mobility and safety, including PROMETHEUS, DRIVE, and MOTIV. He is cooperating with all leading car manufacturers and suppliers to design and evaluate telematic systems. He also gives lectures on man-machine-interface, work psychology, and traffic system technology.

James L. Fozard has conducted research on aging and the development of national programs of long-term health care for older people for more than 30 years. He is best known for his work with longitudinal studies of aging including the VA Normative Aging Study and the National Institute on Aging Baltimore Longitudinal Study of Aging, which he directed for 13 years. Author of over 160 articles and chapters, Fozard was a member of the faculty of the Johns Hopkins University School of Hygiene and Public Health for

10 years and the Psychiatry Department of Harvard Medical School for 12. He received his doctorate in experimental psychology from Lehigh University and did his postdoctoral training at the Massachusetts Institute of Technology. His scientific autobiography, "How Ten Years with Ageless Albino Rats and College Sophomores Led to a 30-Something Year Career in Geropsychology," appears in J. E. Birren and J. F. Schroots (eds.), *A History of Geropsychology through Autobiography*.

Laura N. Gitlin is Interim Codirector and Director of Research of the Senior Health Institute, Jefferson Health System. She is also Director of the Community and Homecare Research Division, and Professor in the Department of Occupational Therapy, College of Health Professions, Thomas Jefferson University, Philadelphia, Pennsylvania. Her research interests include adaptation to disability, family caregiving, home modification and assistive technology use, and home-based interventions. She is the author of 2 books and another forthcoming on physical function in the elderly and more than 70 journal articles and chapters related to the study of family caregivers, device use among the elderly, and home interventions to improve the well-being of elders. Gitlin is the principal investigator and consultant on numerous studies funded by the National Institute on Aging, other federal agencies, and foundations. Recently, she was inducted into the Academy of Research of the American Occupational Therapy Foundation for outstanding research contributions to occupational therapy.

Klaus Großjohann is Managing Director of the German Foundation for the Care of Older People (Kuratorium Deutsche Altershilfe or KDA) in Cologne, the leading non-profit-making, independent consultant for the care and support of the elderly in Germany. He studied sociology, psychology, and political economics in Cologne, Bonn, Berlin, and Cambridge, Massachusetts, and received his degree in sociology from the Freie Universität Berlin. As project manager, and in cooperation with diverse research establishments, he was involved in investigations concerning health, social policy, and social gerontology. He is the author of several publications in this field. More recently, he has been a member of the second, third, and current fourth Commission of the German Federal Government on the situation of older people, and he is vice president of Eurolink Age—a network of organizations and individuals which promotes good policy and practice on aging in the interests of older people in the European Union.

Elke Jansen works as a scientific assistant for the Zentrum für Evaluation und Methoden (ZEM) at the University of Bonn. She received her Ph.D in psychology at the University of Bonn in 2002. At present she manages the interdisciplinary research project FRAME, which investigates leisure-time mobility of elderly people. She also works as an independent psychotherapist.

Paul P. Jovanis is Professor of Civil and Environmental Engineering at Pennsylvania State University, State College, Pennsylvania. He received his Ph.D. in civil engineering from the University of California at Berkeley in 1980. His current research interests focus on a human-centered view of transportation services including older traveler mobility and safety; use, safety, and perception of intelligent transportation systems; and safety of motor carrier driving hours of service. He has advised government organizations at the local, state, and national level in highway safety and intelligent transportation. He has published over 100 papers in these areas, including several which were heavily cited in a recent proposed government rulemaking concerning driving hours.

Günter Kroj is Director of the Behaviour and Safety Department at the Federal Highway Research Institute (BASt). He received his Ph.D. in natural sciences from the University of Bergisch Gladbach, Germany, and his Professor in Psychology from the University of Wuppertal. Between 1990 and 1996, he chaired the Section of German Traffic Psychologists in the Association of German Psychologists. Since 1996, he has been a board member of the Forum of European Road Safety Research Institutes (FERSI). He was the chairman of international and national working parties as well as of workshops and conferences on Interdisciplinary Road Safety Research, and he has published about 200 reports, studies, journal articles, and books in the field of traffic psychology, accident research, and the evaluation of traffic safety programs. He chaired the expert group that drafted the recent German Road Traffic Safety Programme set up by the German Federal Ministry of Transport, Building, and Housing in February 2001.

Andreas Kruse, from 1993 to 1996, was Director of the Institute of Psychology at the University of Greifswald; since 1997, he has been Director of the Institute of Gerontology at the University of Heidelberg. His fields of research include competence, rehabilitation, coping with borderline situations, and care systems for the chronically and terminally ill. He was a member of the first and second and chair of the third Expert Commission on Aging of the Government of the Federal Republic of Germany. He was a member of the Technical Committee of the United Nations concerned with developing the International Agenda of Action on Aging. He has received several national awards for medicine and gerontology, as well as the First Presidential Award of the International Association of Gerontology.

Sibylle Meyer received her Ph.D. in sociology at the Free University of Berlin, Germany. She has worked as a research fellow with the Institut für Zukunftsstudien und Technologiebewertung and with the Technical University of Berlin. Since 1993 she has been, together with Dr. Eva Schulze, Director of the Berlin Institute for Social Research (BIS). She has written numerous books and articles on housework, family, gerontechnology, and new technology and services for private households.

Victor Regnier holds a professorship between the School of Architecture and Gerontology at the University of Southern California in Los Angeles. From 1992 until 1996, he served as Dean of the School of Architecture. He has published 6 books that deal with various aspects of housing for the elderly. In 1999 he received the Gerontological Society of America's Polisher Award for applied research. In 2000 *Contemporary Long Term Care* selected him as one of 5 national leaders whose work has made a difference in the quality of life of older people. As a researcher he has directed 21 projects dealing with the social and behavioral impact of the environment on older people. As a designer he has provided consultation advice on over 250 buildings in 35 states, Canada, Germany, Japan, and England. He is the only person to have achieved fellowship status in both the American Institute of Architects and the Gerontological Society of America.

Graham D. Rowles is Professor of Geography, Behavioral Science, and Nursing; Director of the Ph.D. Program in Gerontology; and Associate Director of the Sanders-Brown Center on Aging at the University of Kentucky. He received his Ph.D. in geography from Clark University in Worcester, Massachusetts. His research focuses on the experience of aging in different environmental contexts. He has conducted in-depth ethnographic research with elderly populations in urban (inner city), rural (Appalachian), and nursing facility environments. His publications include *Prisoners of Space? Exploring the Geographical Experience of Older People* and 4 coedited volumes in addition to more than 50 book chapters and articles. He is a fellow of the Gerontological Society of America and the Association for

Gerontology in Higher Education. Rowles received the 1987 Distinguished Academic Gerontologist Award of the Southern Gerontological Society, and in 2001 he received a Leadership Service Commendation from the American Occupational Therapy Foundation.

Georg Rudinger is Professor of Psychology at the University of Bonn. His main research interests are longitudinal design, analysis, and methodology across the life span (e.g., Cross-European Longitudinal Study of Aging, funded by the European Union); research in the field of applied psychology and multimedia (e.g., Aging and Technology, Likeable and Usable Service Interfaces; Multilateral Security in e-Communication); and mobility and transport (e.g., Seniors in the Future Traffic and Transport System; In-Vehicle-Safety-Devices; Leisure Time Mobility of the Elderly; and Sustainable Transport: Links and Liaisons to America). He has been a guest professor at UCLA, Free University of Berlin, Pennsylvania University, University of Geneva, University of Leipzig (Wilhelm-Wundt-Professor), and University of Leiden. He established the Center of Evaluation and Methodology (CEM) as a unit of the Faculty of Arts and Humanities of the University of Bonn; since April 2000, he has been Dean of the Faculty of Arts and Humanities.

Bernhard Schlag is the Chair of Traffic and Transportation Psychology at the Dresden University of Technology. He received his Ph.D. from the University of Essen. Schlag lectures on general psychology and traffic psychology. He has carried out nearly 50 empirical research projects on behalf of German Federal ministeries, the Commission of the European Community, and industrial partners dealing with mobility and traffic behavior; risk and accident analyses for children, young drivers, and older people; acceptance of innovations; and attitude and behavior change. He has published about 180 papers in scientific journals, monographs, and books. He is a member of the advising groups of the German Federal and Saxonian ministeries. The staff of the Chair of Traffic and Transportation Psychology comprises 9 scientists—6 psychologists, 1 economist, and 2 traffic engineers—enabling an interdisciplinary approach to questions of mobility.

Jane C. Stutts is Manager of Epidemiological Studies at the University of North Carolina Highway Safety Research Center (HSRC). She received her undergraduate degree in psychology from Wake Forest University and her Ph.D. in epidemiology from the University of North Carolina at Chapel Hill. During her 26-year tenure at HSRC she has managed projects spanning a wide range of highway safety areas. Recent research efforts have focused on older drivers, driver distraction, drowsy driving, pedestrian and bicyclist safety, and novice driver education. Her work in the older driver area has emphasized the dual goals of safety and mobility for the aging population.

Patricia F. Waller is Senior Research Scientist at the Texas Transportation Institute Center for Transportation Safety. She was Director of the Transportation Research Institute at the University of Michigan from 1989 to 1999 and is now Senior Research Scientist Emerita and Professor Emerita at the University of Michigan. Previously she was Associate Director for Driver Studies at the University of North Carolina Highway Safety Research Center, Research Professor in the University of North Carolina School of Public Health, and founding director of the University of North Carolina Injury Prevention Research Center. She has been active in the field of transportation and injury control since 1967. Her special interests include older drivers, alcohol and driving, young novice drivers, heavy truck safety, and driver licensing. She is especially interested in integrating injury control and health and human dimensions into national transportation policy.

John F. Watkins is Associate Professor on the faculties of Geography and Gerontology at the University of Kentucky, where he also serves as Director of Graduate Studies in the Ph.D. program in Gerontology. He received his Ph.D. from the University of Colorado-Boulder, specializing in mathematical demography with an emphasis on multistate/multiregional life table and projection models and analyses of complex migration systems. His work includes international examinations of comparative elderly migration networks, family survival strategies and mobility in several Southeast Asian countries, and elderly migration and development outcomes in the United States. His current research employs life history narratives to study notions of the spatial life course and the impact of cumulative place experience on the emergence and transferal of home.

Gerald D. Weisman is Professor of Architecture and Codirector of the Institute on Aging and Environment at the University of Wisconsin-Milwaukee. He received his Ph.D. from the University of Michigan and taught previously at Kansas State and Pennsylvania State Universities. His research interests focus on therapeutic environments for the cognitively impaired and the linkages between architectural research and practice. *Holding on to Home: Designing Environments for People with Dementia*, coauthored by Weisman and Uriel Cohen, was the recipient of a citation in the annual *Progressive Architecture* Awards Program and one of two awards in its category in the American Institute of Architects International Design Book Fair competition. Weisman's work—through the Institute on Aging and Environment at the University of Wisconsin-Milwaukee—has been funded by the American Institute of Architects/Association of Collegiate Schools of Architecture Health Facilities Research Program, the National Office of the Alzheimer's Association, the Helen Bader Foundation, the National Endowment for the Arts, and the Retirement Research Foundation.

Sherry L. Willis, Professor of Psychology at the Pennsylvania State University, earned her Ph.D. in educational psychology from the University of Texas at Austin. Her work has contributed much to the study of cognitive training of older adults. The everyday life experiences of the elderly have been a more recent subject of interest for Willis. She is currently involved in the ongoing ACTIVE study, a controlled trial to test for the effects of different cognitively oriented interventions.

Preface

The idea driving this book is the belief that older people play a critical role in community life and in sustainable community development. Equally important is the fact that aging takes place primarily in the community context. This context provides, as is so often pointed out by M. Powell Lawton, major opportunities as well as constraints for a "good life in old age." More specifically, we believe that living arrangements, living environments, outdoor mobility, and outdoor activities play an important role in aging independently. Living arrangements in old age are characterized by rapidly evolving new options for different patterns of everyday life. Remaining in familiar, sustainable, and well-designed homes is crucial for ensuring autonomy in old age. Outdoor mobility is one of the major challenges facing older adults as well as our whole society. The characteristics of the environment and neighborhood are of particular importance for ensuring mobility in old age when driving is no longer an option. Considering the future of aging theoretically from an environmental gerontology perspective and practically in terms of available technology, the central assumption of this volume is that future "indoor" and "outdoor" environments will become much more intertwined than is the case today. For example, the Internet probably will lead to a new understanding of distance and nearness even in the presence of severe, chronic illness. Hence, merging both of these concerns—living arrangements and mobility—in one volume was an innovative and stimulating enterprise for the authors of this book, and it is our hope that our readers will share this experience.

The book's substance is based on the conference "Aging in the Community: Living Arrangements and Mobility," held in April 2001 in Heidelberg, Germany, and organized by the German Center for Research on Aging at the University of Heidelberg in cooperation with Pennsylvania State University. The conference as well as the preparation of this book received substantial financial support from the German Research Council and the

German-American Academic Council. Additional financial support was provided by the mayor of Heidelberg, the Beamten-Wohnungsgesellschaft Dr. Buschmann, the SRH-Gruppe, and the Schering Forschungsgesellschaft.

It is always difficult to convey the full flavor of a conference. A special feature of this one was a very stimulating interaction between senior and junior scientists as well as between academics and applied researchers. The appendix therefore gives a full listing of all persons contributing to the conference. It is our hope to provide a glimpse into the dynamic interchange via the conceptual papers, state-of the-art reviews, and empirical data gathered in this volume. All of these contributions received a rigorous peer-review process involving all of the participating authors, which led to major revisions and improvements of the material originally presented.

Another unique feature of this book is that it includes a mix of authors from the United States and Germany. There were historical as well as content-related reasons for this. The Heidelberg conference, the basis for this book, was originally designed as an effort to promote linkages between American and German scientists and to foster a collaboration between junior scientists from both countries. Living arrangements as well as issues of outdoor mobility show quite striking similarities and differences between the two cultures (e.g., in terms of attachment to place and automobile driving). It seemed important therefore to explore whether these similarities also hold true for older adults. As for living arrangements, although the cultural background of housing is similar in the United States and Germany (private homes, oriented to the needs of the individual or the family), reasons for moving in old age might be different owing to different habits, environmental opportunities, and distances. There is also a high standard of personal transportation infrastructure in both countries. However, there are pronounced differences between the countries in the availability of public transportation and the importance of driving for ensuring independence in later life.

This book is divided into five parts. Part I introduces the volume with discussions of indoor and outdoor needs of elderly people within their environment. Part II provides the reader with a gamut of basic considerations concerned with aging in socio-physical environments framed within a diversity of scientific disciplines. The book's main topics, living arrangements and mobility, are then treated separately in the two following sections. Thus, Part III focuses on more detailed views of living arrangements, with the goal of specifying the indoor-related needs of older adults. Part IV strives to analyze outdoor-related needs of the older person with particular emphasis on the dynamics of assessing and using the environment through mobility.

Finally, Part V highlights future perspectives of aging independently and ends with a concluding chapter designed to discuss and integrate the contents of the book as a whole.

That said, it seems very obvious that the issues covered in this volume heavily echo the efforts of M. Powell Lawton toward acknowledging societal and community context for securing a good life in old age. Thus, it is only natural that we should dedicate this book to Dr. Lawton, who passed away in January 2001.

K. Warner Schaie, Hans-Werner Wahl,
Heidrun Mollenkopf, and Frank Oswald

PART I

Setting the Field

CHAPTER 1

Research on Living Arrangements in Old Age for What?

Hans-Werner Wahl

The purpose of this chapter is to convey the general message that a person's living arrangement is an important and critical facet of aging in the community as well as of gerontology, particularly *environmental gerontology* (e.g., Wahl, 2001a, 2001b). In order to do so, the chapter reviews issues concerned with living environments, a term used interchangeably with the term living arrangements in this chapter, at a rather general level. Many of the themes mentioned here will be treated in more detail and illustrated with more empirical data in the remaining sections of this book (particularly in those chapters concerned with the living environments of older people).

To start with, living environments represent those places where older people spend their lives and experience their aging, as has been demonstrated by a large body of research on time budgets and daily activities (e.g., Baltes, Maas, Wilms, & Borchelt, 1999; Baltes, Wahl, & Schmid-Furstoss, 1990; Moss & Lawton, 1982). The living environments of older people have many facets and serve a variety of functions. They are places of bonding and making personal attachments, places to experience the feeling of being at home, places of materialized biography, places for reminiscence, and places to express personal lifestyles. They provide opportunities to live as independently as possible and ensure the privacy of life and aging, but they are also places of loneliness and the experience of chronic conditions, of dying and death. Hence, living environments provide a very important physical and spatial structure of opportunities and constraints for the course and outcomes of aging.

The importance of the environment for the aging individual has been described as a Gestalt switch which must be made by researchers as well as practitioners by focusing upon the environment and then examining other dimensions of the older person as background characteristics (Bell, Fisher, & Loomis, 1978). Obviously, both the person and the environment are essential components of the "ecological equation" (Lawton, 1982; Lawton & Nahemow, 1973), and consideration of their interaction (or, as it is often called, transaction; see Parmelee & Lawton, 1990) probably is the most intriguing question for environmental gerontology theory and research. For the present volume, however, it is essential to make a second kind of Gestalt switch, namely, to emphasize the outdoor environment with its opportunities and constraints in lieu of the indoor environment in old age. Obviously again, there is also a relation between both the "indoor" and "outdoor" environment thus leading, in principal terms, to a triple interaction of person × indoor setting × outdoor setting. Addressing this complex relationship instead of treating settings as separate entities is another intriguing question of environmental gerontology.

Exploration of the general importance of living environments for aging in the community can take advantage of a basic distinction suggested by Birren (1996): that between the aged, aging, and age. First, the nature of living arrangements can be seen as a major characteristic of the *aged* (i.e., these arrangements are a crucial social characteristic, indicator, and major determinant of the objective life quality of elders). They provide developmental opportunities and constraints in a very realistic, day-to-day sense. Second, living environments also play a substantial role in their contribution to a better understanding of *aging* as a process. An interesting issue from a life-span developmental perspective concerns the question of "critical phases" during adulthood and old age, in which physical and spatial environmental opportunities and constraints strongly impact upon the aging individual's developmental trajectories and the fulfillment of personal goals in life (e.g., the challenge for an elderly woman, living alone, managing a large household after the occurrence of major disability). Furthermore, living environments play a somewhat different role for the aging of the relatively healthy and competent young-old population (where they primarily assume a stimulating function), compared to the frailer old-old population (where they primarily assume a supportive function). Third, the living arrangements of older people, including environments that have been specifically designed to accommodate the growing diversification and heterogeneity of the elderly (such as assisted living facilities), help us define *age* as a crucial social category of present and future societies.

In the next section of this chapter, following a brief historical overview, a profile of environmental gerontology is suggested based on answers regarding 2 questions critical for the field: (1) What rationale lies behind environmental gerontology, and what are the main challenges of the field? (2) How has current research in environmental gerontology embraced this rationale and addressed the concomitant tasks? In the final section of the chapter, my answers to both of these questions will be used to explore a third question critical for the field: What are future tasks for environmental gerontology? Synergies that result from considering "indoor" and "outdoor" perspectives of aging in the community at the same time, the approach taken in this book, will be treated as an essential aspect of future gerontological research.

ON THE ROLE OF ENVIRONMENTAL GERONTOLOGY WITHIN CURRENT GERONTOLOGY

A brief historical overview will help anchor environmental gerontology within the gerontology research enterprise. The chapter written by Kleemeier (1959) in the *Handbook of Aging and the Individual* can be seen, in a sense, as the "birth" of environmental gerontology. In the 1960s, the first large environmental gerontology data sets (such as Carp, 1966) were generated. Beginning in the early 1970s, the need to understand better the rapidly growing mountain of data became a priority. Lawton and Nahemow's (1973) proposal of the Press-Competence Model is a classic example. Other landmark book chapters were written by Carp (1987) in the influential *Handbook of Environmental Psychology*, Lawton (1977) in the first edition of the *Handbook of the Psychology of Aging*, and Scheidt and Windley (1985) in the second edition of the *Handbook of the Psychology of Aging*. The application of major environmental gerontology findings was discussed in an exemplary contribution by Lawton (1980). Since the 1970s, environmental gerontology has been clearly accepted as a major field of gerontology, and it is well represented in major gerontology textbooks around the world.

Rationale Behind Environmental Gerontology and Main Challenges in the Field

Acknowledging the Physical-Spatial Context of Aging

It is now common in social and psychological gerontology to consider ongoing changes in the interaction of the aging person and his/her environment and in particular the physical and spatial environment, as a crucial facet of the aging process (e.g., Lawton, 1982; Parmelee & Lawton, 1990; Wahl, 2001a, 2001b). This is important to note given the long prevailing tendency in gerontology to assign priority to the person and to neglect the physical and spatial circumstances that provide an important contextual element for aging. In the more traditional version of the ecological approach, older persons were characterized as being particularly vulnerable to environmental press (Lawton & Nahemow, 1973) because of age-related losses in sensory functions, ambulation, and cognition. The victim perspective of person-environment relations, which places strong emphasis on the objective environment, was later reframed as an interplay between "docility" and "proactivity" (e.g., Lawton, 1985). That is, older people were no longer seen only as pawns who were vulnerable to environmental challenges, but also as being capable of compensating and adapting to the disturbances of person-environment relations. As Lawton (1985) has argued, the age-related shrinkage of life space might also serve adaptive functions by allowing density of control in the spatially reduced world of old age. Establishing a "control center" within the home environment (placement of the TV remote control, a book, medication, family photographs, and/or a mobile phone in a concentrated area) illustrates one form of proactive environmental manipulation that can be highly adaptive for a large portion of the elders and particularly the oldest-old.

Parallel to research efforts focusing on the objective environment, another body of work has addressed older people's subjective experience of their surroundings. This body of research is not limited to the study of residential satisfaction; rather, it investigates how aging persons are embedded in their environments, as well as how the environment is biographically anchored within older persons who normally have spent decades in the same place (e.g., Rowles, 1983; Rubinstein, 1998). Obviously, the control and living centers of older people mentioned above are also good examples of the closely intertwined objective and subjective nature of person-environment settings, offering not only support in everyday tasks, but also fertile ground for reminiscence and the pursuit of leisure-oriented activities.

Tentative Definition of Environmental Gerontology and Key Challenges

The ecology of aging is particularly concerned with the description, explanation, and modification of the relationship between the aging person and his/her socio-physical environment including transitions from one environment to another (Wahl, 2001b). An important element of this definition is the emphasis on description, which calls for the collection of data in naturalistic settings of older people, a task crucial to gerontology in general. To be able to explain the relationship between aging individuals and the environment, well-defined theoretical models are needed. Hence, this was and is another crucial task for environmental gerontology (Lawton, Windley, & Byerts, 1982; see also the contributions of Laura N. Gitlin in Chapter 5 and Gerald D. Weisman in Chapter 11 in this volume). Furthermore, modifying the relationship between older persons and their environments (especially by improving their housing) was, from the inception of environmental gerontology, a goal intended to optimize the quality of life of older people (Lawton, 1980, 1983). This value orientation of environmental gerontology is best illustrated by one of Lawton's (1980) statements, "The right to a decent environment is an inalienable right and requires no empirical justification" (p. 160). Finally, the term "socio-physical environment" is important because the physical environment is always closely related to the social and cultural world. Nevertheless, environmental gerontology has traditionally been understood primarily as the study of the physical and spatial environment of older persons.

The tentative definition of environmental gerontology suggested above elicits four interrelated key challenges in this field (see also Wahl, 2001a): (1) Empirical Research—the challenge to develop a consistent and heuristically fruitful empirical research perspective and to ensure progression and a good research standard in the field; (2) Theory—the challenge to develop theoretical models of the person-environment relation in the later years; (3) Comprehensiveness—the challenge to address the broad varieties of older adults and their respective living settings; and (4) Application—the challenge to use existing findings in order directly or indirectly to enhance the life quality of elders by optimizing their living arrangements. How has the current environmental gerontology met these major challenges in the field?

The Challenge to Empirically Address Person-Environment Relations in Old Age

In a recent chapter which appeared in the fifth edition of the *Handbook of the Psychology of Aging* (Wahl, 2001a), the present author suggested a 3 × 3 matrix for organizing the available empirical literature in the field. First, a distinction is suggested between personal home environments, institutional settings, and residential decision. Second, Lawton's (1989) differentiation between three basic functions of the environment in terms of maintenance, stimulation, and support is used to consider research in each of these domains. The environmental function of *maintenance* highlights the important role of constancy and predictability of the environment. The environmental function of *stimulation* typically means the departure from the usual in the environment, the appearance of a novel array of stimuli and their effects on behavior. The environmental function of *support* can typically be seen in the environment's potential to compensate for reduced or lost competencies. Although these environmental functions are closely related to each other in real person-environment interaction, it seems helpful to highlight each of these environmental functions separately in an overview of the literature.

What appears in an analysis of the recent empirical literature published between 1990 and 2001, by applying this conceptual schema, is that all of these respective issues have received some attention (see Wahl, 2001a, for more details). A relatively facet-rich picture of what it means to "feel at home" after decades of aging in the same place is provided by research addressing the *maintenance* function of the environment. For instance, Rubinstein (e.g., Rubinstein, Kilbride, & Nagy, 1992) has identified 3 classes of psychosocial processes which give meaning to the home environment: social-centered (ordering of the home environment based on a person's version of sociocultural rules for domestic order), person-centered (expression of one's life course in features of the home), and body-centered processes (the ongoing relationship of the body to the environmental features that surround it) (see also Oswald, 1996; Rowles, 1983; see also Chapter 9 by Oswald and Chapter 6 by Rowles and Watkins, respectively, in this volume). It is interesting and in a sense hopeful that "feeling at home" can also arise in institutional settings (e.g., Groger, 1995). The consideration of the maintenance function in the institutional setting might be even more important when the issue of the "therapeutic" potential of institutional environments (e.g., special care units) for demented elders is addressed. Although practical work has been much facilitated by specifically designed institutional settings that better serve the demented elderly (e.g., Weisman, 1997), the claim that these new environments actually produce better outcomes is still subject to debate (see also Day, Carreon, & Stump, 2000). According to Zeisel (1999), "The future will tell if the approaches being developed at the end of the twentieth century in environmental design and caregiving for people with Alzheimer's disease and other dementias take hold in the twenty-first century or are discarded as short-lived fads" (p. 129).

Some research addressing the *stimulating* function of the environment can also be found in the available literature. A basic fact to consider in this regard is that most of the older person's day is spent within the home or institutional environment; this is particularly true for the oldest-old (Baltes et al., 1990, 1999; Moss & Lawton, 1982). As a consequence, person-environment interaction processes at the symbolic or overt level have a major impact on the behavioral and emotional functioning of older people, affecting their ability to maintain a high level of competence, live a fulfilled life, and rearrange their environment in order to serve changing needs and goals (e.g., Oswald, 1996; Rubinstein, 1989). As has also been shown for the setting of institutions, features of the physical environment (e.g., room structure) as well as the social environment (e.g., staff behavior) promote social contacts and the maintenance of activity, as well as inhibit negative behaviors such as agitation and verbal disruptions (e.g., Baltes & Wahl, 1992; Cohen-Mansfield, Werner, & Marx, 1990; Day et al., 2000).

Consideration of the *support* function of the environment has been closely associated with environmental gerontology ever since Lindsley's (1964) well-known introduction of the term "prosthetic environment." Interestingly enough, this body of empirical research is smaller than one would assume, given the centrality of this topic for practical application (see also Gitlin, 1998). Physical and spatial characteristics in particular have been shown to be associated with differential levels of independence in the behavioral competence of older people in personal home environments as well as in institutions (e.g., Gitlin, 1998; Netten, 1989; Wahl, Oswald, & Zimprich, 1999).

Residential decision is a third classic issue addressed in the environmental gerontology literature. The question Hamlet might have posed in his old age could have been, "To move or not to move." Interestingly, research has gradually begun to confirm the notion that relocation is a developmental opportunity for the normally aging adult. Although moving is not always easy and depends on a variety of personal motivations and environmental circumstances, it is no longer viewed as an unavoidable trauma or the consequence of severe chronic conditions (e.g., Oswald, Schilling, Wahl, & Gäng, 2002; Ryff & Essex, 1992; Serow, Friedrich, & Haas, 1996). By and large, the maintenance function of the environment is still crucial for older people, reflected by the fact that making a decision to move is still relatively rare in old age (Serow et al., 1996). Once the relocation decision has been faced and finally made, it seems as if stimulation-related motives (regarding a move as a developmental opportunity) become more and more prevalent in today's elders, while support-related motives (associated with the frail aspect of aging) lose their predominance.

To conclude, the recent empirical research, in my estimation (see also Wahl, 2001a), has addressed the basic domains of environmental gerontology (personal home environment, institutional settings, residential decisions) as well as the basic functions that the environment provides for older persons (maintenance, stimulation, support) in considerable intensity and by means of a variety of methods.

The Challenge to Theoretically Address Person-Environment Relations in Old Age

Most of the empirical literature on environmental gerontology is currently framed within a set of theories that might be labeled as classics within the field. Lawton and Nahemow's (1973) Press-Competence Model, which essentially views behavior as a function of personal competence and environmental press, is probably the most widely acknowledged perspective for understanding person-environment relations, with an emphasis on the objective environment. Other theoretical approaches, such as the Person-Environment Congruence Model (Carp & Carp, 1984; Kahana, 1975), that is, understanding behavior as a function of the congruence between personal characteristics and environmental opportunities, as well as Moos's (1976) Social Ecology Model, have been predominantly applied to institutional settings and their objective environmental characteristics. By contrast, the Stress-Theoretical Model (Schooler, 1982) as well as transactional views of older persons in their environments (Rowles, 1983) have stressed the role of evaluative and meaning-oriented processes and thus have addressed the subjective component of the person-environment relation. The need for theoretical pluralism, which is suggested by the old theoretical accounts of the person-environment relation in old age, still appears valid today. A single theory that can account for a broad range of person-environment phenomena has not yet appeared, nor is it likely to anytime soon.

My observation of the field is that it is currently in transition, vacillating between the "good old" theories, such as the Press-Competence Model (Lawton & Nahemow, 1973), and a still unfinished search for substantial conceptual additions, redefinitions, refinements, and updates of already existing approaches as well as the introduction of new ideas (Scheidt & Windley, 1998) that overcome what Lawton (1998) has called the "plateau in theory development" (p. 2). These theoretical challenges echo classic issues of debate within the environmental sciences and environmental psychology in particular, such as the back and forth between an interactional versus transactional worldview and their methodological implications (Parmelee & Lawton, 1990; Wapner, Demick, Yamamonto, & Minami, 2000). They also involve conceptual priorities inferred from the current state of the art of social and behavioral gerontology, such as the strong need for the consideration of interindividual differences, the relation of affect and the environment, and the more fruitful use of concepts such as psychological resilience or control within environmental gerontology studies (Lawton, 1998; Wahl, 2001a).

The Challenge of Comprehensiveness

In earlier work on environmental gerontology (e.g., Carp, 1987), concerns were raised that addressing person-environment interaction in old age should not be restricted to the consideration of elders suffering from severe losses in competence. Instead, a comprehensive account would include the entire gamut of elderly individuals, from different groups of frail elderly to "normal" or "successfully" aging older individuals. Moreover, consideration should be given to various kinds of living contexts, from urban to rural settings and from ordinary housing to highly specific purpose-built living environments, such as assisted living facilities and institutions. A review of the most relevant empirical work in the field (see Wahl, 2001a) shows that elders, ranging from the healthy and active sun-belt movers to very frail Alzheimer patients, have been studied during the 1990s. Research on aging has also investigated a broad variety of ecologies. Environmental gerontology, as well as other areas of psychological gerontology, must nevertheless be characterized as predominately urban in nature; that is, more work concerned with rural settings is needed (Coward & Krout, 1998). In addition, future researchers would do well to examine the new person-environment settings that arise from forthcoming cohorts of older adults (the baby boomers, in particular) and the advent of new technologies and new media (Stokols, 1999). For example, an important question in this regard is how the meaning of home and thus the maintenance function of the home environment will change as a result of Internet use and intelligent home facilities (Vercruyssen, Graafmans, Fozard, Bouma, & Rietsema, 1996).

The Challenge of Keeping the Balance Between Basic Research and Application

The tension between basic science and application in environmental gerontology creates some natural pitfalls as well as opportunities. I believe environmental gerontology to be a shining example of an area of gerontology that has produced results that are directly applicable to various fields, such as planned housing or institutional design. This fact has contributed much to the societal recognition of gerontology in general in recent years. However, there is a tendency for environmental gerontology researchers to become inordinately absorbed by practical needs (and there are many), which results in their being too strongly driven by practical demands instead of theoretical models and the general epistemological state of the field.

TASKS AHEAD FOR ENVIRONMENTAL GERONTOLOGY

At a rather general level, I see, at first, the need for better integration of the physical and the social environment. The need to consider the physical and the social environment with equal emphasis in ecological theorizing has always been emphasized by the big names in social ecology, environmental psychology, and gerontology (such as Barker, Bronfenbrenner, Lawton, Lewin, and Moos). However, most of the current empirical work in environmental gerontology assigns precedence to the physical environment and tends to neglect relations between the physical and social environment. Future theorizing and empirical research therefore needs to consider more thoroughly both the physical and the social environment. Such a stance will require greater collaboration between those interested in social support networks and those interested in physical ecology. Second, I see a great need for better integration of environmental and psychological gerontology. Future theoretical accounts ought to use ecological approaches (which explicitly consider the socio-physical environment) in combination with concepts from psychological gerontology conceptions (typical examples were suggested above). The combination works to the advantage of both fields of research but, in practice, requires increased collaboration between ecologists and developmental and personality psychologists. Third, there is a great need for better integration of micro- and macro-levels of analysis. Research should, for example, more intensively investigate the influence of culture and society on adapting to one's home environment, living and aging in an institution, or deciding to move. Again, in terms of research practice, stronger collaboration between ecologists, sociologists, anthropologists, and social policy researchers will become necessary.

Among the more concrete and still widely unmet research tasks ahead for environmental gerontology, the synergy that results from simultaneously considering "indoor" and "outdoor" perspectives of aging independently deserves a more prominent role in the future. Since older individuals spend most of their time indoors, the outdoor environment is likely to be a highly valued commodity for them (especially for the oldest-old). The meaning of being at home and the meaning of being mobile outside the home are both inseparable components of a single dynamism, linking private to public interaction, individualism to societal participation, and shelter and high control (but also passivity and narrow-mindedness) to openness and new stimulation, but also to risk and loss of control (Mollenkopf, Oswald, & Wahl, 1999). It is also inevitable that neighborhood characteristics serve as facilitators for activities of daily living and leisure activities outside the home environment (e.g., Mollenkopf, Marcellini, & Ruoppila, 1998; Smith, 1991). Nevertheless, the ease with which one pursues such activities is likely to be the product of the aging person and the role and meaning that the indoor environment possesses for him or her. Furthermore, the relation between indoor and outdoor aging will be shaped dramatically by technology in the future. The Internet in particular has already opened new gates to the outside world for many elders, no matter where they live. Thus, instead of examining living environments and outdoor mobility in isolation—which is the prevailing paradigm—the essential questions of future environmental gerontology are certain to evolve from the simultaneous consideration of both areas of inquiry. This book is a step in that direction.

REFERENCES

Baltes, M. M., Maas, I., Wilms, H.-U., & Borchelt, M. (1999). Everyday competence in old and very old age: Theoretical considerations and empirical findings. In P. B.

Baltes & K. U. Mayer (Eds.), *The Berlin aging study* (pp. 384–402). Cambridge: Cambridge University Press.

Baltes, M. M., & Wahl, H.-W. (1992). The dependency-support script in institutions: Generalization to community settings. *Psychology and Aging, 7,* 409–418.

Baltes, M. M., Wahl, H.-W., & Schmid-Furstoss, U. (1990). The daily life of elderly Germans: Activity patterns, personal control, and functional health. *Journal of Gerontology: Psychological Sciences, 45,* 173–179.

Bell, P. A., Fisher, J. D., & Loomis, R. J. (1978). *Environmental psychology.* Philadelphia: Saunders.

Birren, J. E. (Ed.). (1996). *Encyclopedia of gerontology: Age, aging, and the aged.* San Diego, CA: Academic Press.

Carp, F. M. (1966). *A future for the aged.* Austin: University of Texas Press.

Carp, F. M. (1987). Environment and aging. In D. Stokols & I. Altman (Eds.), *Handbook of environmental psychology* (Vol. 1, pp. 330–360). New York: Wiley.

Carp, F. M., & Carp, A. (1984). A complementary/congruence model of well-being or mental health for the community elderly. In I. Altman, M. P. Lawton, & J. F. Wohlwill (Eds.), *Human behavior and environment: Elderly people and the environment* (Vol. 7, pp. 279–336). New York: Plenum Press.

Cohen-Mansfield, J., Werner, P., & Marx, M. S. (1990). The spatial distribution of agitation in agitated nursing home residents. *Environment and Behavior, 22,* 408–419.

Coward, R. T., & Krout, J. A. (Eds.). (1998). *Aging in rural settings: Life circumstances and distinctive features.* New York: Springer.

Day, K., Carreon, D., & Stump, C. (2000). The therapeutic design of environments for people with dementia: A review of the empirical research. *The Gerontologist, 40,* 397–416.

Gitlin, L. N. (1998). Testing home modification interventions: Issues of theory, measurement, design, and implementation. In R. Schulz, G. Maddox, & M. P. Lawton (Eds.), *Annual review of gerontology and geriatrics: Focus on interventions research with older adults* (Vol. 18, pp. 190–246). New York: Springer.

Groger, L. (1995). A nursing home can be a home. *Journal of Aging Studies, 9,* 137–153.

Kahana, E. (1975). A congruence model of person-environment interaction. In P. G. Windley & G. Ernst (Eds.), *Theory development in environment and aging.* Washington, DC: Gerontological Society.

Kleemeier, R. W. (1959). Behavior and the organization of the bodily and external environment. In J. E. Birren (Ed.), *Handbook of aging and the individual* (pp. 400–451). Chicago: University of Chicago Press.

Lawton, M. P. (1977). The impact of the environment on aging and behavior. In J. E. Birren & K. W. Schaie (Eds.), *Handbook of the psychology of aging* (pp. 276–301). New York: Van Nostrand Reinhold.

Lawton, M. P. (1980). *Environment and aging.* Belmont, CA: Brooks-Cole.

Lawton, M. P. (1982). Competence, environmental press, and the adaptation of older people. In M. P. Lawton, P. G. Windley, & T. O. Byerts (Eds.), *Aging and the environment: Theoretical approaches* (pp. 33–59). New York: Springer.

Lawton, M. P. (1983). Environment and other determinants of well-being in older people. *The Gerontologist, 23,* 349–357.

Lawton, M. P. (1985). The elderly in context: Perspectives from environmental psychology and gerontology. *Environment and Behavior, 17,* 501–519.

Lawton, M. P. (1989). Three functions of the residential environment. In L. A. Pastalan & M. E. Cowart (Eds.), *Lifestyles and housing of older adults: The Florida experience* (pp. 35–50). New York: Haworth.

Lawton, M. P. (1998). Environment and aging: Theory revisited. In R. J. Scheidt & P. G. Windley (Eds.), *Environment and aging theory: A focus on housing* (pp. 1–32). Westport, CT: Greenwood Press.

Lawton, M. P., & Nahemow, L. (1973). Ecology and the aging process. In C. Eisdorfer & M. P. Lawton (Eds.), *The psychology of adult development and aging* (pp. 619–674). Washington, DC: American Psychological Association.

Lawton, M. P., Windley, P. G., & Byerts, T. O. (Eds.). (1982). *Aging and the environment: Theoretical approaches.* New York: Springer.

Lindsley, O. R. (1964). Geriatric behavioral prosthetics. In R. Kastenbaum (Ed.), *New thoughts on old age* (pp. 41–60). New York: Springer.

Mollenkopf, H., Marcellini, F., & Ruoppila, I. (1998). The outdoor mobility of elderly people—A comparative study in three European countries. In J. Graafmans, V. Taipale, & N. Charness (Eds.), *Gerontechnology: A sustainable investment in the future* (pp. 204–211). Amsterdam: IOS Press.

Mollenkopf, H., Oswald, F., & Wahl, H.-W. (1999). Alte Menschen in ihrer Umwelt: "Drinnen" und "Draußen" heute und morgen [Older people in their environment: "Inside" and "outside" today and tomorrow]. In H.-W. Wahl, H. Mollenkopf, & F. Oswald (Eds.), *Alte Menschen in ihrer Umwelt: Beiträge zur ökologischen Gerontologie* [Old people in their environment: Contributions to environmental gerontology] (pp. 219–238). Wiesbaden, Germany: Westdeutscher Verlag.

Moos, R. H. (1976). Evaluating and changing community settings. *American Journal of Community Psychology, 4,* 313–326.

Moss, M., & Lawton, M. P. (1982). Time budgets of older people: A window on four life styles. *Journal of Gerontology, 37,* 115–123.

Netten, A. (1989). The effect of design of residential homes in creating dependency among confused elderly residents: A study of elderly demented residents and their ability to find their way around homes for the elderly. *International Journal of Geriatric Psychiatry, 4,* 14.

Oswald, F. (1996). *Hier bin ich zu Hause. Zur Bedeutung des Wohnens: Eine empirische Studie mit gesunden und gehbeeinträchtigten Älteren* [On the meaning of home: An empirical study with healthy and mobility impaired elders]. Regensburg, Germany: Roderer.

Oswald, F., Schilling, O., Wahl, H.-W., & Gäng, K. (2002). Trouble in paradise? Reasons to relocate and objective environmental changes among well-off older adults. *Journal of Environmental Psychology, 22,* 273–288.

Parmelee, P. A., & Lawton, M. P. (1990). The design of special environment for the aged. In J. E. Birren & K. W. Schaie (Eds.), *Handbook of the psychology of aging* (3rd ed., pp. 465–489). New York: Academic Press.

Rowles, G. D. (1983). Geographical dimensions of social support in rural Appalachia. In G. D. Rowles & R. J. J. Ohta (Eds.), *Aging and milieu: Environmental perspectives on growing old* (pp. 111–130). New York: Academic Press.

Rubinstein, R. L. (1989). The home environments of older people: A description of the psychosocial processes linking person to place. *Journal of Gerontology: Social Sciences, 44,* S45–53.

Rubinstein, R. L. (1998). The phenomenology of housing for older people. In R. J. Scheidt & P. G. Windley (Eds.), *Environment and aging theory* (pp. 89–110). Westport, CT: Greenwood Press.

Rubinstein, R. L., Kilbride, J., & Nagy, S. (1992). *Elders living alone: Frailty and the perception of choice.* Hawthorne, NY: Aldine de Gruyter.

Ryff, C. D., & Essex, M. J. (1992). The interpretation of life experience and well-being: The sample case of relocation. *Psychology and Aging, 7,* 507–517.

Scheidt, R. J., & Windley, P. G. (1985). The ecology of aging. In J. E. Birren & K. W. Schaie (Eds.), *Handbook of the psychology of aging* (2nd ed., pp. 245–258). New York: Van Nostrand Reinhold.

Scheidt, R. J., & Windley, P. G. (Eds.). (1998). *Environment and aging theory: A focus on housing.* Westport, CT: Greenwood Press.

Schooler, K. K. (1982). Response of the elderly to environment: A stress-theoretical perspective. In M. P. Lawton, P. G. Windley, & T. O. Byerts (Eds.), *Aging and the environment: Theoretical approaches* (pp. 80–96). New York: Springer.

Serow, W. J., Friedrich, F., & Haas, W. H. (1996). Residential relocation and regional redistribution of the elderly in the USA and Germany. *Journal of Cross-Cultural Gerontology, 11,* 293–306.

Smith, G. C. (1991). Grocery shopping patterns of the ambulatory urban elderly. *Environment and Behavior, 23,* 86–114.

Stokols, D. (1999). Human development in the age of the Internet: Conceptual and methodological horizons. In S. L. Friedman & T. D. Wachs (Eds.), *Measuring environment across the life span* (pp. 327–356). Washington, DC: American Psychological Association.

Vercruyssen, M., Graafmans, J., Fozard, J. L., Bouma, H., & Rietsema, J. (1996). Gerontechnology. In J. E. Birren (Ed.), *Encyclopedia of gerontology: Age, aging, and the aged* (Vol. 1, pp. 593–603). San Diego, CA: Academic Press.

Wahl, H.-W. (2001a). Environmental influences on aging and behavior. In J. E. Birren & K. W. Schaie (Eds.), *Handbook of the psychology of aging* (5th ed., pp. 215–237). San Diego, CA: Academic Press.

Wahl, H.-W. (2001b). Ecology of aging. In N. J. Smelser & P. B. Baltes (Eds.), *International encyclopedia of the social and behavioral sciences* (Vol. 6, pp. 4045–4048). New York: Pergamon/Elsevier Sciences.

Wahl, H.-W., Oswald, F., & Zimprich, D. (1999). Everyday competence in visually impaired older adults: A case for person-environment perspectives. *The Gerontologist, 39,* 140–149.

Wapner, S., Demick, J., Yamamonto, T., & Minami, H. (Eds.). (2000). *Theoretical perspectives in environment-behavior research: Underlying assumptions, research problems, and methodologies.* New York: Kluwer/Plenum.

Weisman, G. D. (1997). Environments for older persons with cognitive impairments. In

G. Moore & R. Marans (Eds.), *Environment, behavior and design* (Vol. 4, pp. 315–346). New York: Plenum Press.

Zeisel, J. (1999). Life-quality Alzheimer care in assisted living. In B. Schwarz & R. Brent (Eds.), *Aging, autonomy, and architecture* (pp. 110–129). Baltimore, MD: Johns Hopkins University Press.

CHAPTER 2

Mobility for What?

K. Warner Schaie

A principal objective of this volume is to examine the role of mobility in the lives of the elderly. We wish to examine obstacles to mobility and ways in which mobility can be enhanced. Before we engage in a detailed examination of these matters, it would seem appropriate to examine the conceptual basis for our focus on the importance of mobility for the elderly. Why is mobility so important in the last stage of life, and what are the objectives and goals of maintaining and enhancing mobility for older persons?

Some would argue that one of the principal requirements for a high quality of independent living in old age is the ability to achieve full access to services, resources, and cultural opportunities. Others would suggest that technological advances now make it possible to obtain information, participate in passive entertainment activities, engage in communication, and initiate the provision of many services without ever leaving the confines of one's home. To address the latter argument one has to examine the fact that many home-based interactions are typically of a virtual kind. Many of us would seriously question whether these virtual interactions can ever possess the interpersonal attributes and physical experiences that most persons find essential to a full life. No matter how important such interactions may be for expanding the intellectual horizons and for providing access to virtual services for the homebound, they do not form the content of the materials I shall address. Furthermore, I will not address issues related to relocation and residential mobility.

In this introductory review I intend to focus instead on some of the psychological and physical advantages of engaging in interactions and experiences that require leaving the confines of one's home. Perhaps the most important advantage here is the ability to maintain a connectedness with a wide spectrum of the community and culture in which we live. For many persons, particularly when their intimate relationships have been constricted through personal losses and failing health, this connectedness remains perhaps the sine qua non of a life that remains worth living.

The mobility characteristics required to maintain connectedness with one's community and culture demand first of all that older individuals retain a physical and psychological personal infrastructure which remains at least minimally effective. Changes in these characteristics will be discussed in later chapters. They are substantial, but they do not confine most elderly to their homes (also see Fozard, 2000; Fozard & Gordon-Salant, 2001).

These mobility characteristics also require that the environment be organized in such a manner that the reduced capability of older organisms can be maximized, both in terms of increasing the compensatory characteristics of the environment and by providing suitable personal and mass transportation structures that support personal mobility. Again much space in this volume will be devoted to considering ways in which external environments can be suitably modified to support the reduced capacity of many older persons (also see Ball & Owsley, 2000; Burckhardt, 2000; Hanowski & Dingus, 2000). Obviously, conditions of physical and cognitive frailty also interact in complex fashion with environmental obstacles (cf. Willis, 2000).

While considering these matters, it is important to keep in mind that the elderly are not a homogeneous population; constraints on mobility will differ at various stages of old age. While there are few mobility constraints for the young-old, increasing constraints become obvious as old-old and very old ages are reached, and as frailty increases. Different solutions for maintaining mobility will therefore be called for, and a transition from being an active traffic participant to that of being a user of transportation provided by others is likely to be inevitable for those achieving a long life.

MOBILITY GOALS FOR THE ELDERLY

Before we can enter into a discussion of the complex issues enumerated above it seems important that we should ask the meta-question of why many of us think that it is of great importance to maintain and enhance the mobility of our older population. Perhaps the overriding objective is to preserve those attributes of personal choice and independence that will permit maintenance of a high quality of life for the elderly. This objective, of course, demands the essential need to maintain basic levels of physical health, intellectual competence, and psychological well-being. It may also require rehabilitative services and prosthetic devices (canes, walkers, or wheelchairs) that allow basic mobility. The meta-goals of mobility, of course, also include the maintenance of independence, the ability of maintaining familiar habits and lifestyles, and maintaining one's independence.

With respect to the particular contributions of personal mobility toward these objectives, we can then point to a number of specific goals of mobility that should be considered. I will discuss six goals that I have identified to be of high salience to many older persons. I should make it clear from the outset that these goals are not exclusive and many others could be added to the list. I also want to emphasize that the priority ranking of these goals will differ from individual to individual, and thus no importance should be assigned to the order in which these goals are listed.

The 6 goals of mobility include the following:

- Reducing personal isolation, including the maintenance of feeling part of one's community
- Participating in cultural and recreational activities (both as a spectator and as a participant)
- Maintaining opportunities to access full choices of goods and services
- Retaining choice of health services and personal care facilities
- Maintaining access to a full range of financial and other personal consultants
- Participating in opportunities for religious worship and other spiritual experiences.

I will try to provide a rationale for why each of these goals of mobility is essential for the maintenance of a high quality of life for the elderly populations in both the United States and Germany.

Reduction of Personal Isolation

Perhaps one of the major psychological issues for older persons is their perceived as well as their actual isolation. Isolation becomes an important issue because the emotional response to this growing isolation tends to be loneliness. Next to physical dependency, loneliness is one of the greatest fears that people associate with old age. In addition, social isolation has also been found to be a major correlate of the deterioration of health in the elderly (Strawbridge, Shema, Balfour, Higby, & Kaplan, 1998).

Much of this isolation coincides with increasing longevity and the sociocultural changes that have occurred over the past century, which have led to the demise of normative extended families. There is a wide variation in coresidence between generations in different countries. For example, China and Japan still have very high rates of coresidence, compared to the United States and Western Europe (cf. Ikels, 1997). Worldwide, there has been a decline over the past 40 years in the proportion of older persons living with their children (Sundström, 1994). This decline has accompanied the move from largely rural to urban environments as well as the increase in career mobility, which make coresidence more difficult (Gille, 1992). Older adults are also more likely to remain in rural environments even when their adult children move to the cities (Norris-Baker & Scheidt, 1994). There has also been a growing resistance to parental coresidence on the part of both generations (Goldscheider & Lawton, 1998; Szinovacz, 1997).

Old people, of course, need love, affection, and social interaction just as much as others at any other age. For many older persons, a marriage may have lasted for 40 years or longer. When a spouse dies, it may be increasingly difficult to find ways to meet the needs fulfilled by the close marital relationship. Hence, other means of reducing isolation such as increased involvement in community organizations and more intense interactions with brothers, sisters, and friends may be essential. Paradoxically, the low level of formal services available in rural areas and small towns may actually lead to greater interaction with neighbors and relatives, who, in these circumstances, become the primary providers of supportive services (Blieszner, McAuley, Newhouse, & Mancini, 1987).

Some older persons seek to reduce social isolation by joining planned retirement communities; however, such communities are relatively expensive and tend to draw mostly the more affluent (Somers & Spears, 1992). It is likely therefore that the affluent baby boomers will increasingly be found in such communities as they reach retirement age (Longino, 1998). Nevertheless, the proportion of the older population seeking this solution will remain limited, and, if these individuals age in place, they will experience the same mobility problems once they are no longer able to use their personal means of transportation, the automobile.

For most individuals, reduction of social isolation is directly related to the maintenance of mobility to be able to interact with valued others beyond the virtual contact that is offered by electronic means. Hence, the ready availability of convenient forms of mass transportation or the maintenance of the ability to use personal transportation become central elements in avoiding or reducing personal isolation.

Participation in Cultural and Recreational Activities

The passive experience of the media explosion is typically experienced by most elders, like the rest of the population, in their homes in front of a television set. There is substantial evidence, however, that the maintenance of cognitive function in old age requires much more active pursuits of intellectual stimulation (Gribbin, Schaie, & Parham, 1980; Schaie, 1996). More often it will involve attending live performances, traveling individually or in a group to sites of cultural and touristic importance, participating in senior colleges, or being active in social and political organizations. In the United States, an important role for seniors has been their participation in volunteer community activities (cf. Schaie, 1995), a role which is attaining increasing importance in Germany as well as in other industrialized societies. All such activities require retention or enhancement of personal mobility.

Recreational activities are also essential for the maintenance of physical health. Ample evidence is available to suggest that physical activities and exercise programs involving group participation are of the utmost importance in maintaining cardiovascular health and in reducing the impact of other chronic diseases, as well as maintaining the strength and flexibility required to avoid the hazards of an active independent life. The success of structured aerobic and strength training programs has been demonstrated even at quite advanced ages (e.g., Blumenthal, 2001; Evans, 2000).

Access to Full Choices of Goods and Services

In order to access community services, health care, and other amenities of life, it is essential to have access to adequate transportation. Because of the lack of frequent and convenient public transportation in the rural areas of the United States, older persons living in nonurban areas are heavily dependent on the use of personal automobiles. In many urban and suburban areas in the United States, public transportation is often minimal and inconvenient, resulting in dependence on the automobile in these areas as well. Because of the limited availability of public transport, maintenance of driving abilities (and driving privileges) is a particularly important requirement for quality living. Because of declines in sensory processes and response speed, many older persons in their late 70s or 80s either give up driving voluntarily or lose their driving license. The resulting reduction in mobility leads to an increased dependence on others. Even more important, the reduction in mobility reduces access to the wide array of goods and services which are now generally available to most of us. Although most elderly do not live in poverty, many must still survive on limited incomes (Atchley, 2000). Mobility, if nothing else, allows price shopping and consequently an expansion of the purchasing power of one's income.

Choice of Health Services and Personal Care Facilities

The provisions for providing and financing health care are very different in the United States and Germany (see Kane, 2000, and Rakowsky, 2002, for descriptions of the impact of the U.S. health care system on the elderly). The cost of transportation to health care facilities may be reimbursable, and many facilities that house older persons with limited mobility do provide transportation to health facilities. Nevertheless there are strong commonalities related to the impact of mobility on taking full advantage of and having choices in using the health care system. When home health care services are available, they are likely to be offered by the least qualified health care and ancillary personnel. Undoubtedly the German *Notarzt* (emergency physician) answering a call will have superior training to the American paramedic, but even he or she is likely to be at the low end of the health care hierarchy in terms of experience and prestige.

Clearly, exercising a choice of health care specialists or health care facilities in all Western societies requires access to transportation, both for normal health care as well as emergency situations. Some older persons' personal preferences will be for nontraditional health care resources, whether naturopaths, acupuncturists, or faith healers. These resources are not necessarily available in close proximity, and a lack of mobility would preclude their use. Mobility restrictions similarly impair access to other personal care specialists, whether these be beauticians, cosmeticians, physical therapists, or health spas.

Access to Financial and Other Personal Consultants

It is certainly possible to pay one's bills and conduct one's investments and other financial transactions over the Internet. Yet many older persons would be quite reluctant to manage their life's savings via the impersonal algorithms of web banking. Most older persons have throughout their lives based their financial decisions on face-to-face interactions with bankers and other financial consultants with whom they have developed a personal relationship of trust and confidence. Given the need to adjust financial planning to a changing societal climate and the demands of providing realistically for an unexpectedly prolonged life expectancy, direct consultation with trusted financial and legal advisers becomes even more pressing (cf. Cutler, Gregg, & Lawton, 1992), and very few of these professional are likely to make house calls.

Similarly, most older persons need to interact with a variety of government agencies in relation to their pensions, retirement benefits, and insurance problems. A great variety of public resources is available to make the lives of older persons easier or to improve the quality of their lives, if only problems of ready access can be solved to such resources which are typically located outside the proximity of one's home.

Direct Participation in Religious Worship or Other Spiritual Experiences

Religious motivation has received little attention until recently from researchers in adult development. This is especially surprising because we know that particularly older adults in the United States report that religious beliefs and activities are quite central to their lives. In a recent Gallup poll, 60% of adults reported religion to be very important in their lives (Newport, 1999). The elderly may attend church less frequently owing to health problems, but they do remain active in other dimensions of religion. Some argue that older persons increasingly satisfy their religious needs by engaging in solitary spiritual activities (Payne & McFadden, 1994), but such recourse does not take advantage of the important role of religious communities as a resource in reducing isolation.

Because of the ritual nature of most religious worship, many persons find it essential to their spiritual welfare to participate in organized religious activities—being a member of a formal religious organization, attending church services, or serving as a Sunday school teacher. This may indeed be one of the principal avenues for the single elderly to retain their feelings of connectedness.

The role of religiosity in old age is of particular interest because various dimensions of religiosity have been associated with physical and mental health concerns, such as well-being, self-esteem, depression, and even mortality (Levin, 1996; Strawbridge et al., 1998). It has been suggested that some aspects of religion may be particularly important for the elderly in buffering the effects of stressors. By promoting a sense of meaning in the face of adversity, religion may be an important asset for helping older adults cope successfully with stressful events that arise in roles they value highly (Krause, 1998).

Again mobility is essential not only to participate in religious rituals or other group activities of a spiritual nature, but also to afford individual choice in being able to hear a favorite charismatic preacher or engage in discipleship with a favorite guru.

SOME CONCLUSIONS

I have argued in these introductory comments that personal mobility is an essential element in maintaining the connectedness of the older person to his or her community and society. Such connectedness was described as being an essential element for the maintenance of sustainable levels of physical and emotional health and the degree of well-being essential for allowing older persons to function independently and to exercise maximum choice in their lives.

The importance of personal mobility in the maintenance of high levels of functioning in the elderly was further elaborated by identifying six goal areas in which mobility is of particular salience: reduction of personal isolation, participation in cultural and recreational activities, access to full choices of goods and services, choice of health services and personal care facilities, access to financial and other personal consultants, and direct participation in religious worship and other spiritual experiences. I have tried to indicate why mobility is so important to attain these goals, and I am now eager to learn how we can better serve our elders by removing mobility-related obstacles to the attainment of these goals.

REFERENCES

Atchley, R. C. (2000). *Social forces and aging* (9th ed.). Belmont, CA: Wadsworth.
Ball, K., & Owsley, C. (2000). Increasing mobility and reducing accidents of older driv-

ers. In K. W. Schaie & M. Pietrucha (Eds.), *Mobility and transportation in the elderly and aging* (pp. 213–250). New York: Springer.

Blieszner, R., McAuley, W. J., Newhouse, J. K., & Mancini, J. (1987). Rural-urban differences in service use by older adults. In T. H. Brubaker (Ed.), *Aging, health, and family: Long-term care* (pp. 162–174). Beverly Hills, CA: Sage.

Blumenthal, J. (2001). Exercise interventions and chronic disease. In K. W. Schaie, H. Leventhal, & S. L. Willis (Eds.), *Social structures and effective health behaviors in the elderly.* New York: Springer.

Burckhardt, J. E. (2000). Limitations of mass transportation systems and individual vehicle systems for older persons. In K. W. Schaie & M. Pietrucha (Eds.), *Mobility and transportation in the elderly and aging* (pp. 97–123). New York: Springer.

Cutler, N. E., Gregg, D. W., & Lawton, M. P. (Eds.). (1992). *Aging, money, and life satisfaction: Aspects of financial gerontology.* New York: Springer.

Evans, W. J. (2000). Effects of exercise on body composition and functional capacity of elderly persons. In K. W. Schaie & M. Pietrucha (Eds.), *Mobility and transportation in the elderly* (pp. 71–90). New York: Springer.

Fozard, J. L. (2000). Sensory and cognitive changes with age. In K. W. Schaie & M. Pietrucha (Eds.), *Mobility and transportation in the elderly* (pp. 1–61). New York: Springer.

Fozard, J. L., & Gordon-Salant, S. (2001). Sensory and perceptual changes with aging. In J. E. Birren & K. W. Schaie (Eds.), *Handbook of the psychology of aging* (5th ed., pp. 241–266). San Diego, CA: Academic Press.

Gille, A. (1992). Living accommodations for the urban elderly. In M. Bergener, K. Hasegawa, S. I. Finkel, & T. Nishimura (Eds.), *Aging and mental disorders: International perspectives* (pp. 56–64). New York: Springer.

Goldscheider, F. K., & Lawton, L. (1998). Family experiences and the erosion of support for intergenerational co-residence. *Journal of Marriage and the Family, 60,* 623–632.

Gribbin, K., Schaie, K. W., & Parham, I. A. (1980). Complexity of life style and maintenance of intellectual abilities. *Journal of Social Issues, 36,* 47–61.

Hanowski, R. J., & Dingus, T. A. (2000). Will intelligent transportation systems improve older driver mobility? In K. W. Schaie & M. Pietrucha (Eds.), *Mobility and transportation in the elderly* (pp. 279–298). New York: Springer.

Ikels, C. (1997). Long-term care and the disabled elderly in urban China. In J. Sokolovsky (Ed.), *The cultural context of aging: Worldwide perspectives* (2nd ed., pp. 452–471). Westport, CT: Bergin and Garvey.

Kane, R. (2000). *The health care system and the self.* In K. W. Schaie & J. Hendricks (Eds.), *Evolution of the aging self: Societal impacts* (pp. 183–203), New York: Springer.

Krause, N. (1998). Stressors in highly valued roles, religious coping and mortality. *Psychology and Aging, 13,* 242–255.

Levin, J. S. (1996). How religion influences morbidity and health: Reflection on natural history, salutogenesis and host resistance. *Social Science and Medicine, 43,* 849–864.

Longino, C. F., Jr. (1998). Geographic mobility and the baby boom. *Generations* (Spring), 60–64.

Newport, F. (1999, December 24). *Gallup Poll: Americans remain very religious, but not necessarily in conventional ways.* Princeton, NJ: Gallup.

Norris-Baker, C., & Scheidt, R. J. (1994). From "our town" to "ghost town"? The changing context of home for rural elders. *International Journal of Aging and Human Development, 38,* 181–202.

Payne, B. P., & McFadden, S. J. (1994). From loneliness to solitude. Religious and spiritual journeys in later life. In L. E. Thomas & S. A. Eisenhandler (Eds.), *Aging and the religious dimension* (pp. 13–37). New York: Springer.

Rakowsky, W. (2002). Impact of health care organization on maintenance & change in health behaviors. In K. W. Schaie, H. Leventhal, & S. L. Willis (Eds.), *Social structures and effective health behaviors in the elderly.* New York: Springer.

Schaie, K. W. (1995). Entwicklung im Alter: Individuelle Voraussetzungen—Gesellschaftliche Konsequenzen [Development in old age: Individual aspects—Societal consequences]. In H. Klose (Ed.), *USA: Altern und Modernisierung)* [Aging and modernization in the USA] (pp. 65–89). Bonn, Germany: Friedrich Ebert Foundation.

Schaie, K. W. (1996). *Intellectual development in adulthood: The Seattle longitudinal study.* New York: Cambridge University Press.

Somers, A. R., & Spears, N. L. (1992). *The continuing care retirement community.* New York: Springer.

Strawbridge, W. J., Shema, S. J., Balfour, J. L., Higby, H. R., & Kaplan, G. A. (1998). Antecedents of frailty over three decades in an older cohort. *Journal of Gerontology: Social Sciences, 53B,* S9–S16.

Sundström, G. (1994). Care by families: An overview of trends. *Social Policy Studies, 14,* 15–55. Paris, France: OECD.

Szinovacz, M. E. (1997). Adult children taking parents into their homes: Effects of childhood living arrangements. *Journal of Marriage and the Family, 59,* 700–717.

Willis, S. L. (2000). Driving competence: The person × environment fit. In K. W. Schaie & M. Pietrucha (Eds.), *Mobility and transportation in the elderly* (pp. 269–278). New York: Springer.

PART II

The Aging Individual and the Environment: Basic Considerations

Enabling Environments for Physical Aging: A Balance of Preventive and Compensatory Interventions

James L. Fozard

Many preventive functions of environmental interventions focus on safety (e.g., a traffic light at an intersection, a grab bar in the bathtub, or an ergonomically designed tool). Most compensatory functions of environmental interventions focus on the unique needs of subgroups of the population (e.g., visual and auditory products and environments for elderly persons or a cane to assist personal mobility). Likewise, interventions with people can have a preventive or compensatory focus. Preventive functions may be based on lifestyle choices (e.g., smoking prevention, exercise, or diet). Compensatory functions may be based on medical treatment, physical rehabilitation, cognitive training, or other interventions. The proper balance of preventive and compensatory interventions for aging and aged persons changes continuously with new knowledge about aging and interventions.

This chapter proposes and describes a "proper balance" of preventive and compensatory interventions that reflects current knowledge about physical aging. Accordingly, it will first review how people adapt to some common challenges of physical aging. Second, a classification of physical aging into three dimensions—structural, control, and information—will be proposed.

The purpose of this classification is to facilitate the discussion in the third part of the chapter, promising preventive and compensatory interventions—both environmental and personal—for the three dimensions of aging resulting from recent scientific advances. The interventions include changes in the lifestyle and health of individuals and in the living and working environment. Because physical aging has a longtime course, the optimal timing of these interventions requires special attention.

ADAPTATIONS TO FUNCTIONAL LIMITATIONS OF PHYSICAL AGING

Many physical activities related to indoor and outdoor personal mobility decrease with age (Verbrugge, Gruber-Baldini, & Fozard, 1996), and, as shown in Table 3.1, the difficulty in carrying them out increases (U.S. Bureau of the Census, 1996). In the two personal mobility tasks, walking and transferring, 50% or less received help as compared to over 70% of those reporting difficulty with getting out, fixing a meal, or doing light housework. Verbrugge and Jette (1994) found that, for persons reporting difficulty performing activities of daily living, help from another person was the most frequently reported source of assistance for both activities involving upper and lower limbs. Canes, walkers, wheelchairs, and handrails were the most frequently reported assistive devices used for activities requiring lower limb activity.

The data in Table 3.1 do not specify the degree of task difficulty, how people adapt to difficulties, or the types of help received. Respondents to the survey include persons who perform the activity, denying its difficulty.

TABLE 3.1   Reported Limitations (%) in Three Age Groups

Task	Mean Age 70		Mean Age 80		Age 85+
	Men	*Women*	*Men*	*Women*	*Both*
Walk	7	10	16	20	35
Get out	6	11	16	26	45
Transfer	5	7	9	13	22
Fix meal	4	5	9	14	28
Housework	5	8	12	18	31

Source: U.S. Bureau of the Census, 1996.

Other people may not complain of a functional limitation partly because they have altered the way in which they accomplish the task prior to responding to the survey. Both possibilities may explain some of the differences between the persons reporting functional limitations and those receiving help in performing the activity. The survey includes persons who continue performing the activity but modify *how* the activity is performed or *how often* it is performed or both, depending on the task demands. Adaptations include modifying the environment, using assistive devices, and obtaining help from other persons.

Wahl, Oswald, and Zimprich (1999) reviewed several approaches to studying how people adapt to the challenges of physical aging. A recently published structured interview schedule, the Physical Functioning Inventory (PFI), determines what adaptations if any are reported by persons when performing three activities of daily living (ADLs), 14 instrumental activities of daily living (IADLs), three personal mobility activities, and three strenuous (moderate, very, most) activities (Whetstone et al., 2001). All questions began, "Do you have difficulty . . . ?" Probes following responses of "yes" or "no" elicit information about *how* and *how often* the activity has been modified. Most people reporting difficulty in carrying out the tasks also reported modifying how the task was performed. Interestingly, about 58% of the group reporting "no difficulty" also reported making modifications. With the exception of one IADL, driving, and reports of walking outdoors, the percentages of persons reporting changes in how often an activity was performed was less than the percentage reporting changes in how the activity was performed. A wide variety of modifications in how tasks are performed were described, particularly for difficulties in getting around and out of the house and performing personal hygiene. When assessing the home to identify needed modifications, the PFI would be a useful companion instrument to the newly developed Comprehensive Assessment Survey Protocol for Aging Residents (CASPAR) (Sanford, 2000).

THREE DIMENSIONS OF PHYSICAL AGING

Changes in how and how often activities are performed in relation to physical aging are largely specific to three dimensions of physical aging. The *structural dimension* includes the skeletal, connective, and muscle tissue— figuratively speaking, the machinery of the body. The *control dimension* includes the endocrine and neural systems which control and coordinate the actions of the body. The *information dimension* includes the visual, auditory, proprioceptive and thermal sensory, and perceptual systems which provide information from the environment. This three-dimensional scheme is based largely on transactional models (Baltes & Baltes, 1990; Lawton & Nahemow, 1973) applied to ergonomics (Corso, 1981; Fozard & Popkin, 1978) and gerontechnology (Fozard, Rietsema, Bouma, & Graafmans, 2000).

Changing the physical and social environment can prevent or delay limitations in function as well as compensate for them. The same is true for changing a person. Currently, compensatory environment interventions are the most widely used for the information dimension, but new opportunities for prevention are emerging. Currently, preventive and compensatory interventions with persons are the most widely used for the structural dimension, but new, longer-range opportunities for prevention are emerging. In the following discussion, the effects of interventions on the control dimensions are blended with interventions for the other two dimensions.

Age-related declines in the three dimensions of physical aging usually occur slowly starting from a wide range of initial levels observed in early adulthood. Incremental changes in many physiological functions over adulthood, which total 25% to 60% between initial and ending values, may require periods of from 5 to 10 years to observe. Accordingly, the optimal timing of preventive measures includes a wide range, depending on the nature of the intervention.

PREVENTIVE AND COMPENSATORY INTERVENTIONS FOR THE THREE DIMENSIONS OF PHYSICAL AGING

Interventions for the Structural and Control Dimensions

Prevention

Exercise and training provide compensation for many age-related changes in the structural and control dimensions. A physiological reserve of strength acquired earlier in life may decrease later functional limitations and lessen the impact of injury. The adage "use it or lose it" applies to the maintenance of strength, but it is also important for building a physiological reserve of strength which can counteract the age-related loss of muscle strength and mass. Long-term strength training can improve and maintain strength in the elderly as well as the young (e.g., Ivey et al., 2000). Even modest exercise such as walking can reduce the development of functional limitations (Miller, Rejeski, Reboussin, Have, & Ettinger, 2000). Two further challenges to the application of this scientific concept include the definition of the time and intensity parameters needed to achieve and maintain a physiological reserve and the definition of the threshold below which reserve should not fall (e.g., Kiryu, Takahashi, & Ogawa, 1997).

Evidence for a longtime course for primary prevention is accruing for bone and muscle. The best defense against excessive age-related loss of bone density is a reserve acquired during the period of life when the density gain exceeds the loss in the bone turnover process. Post-menopausal hormone replacement therapy reduces but does not eliminate loss in bone density (Kaiser, 1997, p. 75). Ongoing clinical trials may identify pharmaceutical interventions that will increase bone density in old age.

Longitudinal research documents significant individual differences in age-related declines in arm and leg strength (e.g., Metter, Conwit, Tobin, & Fozard, 1997). Rantanen and colleagues (1999) reported positive correlations between grip strength measured in middle age and functional limitations observed or reported 25 years later. The percentage of persons with self-reported difficulties or performance increased systematically with lower grip strength.

On the basis of earlier literature on physical frailty, Pendergast, Fisher, and Calkins (1993) estimated that a 70-year-old person needs about 40% of his or her strength at 25 years to be functionally independent. The basis for specifying strength goals for walking is being addressed in several laboratories (e.g., Rantanen and Avela, 1997; Kwon et al., 2001). Within a critical range, knee extensor strength is positively correlated with gait speed. Below and above the critical range, the slope relating strength to gait speed is flat. The excess strength at the high end of the function defines the physiological reserve. In comparison to male age peers, women had less or no physiological reserve over a wide range of ages. Rantanen and Avela (1997) plotted the cumulative distributions of leg power (Watts/kg) observed for 5 gait speed groupings ranging from < 1m/s to > 2m/s. The differences were striking. The tenth, fiftieth, and ninetieth percentiles of strength associated with gait speeds < 1m/s were in round numbers, 1, 2, and 4 W/kg. Corresponding figures for speeds ranging from 1.3m/s to 1.5m/s and > 2m/s were 4, 5, and 12, and 8, 12, and 15 W/kg, respectively. The correlation between knee strength and gait speed is in the moderate range, so other factors influencing strength and gait must be considered in interventions, including nutrition, reduction of joint pain, passive stimulation of muscles, and hormonal therapies (see Evans, 2000, for an excellent review).

A second, more speculative approach to prevention in the control (endocrine) dimension would be based on pharmacological interventions using hormone administration (e.g., growth hormone, DHEA, sex hormones). A landmark study of old men made by Rudman and colleagues (1990) showed the reversal of several signs of aging including loss of muscle mass resulting from administration of growth hormone. Since then there has been a considerable amount of research investigating the preventive as well as the medical application of hormone replacement therapy (Kowal, 1997; Morley, 2001). To date, little clinical research has been directed at comparing the usefulness of the approach either as a substitute for or as a supplement to strength training.

Given the widespread public apathy toward many current public health interventions related to lifestyle changes, the difficulties of implementing a preventive program along the lines proposed would be formidable. The role of technically based equipment in the interventions discussed above would be to improve the monitoring of results, both at the level of strength and muscle quality and at the motivational level. The participation by the elderly in regular programs of physical activity and especially in strength training is very low (Fozard & Heikkinen, 1998). In comparison with machines that provide constant and meaningful information about the progress and status of a person using machines for aerobic training, very little meaningful information is provided by strength training machines beyond the amount of weight used in the training session (Chodzko-Zajko, 2001).

Compensation

As demonstrated by Fiaterone and colleagues (1994), strength training by very frail elderly persons can improve functional ability. However, compensatory interventions—equipment, help from others—remain the most common. Many developments of the equipment and environments that compensate for losses in personal mobility, driving, and home activities are covered in other chapters. Applications of the universal design concept to homes and everyday products have resulted in significant improvements for persons with limitations in function. Where applicable, environmental adaptations such as grab bars are effective partly because they do not limit functioning as much as canes, crutches, and walkers. Many aids to personal mobility were developed to meet the short-term needs of persons recovering from an injury more than for those needing them all the time. Problems of safety and injury secondary to the use of the devices are common. Development of protective hip pads and the tricycle type walking aids, which also serve a useful function for transporting parcels and clothes, are examples of improvements in this area.

Interventions for the Information Dimension

Except for the dangers of long-term exposure to extremes of intense light or sound, little was known about primary prevention of age-associated limitations in sensation. Recent research links cardiovascular functioning to age-related hearing loss and visual function. Other work suggests that visual attention and other cognitive processes can be modified by training. Together these developments provide a relatively novel basis for developing preventive interventions in perceptual processes. The following paragraphs summarize the developments, which are more fully described by Fozard (2001).

Prevention in Hearing

Longitudinal data indicate that for persons who are presumed clinically not to have a history of severe noise exposure, hearing losses typically begin in the 40s and 50s for men and later for women (Morrell, Gordon-Salant, Pearson, Brant, & Fozard, 1996). To improve existing standards for noise-exposure limits, a controlled clinical trial is needed to determine when and how much normal environmental noise contributes to presbycusis. Modern digital hearing-aid technology to monitor and record noise levels continuously at the ear makes a clinical trial possible in a natural setting. The same technology used to protect the user against dangerous levels of noise could be used to suppress noise exposure in an intervention group.

In a cross-sectional population-based study, Cruickshanks and colleagues (1998) related presbycusis to tobacco use; and in a longitudinal study by Brant and colleagues (1996), to elevated systolic blood pressure in men. The number of men developing significant hearing loss over the observation period increased systematically with chronic systolic blood pressures between 120 and 160 mmHg. A planned intervention is needed to confirm the results of this observational study—one that uses contemporary measures of cardiovascular function.

Prevention in Vision

As with hearing, excessive exposure to bright light and cardiovascular problems contribute to age-related visual problems. The amount and duration of exposure to bright light necessary to impair vision is poorly understood—most information comes from studies of occupational groups at risk such as professional fishermen, who are exposed to large amounts of reflected light and ultraviolet radiation from the water. Elevated blood pressure is associated with increases in intraocular pressure, a major risk for glaucoma (McLeod, West, Quigley, & Fozard, 1990). Damage to the retina secondary to diabetes (diabetic retinopathy) is a very serious form of visual impairment. Collectively, these results indicate that visual function is impaired secondary to diseases for which hypertension is itself a primary contributing factor.

Principles of Compensation

Compensations for the information dimension include the following:

- Increasing signal strength by increasing the contrast between signal and background
- Slowing the rate of presentation of information
- Providing redundant information (e.g., simultaneous visual and auditory information)
- Increasing signal distinctiveness by using other sensory channels (e.g., vibration)
- Using smart technology to find right signal strength
- Reducing the requirements for reserve cognitive capacity in complex tasks
- Using skill training and rehabilitation procedures in conjunction with task redesign.

Compensation in Hearing

The most important environmental interventions include reduction of environmental reverberation and masking and the use of hearing aids, including those with multiple microphones (Schieber, Fozard, Gordon-Salant, & Weiffenbach, 1991). Training in listening skills and lip-reading are important adjuncts for hearing-aid users. Only about 20% of those who could benefit from using hearing aids actually use them. Costs and marketing practices contribute to this situation (Fozard & Gordon-Salant, 2001; Moore, 1995). Understanding fast, natural speech and compressed speech without frequency distortion is more difficult in old age. Technology for altering the speech rate in television broadcasting has shown considerable promise for improving speech intelligibility (Miyasaka, 2001).

Compensation in Vision

Studies in the Netherlands, Japan, and the United States have significantly increased knowledge about practical compensatory environmental measures (see Fozard & Gordon-Salant, 2001, for a review). Steenbekkers (1998) determined the size of lower-case Times Roman type needed to read a standard passage by Dutch adults in 2 age groups under the viewing conditions shown in Table 3.2. Overlapping type sizes for the two age groups are approached only in the 100% contrast (black letters on white background) condition at 1,000 lux. As the illumination level decreases from 1,000 to 10 lux, the size type required for reading by the oldest group doubles while that of the youngest stays the same. The effect of poor contrast (10%) is greatest at the lowest level of illumination in both groups. The benefits of improved illumination and contrast are seldom realized in practice (Charness & Dijkstra, 1999).

The effect of illumination and contrast carry over into mobility tasks, both walking (Klein, Klein, Lee & Cruickshanks, 1998) and driving (Dellinger, Sehgal, Sleet, & Barrett-Connor, 2001; Kline, Kline, Fozard, Schieber, & Sekuler, 1992). The contribution of vision to driving is especially

TABLE 3.2   Type Size Needed to Read by 25- and 75-Year-Old Groups Under Three Illumination (lux) Contrast (%) Levels

Lux	10		100		1000	
Age	25	75	25	75	25	75
Contrast						
10	10.0	12.6	4.0	8.0	3.2	6.3
33	5.0	10.0	4.0	8.0	3.2	6.3
100	4.0	8.0	3.2	6.3	3.2	5.0
100	3.2	8.0	3.2	5.0	3.2	4.0

Note: The third row is for white letters on a black background; the fourth row is for black letters on a white background.
Source: Steenbekkers, 1998.

important in reading road signs and in steering a vehicle. Schieber and Kline (1994) found that the legibility of simulated road signs for adults 65 to 79 years old was 0.8 that of 18- to 25-year-old adults in daylight and about half in the more difficult conditions. The authors proposed various ways to redesign signs. Owens and Tyrrell (1999) measured steering errors in a driving simulator under 4 levels of illumination ranging from 1.5 cd/m2 (daylight) to −2.5 cd/m2 (dark, scotopic vision). The number of errors increased with decreasing illumination much more for drivers with mean ages of 72 years than for groups with mean ages of 39 or 24.

Compensation in Complex Tasks

Limitation in vision is but one of many factors contributing to age differences in attention and search, visual guidance of control movements, and maintenance of gait and balance (see Fozard & Gordon-Salant, 2001). Physiological reserve in the control dimension is usually studied by requiring persons to perform a secondary task in addition to the primary task and observing the resulting performance decrement. In practical situations requiring divided attention, older persons are more likely to suffer performance decrements in the primary task than younger ones (Fozard, 2000, pp. 16–19). More recently, Lindenberger, Marsiske, and Baltes (2000) required adults to recall memorized lists of words while sitting, standing, or walking on an oval or complex track. Performance on both tasks declined with age when performed together. The opportunity to practice walking prior to the imposition of the memorization task resulted in relatively less slowing in the walking task for all participants—a finding relevant to the current discussion of interventions.

The contribution of vision to balance increases with age, and it is most pronounced when proprioceptive information is impoverished (Hay, Baird, Fleury, & Treasdale, 1996; Turano, Rubin, Herdman, Chee, & Fried, 1994). At a practical level, Templer (1995) provides a wealth of examples of poor designs of surfaces and lighting of stairs that give insights on how to improve lighting and walking surfaces.

The use of assistive technology in palliative care and provision of comfort and psychosocial support was studied in reference to demands on professional and nonprofessional caregivers by Mann, Offenbacher, Fraas, Tomita, and Granger (1999). The provision of technological aids and environmental interventions was compared to usual care at home for very frail, older patients who had been discharged to home from hospitals or who were receiving home nursing services. Costs, services received, and changes in functioning were monitored for 18 months. Functioning declined in both groups, more so in the control group. The intervention group spent more on environmental materials and modifications. The costs for institutional and home nursing care were higher in the control than in the experimental group. The experimental group used an average of 7.5 times as many devices and modifications as the control group over the 18 months.

SUMMARY AND CONCLUSIONS

During the UN Year of the Elderly in 1999, United Nations General Secretary Kofi Annan articulated an international policy goal for creating "enabling environments for aging." Achieving that goal requires us to consider both environmental and personal interventions that contribute to the prevention of age-related limitations in functioning as well as human and technical help to compensate for them. In order to give operational meaning to "the enabling environment for aging," the many facets of physical aging that reduce independent functioning and health in aging persons were divided into three broad classes: structural (bone and muscle), control (neural, endocrine), and information (vision, hearing, and proprioception). In each dimension the potential for prevention or delaying of physical aging was considered, followed by a discussion of current and proposed compensations.

The quantity and quality of research related to physical aging have increased significantly over the past decade. In the structural and control dimensions, studies indicate both the feasibility and importance of physical activity and strength training in prevention. In the information dimension, new research has identified more opportunities for prevention as well as compensation. Finally, research provides an increased understanding of the applications of technologically based products and environments for prevention and compensation.

The expanding opportunities for interventions create additional challenges for implementing them, especially the ones involving long-term preventive efforts. Significant efforts by program planners and practitioners will be needed to implement programs of prevention based on long-term goals. Advances in technology related to environments and products that can improve vision and hearing may make it easier to take advantage of the many trade-offs among signal-enhancing and noise-suppression approaches to compensatory interventions.

ACKNOWLEDGMENTS

I wish to thank the volume editors for their constructive comments which improved the clarity and exposition of the concepts discussed. Special thanks are due to Professor Ben Hurley of the University of Maryland for his critique and suggestions related to the material on the structural and control dimensions of aging.

REFERENCES

Baltes, P. B., & Baltes, M. M. (Eds.). (1990). *Successful aging: Perspectives from the behavioral sciences.* Cambridge: Cambridge University Press.

Brant, L. J., Gordon-Salant, S., Pearson, J. D., Klein, L. L., Morrell, D. H., Metter, E. J., & Fozard, J. L. (1996). Risk factors related to age associated hearing loss in the speech frequencies. *Journal of the American Academy of Audiology, 7,* 152–160.

Charness, N. S., & Dijkstra, K. (1999). Age, luminance, and print legibility in homes, offices and public places. *Human Factors, 41,* 173–193.

Chodzko-Zajko, W. (2001). Active aging in the new millenium: The role of technology in the promotion of physically active lifestyles in older adults. In K. Sagawa (Ed.), *Proceedings of the International Workshop on Gerontechnology* (pp. 115–120). Tsukuba, Japan: National Institute of Bioscience and Human Technology.

Corso, J. F. (1981). *Aging sensory systems and perception.* New York: Praeger.

Cruickshanks, K. J., Wiley, T. L., Tweed, K. T., Klein, B. E. I., Klein, R., Mares-Perlman, J. A., & Nondahl, D. M. (1998). Prevalence of hearing loss in older adults in Beaver Dam, WI: The epidemiology of hearing loss study. *American Journal of Epidemiology, 148,* 879–886.

Dellinger, A. M., Sehgal, M., Sleet, D. A., & Barrett-Connor, E. (2001). Driving cessation: What older former drivers tell us. *Journal of the American Geriatrics Society, 49,* 431–435.

Evans, W. J. (2000). Effects of exercise on body composition and functional capacity of elderly persons. In K. W. Schaie & M. Pietrucha (Eds.), *Mobility and transportation in the elderly* (pp. 71–90). New York: Springer.

Fiaterone, M. A., O'Neill, E. F., Ryan, N. D., Clements, K. M., Solares, G. R., Nelson, M. E., Roberts, S. B., Kehayias, J. J., Lipsitz, L. A., & Evans, W. J. (1994). Exercise training and nutritional supplementation for physical frailty in very elderly people. *New England Journal of Medicine, 330,* 1769–1775.

Fozard, J. L. (2000). Sensory and cognitive changes with age. In K. W. Schaie & M. Pietrucha (Eds.), *Mobility and transportation in the elderly* (pp. 1–45). New York: Springer.

Fozard, J. L. (2001). Gerontechnology and perceptual-motor function: New opportunities for prevention, compensation, and enhancement. *Gerontechnology, 1(1),* 5–24.

Fozard, J. L., & Gordon-Salant, S. (2001). Changes in vision and hearing with aging. In J. E. Birren & K. W. Schaie (Eds.), *Handbook of the psychology of aging* (5th ed., pp. 241–266). San Diego, CA: Academic Press.

Fozard, J. L., & Heikkinen, E. (1998). Maintaining movement ability in old age. In J. A. M. Graafmans, V. Taipale, & N. E. Charness (Eds.), *Gerontechnology: A sustainable investment in the future* (pp. 48–61). Amsterdam: IOS Press.

Fozard, J. L., & Popkin, S. J. (1978). Optimizing human development: Ends and means of an applied psychology of aging. *American Psychologist, 33,* 975–989.

Fozard, J. L., Rietsema, J., Bouma, H., & Graafmans, J. A. M. (2000). Creating enabling environments for the challenges and opportunities of aging. *Educational Gerontology, 26,* 331–344.

Hay, L., Baird, C., Fleury, M., & Treasdale, N. (1996). Availability of visual and proprioceptive afferent messages and postural control in elderly adults. *Experimental Brain Research, 108,* 129–139.

Ivey, F. M., Tracy, B. L., Lemmer, J. T., Ness-Aiver, M., Metter, E. J., Fozard, J. L., & Hurley, B. H. (2000). Effects of strength training and detraining on muscle quality: Age and gender comparisons. *Journal of Gerontology: Biological Sciences, 55A,* B152–B157.

Kaiser, F. E. (1997). Osteoporosis. *Korean Journal of Gerontology, 7,* 73–75.

Kiryu, T., Takahashi, K., & Ogawa, K. (1997). Multivariate analysis of muscular fatigue during bicycle ergometer exercise. *Transactions on Biomedical Engineering, 44,* 665–672.

Klein, B. E., Klein, R., Lee, K. E., & Cruickshanks, K. J. (1998). Performance-based and self-assessed measures of visual function as related to history of falls, hip fractures, and measured gait time. *Ophthalmology, 105,* 160–164.

Kline, D. W., Kline, T. J. B., Fozard, J. L., Schieber, F., & Sekuler, R. (1992). Aging and driving: The problems of older drivers. *Journal of Gerontology, 47,* P27–P34.

Kowal, J. (1997). Reversible frailty: Hormonal senescence. *Korean Journal of Gerontology, 7,* 76–78.

Kwon, I., Oldaker, S., Schrager, M. A., Talbot, L. A., Fozard, J. L., & Metter, E. J. (2001). Relationship between muscle strength and self-paced gait speed: Age and sex effects. *Journal of Gerontology: Biological Sciences, 56,* B398–B404.

Lawton, M. P., & Nahemow, L. (1973). Ecology and the aging process. In C. E. Eisdorfer & M. P. Lawton (Eds.), *The psychology of adult development and aging* (pp. 619–674). Washington, DC: American Psychological Association.

Lindenberger, U., Marsiske, M., & Baltes, P. B. (2000). Memorizing while walking. *Psychology and Aging, 15,* 417–436.

Mann, W. C., Offenbacher, K. J., Fraas, L., Tomita, M., & Granger, C. V. (1999). Effectiveness of assistive technology and environmental interventions in maintaining independence and reducing home care costs for the frail elderly: A randomized controlled trial. *Archives of Family Medicine, 8,* 210–217.

McLeod, S. D., West, S, K., Quigley, H. A., & Fozard, J. L. (1990). A longitudinal study of the relationship between intraocular pressure and blood pressure. *Investigative Ophthalmology and Visual Science, 31,* 2351–2366.

Metter, E. J., Conwit, R., Tobin, J., & Fozard, J. L. (1997). Age-associated loss of power and strength in the upper extremities in women and men. *Journal of Gerontology: Biological Sciences, 52A,* B267–B276.

Miller, M. E., Rejeski, W. J., Reboussin, T. R., Have, T., & Ettinger, W. H. (2000). Physical activity, functional limitations and disability on older adults. *Journal of the American Geriatrics Society, 48,* 1264–1273.

Miyasaka, E. (2001). Some applicable trials for realization for human-friendly broadcasting. In K. Sagawa (Ed.), *Proceedings of the International Workshop on Gerontechnology* (pp. 23–26). Tsukuba, Japan: National Institute of Bioscience and Human Technology.

Moore, B. J. C. (1995). *Perceptual consequences of cochlear damage.* Oxford: Oxford University Press.

Morley, J. E. (2001). Andropause: Is it time for the geriatrician to treat it? *Journal of Gerontology: Medical Sciences, 56A,* M263–M265.

Morrell, C. H., Gordon-Salant, S., Pearson, J. D., Brant, L. J., & Fozard, J. L. (1996) Percentiles for cross-sectional and longitudinal changes in hearing level. *Journal of the Acoustical Society of America, 100,* 1949–1967.

Owens, D. A., & Tyrrell, R. A. (1999). Effects of luminance, blur, and age on nighttime visual guidance: A test of the selective degradation hypothesis. *Journal of Experimental Psychology: Applied, 5,* 1–14.

Pendergast, D. R., Fisher, N. M., & Calkins, E. (1993). Cardiovascular, neuromuscular and metabolic alterations with age leading to frailty [Special issue]. *Journal of Gerontology, 48,* 61–67.

Rantanen, T., & Avela, J. (1997). Leg extension power and walking speed in very old people living independently. *Journal of Gerontology: Medical Sciences, 52A,* M325–M331.

Rantanen, T., Guralnik, J. M., Foley, D., Masake, K., Leville, S., Curb, J. D., & White, L. (1999). Midlife handgrip strength as a predictor of old age disability. *Journal of the American Medical Association, 281,* 558–560.

Rudman, D., Feller, A. G., Nagraj, H. S., Gerfans, G. A., Lalitha, P. Y., Goldberg, A. F., Schlenker, R. A., Cohn, L., Rudman, I. W., & Mattson, D. E. (1990). Effect of human growth hormone in men over 60 years old. *New England Journal of Medicine, 323,* 1–6.

Sanford, J. A. (2000). Home modifications for elders: Bringing together differing approaches to assessment. *Maximizing Human Potential, 8*(1, Summer), 2, 8. San Francisco, CA; American Society on Aging.

Schieber, F., Fozard, J. L., Gordon-Salant, S., & Weiffenbach, J. (1991). Optimizing the sensory-perceptual environment of older adults. *International Journal of Industrial Ergonomics, 3,* 133–162.

Schieber, F., & Kline, D. W. (1994). Age differences in the legibility of symbol highway signs as a function of luminance and glare level: A preliminary report. In *Proceedings of the Human Factors and Ergonomics Society, 38th Annual Meeting* (pp. 133–135). Santa Monica, CA: Human Factors and Ergonomics Society.

Schieber, F., Kline, D. W., Kline, T. J. B., & Fozard, J. L. (1992). The relationship between contrast sensitivity and the visual problems of older drivers. In Society of Automotive Engineers (Ed.), *Technical Paper 920613* (pp. 1–7). Warrendale, PA: Society of Automotive Engineers.

Steenbekkers, L. P. A. (1998). Visual contrast sensitivity. In L. P. A. Steenbekkers &

C. E. M. van Geifsterveldt (Eds.), *Design-relevant characteristics of ageing users* (pp. 131–136). Delft, The Netherlands: Delft University of Technology Press.

Templer, J. (1995). *The staircase: Studies of hazards, falls and safer design* (Volumes 1, 2). Cambridge, MA: MIT Press.

Turano, K., Rubin, G. S., Herdman, S. J., Chee, E., & Fried, L. P. (1994). Visual stabilization in the elderly: Fallers vs. non-fallers. *Optometry and Vision Science, 71,* 761–769.

U.S. Bureau of the Census. (1996). *Current population reports, special studies, 65+ in the United States.* Washington, DC: U.S. Government Printing Office (pp. 23–190, Table 3.8).

Verbrugge, L. M., Gruber-Baldini, A. L., & Fozard, J. L. (1996). Age differences and age changes in activities: The Baltimore Longitudinal Study of Aging. *Journal of Gerontology: Social Sciences, 51B,* S30–S41.

Verbrugge, L. M., & Jette, A. M. (1994). The disablement process. *Social Science and Medicine, 38,* 1–14.

Wahl, H.-W., Oswald, F., & Zimprich, D. (1999). Everyday competence in visually impaired older adults: A case for person-environment perspectives. *The Gerontologist, 39,* 140–149.

Whetstone, L. M., Fozard, J. L., Metter, E. J., Hiscock, B. S., Burke, R., Gittings, N. E., & Fried, L. P. (2001). The Physical Functioning Inventory: A procedure for assessing physical function in adults. *Journal of Aging and Health, 13,* 467–493.

CHAPTER 4

Psychological Issues of Aging Independently

Andreas Kruse

In this chapter, aging independently is discussed from four different perspectives: neuropsychology, cognitive psychology, personality psychology, and ecopsychology. This discussion begins with the construct of plasticity, which is central for understanding the development of new behavior schemata, the compensation of developmental losses, and the effects of stimulation and training on sensorimotor and cognitive functioning. The second section proceeds from a multidimensional model of cognitive structure and development. It is argued that life competencies acquired in earlier ages do more than simply promote successful aging. To be precise, a psychological definition of productivity leads one to the insight that the successful use of life competencies creates a productive context for younger peoples' development. The third section, which takes the perspective of personality psychology, focuses on older peoples' inner experiences of aging (subjective perceptions of resources, gains, barriers, and losses). The section on ecopsychological aging research concentrates on empirical studies that illustrate the impact of the physical and institutional environment on everyday competence and well-being. In the final section, it is argued that competence can be defined only by integrating the perspectives discussed above. This definition stresses the responsibility of both the individual and society for a good life in old age. Institutional subsidiarity is discussed as a possible basis for deciding when state intervention is required to strengthen individual resources.

PLASTICITY

From a neuropsychological view, aging is a process of morphological (structural) and functional change in separate nerve cells and in groups of cells. Morphological change includes the loss of nerve cells, dendrites, and synapses. Functional change includes a decrease in the resting potential and the speed of arousal transmission. Moreover, inhibitory strength is reduced, leading to lessened precision of arousal transmission. This is only one side of the coin; the other side is the nerve cell's capacity to change (or plasticity), which is reflected in the effects of rehabilitation and cognitive training. Plasticity is a key element of the central nervous system which also applies to late phases of life. Regarding rehabilitation, plasticity implies the capacity of surrounding areas to take over for destroyed brain areas. Here I must stress the necessity of intense rehabilitation which involves maximal stimulation and training of the individual throughout the day: only continuous rehabilitation can stimulate the growth of new dendrites and new nerve cell groups (Ronning & Guldvog, 1998). With respect to cognitive training, plasticity implies the individual's ability to learn new cognitive strategies and to alleviate age-related losses in fluid intelligence (Baltes, Kühl, & Sowarka, 1992). With respect to orientation in a new environment, plasticity implies the individual's capacity to adapt—that is, to develop the cognitive and psychomotor images that are necessary to deal effectively with environmental demands and opportunities (Gitlin, 1998).

Functional plasticity refers to the increased resting potential of neurons (on the basis of which cellular excitation processes can be accelerated). Morphological plasticity refers to the production of new synapses and the enrichment of dendrite growth in continuous activation processes. However, if there is a lack of continuous stimulation of sensory, sensorimotor, and cognitive functions, the probability of losses in cognitive and everyday competence—especially in very old age—increases dramatically. Losses resulting from insufficient stimulation and training can be traced back to the reduced capacity of the synapses and to a reduced number of dendrites (Näätänen, 1992). A certain amount of stimulation and activation, as well as a certain amount of training in cognitive and everyday competencies, is a necessary condition for maintaining an independent and responsible life in old age (Lawton, 1989; Wahl, 1998).

POTENTIALS AND LIMITS OF
COGNITIVE DEVELOPMENT

Baltes (1987) proposed a two-component model of intellectual development which differentiates between the mechanics and pragmatics of intelligence and focuses on the impact of biological and cultural factors on intellectual performance. The developmental processes in the two components differ in old age: there is a substantial decrease of functioning of the cognitive mechanics, but a relatively high stability of the cognitive pragmatics. When knowledge and training, which were developed in earlier phases of life, continue to be used, a further increase in the pragmatics of intelligence is possible even in old age. As shown by the Berlin Aging Study (BASE), the multidimensional structure of cognitive functioning can also be confirmed for the very old with a cluster of three functions representing the mechanics (reasoning, perceptual speed, memory) and a cluster of two functions representing the pragmatics of intelligence (fluency, knowledge). On the other hand, results of this study also show (1) a higher covariance between these functions in the very old (85–103 years) than in the old (70–85 years), supporting the assumption of a general cognitive ability factor, and (2) significant decrements both in mechanics as well as in pragmatics performances with a higher variability and a greater decline in mechanics compared to pragmatics functions (Lindenberger & Reischies, 1999; Smith & Baltes, 1999).

Proceeding from the question of whether performance deficits in older adults are caused by constraining biological influences in old age or are influenced by environmental and societal conditions, Kliegl, Mayr, and Krampe (1994) differentiated tasks into those representing sequential complexity (varying the number of steps necessary for task solution) and tasks representing coordinative complexity (regulation and surveillance of information between solution steps). In support of Salthouse's (1985) theory of cognitive slowing in old age, they found significantly larger age-related slowing (better: they found older individuals to be significantly slower than others) on tasks involving coordinative complexity.

The strong relation between sensory and cognitive functioning in old age, also found in BASE (Lindenberger & Baltes, 1997), points to the presence of general aging processes of the brain. The relation between sensory measures and mechanical intelligence components proved to be much stronger than relations to social-structural variables, which played a more prominent role in pragmatics functions.

The Testing the Limits paradigm is an effective means of identifying age differences in memory functioning. This paradigm specifies that learning and performance differences between old and young persons should be most pronounced when subjects are pushed to maximum performance levels, under the assumption that younger persons possess greater reserve capacity than older persons. In a series of training studies, Kliegl, Smith, and Baltes (1989) found strong support for this hypothesis. Older people can make amazing training gains, but they are not able to touch the performance level attainable by younger subjects undergoing the same training procedure.

I use "life competencies" to refer to experiences, strategies, and knowledge systems that people have acquired in earlier phases of the life span. Life competencies, honed in the context of effective coping, enable people to maintain or reestablish a personally satisfying perspective on their lives when confronted with serious problems, tasks, and challenges in later years. Acquiring life competencies at earlier ages is a basic requirement for successful development in advanced age (e.g., effective coping with demands of life in old age). Such demands include practical and psychological as well as interpersonal and ethical demands (Kruse, 2001). Consequently, our understanding of life competencies is not limited to the experiences, strategies, and knowledge systems acquired in the context of occupational activities. Life competencies are also reflected by ethical judgments, voluntary activities, and the willingness to assume responsibility for oneself, others, or society. Empirical findings show that active coping with developmental tasks and the opportunities/limitations of an active life can lead to the establishment of expert knowledge or wisdom with respect to questions of living (see Smith & Baltes, 1990). Expert knowledge or wisdom is not limited to old age; it can be developed in earlier phases as well. The only prerequisite for the development of expert knowledge or wisdom is conscious and responsible preoccupation with a multitude of problems, tasks, and challenges at different life stages and different contexts of development. I use the term "human capital" to refer to the significance of life competencies for society and culture; in other words, the processes of initiating societal and cultural change and the extent to which societal and cultural change is determined by life competencies of the old. Societal and cultural development depends on the opportunity to display individual life competencies. This requires relevant infrastructural conditions; for example, opportunities for volunteers to qualify and to use given experiences, strategies, and knowledge systems effectively (Kruse & Schmitt, in press). The term "productivity" is not restricted to participation in the labor market, to voluntary activities, or to manual (tangible) expressions of productivity. Instead, an adequate definition of productivity must include intellectual, emotional, and motivational expressions of productivity (Montada, 1996). By using an extended definition of productivity, several aspects of leading a productive life in old age can be distinguished: (1) being interested in the development, living conditions, and vital interests of younger people, (2) transmitting information to younger generations, and (3) reflecting the experiences and knowledge systems of younger generations. These aspects are examples of intellectual and emotional productivity in old age, since intergenerational discourses can initiate emotional and intellectual differentiation in older and younger participants. Moreover, older people can provide younger people with a good example of how to cope with problems and difficulties. They can build a productive context for others and provide an illustrative example of emotional and motivational aspects of productivity (Kruse 1996; Staudinger, 1996).

THE AGING SELF

The results of a survey, Images of the Elderly and Social Structure, conducted by Kruse, Rudinger, and Schmitt (in press), illustrates images of the elderly in German society. The random sample (nearly 1,300 subjects) was collected on the basis of the following characteristics: age (45 to 75 years), gender, habitation in eastern or western Germany, habitation in urban or rural regions, habitation in regions with high or low unemployment, and occupational and social status.

Table 4.1, which presents the results of a regression analysis, illustrates the power of social-structural variables and individual resources in predicting three dimensions of the self-concept: (1) perceptions of age-related losses (6 items, $\alpha = 0.79$), (2) perceived potentials of leading a productive and responsible life (4 items, $\alpha = 0.70$), and (3) perceived barriers to leading a productive and responsible life (4 items, $\alpha = 0.72$).

Two aspects seem to be noteworthy. First, the predictive power of the social-structural variables (areas with high versus low unemployment, living in the eastern versus western part of Germany, education, household income) is high for the dimension "perceived barriers to leading a productive and responsible life." This result supports the hypothesis that the subjectively perceived opportunities to be productive in one's own social network is influenced by objective life conditions since these constitute not only the opportunities and limitations of an independent, self-responsible, and personally meaningful (or productive) life, but also chances and limitations of social participation and shared responsibility. Second, the predictive power

TABLE 4.1   Predicting Dimensions of Age-Related Self-Concept from Individual Resources and Socio-structural Variables

Predictors	Perceptions of age-related losses	Perceived potentials of leading a productive and responsible life	Perceived barriers of leading a productive and responsible life
	β	β	β
Areas with high versus low unemployment	−.02	−.04	.11**
Eastern versus western part of Germany	.09	−.04	.29**
Chronological age	.18**	.00	.12**
Sex	−.06	.02	.08*
Subjective health status	−.36**	.18**	−.16**
Education	−.10**	.21**	−.10*
Income of household	.00	.08	−.14**
Perceived social integration	.25**	−.18**	.25**
R^2 (adj.)	.32	.15	.33

Note: Results from multiple regression analysis.
*$p < .05$; **$p < .01$.
Source: Kruse, Rudinger, & Schmitt, in press.

of the subjectively experienced resources (subjective health status, perceived social integration) is very high for the dimension "perceptions of age-related losses." This result supports the hypothesis that perception of the aging process is influenced by the subjective interpretation of personal resources—for example, in the areas of health and social relationships.

In the Interdisciplinary Longitudinal Study on middle and later adulthood (Martin et al., 2000), 5 patterns of aging were differentiated on the basis of 10 characteristics of the subjectively experienced situation. These were described in the following way: (1) healthy and responsible aging (30.9%), (2) compensatory aging (25.1%), (3) accepting one's own aging (19.6%), (4) healthy and happy aging (12.5%), and (5) physically and socially stressful aging (11.9%) (Minnemann, Schmitt, Sperling, & Jüchtern, 1997). When interpreting these patterns, it should be noted that they were observed in a group of 500 persons aged 61 to 63 years at the time of the survey (i.e., among a group of the "young" or "new" elderly). More than 40% of the people who took part in this study described their present situation in terms of "healthy and responsible aging" or "healthy and happy aging." A further 25% of the people perceived limitations in their present situation, mostly due to the consequence of retirement, the loss of contacts to previous working colleagues, and health problems. At the same time, the participants stated that they had succeeded in compensating for these limitations by developing new interests and activities and by changing their perspective on life. Finally, nearly a third of the sample accentuated significant limitations in the current situation which were experienced as burdensome. The major part of this group was in a position to come to terms with these limitations; age-related limitations were a profound negative influence on one's life and life perspective for only a minority of persons in this group.

How do individuals experience very advanced age? In the BASE study, self-definitions of elderly and very old people generally emphasize activity and the present (Freund & Smith, 1997). Even for those 85 years old and older, positively evaluated characteristics and qualities remained predominant. However, the ratio between positively and negatively evaluated attributes becomes less favorable in advanced age, largely as a consequence of poor health and losses in vision and hearing. Moreover, the number of different aspects by which people define themselves declines with increasing age. The richness of the definition of the self, by referring to a wide variety of different aspects of self, is unable to protect the aging adult from the effects of substantial illness burdens and marked limitation of sensory capacities. The limitations of psychological resilience as a resource of psychological adjustment became clear in these findings.

To what extent do older people interpret their old age as a phase of life in which positive as well as negative changes in personality and life situation are to be expected? In a survey on the personal and social resources of the elderly (Kruse & Schmitt, in press), subjectively experienced gains and losses were analyzed. The survey included 450 persons (age range: 60 to 100 years). Ten "gains" and 16 "losses," as perceived by older people, were identified. Six gains were reported by at least one-fifth of the total sample (rank ordered in the frequency named): (1) change in the criteria (level of aspiration) required to bring commitment in life, (2) maintenance of a positive and affirmative attitude despite experienced losses, (3) more realistic assessment of limitations to own activities, increasing acceptance of these limitations, and the discovery of new opportunities for activity, (4) increasing ability to accept unfulfilled wishes and expectations in life and to make compromises, (5) increasing ability to reevaluate earlier events and experiences, and (6) declining obligations in family and work. The following 6 losses were reported by at least one-fifth of the total sample (again the rank order is of frequency named): (1) experienced or feared loss of intimate confidants (relatives and friends), (2) increase in illnesses and decrease in physical capability, (3) chronic pain often perceived as "strong" or "very strong," (4) uncertain future owing to the feared loss of the husband/wife, (5) uncertain future owing to the fear of becoming chronically ill and frail, and (6) reduced capacity in memory, especially in short-term memory. These results suggest that subjectively experienced losses increase from the youngest (60 to 70 years) to the oldest age groups (90 to 100 years). An increase in illnesses and a decline in physical capability were reported by 38% of the 80- to 100-year-olds, but by only 21% of the 70- to 79-year-olds, and by only 9% of the 60- to 69-year-olds. In addition, chronic pain was reported by a relatively high proportion of those 80 years old and older (see also Ferrel & Ferrel, 1996; Heuft, Kruse, & Radebold, 2000). A particularly large increase in experienced memory losses was reported by the age group of the 70- to 79-year-olds compared to the 80- to 100-year-olds.

Analyses of personal goals or of subjectively experienced gains and losses attempt to peek into the "inside" of aging, that is, into the special manner in which older people themselves perceive the aging process (Thomae, 1996). Birren (1999) characterizes the necessity of analyzing the inside of aging as follows:

> Aging can be looked at in two ways. We can talk about the problems of aging or about the potentials of aging. Longevity catches many older people by surprise. There is no model for them to follow. Many of us are doing studies by looking at the outside of aging. Looking at the aging individual, looking at the disease processes. Another thing we have to explore is the inner experience of aging. Looking at the inside of aging. It is an interpretation of life by individuals. We tend to project onto the older person their problems as we see them, not the way the older person is viewing them. (Birren, 1999, p. 2)

Though demands and losses may increase in advanced age, this does not mean that people in this phase of life are unable to resist such demands and losses and sustain or reestablish a bearable (better: meaningful) perspective on life. The fact that a fairly large proportion of very old describe positively valued characteristics and gains in old age serves as an indicator of this resistance: the phenomenon of resilience in old age (Staudinger, Marsiske, & Baltes, 1995).

Kruse and Schmitt (1998) examined psychological well-being in spite of dependency from a perspective which integrates personal (internal) and environmental (external) resources. The significance of perceived stress, personal and environmental resources as predictors of depressivity, lonely dissatisfaction, agitation (assessed via the respective scales of the Philadelphia Geriatric Center Morale Scale), and subjective aging (assessed via the Nuremberg Age Inventory) was analyzed by means of multiple regression analysis. The predictive power of stress was no longer significant when personal and environmental resources were entered in multiple regression analysis. Focusing on personal resources, a coping pattern accentuating activity, personal ability, and control was the best predictor of psychological well-being. Concerning environmental resources, most of the predictive power was due to perceived quality of medical treatment and social services. Multiple regression analysis with assimilative coping and perceived quality of medical treatment and social services as predictors of subjective aging showed two significant main effects that explained 30% of the variance.

Proceeding from the assumption that the effects of personal variables depend on environmental conditions and vice versa, a further regression analysis was conducted with the interaction of assimilative coping and perceived quality of medical treatment and social services as an additional predictor (see Table 4.2).

The significant interaction term indicates that the effectiveness of assimilative coping depends on the quality of medical treatment and social services. If this quality is high, assimilative coping contributes to a more

TABLE 4.2   Predicting Subjective Aging from Assimilative Coping (Tenacious Goal Pursuit) and Perceived Quality of Medical Treatment and Social Services

Predictor(s)	B	R^2
Assimilative coping (Tenacious Goal Pursuit)	3.30**	
Perceived quality of medical treatment and social services	2.45**	
Assimilative coping (Tenacious Goal Pursuit) × Perceived quality of medical treatment and social services	−1.34**	.41

Note: Results from multiple regression analysis.
**$p < .01$.
Source: Kruse & Schmitt, 1998, p. 122.

optimistic perspective of one's own aging process. If the quality of medical treatment and social services is low, assimilative coping seems to contribute to a more pessimistic perspective of one's own aging process.

PHYSICAL ENVIRONMENT AND EVERYDAY COMPETENCE

In planning "good" or "age-friendly" living environments, it is necessary to take into account the inter-individual heterogeneity of the elderly. This heterogeneity is observed not only in the area of competence, but also in the areas of needs and motives. What environmental criteria must be met for the individual to be satisfied with housing conditions? To what extent is the individual striving to adapt the environment to his or her goals in life ("proactivity") (Lawton, 1989; Wahl, 2001)? It is an important task of ecological gerontology to encourage planners, decision makers, and policy makers to be more sensitive to the influence of living environment on competence, well-being, and social integration in old age. Creating age-friendly living environments can be understood as a key element of subsidiarity (Wahl, Mollenkopf, & Oswald, 1999). Our understanding of society's responsibility for creating age-friendly environments must not be restricted to economic support, but should include counseling centers for older people. In the process of counseling, 2 aspects should be taken into account: everyday competence (the type of environment and technical support optimal for the individual pattern of competence), and personal needs and motives (the criteria for good housing conditions which the individual has developed over the life course) (Oswald, 1998).

In a study of opportunities and limitations of independent living in old age (number of participants: 1,092; age range: 59 to 89 years), Schmitt, Kruse, and Olbrich (1994) analyzed the relation between physical environment and functional (or everyday) competence. The analysis showed that greater independence (and thus fewer care needs) in ADL and IADL was correlated with better housing conditions.

Table 4.3 illustrates the person-environment relation: patterns of everyday competence are strongly associated with housing conditions. Although higher social status was correlated with both poorer housing conditions and poorer levels of ADL and IADL, the relationship between everyday competence and objective housing conditions remained significant after controlling for education and income. Therefore, it was hypothesized that com-

TABLE 4.3   Objective Housing Conditions in Three Patterns of Competence

Objective housing conditions	High competence in most activities of daily living (n = 619)	Reduced competence in some activities of daily living (n = 322)	Reduced competence in most activities of daily living (n = 151)
Very good	27 (4.4%)	7 (2.2%)	—
Good	241 (38.9%)	69 (21.4%)	16 (10.6%)
In-between	266 (43.0%)	138 (42.9%)	67 (44.4%)
Bad	76 (12.3%)	85 (26.4%)	51 (33.8%)
Very bad	9 (1.5%)	23 (7.1%)	17 (11.2%)

Source: Schmitt, Kruse, & Olbrich, 1994, p. 383.

petence in performing activities of daily living could be significantly increased by intervention measures that focus on the physical environment (a similar conclusion can be drawn from Mann, Ottenbacher, Fraas, Tomita, & Granger, 1999).

In further analyses, we compared an objective assessment and older people's perceptions of housing conditions. This comparison is important for understanding the subjective criteria of "good life" and "good living conditions." Moreover, this comparison is necessary in planning intervention programs. As shown in Table 4.4, older people in general are more satisfied with their housing conditions than could be expected from objective assessment. Only low correlations can be found between objective and subjective measures of housing conditions. The degree of satisfaction with housing conditions seems to be a poor predictor for the need of environmental interventions that might increase competence.

COMPETENCE AND SUBSIDIARITY

Elsewhere, I proposed defining competence as the individual's ability to maintain or regain an independent, self-determined, personally meaningful, and task-related life in a stimulating, supportive, and motivating physical, social, and infrastructural environment (Kruse, 1996). This definition places emphasis on the individual's autonomy with respect to (1) self care, instru-

TABLE 4.4   Satisfaction with Housing Conditions in Three Patterns of Competence

Satisfaction with objective housing conditions	High competence in most activities of daily living (n = 619)		Reduced competence in some activities of daily living (n = 322)		Reduced competence in most activities of daily living (n = 151)	
Very satisfied	370	(59.8%)	177	(55.1%)	103	(68.2%)
Satisfied	164	(26.5%)	89	(27.6%)	32	(21.2%)
In-between	61	(9.9%)	37	(11.5%)	12	(7.9%)
Dissatisfied	17	(2.8%)	14	(4.3%)	2	(1.3%)
Very dissatisfied	7	(1.1%)	5	(1.6%)	2	(1.3%)

Source: Schmitt, Kruse, & Olbrich, 1994, p. 385.

mental and leisure time activities; (2) coping with developmental tasks, difficulties, and problems; and (3) taking advantage of situational opportunities for a personally meaningful life (Baltes, 1996). It also stresses the significance of the environment in offering opportunities for acting responsibly in stimulating, supporting, and motivating the individual (Lawton, 1989; Wahl, 1998). Taken together, competence refers exclusively neither to individual abilities and skills nor to environmental characteristics. Instead, competence results from a person-environment interaction. This interaction is important not only from a psychological but also from a social and political view. The definition of competence stresses the responsibility of both the individual and society for a good life in old age. In terms of social policy, determining the appropriate structures for the balance of individual and societal responsibility should be guided by the principle of institutional subsidiarity (Bäcker, Bispinck, Hofemann, & Naegele, 2000). Subsidiarity is defined as a principle of social organization, wherein the individual and the immediate community are the primary agents of intervention, and the state intervenes only when there is no other alternative. Preferably, the individual's resources should be improved so that he or she is able to lead an independent, self-determined, and personally meaningful life. Here it is important to assist the individual in creating or changing environmental conditions in accordance with personal values and goals. Where the individual is unable to help himself, assistance should be sought first from family members, neighbors, self-help groups, and voluntary welfare organizations; the state should be called upon as a last resort. This premise becomes all the more important in the case of high vulnerability—a risk that increases in advanced old age. Vulnerability is a demand not only upon the individual, but on society (Baltes, 1999). To what extent does society provide support for the individual in his or her effort to sustain or regain an independent and personally responsible existence? How clearly defined is the obligation of society to use resources from the social security system (for example, health insurance) to support old people? Given the demographic development in many developed countries: to what extent will decision makers and policy makers be prepared to be advocates for the elderly when resources available to the social security system become more severely limited than they are today (Walker, 1999)? Will the needs of people who rely on comprehensive treatment, rehabilitation, and long-term care still be adequately represented and acknowledged in public discourse?

CONCLUSION

This chapter not only emphasized the concept of independence, but also dealt with the concepts of responsibility for oneself and of shared responsibility. With the concept of independence, I referred to the individual's ability to cope successfully with the tasks and challenges of daily life without relying on the help of others. With the concept of self-responsibility, I referred to individuals' abilities and motivations to lead their daily lives in congruence with personal needs, norms, and values and to reflect upon questions of their own personalities and identities as well as the possibilities and limitations inherent in their personal life situations. With the concept of shared responsibility, I referred to an individual's ability and motivation to assume the perspective of other people, to advocate for others, and to contribute to the attainment of other people's needs.

The concepts of independence, responsibility for oneself, and shared responsibility reflect different facets of competence and subsidiarity. The concept of competence is central for understanding person-environment interactions and their influence on independence, self-determination, and social participation. With respect to subsidiarity, older persons should be regarded as a resource for society, as many of them engage in voluntary work which contributes to dealing with the demands and problems of the community. It is an important societal task to use the productive potential of the elderly.

REFERENCES

Bäcker, G., Bispinck, R., Hofemann, K., & Naegele, G. (2000). *Sozialpolitik und soziale lage in Deutschland* [Social politics and social circumstances in Germany] (3rd ed.). Opladen, Germany: Westdeutscher Verlag.

Baltes, M. M. (1996). *The many faces of dependency in old age.* Cambridge: Cambridge University Press.

Baltes, M. M., Kühl, K. P., & Sowarka, D. (1992). Testing for limits of cognitive reserve capacity: A promising strategy for early diagnosis of dementia. *Journal of Gerontology, 47,* 165–167.

Baltes, P. B. (1987). Theoretical propositions of life-span development psychology: On the dynamics between growth and decline. *Developmental Psychology, 23,* 611–626.

Baltes, P. B. (1999). Alter und Altern als unvollendete Architektur der Humanontogenese [Old age and aging: The unfinished architecture of human ontology]. *Zeitschrift für Gerontologie und Geriatrie, 32,* 443–448.

Birren, J. E. (1999). The inner experience of ageing—implications for productive ageing and eldercare. *Age Concerns, 5*(14), 1–2.

Ferrel, B. R., & Ferrel, B. A. (Eds.). (1996). *Pain in the elderly.* Seattle, WA: IASP Press.

Freund, A., & Smith, J. (1997). Die Selbstdefinition im hohen Alter [The self-definition in old age]. *Zeitschrift für Sozialpsychologie, 28,* 44–59.

Gitlin, L. N. (1998). Testing home modification interventions: Issues of theory, measurement, design, and implementation. In R. Schulz, G. Maddox, & M. P. Lawton (Eds.), *Annual review of gerontology and geriatrics: Focus on interventions research with older adults* (Vol. 18, pp. 190–246). New York: Springer.

Heuft, G., Kruse, A., & Radebold, H. (2000). *Gerontopsychosomatik* [Gerontopsychosomatics]. Munich, Germany: Reinhardt.

Kliegl, R., Mayr, U., & Krampe, R. T. (1994). Time-accuracy functions for determining process and person differences: An application to cognitive aging. *Cognitive Psychology, 26,* 134–164.

Kliegl, R., Smith, J., & Baltes, P. B. (1989). Testing-the-limits and the study of adult age differences in cognitive plasticity of a mnemonic skill. *Developmental Psychology, 25,* 247–256.

Kruse, A. (1996). Alltagspraktische und sozioemotionale Kompetenz [Everyday and socioemotional competence]. In M. Baltes & L. Montada (Eds.), *Produktives Leben im Alter* (pp. 290–322). Frankfurt, Germany: Campus.

Kruse, A. (2001). Psychology of adult education. In N. J. Smelser & P. B. Baltes (Eds.), *The international encyclopedia of the social and behavioral sciences* (Vol. 6, pp. 4223–4227). Oxford: Elsevier Science.

Kruse, A. (2002). Produktives Leben im Alter: Der Umgang mit Verlusten und der Endlichkeit des Lebens [Productive living in old age: Dealing with loss and the finitude of life]. In R. Oerter & L. Montada (Eds.), *Entwicklungspsychologie* (5th ed., pp. 983–996). Weinheim, Germany: Psychologie Verlags Union.

Kruse, A., Rudinger, G., & Schmitt, E. (in press). *Bilder des Alters und gesellschaftliche*

Entwicklung [Images of aging and societal development]. Weinheim, Germany: Psychologie Verlags Union.

Kruse, A., & Schmitt, E. (1998). Die psychische Situation hilfsbedürftiger älterer Menschen—eine ressourcenorientierte Sicht [The psychological situation of the older individual in need of care—a resource-oriented perspective]. *Zeitschrift für Klinische Psychologie, 27,* 118–124.

Kruse, A., & Schmitt, E. (in press). Perceived gains and losses in old age: Individual productivity and social responsibility. *Ageing & Society.*

Lawton, M. P. (1989). Environmental proactivity and affect in older people. In S. Spacapan & S. Oskamp (Eds.), *Social psychology and aging* (pp. 135–164). Beverly Hills, CA: Sage.

Lindenberger, U., & Baltes, P. B. (1997). Intellectual functioning in old and very old age: Cross-sectional results from the Berlin Aging Study. *Psychology and Aging, 12,* 410–432.

Lindenberger, U., & Reischies, F. M. (1999). Limits and potentials of intellectual functioning in old age. In P. B. Baltes & K. U. Mayer (Eds.), *The Berlin Aging Study* (pp. 329–359). New York: Cambridge University Press.

Mann, W. C., Ottenbacher, K. J., Fraas, L., Tomita, M., & Granger, C. V. (1999). Effectiveness of assistive technology and environmental interventions in maintaining independence and reducing home care costs for the frail elderly: A randomized trial. *Archives of Family Medicine, 8(3).*

Martin, P., Ettrich, K. U., Lehr, U., Roether, D., Martin, M., & Fischer-Cyrulies, A. (Eds.). (2000). *Aspekte der Entwicklung im mittleren und höheren Lebensalter* [Aspects of development in middle and later adulthood]. Darmstadt, Germany: Steinkopff.

Minnemann, E., Schmitt, M., Sperling, U., & Jüchtern, J. C. (1997). Formen des Alterns: Sozialer, gesundheitlicher und biographischer Kontext [Forms of aging: Social, health, and biographical contexts]. *Zeitschrift für Gerontopsychologie und-psychiatrie, 10,* 251–257.

Montada, L. (1996). Machen Gebrechlichkeit und chronische Krankheit produktives Altern unmöglich? [Do frailty and chronic illness make productive aging impossible?] In M. Baltes & L. Montada (Eds.), *Produktives Leben im Alter* (pp. 382–392). Frankfurt, Germany: Campus.

Näätänen, R. (1992). *Attention and brain function.* Hillsdale, NJ: Lawrence Erlbaum.

Oswald, F. (1998). Erleben von Wohnalltag bei gesunden und gehbeeinträchtigten Älteren [The subjective experience of everyday living among healthy and mobility impaired elderly]. *Zeitschrift für Gerontologie & Geriatrie, 31,* 250–256.

Ronning, O. M., & Guldvog, B. (1998). Stroke units versus general medical wards in 12- and 18-month survival: A randomized, controlled trial. *Stroke, 29,* 779–784.

Salthouse, T. A. (1985). *A theory of cognitive aging.* Amsterdam: North Holland.

Schmitt, E., Kruse, A., & Olbrich, E. (1994). Formen der Selbständigkeit und Wohnumwelt—ein empirischer Beitrag aus der Studie "Möglichkeiten und Grenzen selbständiger Lebensführung im Alter" [Forms of autonomy and living environments—an empirical contribution from a study entitled "Potentials and Limits to Autonomous Functioning in Old Age"]. *Zeitschrift für Gerontologie & Geriatrie, 27,* 381–389.

Smith, J., & Baltes, P. B. (1990). Wisdom-related knowledge: Age/cohort differences in response to life-planning problems. *Developmental Psychology, 26,* 494–505.

Smith, J., & Baltes, P. B. (1999). Trends and profiles of psychological functioning in very old age. In P. B. Baltes & K. U. Mayer (Eds.), *The Berlin Aging Study* (pp. 197–226). New York: Cambridge University Press.

Staudinger, U. (1996). Psychologische Produktivität und Selbstentfaltung im Alter [Psychological productivity and self-development in later life]. In M. M. Baltes & L. Montada (Eds.), *Produktives Leben im Alter* (pp. 344–373). Frankfurt, Germany: Campus.

Staudinger, U., Freund, A., Linden, M., & Maas, I. (1999). Self, personality, and life regulation: Facts of psychological resilience in old age. In P. B. Baltes & K. U. Mayer (Eds.), *The Berlin Aging Study* (pp. 302–328). New York: Cambridge University Press.

Staudinger, U., Marsiske, M., & Baltes, P. B. (1995). Resilience and reserve capacity in later adulthood: Potentials and limits of development across the life span. In D. Cicchetti & D. Cohen (Eds.), *Developmental psychopathology,* Vol. 2: *Risk, disorder and adaption* (pp. 801–847). New York: Wiley.

Thomae, H. (1996). *Das Individuum und seine Welt* [The individual and his world] (3rd ed.). Göttingen, Germany: Hogrefe.

Wahl, H.-W. (1998). Alltagskompetenz: Ein Konstrukt auf der Suche nach einer Identität. [Everyday competence: A construct in search of an identity]. *Zeitschrift für Gerontologie & Geriatrie, 31,* 243–249.

Wahl, H.-W. (2001). Environmental influences on aging and behavior. In J. E. Birren & K. W. Schaie (Eds.), *Handbook of psychology and aging* (5th ed., pp. 215–217). San Diego: Academic Press.

Wahl, H.-W., Mollenkopf, H., & Oswald, F. (Eds.). (1999). *Alte Menschen in ihrer Umwelt* [Older individuals in their environment]. Opladen, Germany: Westdeutscher Verlag.

Walker, A. (1999). Ageing in Europe—challenges and consequences. *Zeitschrift für Gerontologie & Geriatrie, 32,* 390–397.

CHAPTER 5

M. Powell Lawton's Vision of the Role of the Environment in Aging Processes and Outcomes: A Glance Backward to Move Us Forward

Laura N. Gitlin

D r. M. Powell Lawton was a visionary and an important pioneer in environmental psychology. He imparted to the gerontological community a legacy of seminal theories, multidimensional constructs, widely used scales, and assessment tools. His remarkable productivity attests to the awe-inspiring intellectual energy, breadth, and depth that he brought to key areas of research on growing old. Of most importance, however, was his personal mandate and his fundamental premise as a scientist: the imperative to improve the life quality of older people through research and the development and application of theoretical frameworks.

A recent book of insightful essays collected in honor of Lawton, written by those who worked with or who were mentored by him, highlights the many dimensions of aging that he influenced (Rubinstein, Moss, & Kleban, 2000). These pivotal areas included, but are not limited to, quality of life, environment and aging, affective well-being, human development, caregiving, community and program development, and end-of-life decision making. This chapter describes merely one of his many domains of concern—the role of the environment on aging processes and outcomes as a basis from which to identify the next research steps in examining living environments. Specifically, this chapter briefly reviews Lawton's ecological theory of aging, in particular the competence-environment press framework, and his model of the "good life." These macro-level theoretical constructs are useful starting points in considering living environments for older people, the focus of this book. Obviously, these constructs have been copiously articulated, elaborated, and refined over the past 30 years by Lawton and others. More recently is the comprehensive review of environment and aging research provided by Wahl in the fifth edition of the *Handbook of the Psychology of Aging* (2001). Thus, for the purposes of this chapter, only selected features of these models are highlighted here as they relate to the general theme of this book and as they help inform a perspective on future directions on research on living environments. Noteworthy is that Lawton himself revised and refined the constructs discussed here throughout his long career in view of emerging empirical evidence and further theoretical reflection. Thus, in the spirit of Lawton, this chapter takes a brief look back as a way of identifying specific areas for future research and ways to move forward to address the complex theoretical and methodological challenges of research on living environments.

ECOLOGICAL THEORY OF AGING

Celebrated throughout Lawton's research is the role of living environments in supporting everyday competencies and the life quality of people as they age (Lawton, 1981, 1983). The environment, defined broadly as "all that lies outside the individual," has a unique function in the schemata of Lawton's work. It serves not only as the backdrop or context of behavioral performance but, more important, as an active agent in shaping behavioral outcomes. Lawton argued that the built environment has essential characteristics that can be objectively observed and quantified and that exert varying degrees of influence over behavior and daily performance. Environments vary in their degree and type of impact depending on a number of factors including the person's level of competency, personal appraisals, and the characteristics of the ongoing interactions or transactions that transpire between persons and environments. Thus, not all environments afford life quality, and understanding the dynamic interplay of environment and persons becomes particularly important in order to advance better living arrangements. Also, Lawton's early research on neighborhood characteristics and relocation decisions suggests that he envisioned both inside and outside environments and mobility within each as important areas of investigation.

Core to Lawton's work on the environment was his ecological theory of aging. Essentially, his ecology of aging perspective represented an adaptation theory that was applicable to any age, although it was initially developed with the elderly in mind (Nahemow, 2000). It proposes a dynamic, transactional relationship between individuals and their living environments, the outcome of which is either a positive or negative valence (Lawton, 1982). Lawton and Nahemow (1973) captured these processes by proposing a competence-environmental press framework which was graphically portrayed in a simple, eloquent model. In this model, the y-axis refers to a person's level of competency (high to low), a construct Lawton had carefully explicated in his early research endeavors. He conceptualized competency as composed of 5 categories of behavior ordered hierarchically, each reflecting increasing levels of difficulty (biological, functional health, cognition, time use to the most complex, social behavior); and he developed a range of assessment tools that measured these components.

The x-axis of the competence-environment model refers to the level of demand or press from high to low (moving right to left) that is imposed by an environment. Lawton defined different dimensions of the environment as discussed below, but this aspect of the model remained the least developed conceptually and with regard to the advancement of assessment tools. Also portrayed cutting through the graphic diagonally from left to right is a band reflecting the "zone of adaptation." This zone narrows at the base of the model reflecting the intersection of low competence and low environmental press and broadens at its apex or top of the model reflecting higher levels of competencies and tolerance for a higher level of environmental press.

A central tenet of this model is that as persons' competencies decline, the demand structure of the environment becomes increasingly imposing, resulting in the high potential for negative adaptive outcomes. This tenet, formally referred to as the *docility hypothesis*, generated much discussion and influenced the development of specialized living settings particularly for persons with dementia. Nevertheless, it also met with some objection in that the docility hypothesis did not account for the proactive behaviors adapted by persons to maintain a just-right fit with environmental pressures and to adjust to and regulate declining competencies. Lawton expanded his vision by subsequently positing the proactivity hypothesis in support of the self-regulatory abilities of older people which, in turn, reaffirmed the dynamic processes of person-environmental interactions (Lawton, 1989, 1990a, 1990b).

The competence-environmental press framework has since been used as a heuristic model to understand the relationship between persons with specific characteristics and special living environments. Specifically, it has been applied to research on families with dementia and their living arrangements and special dementia units (Gitlin, Corcoran, Winter, Boyce, & Hauck, 2001; Weisman, Chaudhury, & Diaz, 2000). Moreover, the model provides a compelling theoretical rationale for the use of the environment as a therapeutic modality and, in particular, as a justification for modifying features of living environments to adjust imbalances. Competent behavior may be enhanced by strategies that alter different dimensions of the objective environment and/ or a person's interaction with the environment. For example, a person can adapt different behaviors within his or her environment (e.g., sit while performing an activity), use an assistive device (e.g., mobility aid), or proactively rearrange or structurally alter physical features (e.g., lower cabinets, widen doors).

THE GOOD LIFE

Another construct of relevance to the theme of this book is the *good life* or its more recent label, the *quality of life*. Lawton defined the good life as the "multidimensional evaluation, by both intrapersonal and social-normative criteria, of the person-environment system of an individual in time past, current and anticipated" (Lawton, 1991, p. 6). The good life is composed of 4 overlapping sectors: the objective environment, the perceived quality of life, behavioral competence, and psychological well-being. Each sector has its own internal structure, set of dimensions, and relationships, which have been extensively examined and for which Lawton developed assessment tools. While numerous quality-of-life models have since been developed, Lawton's vision remains unique in two important ways: it is multidimensional and it views the objective environment as an essential contributor to well-being.

Lawton defined the "objective environment" as "all that lies outside the individual and is capable of being counted or rated consensually by observers other than the subjects" (Lawton, 1983). He identified 5 dimensions of the objective environment: personal, group, suprapersonal, social, and physical. Not all these 5 dimensions have been carefully articulated. Unlike the other quality-of-life sectors in which he advanced different measures of their dimensions, he did not develop measures for each environmental aspect.

At the hub of Lawton's good-life model is the ongoing dynamic of person-environment transactions. That is, Lawton conceptualized person-environment transactions as driving the good-life model, thus emphasizing the constantly changing balance between personal competencies, environmental forces, psychosocial adaptation, and perceived life quality.

IMPLICATIONS FOR AGING AND LIVING ENVIRONMENTS

These constructs and models have several important implications for understanding aging processes and living environments. Foremost, these models highlight the centrality of the environment to aging processes and well-being. Specifically, Lawton's work advocates the interconnectedness of living environments and outcomes, such as life quality, and suggests that the study and understanding of well-being in older adulthood is not complete without the integration of an environmental perspective. As such, a key research challenge moving forward is the need to develop new theories that incorporate the environment as an essential ingredient and account for its impact on domains of quality of life. Such theoretical models would facilitate programs of research that test the potential relationships of environmental dimensions to well-being as predictors, mediators, and outcomes.

A related point is the implication for the need to examine empirically the relationships between the environmental sector and other segments of the good-life model and their respective dimensions (e.g., behavioral competence, perceived quality of life, and psychological well-being). The relationship between objective environments and these other good-life quadrants remains understudied. More specifically, the particular dimensions of environments that impact specific clinical populations with regard to their behavioral competence, perceived quality of life, and psychological well-being need careful explication. Hence, the challenge remains to link conceptually and empirically personal characteristics to dimensions of living environments not only to explicate fully the role of environments in the lives of older people but also to identify approaches to optimizing living arrangements.

Furthermore, Lawton's work suggests the need to place the study of living environments within a multidimensional context. A multidimensional approach facilitates an understanding of the gains and limitations of the use of environmental adjustments as a strategy for promoting aging in place. That is, placing the study of environmental redesign in a multidimensional quality-of-life model transforms this approach from a rehabilitative, restorative, or compensatory medical perspective to a holistic social model that emphasizes the interrelated actions available to older people for adapting to faltering competencies. Moreover, placing the study of person-environment adjustments within a broad conceptual framework, such as Lawton's goodlife model, provides a framework for specifying the structure of expected psychological and health-related changes or the relationship between objective environmental conditions and the multiple dimensions of well-being for older adults with different levels of behavioral competencies (Gitlin, 2000).

Yet another implication of Lawton's models described above is the obligation to understand both the "intrapersonal aspects" and "internal standards" individuals apply to their objective environments and objective personal needs. Both types of appraisals, subjective and objective, are important to understand effectively the adaptive mechanisms used by older people including relocation or environmental redesign and the ways in which to intervene effectively to assist older people to age in place in a particular living environment.

FOUR CHALLENGES FOR MOVING FORWARD

Based on the above discussion, 4 interrelated challenges for future research on living environments can be articulated: theoretical development, measurement development, understanding and regulating person-environment transactions, and the clinical application of environment in health care delivery.

Theoretical Developments

Placing the environment within theoretical structures is perhaps the primary challenge of future research which, in turn, will drive the advancement of the field of environment and aging. Contemporary attempts to integrate environmental factors into theoretical models have been promising. Recently, the World Health Assembly of the World Health Organization (WHO) approved major revisions to the international system of classifying disability. It has adopted a new disease classification system referred to now as the International Classification of Functioning, Disability, and Health (ICF). This model posits 4 interconnected structures that impact health and human functioning: the body (e.g., body systems and structures), activities (range of activities from simple to complex), participation (areas of life in which a person is involved, has access to, or for which there are societal barriers or opportunities), and the environment. Within this scheme, environmental factors compose the physical, social, and attitudinal context in which people live and carry out their lives. These factors are external to persons and can have either a positive or negative influence on performance. Future research is necessary to characterize the way in which environmental factors interact with body structures, activities, and participation. The change from the disablement model (Verbrugge & Jette, 1994) to the ICF provides a basis for understanding both health and illness in an environmental context.

Another example of the expansion of a theory to include an environmental perspective is the caregiver stress health process model developed by a research initiative, Resources for Enhancing Alzheimer's Caregiver Health (REACH). The goal of REACH, a multisite study funded by the National Institute on Aging and the National Institute for Nursing Research, is to characterize and test the feasibility of the most promising behavioral, social, technological, or environmental interventions for family caregivers of persons with Alzheimer's disease or related disorders. REACH expanded an existing theory of caregiver stress processes to capture the interactions among the caregiver, care recipient, and the physical and social environment and to link objective environmental stressors to health outcomes (Schulz & Ory, 2000). As shown in Figure 5.1, the primary stressors in this model include the functional limitations and behavioral problems of the care recipient and related social and environmental stressors (e.g., multiple roles, physical setups). The model suggests that caregivers evaluate whether these objective demands pose a potential threat and if they have sufficient coping capabilities to manage these demands. If caregivers perceive the demands as threatening and their coping resources as inadequate, the model suggests that caregivers will experience stress. In turn, the appraisal of stress is assumed to contribute to negative emotional, physiological, and behavioral responses which place the individual at risk for physical and psychiatric disease. Interventions can therefore be designed to have an impact at each level of the stress model. An intervention that involves modifying the physical or social environment of the home targets the primary source of stress in the model (Gitlin et al., 2001; Gitlin & Gwyther, 2003). Thus, the expansion of a basic stress process model to include the environment provides a broader understanding of the particular aspects of caregiving that may be targeted for intervention as well as the potential role of the environment in the experience of stress.

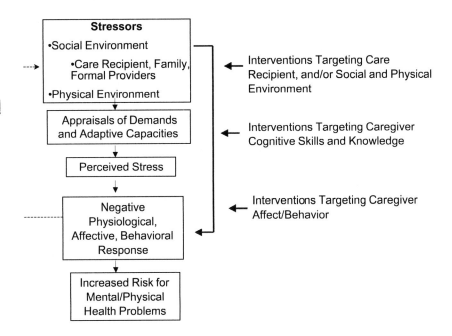

FIGURE 5.1.   REACH Stress Health Process Model.
Source: Schulz and Ory, 2000, p. 56.

Measurement Development

Another critical challenge is that of measurement. The lack of psychometrically sound measures of the environment has hindered the study of the relationship of environmental conditions to behaviors as well as the understanding of the influence of context on daily performance. Moreover, the extreme variation in living environments, and in particular the home, and the tendency of individuals to underreport detrimental conditions highlights the need for a standard metric for use in research and clinical practice. Nevertheless, the way in which we conceptualize and operationalize the environment remains a daunting task.

Measures with adequate psychometric properties have been developed to evaluate dementia patients in residential environments (Norris-Baker, Weisman, Lawton, Sloane, & Kaup, 1999). These tools evaluate a range of environmental dimensions, such as its support of safety, orientation or way finding, physical functioning, comfort, and "person-hood." For home environments, however, only a few environmental assessments have been developed, for which the primary reference group has been physically frail elders (Letts et al., 1994; Tideiksaar, 1986). In most of these assessments, home safety is the primary environmental dimension measured and for which psychometric adequacy has been evaluated (Mann, Hurren, Tomita, Bengali, & Steinfeld, 1994; Oliver, Blathwayt, Brackley, & Tamaki, 1993). Results of these studies show that consistency in ratings varies by the type of hazardous condition observed. For example, Clemson, Roland, and Cumming report excellent agreement among raters for items such as floor coverings, lighting by beds, tub bars and shower rails and low levels of agreement for floor surfaces, presence of pets, external and internal rails, and ramps (Clemson, Roland, & Cumming, 1997). Another study reported inconsistency in raters for observations of grab bars in bathrooms (Sattin, Rodriquez, DeVito, & Wingo, 1998).

These measures have not addressed the important issues of what constitutes an environmental hazard, whether observed hazards represent the same level of risk to older people, whether some environmental conditions present a greater risk depending on a person's level of competency, or whether specific hazards are actually associated with fall or injury events. For example, we do not know if a high door threshold places an older person at higher risk than inadequate illumination or glare. One condition may be inherently more hazardous than another for older people, and the level of risk may vary based on health status (Gitlin, 1998).

Although most home assessments concern physically frail elders, a new tool, the Home Environmental Assessment Protocol (HEAP), is designed to assess the physical features of home environments that support or hinder daily functions of persons with dementia. The HEAP consists of 192 items which are summed into separate indices representing the number of hazards, adaptations, and level of clutter and comfort in 8 areas of the home. Adequate interrater agreement was obtained for hazards; excellent interrater agreement was found for items assessing the presence or absence of adaptation, clutter, and comfort items. Also, measured attributes were related to cognitive and functional status in the expected direction (Gitlin, Schinfeld et al., 2002).

In summary, measures have been successfully developed for certain environmental dimensions important to life quality such as safety, security, and accessibility. However, the measure of attributes contributing to what Lawton referred to as higher-order competencies (engagement, stimulation, satisfaction, novelty, comfort, and personal control), with the exception of a few tools developed for special dementia units, remain relatively unexplored. The most important challenge remains to develop a reliable and valid metric to capture the transactional properties of persons and environments. This may be particularly important for the measure of physical function in which the "context" of performance has been neglected. Few functional assessment tools account for the impact of the environment as part of the measurement of dependence or difficulty in carrying out daily living activities (Gitlin, in press). Finally, of import, is the measure of the subjective experience of the environment and related concepts, such as place attachment, in order to understand its effect on person-environment transactions.

Understanding and Intervening in Person-Environment Transactions

Yet another complexity is examining the relationships among a person, the physical environment, (particularly the home), and the adaptive mechanisms used by an older person. Linking a person's competencies to environmental conditions remains a fundamental challenge. While the competence-environmental press framework serves as a useful heuristic model, in its empirical application to real life person-environment transactions, it does not have precision.

Recent research has begun to document linkages between persons and home environmental features. For example, a recent study of community-living elders with functional limitations shows that having pain, being physically frail, being female, and being a minority member are associated with having numerous home environmental problems (e.g., poor access to living areas, hazards) (Gitlin, Mann, Tomita, & Marcus, 2001). Other research has documented the mediating role of living environments in supporting everyday competence, particularly in elders with sensory deficits (Wahl, Oswald, & Zimprich, 1999). Still other recent research documents the proactive behaviors adapted by older people with physical disability in shaping their environment to support everyday competence (Gignac, Cott, & Badley, 2000).

Maximizing the ability to age in place by helping older people regulate or modify person-environment transactions is also another challenging area for which there is still little research. One recent study shows that, following intervention, families of persons with dementia report less upset and greater efficacy in controlling behavioral problems (Gitlin et al., 2001). Another study shows that home interventions involving modification slow the rate of functional decline (Mann, Ottenbacher, Fraas, Tomita, & Granger, 1999). Figure 5.2 illustrates the basic premise of intervention research building on the competence-environment dialectic. Still more research is necessary to determine the best practices or a combination of intervention strategies, the range of benefits evinced by older people, and who benefits and why from adjusting home environments.

Clinical Application

Lawton's vision was to improve the lives of older people by developing strong theoretical constructs to guide clinical practice. The challenge still remains to link Lawton's meta-theoretical constructs to microlevel clinical principles. Certainly, recent research provides the empirical evidence as to the importance of integrating an environmental perspective with health care models. For example, environmental redesign has been shown to be an important component of minimizing delirium in acute hospitalizations of the elderly (Inouye, Bogardus, Baker, Leo-Summers, & Cooney, 2000), a multifactorial approach to preventing falls (Tinetti et al., 1994), supporting functionality of patients with chronic illness, and in dementia care.

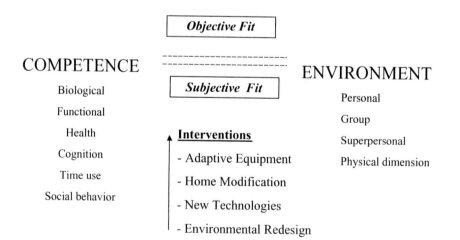

FIGURE 5.2.   Intervention research building on the environmental dialectic.

Finally, another implication of Lawton's work for clinical applications concerns the organization of long-term care. Given that the relationship between persons and their environments is dynamic, reciprocal, and constantly changing, continual assessments and adjustments to maintain a zone of adaptation may be an important approach to long-term care.

CONCLUSION

Looking backward, Lawton early in his research career advanced a fundamental paradigm, the ecology of aging, and a multidimensional quality-of-life model, which he continued to refine and advance. His research provided the gerontological community with such basic working conceptual tools as environmental press, proactivity, competency, and a multidimensional good-life model from which to move forward in research on living arrangements. His macrotheoretical constructs provide a broad framework for the study of persons and living environments and a rationale for developing interventions that adjust person-environment transactions to maximize well-being and support aging in place.

As we build on his opus, we face numerous critical challenges. A fundamental concern is advancing sound theories of the role of the environment in the lives of older people as well as conceptual and operational definitions for guiding the measurement of its dimensions. We must develop conceptual and operational definitions that adequately quantify the dynamical processes captured graphically in the competence-environment press model.

A final point is that placing the study of living arrangements within a broad multidimensional life quality framework, as suggested by Lawton, maximizes the potential to understand the reciprocity between environments and persons and identify both proximal and distal outcomes on life quality of interventions designed to enhance aging in place.

REFERENCES

Clemson, L., Roland, M., & Cumming, R. G. (1997). Types of hazards in the homes of elderly people. *Occupational Therapy Journal of Research, 17,* 200–213.

Gignac, M. A. M., Cott, C., & Badley, E. M. (2000). Adaptation to chronic illness and disability and its relationship to perceptions of independence and dependence. *Journal of Gerontology: Psychological Sciences, 55B,* P362–372.

Gitlin, L. N. (1998). Testing home modification interventions: Issues of theory, measurement, design, and implementation. In R. Schulz, G. Maddox, & M. P. Lawton (Eds.), *Annual review of gerontology & geriatrics: Focus on interventions research with older adults* (Vol. 18, pp. 190–246). New York: Springer.

Gitlin, L. N. (2000). Adjusting "person-environment systems": Helping older people live the "good life" at home. In R. Rubinstein, M. Moss, & M. H. Kleban (Eds.), *The many dimensions of aging: Essays in honor of M. P. Lawton* (pp. 41–54). New York: Springer.

Gitlin, L. N. (in press). *Physical function in the elderly: A comprehensive guide to its measurement.* Austin, TX: Pro-Ed.

Gitlin, L. N., Corcoran, M., Winter, L., Boyce, A., & Hauck, W. (2001). A randomized, controlled trial of a home environmental intervention: Effect on efficacy and upset in caregivers and on daily function of persons with dementia. *The Gerontologist, 41,* 4–14.

Gitlin, L. N., & Gwyther, L. P. (2003). In-home interventions: Helping caregivers where they live. In D. Coon, D. Gallagher-Thompson, & L. Thompson (Eds.), *Innovative interventions to reduce caregiver distress: A clinical guide* (pp. 139–160). New York: Springer.

Gitlin, L. N., Mann, W., Tomita, M., & Marcus, S. (2001). Factors associated with home environmental problems among community-living elders. *Disability and Rehabilitation, 23,* 777–787.

Gitlin, L. N., Schinfeld, S., Winter, L., Corcoran, M., Boyce, A., & Hauck, W. (2002). Evaluating home environments of persons with dementia: Interrater reliability and validity of the Home Environmental Assessment Protocol (HEAP). *Disability and Rehabilitation, 24,* 59–71.

Inouye, S. K., Bogardus, S. T., Jr., Baker, D. I., Leo-Summers, L., & Cooney, L. M. (2000). Hospital Elder Life Program: A model of care to prevent cognitive and functional decline in older hospitalized patients. *Journal of the American Geriatrics Society, 48*(12), 697–706.

Lawton, M. P. (1981). An ecological view of living arrangements. *The Gerontologist, 21*(1), 59–66.

Lawton, M. P. (1982). Competence, environmental press, and the adaptation of older people. In M. P. Lawton, P. G. Windley, & T. O. Byerts (Eds.), *Aging and the environment: Theoretical approaches* (pp. 33–59). New York: Springer.

Lawton, M. P. (1983). Environment and other determinants of well-being in older people. *The Gerontologist, 23,* 349–357.

Lawton, M. P. (1989). Environmental proactivity in older people. In V. L. Bengston & W. Schaie (Eds.), *The course of life: Research and reflections* (pp. 15–23). New York: Springer.

Lawton, M. P. (1990a). Aging and performance of home tasks. *Human Factors, 32*(5), 527–536.

Lawton, M. P. (1990b). Residential environment and self-directedness among older people. *American Psychologist, 45*(5), 638–640.

Lawton, M. P. (1991). A multidimensional view of quality of life in frail elders. In J. E. Birren, J. E. Lubben, J. C. Rowe, & D. E. Deutchman (Eds.), *The concept and measurement of quality of life in the frail elderly* (pp. 3–27). San Diego, CA: Academic Press.

Lawton, M. P., Brody, E. M., & Turner-Massey, P. (1978). The relationships of environmental factors to changes in well-being. *The Gerontologist, 18*(2), 133–137.

Lawton, M. P., & Nahemow, L. (1973). Ecology and the aging process. In C. Eisdorfer & M. P. Lawton (Eds.), *The psychology of adult development and aging* (pp. 619–674). Washington, DC: American Psychological Association.

Letts, L., Law, M., Rigby, P., Cooper, B., Stewart, D., & Strong, S. (1994). Person-environmental competence amongst independent elderly households. *American Journal of Occupational Therapy, 48,* 608–618.

Mann, W. C., Hurren, D., Tomita, M., Bengali, M., & Steinfeld, E. (1994). Environmental problems in homes of elders with disabilities. *Occupational Therapy Journal of Research, 14,* 191–211.

Mann, W. C., Ottenbacher, K. J., Fraas, L., Tomita, M., & Granger, C. V. (1999). Effectiveness of assistive technology and environmental interventions in maintaining independence and reducing home care costs for the frail elderly. *Archives of Family Medicine, 8,* 210–217.

Nahemow, L. (2000). The ecological theory of aging: Powell Lawton's legacy. In R. L. Rubinstein, M. Moss, & M. H. Kleban (Eds.), *The many dimensions of aging: Essays in honor of M. P. Lawton* (pp. 22–40). New York: Springer.

Norris-Baker, C., Weisman, G. D., Lawton, M. P., Sloane P., & Kaup, M. (1999). Assessing special care units for dementia: The professional Environmental Assessment Protocol. In E. Steinfeld & G. S. Danford (Eds.), *Enabling environments: Measuring the impact of environment on disability and rehabilitation* (pp. 16–182). New York: Plenum.

Oliver, R., Blathwayt, J., Brackley, C., & Tamaki, T. (1993). Development of the safety assessment of function and the environment for rehabilitation (SAFER) tool. *Canadian Journal of Occupational Therapy, 60,* 78–82.

Rubinstein, R. L., Moss, M., & Kleban, M. H. (Eds.). (2000). *The many dimensions of aging: Essays in honor of M. P. Lawton.* New York: Springer.

Sattin, R. W., Rodriquez, J. G., DeVito, C. A., & Wingo, P. A. (1998). Home environmental hazards and the risk of fall injury events among community-dwelling older persons. *Journal of the American Geriatric Society, 46,* 669–676.

Schulz, R., & Ory, M. (Eds.). (2000). *Handbook on dementia caregiving: Evidence-based interventions for family caregivers.* New York: Springer.

Tideiksaar, R. (1986). Preventing falls: Home hazard checklists to help older patients protect themselves. *Geriatrics, 41,* 26–28.

Tinetti, M. E., Baker, D. I., McAvay, G., Claus, E. B., Garrett, P., Gottschalk, M., Koch, M. L., Trainor, K., & Horwitz, R. I. (1994). A multifactorial intervention to reduce the risk of falling among elderly people living in the community. *New England Journal of Medicine, 331,* 821–827.

Verbrugge, L. M., & Jette, A. M. (1994). The disablement process. *Social Science and Medicine, 38,* 1–14.

Wahl, H.-W. (2001). Environmental influences on aging and behavior. In J. E. Birren & K. W. Schaie (Eds.), *Handbook of the psychology of aging* (5th ed., pp. 215–237). New York: Academic Press.

Wahl, H.-W., Oswald, F., & Zimprich, D. (1999). Everyday competence in visually impaired older adults: A case for person-environment perspectives. *The Gerontologist, 39,* 140–149.

Weisman, G. D., Chaudhury, H., & Moore, K. D. (2000). Theory and practice of place: Toward an integrative model. In R. Rubinstein, M. Moss, & M. H. Kleban (Eds.), *The many dimensions of aging: Essays in honor of M. P. Lawton* (pp. 3–21). New York: Springer.

CHAPTER 6

History, Habit, Heart, and Hearth: On Making Spaces into Places

Graham D. Rowles and John F. Watkins

E ach person's life is framed in *time* and *space*. Our allocation of time may be the biblical three score and ten years; it may be cut short by a fatal teenage motor accident, or it may be extended well into our tenth decade by a favorable genetic disposition, good living, and medical technology. Our space may be limited to lifelong residence in a single urban neighborhood or rural settlement. Alternatively, it may span the globe and be limited only by our ability and inclination to travel vast distances. Time and space, however, are sterile; they are merely the metric, the spatio-temporal stage upon which life is played out.

A life becomes significant only as an individual story evolves within a unique space-time continuum imbued with meaning. The manner in which a particular life story unfolds is determined by a plethora of factors including genetics, physiological prowess, cognitive ability, personality, and other characteristics of the individual. From birth onward, each life story is also shaped by the environment: the physical setting, the social and economic context, and the cultural milieu. As we grow up, and as we grow old, the trajectory of life experience and the meaning of our story both to ourselves and to others evolve as a complex, ever-changing transactional relationship between personal and environmental factors as we forge an identity and establish our own distinctive manner of being in the world.

Within this broad rubric, the life events and experiences that define who we are as self-actualizing persons become entwined with the selective construction of our life story through two fundamental processes. The first of these is the creation and maintenance of a personal history and sense of "being in time." A growing literature in the social and behavioral sciences focuses on the creation and interpretation of biographies, autobiographies, and personal narratives as windows into the human condition (Birren, Kenyon, Ruth, Schroots, & Svensson, 1996; Kenyon, Clark, & deVries, 2001; Rybarczyk & Bellg, 1997). The second process is the repeated transformation of the spaces of our lives into the places of our lives in a complex and cumulative dynamic process that extends throughout the life course and determines our sense of "being in place." Far less has been written on this topic, although a few informative studies have appeared in recent years (Altman & Low, 1992; McHugh & Mings, 1996; Rowles & Ravdal, 2002; Watkins, 1999; Wheeler, 1995). In concert, these two processes forge an identity and sense of "being in the world" that is integrally linked to well-being.

In this chapter, we focus primarily on the latter theme. We synthesize current knowledge about being in place and the manner in which—for each individual—this phenomenon evolves over the life course, becomes manifest in old age, and is affected by personal and environmental change. We present a conceptual life course model that views being in place as a function of the way in which spaces are repeatedly transformed into places as we move through the environments of our life. We hypothesize that each move to a new setting (or adjustment to change in a current one) involves a process of inhabiting the new or reconfigured space in a manner that involves transference of past environmental experience, integration of new circumstances, and redefinition of our being in place.

BEING IN PLACE

Being in place is a state of existence often characterized by feeling comfortable, at home, and at one with one's environment (Rowles, 1991). A variety of complementary elements are involved. First is the establishment of a *physical intimacy* and familiarity with spaces through habitual use (Clark, 2000; Kielhofner, 1995; Ludwig, 1997; Rowles, 2000). For example, as we spend more time in our residence, the rhythm and routine of repeated daily use establishes ease in moving about within its confines. We arise each morning, complete our daily ablutions, finish our breakfast and coffee, and navigate our way to work with hardly a concerted thought. Over time, such behavioral ritual becomes taken for granted and habitual as our body develops an inherent awareness of the space that transcends our consciousness (Seamon, 1980).

Being in place is rarely a solitary affair. Commonly, it involves sharing space with others—our spouse, children, and others who live in our abode, as well as visitors we receive. Through interactions with others in a space, it gradually comes to assume a *social meaning* as, with the passage of time, there become established a set of social rules, daily rituals of interaction, and norms of behavior in the space—ways in which our social life is constructed and conducted (Rowles, 1983; Rubinstein, 1989; Sixsmith, 1986). The space becomes a behavior setting (Norris-Baker, 1998).

Finally, being in place has an *autobiographical* component (Marcus, 1992, 1995; Rowles, 1983; Sixsmith, 1986). Spaces assume meaning as a result of the accumulation in consciousness of events that transpire within them. The space of our home becomes the place where we raised our children. We vividly recall the children's parties in the family room; the scuffing on the wall serves to remind us. We remember repainting the living room with our now-deceased spouse as we stare at his photograph on the mantle. The front porch assumes significance as the location where our daughter's wedding photographs were taken. Through habitation and the selective remembrance of events, every nook and cranny becomes imbued with an identity that roots us in place. The artifacts we treasure and the places where events transpired become cues to vicariously experienced environments, places displaced in time and space to which we may return at will through reminiscence (Rowles, 1978). A sense of autobiographical "insideness," of being part of the place and of the place being a part of the self, becomes part of our persona (Hay, 1998; Rowles, 1983; Rubinstein, 1989).

Although there may be some variations in specific manifestations among cultures, physical intimacy, social immersion, and autobiographical insideness are universal, cross-culturally relevant dimensions of a person's being in place. But how is a sense of being in place created? What human imperatives and experiential processes contribute to its evolution over time? We suggest that being in place results from the repeated and cumulative process of making spaces into places.

MAKING SPACES INTO PLACES

Making spaces into places, the art of place making, is a skill that evolves over the life course. Four interwoven elements are involved: history, habit, heart, and hearth.

History

Each of us has a history of transforming spaces into places. We do this both on a transitory, ephemeral level (when we take a favorite pillow or artifact from home to facilitate our sleep and feel "at home" in an unfamiliar motel), and on a more permanent, substantial basis (when we change residence and personalize a new structure). Some people's life history involves frequent relocations. Such people become experienced place makers, adept at sustaining links with places of their past even as they accommodate to new settings. With each relocation, they transfer a part of their past and blend it into each new setting with increasing ease. Maintaining links with places of the past may involve transferring treasured artifacts including photographs and memorabilia that serve as cues to personal history and provide an ongoing sense of identity (Boschetti, 1995; Paton & Cram, 1992). Transference may involve learned strategies for becoming involved in the local social milieu such as making a conscious effort to visit new neighbors (Reed & Payton, 1996). Over our life course, we develop routine ways of accommodating to the stress of severance from the places of our past. We become accustomed to maintaining contact with previous settings through periodic return visits, telephone calls to former neighbors, or ongoing correspondence. Through such processes, our history often provides us with expertise in accommodating to change and making spaces into places. Such expertise is not necessarily developed by all individuals. For some people, a very high frequency of moves through life might prohibit effective employment of accommodation strategies and lead to a sense of separation and impermanence resulting in an inability to identify with any environment. Such individuals may become alienated from place and come to inhabit a "placeless" world (Chandler, 1989; Relph, 1976).

In contrast to those with a history of frequent and successful relocations, people with lengthy residence in a few environments or even a single setting may experience difficulty in abandoning the familiar and transforming new spaces into places. Relocation may be particularly traumatic for elders with a history of lifelong residential stability because they may lack place-making skills.

Habit

A second element of transforming spaces into places is habituation—the manner in which, over time, we come physically to possess the spaces of our lives. Through the rhythm and routine of daily pathways, physical intimacy with an increasingly familiar setting gradually becomes taken for granted. We develop an ability to climb the stairs in the dark without having consciously to count the number of steps. Indeed, the significance of such habituation is made acutely apparent on occasions when our automatic pilot breaks down and we take an extra step!

Similarly, spaces may be transformed into places through social habituation. Home becomes a social place because of the comfortable easiness with which we habitually interact with those who share our residence. It becomes taken for granted that there is little talk at breakfast, that we hug (or do not hug) when we leave for work, that we dine together on Friday evenings, that we talk with our neighbor as we rake up autumn's leaves. We create the social culture of the places we inhabit through ongoing interaction and subtle, often subconscious negotiation with those with whom we share a space (Hay, 1998; Hochschild, 1973; Sixsmith, 1986).

Habit is even important in developing and sustaining autobiographical affiliation with place. Each room of our dwelling becomes imbued with the memories of events that are routinely triggered when we enter the space (Marcus, 1992). The images we repeatedly resurrect in consciousness are patterned, routinized; they are "habits of the mind" reflecting an array of incidents in our lives selectively although implicitly chosen to represent who we are—to define our persona (Rowles, 2000).

Heart

A third process contributing to transforming spaces into places is emotional bonding (Altman & Low, 1992; Rubinstein & Parmalee, 1992; Zingmark, Norberg, & Sandman, 1995). Emotional attachment may result from cues generated simply from being in the space where a traumatic or ecstatic event occurred. More often it is consciously created by the manner in which the space is manipulated and filled with items having emotional significance. We surround ourselves with pictures of loved ones and memorabilia accumulated during significant phases of our life (Boschetti, 1995; Csikszentmihalyi & Rochberg-Halton, 1981). We create place as an emotional repository for all that we are.

Hearth

Physical intimacy, a sense of social immersion and belonging, and psychological attachment are all embraced within a need for centering or rootedness that may reflect a basic human territorial instinct—an inherent imperative for the creation of a place of ownership and possession, a place that is ours, a home. Many writers have emphasized the importance of the hearth as a place of centering: home becomes a location from which we venture forth and to which we often long to return (Altman & Werner, 1985; Buttimer, 1980; Marcus, 1995; Rubinstein, 1989). Our hearth becomes a place of safety and security. As the space of our dwelling becomes ever more permanently possessed, it becomes the fulcrum of our being in place. Indeed, for some, the hearth becomes sacred (Bachelard, 1969; Buttimer, 1980; Eliade, 1959; Zingmark et al., 1995).

REMAKING PLACE

Establishment of a sense of being in place through transformation of spaces into places tends to generate a high level of residential inertia. For many, the outcome is a preference for aging in place. Indeed, in much of the Western world, an aging-in-place imperative has become the underlying motif of residential policy (Callahan, 1992; Tilson, 1990). Although the majority of elders are able to age in place, for some, increasing physical frailty or environmental change necessitates either radical reorientation of customary modes of being in place or relocation. Especially under circumstances where such relocations are involuntary, there may be a significant disruption of an often long-established sense of being in place, and the remaking of place may become problematic.

On the other hand, most elders are adept at transforming spaces into places, particularly if they have experienced several successful relocations during their life course. Wheeler (1995, p. 119) describes this phenomenon for elders who relocated to a North Carolina continuing care retirement community:

> A relationship exists between an individual's feelings about past residential experiences and his/her feelings about his/her current place of residence. . . . [F]actors related to the physical and social environments experienced in the informants' first place of residence can be identified in their current place of residence. Each subsequent residential experience is added to the individual's information base. The information, in turn, is used as a reference by the individual throughout his or her entire life.

The mechanisms of transference are threefold. First, there is *conscious memory*. We transport our history—the places of our past—by selectively remembering life experiences (the events and the places where those events transpired). Each of us carries a reservoir of myriad place experiences, many of which can be resurrected on cue and some of which remain latent (Marcus, 1992; Rowles & Ravdal, 2002). We use our remembrance of place in constructing and maintaining our contemporary sense of self—wherever we may be located in contemporary space. Provided that we remain cognitively intact, remembrance of the places of our past cannot be taken from us. Recent research suggests that even persons with Alzheimer's disease may retain memories of place and home and that such memories may be accessible (Usita, Hyman, & Herman, 1998; Zingmark, Norberg, & Sandman, 1993).

Second, it is possible to transfer adaptively elements of *implicit memory*, our body's awareness of space to each new setting. This is accomplished by many elders who, following relocation, subconsciously choose to recreate place by arranging their furniture in a configuration remarkably similar to that existing in their former residence (Hartwigsen, 1987; Toyama, 1988).

Conscious and implicit memory is reinforced by a third, overt, mechanism: the selective *transfer of possessions* to each new environment (Belk, 1992; Boschetti, 1995). In the case of elders who tend to move from spacious dwellings to residences with progressively less space, this is sometimes a highly conscious process of divestiture that involves a carefully reasoned but emotionally taxing reduction of inventory and placing priority on retaining items of particular personal significance (Morris, 1992). One outcome may be an intensification of the meaning of the items retained. For many elders, the remaking of place becomes a highly conscious and distinctive process of environmental manipulation. Elements of this process are illustrated in the following case study.

REBECCA O'RIORDAN

Rebecca O'Riordan, an 82-year-old widow, moved to Highbury Manor, a continuing care retirement community, approximately a year ago, not long after the death of her husband. Figure 6.1 shows her space—a space identical to the space allotted to other residents of the community. Figure 6.2 depicts her place—a place constructed through a transformation that embraces her history, nurtures a comfortable pattern of habitual behavior, evokes warm emotions, and forms the center of her world.

Clear evidence of Rebecca's contemporary "being in the world" is man-

FIGURE 6.1.   Rebecca O'Riordan's space.

ifested in a collage of recent family photographs which adorns the refrigerator door, and in the practicality of many items of furniture including the
large bureau she brought with her specifically to hold her prized collection
of ceramic birds. As we look more closely, the critical role of time and
history becomes apparent. As she noted, "You bring certain pieces for convenience. Certain pieces you choose for sentimental reasons." There is her
mother's lamp. There is the spinning wheel she used when the family lived
in a steel town near Pittsburgh.

Many of the items evoke stories (see Figure 6.3). The grandfather clock,
a family heirloom, was received as a surprise gift on the day her first daughter was born in 1942. Her husband refinished the case; "Of course, we
worked together on it. It was really fun to see this wood come up." She tells
the story of the old washstand that was adapted to house her television (see
Figure 6.4). "We bought it at an old antique shop in Hamilton, Ohio, that

FIGURE 6.2.   Rebecca O'Riordan's place.

was owned by my friend's sister. Well I just thought it was a neat piece. I never thought we'd adapt it to a TV but we did, in the early sixties."

She turns to a table (see Figure 6.5).

It originally had one leaf. We thought it was cherry but found it was walnut. So he [her husband] took the big leaf, made two small ones, cut off the sausage legs and made a coffee table. The reason I'd never give this up? On Saturday nights we put the leaves up and we had hamburgers, home made French fries and home made milk shakes. And in the winters we'd make a fire in the fireplace and they [her children] roasted marshmallows and they thought this was the most wonderful meal of the week.

FIGURE 6.3.   The grandfather clock.

As she mused it was clear that, for a time, she had reentered a world displaced in time and space. The table itself, and the photographs she kept on it—the photograph of a granddaughter's wedding, the picture of her husband, the faded photograph taken when they were courting—all served as cues for reentry into the past and reinforcement of her identity.

TOWARD A LIFE COURSE MODEL

It is important to place these observations within a broader theoretical context. We propose an experience-based life course model of being in place and the manner in which spaces are repeatedly transformed into places through the evolving trajectory of an individual's life. We take as a starting

FIGURE 6.4. The old washstand.

point the transactional framework employed by most existing aging/environ-
ment theories (see, for example, Kahana, 1982; Lawton & Nahemow, 1973;
Scheidt & Norris-Baker, 1990; Norris-Baker & Scheidt, 1994). Specifically,
our baseline is a modification of the transactional "attunement" or code-
velopment model of Kindermann and Skinner (1992) (see Figure 6.6). In
order to represent a life course perspective, the x-axis represents Age/Time.
Each individual (open circle) and context (shaded circle) observation represents a 5-year age period extending from 5 to 90. Influence/Exchange
Magnitude (the y-axis) refers to the lagged arrows representing the evolving
transactional relationship between the individual and the environmental context, with longer arrows representing a greater magnitude of influence. This
transactional model places reciprocal exchanges between changing individuals and their changing context within a developmental perspective. As the

FIGURE 6.5.   The table.

individual changes in capability or inclination, he or she may modify the
context (perhaps relocate into a continuing care retirement community as
did Rebecca O'Riordan). Changing the environmental context may also involve more immediate manipulation. For example, Rebecca may choose to
move her photographs closer to the chair in which she spends so much of
the day so that she can see more clearly the image of her late husband and
the photograph of her granddaughter's wedding party.

   Three event scenarios, each representing potentially disruptive relocation
events, are built into the model as presented. Event A represents an
employment-related move, event B a retirement migration, and event C a
long-term care "movement for assistance" relocation. In each case, we
hypothesize that there results an imbalance or lack of congruence between
the individual and the environmental context. As the individual accommo-
dates to the new setting, and through habitation transforms the new space
into a place, there is progression toward stasis and person-environment congruence.

   In the upper portion of Figure 6.6 we add a representation of the reservoir
of place images constituting the individual's environmental experience. Each
column represents the totality of environmental experiences of the individual
that are available in consciousness (shaded area) or that remain latent or

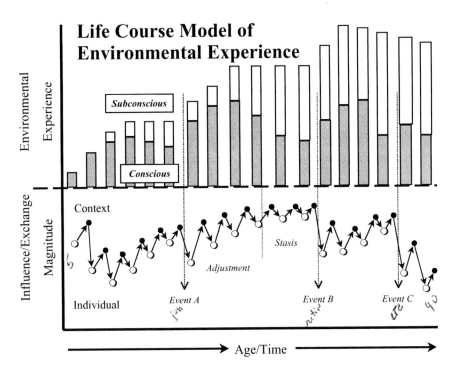

FIGURE 6.6. Life course model of environmental experience.

relegated to the subconscious (open area). There is some evidence that major life transitions, which would include relocation, are associated with increased propensity for reminiscence and the resurrection of places of the past in consciousness (Lieberman & Falk, 1971; see also Chaudhury, 1999, p. 239). We hypothesize that relocation, or a comparable disruptive in situ environmental change, results in heightened environmental awareness and increased utilization of the reservoir of environmental experience (including formerly latent experiences raised to consciousness by the event) that the individual has accumulated over his or her life course. Such environmental experience represents a combination of accumulating new experiences, the sloughing off of now redundant elements of being in the abandoned space, and selective resurrection and transference of prior environmental experience in the process of transforming new spaces into places. The outcome is a renewed and redefined sense of being in place. With progressive adjustment and movement toward individual-context stasis, a greater portion of an individual's environmental experience lapses into the subconscious. This marks habituation in place and the taken-for-granted affinity that gradually develops with increasing familiarity.

SOME IMPLICATIONS

The proposed conceptual model provides a holistic process-oriented framework for developing a genre of empirical research studies that seek to integrate fully overt patterns of relocation behavior, the cognitive representations that underlie such behavior, and personal history-related emotions, memories, and self-defining sources of identity that condition adjustment to new settings in old age. We consider that it also has the potential to stimulate new theory in gerontology which will allow us to move beyond rather static extant models of the evolving person-environment transaction by explicitly linking the dimensions of time and space and considering relocation within a life course perspective.

Many critical issues remain to be addressed. It is important to confirm that an imperative for being in place and a propensity for place making is, indeed, an inherent and universal component of human identity and being in the world that is applicable across cultures and generations. Within this rubric, there are several key issues. With respect to individual variability, why do some individuals seem to have the propensity to develop strong, resilient, and adaptable affinities for place while relocation for others may become an ecological crisis resulting in pathological outcomes as a home attachment that initially developed subconsciously becomes conscious (Giuliani, 1991; Peled & Schwartz, 1999, p. 88)? What is the outcome for elders when place making fails? What are the effects of critical extraneous events leading to involuntary displacement such as wars, natural disasters, and other life-changing events on the ability of elders to transform spaces into places and hence retain a sense of identity through place (Fullilove, 1996)? And what is the effect of time itself on the processes of place making among elders? Can we anticipate significant cohort differences in ability and propensity for transforming spaces into places as a result of differences among increasingly mobile successive generations of elders?

At what point does an elder's ability to adapt to a changing familiar environment become problematic? For example, having lived in a familiar and meaningful community residence for decades may become maladaptive and even dangerous for some persons with dementia. There is a closely related moral issue here: can we allow ourselves to let the ability of people to transform even the worst of spaces into places that are tolerable become an excuse for inaction in intervening to improve suboptimal environments?

Finally, moving to a theoretical level, there may be a distinct relationship between place making and the more general psychological processes of adaptation (Baltes, 1997; Lazarus & Folkman, 1984; Peirce, 1995; Wahl, 2001). Processes of place making and remaking may represent inherent strategies for coping with loss and the stress of personal and environmental change. For example, the case of Rebecca O'Riordan provides some evidence to suggest that transformations of place through increased concern with treasured artifacts and remembrances of the deceased can become an integral component of adjusting to bereavement. Can place making be viewed as an element of more general models of coping? Is place making a stable component of individual personality and identity, or is this an ability that evolves in a systematic manner over the life course?

Assuming that each of these issues can be satisfactorily clarified, how does a deeper understanding of the processes whereby elders transform spaces into places help us understand pragmatic problems associated with mobility and the changing living arrangements of elders? We contend that it makes a critical difference—between designing and allocating spaces in which elders "exist" in settings severed from their past and nurturing the creation of places where they "live" in a milieu that reinforces the richness of their life history. It is the difference between elders who are alienated from place and elders who retain a sense of being "in" rather than "out" of place. Most important, the perspective offers the prospect of an array of practical, theoretically grounded place therapies which minimize the disruptive effects of environmental change on the lives and well-being of elders (Scheidt & Norris-Baker, 1999).

Perhaps the most important intervention is *recognition* among professionals of the complexity of elders' relationships with the places of their lives and the manner in which a sense of being in place is disrupted by environmental change. There is also considerable unrealized potential for designing spaces that can become places—*environmental designs* which incorporate ample options for the storage and display of identity-reinforcing photographs and treasured artifacts (Hunt & Pastalan, 1987). A third option is *behavior-setting therapies* which focus on strategies to ensure the survival of threatened spaces that have become key places for social interactions among small groups of elders (Scheidt & Norris-Baker, 1999). On a larger scale, there are options for *community therapy* oriented toward maintaining the identity of traditional neighborhoods through boosterism and rekindling a sense of

FIGURE 6.7.   Her place in the future.

community history, identity, and pride (Hummon, 1992; Norris-Baker & Scheidt, 1994; Scheidt & Norris-Baker, 1999).

Shifting focus from the manipulation of the environmental context to the elders themselves, *relocation preparation and adjustment* strategies, ranging from preliminary visits and the anticipatory modeling of relocation (Hunt & Pastalan, 1987; Pastalan, 1983), through the processes of "constructing familiarity" (Reed & Payton, 1996), to psychotherapy based on an "ecoanalysis of the home" (Peled & Schwartz, 1999), have met with some success. Such strategies are designed to prepare elders to deal with the consequences of relocation by providing counseling support and assistance in the process of separation from familiar place and the recreation of place. Complementary to such place therapy is the need for a reappraisal of the overwhelmingly negative tone of most studies of relocation. In many cases, relocation can lead to positive outcomes (Kahana & Kahana, 1983). Indeed, the *enhancement of potentially positive outcomes* can often ameliorate negative impacts of severance from place (Scheidt & Norris-Baker, 1999, p. 5).

A valuable proactive place therapy involves a deliberate focus on *artifact transference* (McCracken, 1987; Wapner, Demick, & Redondo, 1990). There is considerable potential for interventions to assist and support elders in choosing key items to accompany them to new settings—items that facilitate the transference and re-creation of a sense of place. One of the dangers in efforts to assist elders to accommodate to new settings is the propensity to deny the existence of old ones. There is an increasing recognition of the therapeutic importance of *retaining links* with prior environments—through return visits, telephone calls to former neighbors, and the encouragement of reminiscence and vicarious re-immersion in physically abandoned environments (Burnside & Haight, 1994; Chaudhury, 1999).

Finally, it is fitting that a chapter focused on the integration of space and time should conclude with a recognition of the degree to which many elders' sense of being in place may be framed in relation to *projecting into the future*. Such a projection may be an important element of place making. The place Rebecca created in her apartment was not only an amalgam of her present and her past; it provided a launching pad for her place in the future. On the back of numerous items, including a large framed picture which, upon Rebecca's death, was to be given to her oldest daughter (see Figure 6.7), Rebecca had taped instructions regarding her wishes. Such activity has provided a physical assurance of some continuity of her place in the future lives of her children and hence of her identity beyond her death.

REFERENCES

Altman, I., & Low, S. M. (Eds.). (1992). *Place attachment*. New York: Plenum Press.

Altman, I., & Werner, C. M. (Eds.). (1985). *Home environments*. New York: Plenum Press.

Bachelard, G. (1969). *The poetics of space*. Boston: Beacon Press.

Baltes, P. B. (1997). On the incomplete architecture of human ontogeny: Selection, optimization, and compensation as foundation of developmental theory. *American Psychologist, 52,* 366–380.

Belk, R. W. (1992). Attachment to possessions. In I. Altman & S. M. Low (Eds.), *Place attachment* (pp. 37–62). New York: Plenum Press.

Birren, J. E., Kenyon, G. M., Ruth, J., Schroots, J. J. F., & Svensson, T. (Eds.). (1996). *Aging and biography: Explorations in adult development*. New York: Springer.

Boschetti, M. A. (1995). Attachment to personal possessions: An interpretive study of the older person's experiences. *Journal of Interior Design, 21*(1), 1–12.

Burnside, I., & Haight, B. (1994). Reminiscence and life review: Therapeutic interventions for older people. *Nurse Practitioner, 19*(4), 55–61.

Buttimer, A. (1980). Home, reach and the sense of place. In A. Buttimer & D. Seamon (Eds.), *The human experience of space and place* (pp. 166–187). New York: St. Martin's Press.

Callahan, J. J. (1992). Aging in place. *Generations, 16,* 5–6.

Chandler, J. (1989). Marriage and the housing career of naval wives. *Sociological Review, 37,* 253–276.

Chaudhury, H. (1999). Self and reminiscence of place: A conceptual study. *Journal of Aging and Identity, 4*(4), 231–253.

Clark, F. A. (2000). The concepts of habit and routine: A preliminary theoretical synthesis. *Occupational Therapy Journal of Research, 20* (Supplement 1), 123S–137S.

Csikszentmihalyi, M., & Rochberg-Halton, E. (1981). *The meaning of things: Domestic symbols and the self.* New York: Cambridge University Press.

Eliade, M. (1959). *The sacred and the profane.* New York: Harcourt, Brace & World.

Fullilove, M. T. (1996). Psychiatric implications of displacement: Contributions from the psychology of place. *American Journal of Psychiatry, 153*(12), 1516–1523.

Giuliani, M. V. (1991). Towards an analysis of mental representations of attachment to home. *Journal of Architecture and Planning Research, 8,* 133–146.

Hartwigsen, G. (1987). Older widows and the transference of home. *International Journal of Aging and Human Development, 25*(3), 195–207.

Hay, R. (1998). Sense of place in developmental context. *Journal of Environmental Psychology, 18*(1), 5–29.

Hochschild, A. R. (1973). *The unexpected community.* Englewood Cliffs, NJ: Prentice Hall.

Hummon, D. M. (1992). Community attachment, local sentiment and sense of place. In I. Altman & S. M. Low (Eds.), *Place attachment* (pp. 253–278). New York: Plenum Press.

Hunt, M. E., & Pastalan, L. A. (1987). Easing relocation: An environmental learning process. In V. Regnier & J. Pynoos (Eds.), *Housing the aged: Design directives and policy considerations* (pp. 421–440). New York: Elsevier.

Kahana, E. (1982). A congruence model of person-environment interaction. In M. P. Lawton, P. G. Windley, & T. O. Byerts (Eds.), *Aging and the environment: Theoretical approaches* (pp. 97–121). New York: Springer.

Kahana, E., & Kahana, B. (1983). Environmental continuity, futurity, and adaptation of the aged. In G. D. Rowles & R. J. Ohta (Eds.), *Aging and milieu: Environmental perspectives on growing old* (pp. 205–228). New York: Academic Press.

Kenyon, G., Clark, P., & deVries, B. (2001). *Narrative gerontology: Theory, research and practice.* New York: Springer.

Kielhofner, G. (1995). Habituation subsystem. In G. Kielhofner (Ed.), *A model of human occupation: Theory and application* (2nd ed., pp. 63–81). Baltimore, MD: Williams & Wilkins.

Kindermann, T. A., & Skinner, E. A. (1992). Modeling environmental development: Individual and contextual trajectories. In A. B. Asendorpf & J. Valsiner (Eds.), *Stability and change in development: A study of methodological reasoning* (pp. 155–190). Newbury Park, CA: Sage Publications.

Lawton, M. P., & Nahemow, L. (1973). Ecology and the aging process. In C. Eisdorfer & M. P. Lawton (Eds.), *The psychology of adult development and aging* (pp. 619–674). Washington, DC: American Psychological Association.

Lazarus, R. S., & Folkman, R. S. (1984). *Stress, appraisal and coping.* New York: Springer.

Lieberman, M. A., & Falk, J. M. (1971). The remembered past as a source of data for research on the life cycle. *Human Development, 14,* 132–141.

Ludwig, F. M. (1997). How routine facilitates wellbeing in older women. *Occupational Therapy International, 4*(3), 213–228.

Marcus, C. C. (1992). Environmental memories. In I. Altman & S. M. Low (Eds.), *Place attachment* (pp. 87–112). New York: Plenum Press.

Marcus, C. C. (1995). *House as a mirror of self: Exploring the deeper meaning of home.* Berkeley, CA: Conari Press.

McCracken, A. (1987). Emotional impact of possession loss. *Journal of Gerontological Nursing, 13*(2), 14–19.

McHugh, K. E., & Mings, R. C. (1996). The circle of migration: Attachment to place in aging. *Annals of the Association of American Geographers, 86*(3), 530–550.

Morris, B. R. (1992). Reducing inventory: Divestiture of personal possessions. *Journal of Women and Aging, 4*(2), 79–92.

Norris-Baker, C. (1998). The evolving concept of behavior settings: Implications for housing older adults. In R. J. Scheidt & P. G. Windley (Eds.), *Environment and aging theory: A focus on housing* (pp. 141–160). Westport, CT: Greenwood Press.

Norris-Baker, C., & Scheidt, R. J. (1994). From "our town" to "ghost town"? The changing context of home for rural elders. *International Journal of Aging and Human Development, 38,* 181–202.

Pastalan, L. A. (1983). Environmental displacement: A literature reflecting old-person–environment transactions. In G. D. Rowles & R. J. Ohta (Eds.), *Aging and milieu: Environmental perspectives on growing old* (pp. 189–203). New York: Academic Press.

Paton, H., & Cram, F. (1992). Personal possessions and environmental control: The experiences of elderly women in three residential settings. *Journal of Women and Aging, 4*(2), 61–78.

Peirce, A. G. (1995). The complex nature of stress, coping, and adaptation. *Nursing Leadership Forum, 1*(3), 84–89.

Peled, A., & Schwartz, H. (1999). Exploring the ideal home in psychotherapy: Two case studies. *Journal of Environmental Psychology, 19,* 87–94.

Reed, J., & Payton, V. R. (1996). Constructing familiarity and managing the self: Ways of adapting to life in nursing and residential homes for older people. *Ageing and Society, 16,* 543–560.

Relph, E. (1976). *Place and placelessness.* London: Pion Limited.

Rowles, G. D. (1978). *Prisoners of space? Exploring the geographical experience of older people.* Boulder, CO: Westview Press.

Rowles, G. D. (1983). Place and personal identity: Observations from Appalachia. *Journal of Environmental Psychology, 3,* 219–313.

Rowles, G. D. (1991). Beyond performance: Being in place as a component of occupational therapy. *American Journal of Occupational Therapy, 45,* 265–271.

Rowles, G. D. (2000). Habituation and being in place. *Occupational Therapy Journal of Research, 20* (Supplement 1), 52S–67S.

Rowles, G. D., & Ravdal, H. (2002). Age, place and meaning in the face of changing circumstances. In R. S. Weiss & S. A. Bass (Eds.), *Challenges of the third age:*

Meaning and purpose in later life (pp. 81–114). New York: Oxford University Press.

Rubinstein, R. (1989). The home environments of older people: A description of the psychosocial processes linking person to place. *Journals of Gerontology, 44,* S45–S53.

Rubinstein, R., & Parmalee, P. A. (1992). Attachment to place and the representation of the life course by the elderly. In I. Altman & S. M. Low (Eds.), *Place attachment* (pp. 139–163). New York: Plenum Press.

Rybarczyk, B., & Bellg, A. (1997). *Listening to life stories: A new approach to stress intervention in health care.* New York: Springer.

Scheidt, R. J., & Norris-Baker, C. (1990). A transactional approach to environmental stress among older residents of rural communities. *Journal of Rural Community Psychology, 11*(1), 5–30.

Scheidt, R. J., & Norris-Baker, C. (1999). Place therapies for older adults: Conceptual and interventive approaches. *International Journal of Aging and Human Development, 48*(1), 1–15.

Seamon, D. (1980). Body subject, time-space routines, and place ballets. In A. Buttimer & D. Seamon (Eds.), *The human experience of space and place* (pp. 148–165). London: Croom Helm.

Sixsmith, J. (1986). The meaning of home: An exploratory study of environmental experience. *Journal of Environmental Psychology, 6,* 281–298.

Tilson, D. (Ed.). (1990). *Aging in place: Supporting the frail elderly in residential environments.* Glenview, IL: Scott, Foresman.

Toyama, T. (1988). *Identity and milieu: A study of relocation focusing on reciprocal changes in elderly people and their environment.* Stockholm, Sweden: Department for Building Function Analysis, the Royal Institute of Technology.

Usita, P. M., Hyman, I. E., & Herman, K. C. (1998). Narrative intentions: Listening to life stories in Alzheimer's disease. *Journal of Aging Studies, 12*(2), 185–197.

Wahl, H.-W. (2001). Environmental influence on aging and behavior. In J. E. Birren & K. W. Schaie (Eds.). *Handbook of the psychology of aging* (pp. 215–237). New York: Academic Press.

Wapner, S., Demick, J., & Redondo, J. P. (1990). Cherished possessions and adaptation of older people to nursing homes. *International Journal of Aging and Human Development, 31*(3), 219–235.

Watkins, J. F. (1999). Life course and spatial experience: A personal narrative approach in migration studies. In K. Pandit & S. D. Withers (Eds.), *Migration and restructuring in the United States* (pp. 294–312). Boulder, CO: Rowman and Littlefield.

Wheeler, W. M. (1995). *Elderly residential experience: The evolution of places as residence.* New York: Garland.

Zingmark, A., Norberg, K., & Sandman, P.-O. (1993). Experience of at-homeness and homesickness in patients with Alzheimer's disease. *American Journal of Alzheimer's Care and Related Disorders and Research, 8*(3), 10–16.

Zingmark, A., Norberg, K., & Sandman, P.-O. (1995). The experience of being at home throughout the lifespan: Investigation of persons 2 to 102. *International Journal of Aging and Human Development, 41*(1), 47–62.

PART III

Aging Independently "Indoors": Living Arrangements

Purpose-Built Housing and Home Adaptations for Older Adults: The American Perspective

Victor Regnier

The history of purpose-built housing for elders in the United States stretches back about 50 years. Although early buildings constructed with the express purpose of supporting the needs of older people can be traced to the later part of the nineteenth century, it was not until the 1950s and 1960s that the demand for housing for older people justified research and the development of a literature relating to this topic. The term "purpose-built" means that the environmental, psychological, social, and supportive needs of elders were considered when specific design and programming decisions were made. Today, the term "age-restricted" is often used interchangeably with purpose-built to define settings that are inhabited by elders. The vast majority of age-restricted settings have been created expressly for older people, but the term purpose-built connotes a filter which separates those settings where older people live with others of the same age from environments which were designed with the needs of older people in mind. Purpose-built housing for elders includes a number of different housing types. These housing categories vary depending on the age of the recipient and on the amount and type of care and assistance provided. They range from senior apartments to skilled nursing facilities. In general, the most common categories from most independent to most dependent include the following: retirement subdivisions, retirement communities, senior-only apartments, congregate housing, board and care housing, assisted living arrangements, continuing care retirement communities, dementia-specific special housing, and skilled nursing facilities. Dozens of other labels are used to describe other variations of purpose-built housing, including retirement hotels, cooperative housing, accessory apartments, foster care housing, and intermediate care nursing. Most of these, however, represent a very minor segment of the purpose-built elder housing universe.

There are over 34 million people in the United States over the age of 65. It is not a surprise to many that the vast majority of these older people live in the community in ordinary housing which has not been engineered for their needs. In fact, outside of nursing homes, only about 10% of the elderly live in housing stock that would be considered "purpose-built" or "age-restricted." However, we do not have very accurate estimates of these numbers. A recent Harvard Joint Center for Housing Studies analysis (Schafer, 2000) and American Seniors Housing Association statistical digest (Schless & Preede, 2000) provide some insights about basic statistics. From these 2 reports, we can surmise that purpose-built housing can be boiled down to 6 major housing types: retirement communities and subdivisions, senior apartments, congregate housing, assisted living, continuing care retirement communities, and skilled nursing facilities (see Table 7.1).

Approximately 5% of people 65+ live in nursing homes, and 10% of the 65+ population live in the other 5 housing types. Estimates of the number of nursing home beds are reasonably accurate because nursing homes are required to be licensed in every state. Nursing home environments are, for the most part, excluded from discussion in this chapter. For more details on nursing home environments, see Chapter 11. The other numbers are clearly

TABLE 7.1   Seniors Housing Property Types and Estimated U.S. Supply in 2000

Housing type	Percentage	Number of units
Senior apartments	12.5	400,000
Assisted living	15.6	500,000
CCRCs	18.8	600,000
Congregate care	21.8	700,000
Other age-segregated communities	31.3	1,000,000
Total	100.0	3,200,000

Source: Taken partially from Schless & Preede, 2000, p. 12.

"estimates" based on survey and census data. Industry studies, such as *ALFA's Overview of the Assisted Living Industry* (Assisted Living Federation of America [ALFA], 2000), estimate the assisted living population is between 611,300 and 777,800. Estimates of the capacity of continuing care retirement communities are relatively accurate. Between 1,900 and 2,000 of these housing arrangements have been identified in the United States. The number of senior apartments, congregate care, and retirement community dwellers have yet to be verified by any careful inventorying.

The American Seniors Housing Association (ASHA) estimates that in the period from 1997 to 2000, approximately 200,000 units of 4 types of age-restricted housing have been added to the national inventory (Schless & Preede, 2000). The 4 types include: assisted living, congregate housing, continuing care retirement communities, and senior apartments. Assisted living has accounted for two-thirds of the total 4-year inventory. Consistent with economic trends and financing difficulties experienced in this sector recently, the inventory of completed units in the year 2000 was about half as many as in 1999. The absorption of new assisted living units has slowed, and all providers have been challenged to compete in markets which are over-subscribed. The main question is what will happen in the next few years in this sector.

TRENDS AND THE NEW TYPES OF HOUSING BEING DEVELOPED

Assisted Living

Assisted living facilities have been chronicled for a 4-year period by ALFA (2000) in a national overview study. The latest study, published in 2000 for data compiled in 1999, provides a good snapshot of assisted living facilities throughout the country. The average project size is 52.5 units. The majority of the units are studios (61%) which average about 300 square feet in size. Approximately 57% of the gross building area is devoted to residential units, and 43% to common areas according to ASHA (2000). Residents average 83 years of age and have difficulties with at an average of 3 activities of daily living (ADLs). Approximately 26% experience problems with incontinence, 41% need a walker or wheelchair to get around, and 45% have cognitive impairments. Sixty-five percent need help with bathing, and 29% need help with toileting.

A number of national trends are generally recognized by industry leaders as characterizing the future of assisted living. Thirty of these trends have recently been chronicled (Regnier, 2002), representing general industry trends, building and management trends, and international trends from the experience of Northern Europeans. The Scandinavian countries continue to lead the world in the development of highly innovative buildings and systems, and these will likely be emulated in the United States in the decade ahead. Six of the more critical considerations and trends include the following.

Residents Will Continue to Be Sicker, More Chronically Ill, and More Demented

As assisted living facilities compete for more of the limited market of middle-decade 80-year-olds (82–87 age range), the settings that can handle the more acutely ill residents will be more successful at attracting private-pay residents from the more than 1.7 million beds of skilled nursing.

Facilities Will Broaden Their Role to Include Home Care That Supports Older People in the Local Neighborhood

As new technology and systems are developed to cater to the homebound senior, this sector will become more competitive. Clearly, older people prefer to stay in their own homes, and this preference grows to over 90% for the 85+ population (American Association of Retired Persons [AARP], 1996). The cost of assisted living, which can be as much as 2 to 4 times as expensive as living at home, provides further resistance to moving to such a facility.

The Dementia Population Will Increasingly Become the Major Component of Assisted Living

The Alzheimer's Association estimates that 100,000 cognitively impaired residents will be added to the general population every year for the next 20 years (ASHA, 2000). Barring a cure or substantial new drug therapies, these residents will be less able to maintain themselves with home care support in the community. Assisted living will continue to be more attractive and less expensive than skilled nursing care for this population. As residents become more physically impaired and their care regimens more complex, a small percentage are likely to move to nursing homes.

More Variety in Type, Size, Program, Location, and Style

Because assisted living, unlike skilled nursing, represents housing and not a health care environment, variety abounds. Future settings will be oriented toward the different preferences of a new and emerging group of more demanding older consumers.

Physical Therapy and Exercise Regimens Will Become Increasingly More Attractive to Consumers and Providers

Research showing the benefits of strength training, aerobic capacity building, and bone density increases make it clear how important exercise is in maintaining competency. Providers will readily offer these services for a fee. Another side benefit is that an increase in competency will lengthen housing tenure.

Family Partnerships and Integration Will Become Increasingly Common

This will be true as more community-based models are developed. As providers pursue projects in Asia, Pacific Rim countries, and Southern Europe, new ideas about how to integrate family members into these environments will evolve. Family partnerships may also become important as providers seek new and innovative approaches to deal with middle- to low-income populations. Assisted living facilities currently are more "family friendly" than skilled nursing homes.

Continuing Care Retirement Communities

Continuing care retirement communities (CCRCs), a unique building type in the United States, combine independent housing with assisted living and skilled nursing facilities. These have developed in an effort to provide continuity for residents between levels of care and because building codes encourage the separation of people with differing competencies into different buildings. There are approximately 2,000 CCRCs throughout the country.

They are generally large in size compared with congregate care or assisted living facilities. ASHA (2000), in its annual State of Seniors Housing analysis, reports the average building complex is 261 units/beds. The typical project is 164 units of independent housing, 37 assisted living units, and 60 nursing care beds. Residents have a range of competencies that go from totally independent to medically indigent including residents with dementia. CCRCs are more residentially stable with an average length of stay of approximately 5 years. ASHA (2000) data also shows that nearly half of the CCRCs are nonprofit enterprises.

CCRCs in general are older, larger, and more expensive settings than assisted living or congregate environments. ASHA (2000) estimates the median age of their building sample at 15 years versus the 5 years that characterizes assisted living. Because they are larger, CCRCs require almost 4 times as much land area (15 acres, median). According to Schless and Preede (2000), CCRC projects developed between 1994 and 1999 cost $40.4 million compared to assisted living projects, which averaged $9.3 million. All of these factors have made financing, land acquisition, and marketing more of a challenge. The following trends are associated with new projects.

Equity-Based or Rental Arrangements

Tax advantages, greater legal control, and the opportunity to participate in appreciation have made ownership more attractive than a life care fee. Others, who have less saved, find a lease preferable and more affordable than a life care entry fee. Traditional life care fees have been substantially reconceptualized by most providers to reduce risk.

Partial Continuum Projects

Eliminating the nursing component of the CCRC has become more common, especially in states where a certificate of need for nursing is required. Minimum nursing home sizes of from 40 to 60 beds often mean that CCRCs must offer nursing care to people living in the community to maintain a full census. Furthermore, assisted living and dedicated dementia units are reducing the pipeline for nursing care. For the few residents who need this type of care, beds can be more inexpensively contracted in other facilities in the community.

Changing Focus from Clubs and Activities to More Physically and Intellectually Challenging Lifestyles

Mirroring a trend in retirement communities, the focus in new (younger) buildings is on activities that relate to intellectual stimulation and physical fitness. It is not uncommon to find a swimming pool, spa, fitness room, masseuse, Internet café, and gardening facility along with more passive pursuits. "Crafts" are being replaced with investment clubs, exercise groups, elderhostel travelers, and degree-pursuing residents.

Building Types Focusing on High-Density Arrangements

One can still find facilities with cottages, but land prices and the desire to have secure properties which are not too far out in exurban communities have required more attached, multistory building forms. More high-density high-rise structures are being considered than in the past as the desire to move to cities has increased as crime rates have decreased.

Independent Retirement Communities

These communities have been extremely difficult to monitor and inventory. The University of Michigan study of retirement communities (Hunt, Feldt, Marans, Pastalan, & Vakalo, 1984) remains one of the best studies to date, and it is very much out of date. In that study, 3 types of "retirement communities" were identified: retirement new towns, retirement villages, and retirement subdivisions. At that time (early 1980s), the study estimated that at least half of the 1,000,000 people living in the 2,400 retirement communities in the United States that they inventoried fell into one of these 3 categories.

Although a number of new providers are currently developing retirement communities, the Del Webb Corporation continues to maintain a lead over all other competitors in terms of housing design and a clear understanding of the market. From 1986 to 1995, according to *Builder* magazine, it was the fastest-growing homebuilder in America (Freedman, 1999). The success of Del Webb resulted not only from building attractive, well-priced housing but their ability to anticipate the future by understanding the desires of older consumers. Each year they receive input from 25,000 to 30,000 older people through 25 surveys and 180 focus groups (Herron, 1997). The following represent some of the trends associated with the Del Webb community of today.

Focus on Development of Smaller Communities in Frost-Belt as well as Sun-Belt Locales

Communities are often large subdivisions which focus on a population of from 2,500 to 3,000. Cities are selected on the basis of a desire for a retirement community lifestyle rather than an escape to a sun-belt locale. Smaller parcels (500 acres) are easier to purchase, and smaller communities require less risk and are easier to finance. Nevertheless, they are large enough to accommodate first-rate amenities.

One- and Two-Bedroom Units with Modern Kitchens and Bathrooms in a Densely Planned Context

The formula to success is to create an open plan with 9-foot ceilings and clerestory windows. Connections to the outside are made through 8-foot sliding glass doors, and special attention is paid to bathrooms and kitchens. These 2 rooms contain all of the design elements that "move-up" buyers have come to expect from contemporary housing while being sensitive to the need for aging in place. For example, wheelchair-adaptable fixtures and equipment are specified and carefully arranged.

Programs and Amenities Tied to Recreation, Education, Culture, and Travel

A golf course continues to provide the focus for most Del Webb communities, but linkages with local universities and colleges as well as exercise facilities are an extremely important part of the new lifestyle. Many of these communities are oriented toward volunteer organizations which allow residents to help one another. Interdependence has been fostered throughout the years with the resultant creation of a community-based desire to help one another.

Housing Subdivisions Commonly Known as Age-Targeted, Not Age-Restricted Communities

These retirement communities are for people who want the amenities but are put off by the traditional concept of a community restricted to people over the age of 55. These communities are designed to be open to all ages but attract 80% of their constituency from 55+ buyers. They are ad-hoc retirement communities which do not label themselves as such. Thus, they tap a segment of the pre-boomer market who have rejected the traditional retirement community (Suchman, 2001).

Cohousing for Seniors

Cohousing is beginning to become more popular in the United States, but the experiences of Denmark may provide a better source of understanding. In Denmark, cohousing was started as a way to create a more fulfilling shared lifestyle. By the beginning of the 1990s, there were more than 2,000 cohousing units for elders in Denmark and a strong commitment to create more (Boligtrivsel I Centrum, 1994). The experience has been a very positive one with these settings taking on a social life of their own which often stresses interdependency. Recent evaluations have shown mixed results with regard to social cohesiveness (Palsig, 2000). There is a lot of variety in senior cohousing arrangements with regard to sharing tasks and duties. Because residents come together (such as in a condominium association) to make self-governance decisions, everyone knows everyone else. The amount of sharing and interdependence, however, differs from one setting to the next.

Molleparken is typical of a successful senior cohousing venture. The building is a 2-story, L-shaped configuration with a covered but not air-conditioned or heated glass atrium. The outdoor/indoor atrium space between units is approximately 20 feet wide. An elevator provides access to second-floor units. Every unit is self-contained, but they all share a common living room, dining room, and kitchen. Although there is no grand tradition of sharing meals, residents have a collective meal together about once a week. There is a management board and a commitment to help one another. Residents share rides with one another and help out if someone is temporarily ill. If someone needs ongoing help, he or she must seek home help from the local municipality.

There are 28 one- and two-bedroom dwelling units for the resident population of 37, with an average age of 73. The building contains 10 couples, and a few residents still work part-time. The glass-enclosed atrium is a great place to spend time, and because it is so visible from the apartment units, it often stimulates conversations and chance encounters with other residents. Places like Molleparken are developing strong social connections among residents who choose to live with one another. Most hope that the additional informal relationships combined with the ubiquitous and well-funded Danish home care system with allow them to stay here until they die.

The Cheesecake of Mendicino County, California, is a senior cohousing project 100 miles north of San Francisco. This project is an example of a similar albeit much smaller-scale effort of a group of 5 Californians to develop a housing environment where they would be able to live a communal retirement lifestyle (Landecker, 1994). These individuals chose an 11-acre site for the 6,000-square-foot development. One couple became residents initially, and the others, upon their retirements, were to join them within the 10 years. Common areas include a living room, dining room, kitchen, laundry, shower, workshop, and library. The complex consists of 3 buildings including a 2-story lodge, a 1-story bedroom wing, and a 1-story workshop. The lodge has a group living room, kitchen, and dining room on the first floor with 2 small bedrooms on the second floor. The bedroom wing contains 4 other small bedrooms linked together by a deck to the lodge. The small bedrooms and the need to share accommodations make it a bit reminiscent of a weekend retreat rather than a retirement setting.

Housing on College and University Campuses

According to Lee Pastalan (2000), who is developing a national data base that chronicles these types of environments, there are between 50 and 100 elderly housing centers that either exist or are taking shape on campuses throughout the United States. Some of the best-known facilities include those located on or near the campuses of the University of Indiana, the University of Washington, Notre Dame, Cornell, Haverford College, Ithaca College, La Salle College, the University of Virginia, Arizona State University, Penn State University, Duke University, and the University of Michigan. Several colleges are either pursuing plans or have housing units under construction. One of the best-known developments in the "planning stage" is at Stanford University. They have recently shifted into a more active development startup stage.

The best projects appear to be those that are located on university property or have locations that are very near campus (Suchman, 2001). When the university participates as a partner, there is almost always better integration with university programs. These projects cover the gamut of types and styles. Most of them are CCRCs, but some are equity-based or rental apartments. Most older people move to these settings to be near the campus and its programs. Many of them are interested in educational programs sponsored by the university. Others are interested in self-exploration and personal growth. A few are even interested in pursuing degrees. Many are Emeriti faculty or retired staff who want to continue a relationship with the institution. Pastalan, with a 25% continuing faculty appointment at the University of Michigan, is a self-proclaimed member of the "gray militia" who, along with several other retired faculty members, are actively mentoring students.

The universities find the participation of elderly students a force that creates greater diversity in the classroom. Many find the roles established by an Emeriti center useful for faculty or staff who would still like to volunteer their services to the university. Others recognize that older people are often in a position to make a charitable contribution to the university. The University of Southern California Andrus Gerontology Center has received 14 endowed chairs in the last 10 years as a result of their relationship with older donors. The residents of Green Hills, a CCRC near Iowa State University, have made contributions totaling $3 million to the university in the last 5 or 6 years. Clearly this type of university-based elderly housing relationship will continue as more institutions see the utility of links and connections between seniors and campus activities. Although this is a very small segment of the U.S. elder population, it nonetheless represents a growing and influential sector.

Service House Models in Northern Europe: New Perspectives for the United States

One of the great lessons to be learned from Northern Europe is the seamless connection that has developed between housing and services. To most Scandinavians, housing is just another type of service which can support the independence of older people in the community. Most of their projects are mixed-use community centers which contain a restaurant, a swimming pool, a senior center, an outpatient rehabilitation setting, a home care agency, a meals-on-wheels program, and exercise equipment. These services are available to people in the community as well as the individuals who live in attached housing.

The Danes even organize their services in assisted living housing by using home care personnel. In their minds, the only difference between living here and in the community is that service housing can be accessed quickly and easily because it is attached to the service center. Residents are invited to use the restaurant, but they can have their meals delivered to their own apartments.

The Virranranta project in Kuruvesi, Finland, is a good example of a modern service house in a small, central Finnish town (Regnier, 2002; Verderber & Fine, 2000). This project contains 50 units of elder housing attached to a central building where most of the services described above are available. The housing is split into 2 types. At one end are 10 service apartments for the elderly. These are 1-bedroom, 550-square-foot units, and the residents living here are expected to take meals in the central dining room. At the other side of the centrally located service center are 5 small group homes of 8 units each. Two clusters are for people with dementia, 2 clusters are for people with physical impairments, and 1 is for short-stay or respite care. The physical therapy room is used in conjunction with these units to support people who are undergoing therapy as they make a transition back to their own homes. Each cluster of dwelling units is self-contained with its own kitchen, dining room, living room, and garden room. Residents can walk to other destinations in the service house, but they spend most of their time in this cluster.

Settings of this type are absent in the United States, but they could be very helpful in making the transition from a home to a group living arrangement much better. Many assisted living providers are currently exploring ways to broaden their reach into the community to help people who are not quite ready to move into assisted living.

Apartments for Life: Implications for the United States

In the Netherlands, a new housing type has been undergoing development. The building codes in Europe, which are based on an all masonry construction envelope, allow for various competency levels to be supported in the same residential type housing. This has led to an interesting aging-in-place model which allows residents to receive differing levels of care from no services to nursing home support in apartments with about 750 square feet.

The Humanitas Bergweg project in Rotterdam supports older frail people in a normalized apartment context (Regnier, 2002). The 195-unit development consists of 2 housing blocks which are separated by an air-conditioned and heated atrium. One of the housing blocks is a tower that swoops from 4 to 12 stories in its 450-foot length. The other is a 4-story single-loaded corridor housing block. The atrium, 4 stories in height, is open on both sides to these corridors. A third of its population is receiving nursing care, a third is receiving personal care assistance, and a third is receiving no help.

The dwelling units are designed to be modified as residents age in place. The bathroom is large enough to accommodate a wheelchair as well as a stretcher bather. The philosophy of care is targeted toward encouraging residents to take as much responsibility as possible for their own self-care needs. The 3 types of residents are scattered throughout the building complex rather than segregated on separate floors or in one particular area. The atrium, a public environment, is open to everyone in the neighborhood. A restaurant, lounge, and bar are available to residents and community members, along with an array of professional services, such as doctors, physical therapists, and occupational therapists.

There is no reason why a system of this sort could not succeed in the United States. The safety and fire systems that are available today are safe enough to make this type of mixed-use facility easy to implement relatively inexpensively. The Dutch believe that, in the future, more older people will opt for this type of housing rather than the smaller, more service-intensive assisted living style buildings. This type of housing, however, does not appear to be that successful with older, demented residents.

Supported and Shared Housing

The Harvard Joint Center report also discusses 2 types of housing arrangements that are often overlooked or poorly documented: supported housing and shared housing (Schafer, 2000). Together, they account for 15% of the total housing for older people in the United States. Both types represent conventional housing where services or assistance is provided to older residents.

Supported housing is provided to 5% of the 70+ senior population. These are older people who are receiving assistance from outside the home provided by a non-family member or an organization. They are typically residents of single-family housing or apartments (two-thirds of the units are owner occupied and one-third are rented). This type of housing assistance works well for individuals who have good cognitive skills but problems with the activities of daily living. The Danes have established a very well-organized system of home health care support which is targeted to this sector of the population.

Shared housing is provided to 10% of 70+ senior population. These are individuals who have either moved in with a non-elderly person or who have a younger helper living with them. The purpose of the coliving arrangement is to provide assistance for the older person. Residents having difficulties with ADLs and those without children nearby favor this type of an arrangement. Although many of these arrangements involve family members, one-third do not involve them. The housing stock that supports this arrangement is generally large with 45% to 50% of the units having 6 or more rooms.

Home Modifications

The need for home modifications is fueled by the desire to make housing safer, more accessible, and more supportive for older, frail people. More than a quarter of the population aged 75 to 84 experience difficulty in performing activities of daily living; this increases to more than 50% for the 85+ cohort. Great strides have taken place in the last decade in retrofitting housing with aids, but more needs to be done. For example, 23% of the housing occupied by older people have grab bars (Pynoos, 2000); however, only 9% have wheelchair adaptations, 5% to 8% call devices, 8% railings, and 5% ramps at the street.

More important, only about half of the disabled elderly have the modifications they need. Items such as the following represent what 50% of the disabled elderly need to make their dwelling units safer and more supportive: lever door handles, better kitchen access, faucets that are easy to manipulate, more accessible cabinets, stair lifts or elevators, wide 36-inch doors, better bathroom access, and ramps in addition to steps. Given these statistics, a surprisingly high number of older people are satisfied with the safety of their neighborhood or their housing, and only 3% to 5% are unhappy with these issues (Schafer, 2000).

Home modifications are also important in reducing hazards in the environment. The bathroom, the kitchen, and stairs between floors are clearly the most hazardous environments. Sixty percent of the bathrooms have 2 or more hazards like throw rugs or obstructed pathways (Pynoos, 2000). Stairs are also a major impediment. More than 60% of the elderly do not move after age 60 (Schafer, 2000). The vast majority of the housing stock they inhabit is old. It suffers from problems remedied by today's handicap-accessible housing. Typical problems include items such as small bathrooms and bathtubs, narrow bathroom and bedroom doors, steep internal stairs, and the lack of ramp access to the front and rear entries.

Making adjustments to the environment is complicated by a number of factors. One problem is that the reimbursement for making changes is limited. The costs of environmental adaptations are especially problematic for low-income homeowners who are not used to paying for such improvements. Older residents tend to replace broken and damaged equipment and material but rarely invest in improving the environment through additions or qualitative adjustments (Schafer, 2000).

Another problem is the fragmented service delivery system for home modifications. The absence of state and local coalitions representing the interests of older people make it difficult to improve the patchwork system that exists. The lack of trained personnel is also a problem. Information sources on the Internet and the commitment of professional organizations such as the National Association of Home Builders (NAHB) are focusing attention on these issues. Approximately 20% of the new home buyers in the United States are over the age of 55. This has caught the attention of a range of providers and suppliers (National Association of Home Builders Research Center, 2002). Finally, older people often do not wish to make changes to their homes. They may think that modifications make the place look less cozy and residential. They are reluctant to make changes that remind them of their disabilities.

CONCLUSIONS AND FUTURE DIRECTIONS

1. More and different types of housing and service arrangements will be available, and consumers will have more choices in the future. Housing is different by region, type, size, and location while skilled nursing facilities are almost identical throughout the country in terms of configuration and organization. Because new service arrangements (assisted living, congregate care, and so on) take their lead from housing, they are likely to be more varied. Also as we move in the direction of segmenting and understanding market forces better, we will arrive at more appropriate settings by place and market segment. Hotels and motels in the United States have done a good job of segmenting the market. Lots of choices are available for a range of financial capabilities and desires.

We are likely to see projects that are large (over 100 units) and small (40 to 60 units appears to be the smallest feasible size). We are likely to find buildings which operate from the same average square footage per unit figure of from 750 to 850 square feet, of which 35% to 50% is devoted to common space. Dwelling units will probably be the recipient of this displaced area. We will also see buildings in urban areas with perhaps smaller footprints and little parking and buildings in exurban contexts that are 1 story, with lots of parking and perhaps less expensive units.

High-service and low-service buildings will probably evolve as affordability becomes an issue. Keep in mind that cost categories shift as the level of service increases. A typical rule of thumb in an assisted living building has 35% of the cost in the building and maintenance. In a nursing home, costs shift to 25% building and 75% service. Future buildings will be oriented toward health, engagement, and activity while others will take the more traditional approach of passivity, support, and pampering. Finally, options will be oriented toward equity-based choices or rental units. This is particularly true for apartment-for-life projects which will capture residents at an earlier age.

2. There will be a move toward creating more integration between home and purpose-built structures. This will probably first occur as outreach projects from current facilities and will evolve into something that is more akin to the northern European service house models discussed earlier in this chapter. The big difference in the United States will be the sponsorship. Much will come from the private or nonprofit sector and be oriented toward private-pay individuals. The government will play a minor role in system creation. It is more likely to be a financial partner supporting care through subsidies and third-party payments. Hospitals seeking patients, CCRCs seeking more community involvement, and existing facilities seeking a pipeline to new residents will be claiming new territory. Most of these businesses will seek to develop a relationship with residents before they need help or before they need to move into a care setting that operates around the clock.

Baby boomers (those born between 1947 and 1964) who move into retirement as recipients rather than money/resource managers will expect to pay for help and support. Boomers solved conflicts with 2-person working couples by purchasing help (child care) and using technology (cell phones and beepers). They will use these strategies again to balance their own needs (Schafer, 2000). The upcoming generation may be in better shape physically and may be better positioned to avoid long periods of morbidity. Keep in mind that assisted living is generally 2 to 4 times as expensive as living at home. They can afford to ramp up services quite a bit before they start to compete with a highly supportive personal care setting.

3. Retirement communities will continue to evolve with less single-minded focus on recreation. Retirees have made major shifts from the early days of the initial Del Webb facilities of the late 1950s and early 1960s. The basic housing stock is much larger, utilizes the most contemporary equipment, and provides various creature comforts. Plans are open with

rooms flowing into one another. Views outside connect with the inside, and clerestories and skylights introduce light into dark/private areas of the plan.

Retirees are more likely to travel, have experience with other cultures, and use computer/Internet resources avidly. They are more likely to be interested in self-discovery and self-expression (art, poetry, autobiographies, and so on) as much as their predecessors were interested in playing cards and lawn bowling. On the other hand, they will likely be more "other" oriented (Wolfe, 1990). They may actively seek ways to help others through volunteering or through financial support. As mentioned earlier, universities have become prime candidates for affiliations. Where in the past the church was the trusted institution, tomorrow the university will have a similar role in society. Today the major fund-raising recipients are increasingly universities rather than religious institutions. When philanthropists give money to guarantee a better future, it is often through education, not through religion. A stronger focus on beauty, pleasure, and healthful behaviors is also likely to occur. Facilities today are well aware of the relationship between exercise and morbidity. Swimming pools, therapy rooms, exercise pavilions, spa pools, and massage therapy are common services. In Sweden, where the government reimburses a broader range of therapeutic interventions, massage therapy and aromatherapy are popular in rehabilitation facilities that are like spas in the United States. Better nutrition monitoring and preventive health are also likely to become important lifestyle attributes of successful new buildings.

4. New technologies will be used to minimize reliance on formal staff. In Northern Europe there is a significant move toward making independent housing electronically linked to a central authority. This allows residents to control their lives more independently. Using services at the margin of need, like the apartments-for-life program described earlier, shifts responsibility more toward the older person. This eliminates the learned helplessness response that often occurs in highly supportive planned arrangements like nursing homes and assisted living. When residents are more responsible for monitoring their own needs, they will stay more actively engaged by exercising those behaviors that define independent living.

Communications technologies will continue to develop and will make buildings and people safer. Ordering services when they are needed will become a more common strategy for providing assistance. Devices for lifting and moving people and materials will increasingly be the domain of machines designed to operate within a normal residential context. These devices will probably evolve from the crude wheelchairs and lifting devices that are currently available. As robotic technology becomes more sophisticated, more miniaturized, and programmable within relatively unstructured environments, these devices will be of increasing importance (Brooks, 2002). The savings which can accrue as a result of staying out of assisted living and nursing care environments is substantial. A device which may cost between $1,500 and $2,000 per month is still cheaper than a well-trained full-time (40 hours per week) personal care assistant. Tethered to a control center, these devices could monitor, support, and complement other people and devices. These strategies may be less effective for the mentally impaired.

5. Assisted living will change and evolve. These changes will involve an increasingly heavier focus on replacing caregiving labor with devices and materials that save time. New communications strategies, robotic helping devices, and advanced medical maintenance procedures will be oriented toward vesting fewer but more highly trained individuals with the responsibility of overseeing people in their homes and in group housing arrangements. There will be more emphasis on family partnerships as the number of Latino and Asian families with older dependent parents increases. Strategies like a Children-Caregiver Association (CCA), similar to the Parent-Teacher Associations (PTA) common in public and private schools, will formally integrate families into these settings.

More emphasis on physical therapy and exercise will keep residents healthier and will increase their tenure. These kinds of priorities will increase the physical movement and activity in settings which traditionally have focused on passive pursuits (watching television, listening to music, playing cards, making crafts). More emphasis will be placed on dealing with dementia, because mentally confused residents are the least able to live independently with communication and electromechanical assistance in the community. The assisted living environments of tomorrow will become more community based providing advice, assistance, temporary respite, rehabilitation through short-stay visits, and services for end-of-life (hospice) care.

6. Home modifications will be combined with care strategies to keep people independent in their homes for a longer period of time. These interventions will increasingly manage safety by mitigating risk. Multiple-level approaches will be taken which involve "care and repair." For example, strategies for reducing falls will involve eliminating obvious risks, replacing floor coverings with more resilient coatings and coverings, specifying clothing with the appropriate padding, prescribing nutritional supplements and exercises that increase bone density, and monitoring risky behaviors that can lead to a fall or accident.

These approaches will be fundamentally different from those we see today. Adding a grab bar and building a ramp will still be needed, but making a building more accessible and safer will require thinking from a multidimensional perspective. Older people in the future will probably see the benefit of spending money on these interventions as safer, more foolproof approaches are demonstrated.

REFERENCES

American Association of Retired Persons (AARP). (1996). *Understanding senior housing.* Washington, DC: AARP.

American Seniors Housing Association (ASHA). (2000). *The state of seniors' housing.* Washington, DC: ASHA.

Assisted Living Federation of America (ALFA). (2000). *ALFA's overview of the assisted living industry.* Fairfax, VA: ALFA.

Boligtrivsel I Centrum. (1994). *Co-housing for senior citizens in Europe.* Copenhagen, Denmark: BIC.

Brooks, R. (2002). *Flesh and machines: How robots will change us.* New York: Pantheon Books.

Freedman, M. (1999). *Prime time: How baby boomers will revolutionize retirement and transform America.* New York: Public Affairs.

Herron, M. (1997). Del Webb: Marketing powerhouse. *Builder, 20*(9), 96–98, 100, 102, 104, 106.

Hunt, M., Feldt, A., Marans, R., Pastalan, L., & Vakalo, K. (1984). *Retirement communities: An American original.* New York: Haworth Press.

Landecker, H. (1994). Common ground, *Architecture, 83*(10), 76–81.

National Association of Home Builders (NAHB) Research Center. (2002). *2002 directory of accessible building products.* Upper Marlboro, MD: The Center.

Palsig, S. (2000). *Co-housing in Denmark.* Copenhagen, Denmark: Danish Center for Gerontology.

Pastalan, L. (2000). *The importance of senior residential/retirement communities on or near a college/university campus.* Ann Arbor, MI: National Center on Housing and Living Arrangements for Older Americans.

Pynoos, J. (2000). *Home modifications.* Los Angeles: Andrus Gerontology Center.

Regnier, V. (2002). *Design for assisted living: Guidelines for housing the physically and mentally frail.* New York: Wiley.

Schafer, R. (2000). *Housing America's seniors.* Boston: Joint Center for Housing Studies of Harvard University.

Schless, D., & Preede, K. (2000). *Seniors housing statistical digest.* Washington, DC: American Seniors Housing Association (ASHA).

Suchman, D. (2001). *Developing active adult retirement communities.* Washington, DC: Urban Land Institute.

Verderber, S., & Fine, D. (2000). *Healthcare architecture in an era of radical transformation.* New Haven, CT: Yale University Press.

Wolfe, D. (1990). *Serving the ageless market: Strategies for selling to the fifty plus market.* New York: McGraw-Hill.

CHAPTER 8

Purpose-Built Housing for Older Adults: The German Perspective

Klaus Großjohann

I will begin this chapter by first briefly outlining the most important quantitative data currently pertaining to purpose-built housing for the elderly in Germany and, second, by discussing the main challenges that are likely to emerge in this sector, both in the immediate future and in the longer term. I will discuss trends, lines of development, and tendencies linked to financial considerations that can only be alluded to here.

THE CURRENT STATE OF HOUSING FOR GERMAN ELDERLY

It is a fact that there is no absolute dividing line between living at home, either as an owner-occupier or as a renter, and living in an institutional setting. The dividing line that does persist, exists primarily for financial reasons (Bundesministerium für Familie, Senioren, Frauen und Jugend [BMFSFJ] [Federal Ministry for Family Affairs, Senior Citizens, Women and Youth], 1998; Großjohann & Stolarz, 1998). A top-down analysis can identify various ways of compensating for psychological and physical restrictions, as well as a dependence on assistance, care, help, and nursing facilities within each of the forms of living discussed here. The degree of dependency on institutions usually increases from a "normal" residential setting to the hospice; however, even very old people in need of care and nursing can continue living at home with the assistance of their relatives, voluntary helpers, and professional outpatient services.

There has been a great improvement in noninstitutional specialist housing in the past 10 to 15 years. A new type of purpose-built housing for older adults has emerged which combines two elements: *self-reliant housing* and the provision of services and care. Hitherto, this had not been possible: older people had the choice of either living independently or receiving care, because the German version of sheltered housing (*Altenwohnung*) did not include any care provision. Care was provided only within institutional settings, such as old people's homes and nursing homes. In nursing homes, self-reliance was excluded by definition. The new type of "assisted housing" (*Betreutes Wohnen*) has closed this gap. This explains why there has been such a rapid development of this sector in Germany, as indeed in many other countries. Over a relatively short period of time, a considerable number of the elderly, about 150,000, have taken up residence in these households (see Table 8.1). The success story of assisted housing mirrors the growing desire of older people to remain independent as long as possible, while also en-

TABLE 8.1   Forms of Housing Where Older People (65+) Live Today

Form of housing	Number of older people	Share of the total of older people (%)
1. General housing	11.6 million	92.1
2. Self-reliant housing (noninstitutionalized specialist housing)	320,000	2.6
Sheltered housing (*Altenwohnung*)	170,000	1.4
Assisted housing (*Betreutes Wohnen*) (rough estimate)	150,000	1.2
3. Homes for older people (institutionalized specialist housing)	661,000	5.3
Nursing homes	375,000	3.0
Old people's homes	204,000	1.6
Residential homes	82,000	0.7

joying company and feeling safe in the knowledge that help is available if needed.

A parallel development to assisted housing has emerged, known as "communal housing." The spatial arrangements are similar to those of assisted housing; self-reliant flats as well as communal areas are provided. The difference is that communal activities and mutual support are given greater emphasis. In this form of housing, the residents themselves organize their daily routines; in fact, they are even responsible for the development of the housing project. The residents can choose with whom they want to live, and often the result is a much greater variety in the social composition of the unit, both in terms of age and income. This type of purpose-built housing is not included in Table 8.1 only because the number of residents is still rather small. I have mentioned it here because it underlines the growing self-confidence of the mainly younger elderly. They wish not only to choose where they live, but also to take an active part in the administration of their place of residence.

Since the vast majority of older adults remain in their normal houses, as shown in Table 8.1, non-purpose-built housing has been given increased attention as a form of housing for older people. To assist older people in making their houses more suitable, counseling services for housing adaptation have been established. There are about 200 such schemes around the country.

These developments have, among others, greatly improved older persons' opportunities to either remain in their own houses or move to a more suitable environment where they can continue to lead independent lives even if they become frail. Although this trend has improved the lot of many very old people, it is usually not an option for those who already have severe care needs and who cannot manage their own households anymore. If this situation occurs, there is only one choice: to move (usually involuntarily) to an institutional care setting. It is at this point that problems arise, because most of the above-mentioned improvements come to a stop at the door of the nursing home. Sadly, self-reliance is not a priority in institutional care. However, it is equally important to extend the positive developments that are taking place in the field of caring for the elderly to institutional settings. For this reason, I would now like to consider this aspect of purpose-built housing.

A first glance at the quantitative data raises questions about the importance of *nursing homes*, since only 3% of those over 65 reside in nursing homes (Table 8.1). However, one must note that the average age of entry to old people's homes in Germany is well over 80. If the comparison is based on the total number of persons over 80, the proportion of people who reside in homes at this advanced age provides a much clearer, more realistic estimate of the need for such homes. It is also fair to assume that the policy, pursued for many years, of postponing a move into a home by improving outpatient services, has resulted in the tendency of the elderly to resist leaving their homes and moving into an old people's home. This trend is also reinforced by the cost of nursing home care, which remains very high. Indeed, long-term care insurance covers only the costs of specific nursing care, and the elderly themselves have to cover the so-called *accommodation costs* (unless they are underprivileged, in which case, such costs are covered by the social security fund). Frequently, relatives are also required to bear part of the nursing home costs. It is important to note that for many of the very old, those over 80, the old people's home remains an important setting. As the number of very old people in Germany rises, there will be a continuing need for a large number of old people's homes. I will return to this point later.

Providing appropriate living conditions for those elderly who need help, assistance, and nursing brings us face to face with a major challenge that is quantitative as well as qualitative in nature. It is helpful, at this point, to consider Table 8.2.

Table 8.2 shows the current and projected numbers of elders residing mainly in conventional nursing homes. If these facilities were planned and built prior to 1980, their architecture and the life that goes on inside them are oriented toward the principles and functionality of a hospital. Some of these homes require modernization to create better, homelike conditions and provide rehabilitation facilities. The major stumbling block that is still fre-

TABLE 8.2   Projected Need for Nursing Homes

Year	Homes	People aged 65+	
		Millions	*In homes*
1970	5,000	7.94	216,000
2000	8,000	13.6	557,000
2010		16.2	648,000
2020		17.4	783,000
2030		20.4	880,000
2040		21.3	980,000
2050		20.1	1,100,000

quently found in the philosophy of homes for the elderly is that their focus remains concentrated on *nursing functions*, although this focus should have been redirected long ago toward the concept of *personal* or *one-to-one care*. One reason for this failure to refocus has been the inadequate level of staff qualification, which can be mentioned only briefly here.

AN ARCHITECTURAL VIEW OF NEEDS FOR RESTRUCTURING AND MODERNIZING NURSING HOMES

I will select several examples that illustrate certain aspects of the architectural infrastructure of currently existing nursing homes. The most urgent need is to modernize the *first-generation* old people's homes, as well as the *second-generation* homes built in the 1970s according to hospital designs. In some of these homes, more than 50% of the old people live in twin-bed rooms, which reduces the possibility of creating a pleasant, homelike atmosphere and, in most instances, allows little accommodation for the application of modern nursing, assistance, and therapy concepts.

When existing homes are modernized, it can be assumed that the costs will amount to approximately 80% of the costs of building an entirely new facility. For example, in the state of North-Rhine/Westphalia, it is expected that the modernization of existing old people's homes will cost DM 7 billion over the next decade. For all of Germany's western states (i.e., excluding eastern Germany), it can be assumed that the total cost will exceed DM 20 billion. The financial demand in the eastern states is considerably less, because of the huge wave of modernization that occurred immediately after German reunification.

Projected demographic trends show that new homes will be needed. Hundreds of thousands of new beds will have to be created in old people's homes over the next few decades. By extrapolating current numbers of recipients of long-term care insurance, based on the frequency of care-need in 1998 and the results of the most recent population forecast, all other things being equal, more than 10,000 beds in old people's homes will need to be created annually from now through 2050. The task now is to find solutions that will incorporate both the provision of new homes and an adequate response to the pressure for modernization of existing ones.

IMPLICATIONS OF THE GROWING
INCIDENCE OF DEMENTIA

We can hope that transfer to a nursing home for some people in need of care can be postponed or even avoided altogether by better outpatient help and treatment and by supportive caregiving relatives, but we must be aware of the limits imposed by the occurrence of dementia. Relatives and volunteer helpers are limited in their ability to care for those who are in an advanced state of dementia; hence, their transfer to a nursing home often becomes unavoidable. For example, we are currently conducting a study funded by the Federal Ministry for Family Affairs, Senior Citizens, Women and Youth to identify effective major and minor measures to support the elderly with dementia and have a beneficial effect on the quality of their lives. Those activities range from memory-training and self-maintenance therapy to humor therapy and pet therapy. An important advance is being introduced in Germany, using a process developed in England by Tom Kitwood (Kitwood, 2000) and his team at the University of Bradford. This process involves behavior observations and measuring relative well-being. Known as Dementia Care Mapping, its broad use will help those with dementia to overcome passivity and resignation.

We know that certain milieus promote the well-being of dementia sufferers and tend to improve the ability of the nursing staff to provide adequate interventions. These are milieus designed to simulate a high level of normality and a close link with the demented person's previous living circumstances. Such an approach is difficult to introduce in conventional hospitals and ordinary nursing homes in Germany. These facilities have too little resemblance to the elderly person's previous milieu, or they neglect his or her need for a homey atmosphere and a feeling of being sheltered. They are organized along functional lines, with 80 to 100 beds along anonymous corridors with a sterile style of architecture. We have for some time been lobbying for the development of more homelike communities, where the focus is on the normal life of a household—eating and drinking, conversations, and a high level of communication. Ideas originating from the Netherlands, based on the concept of the *Hofje* (Kuratorium Deutsche Altershilfe [KDA] [German Foundation for the Care of Older People], 2000b) or the concept of *Cantous* in France (Kuratorium Deutsche Altershilfe, 2000a) which practice a high level of normality and an above-average level of commitment by relatives, have contributed to the development of the home community concept.

HOME COMMUNITIES: AN ALTERNATIVE DESIGN AND ORGANIZATIONAL CONCEPT FOR OLD PEOPLE'S HOMES

The home communities concept is informed by the principles underlying good outpatient care. It provides an organizational model for improving the quality of life for those in need of residential nursing care. Intensive discussions are being held among specialists in the field to determine whether home communities should become the model for old people's homes, whether they should be financed by long-term care insurance, and whether they should be operating primarily on an inpatient basis. This discussion was instigated by the German Foundation for the Care of Older People (KDA) in Cologne. The home community concept is known as the *fourth generation* in the design of homes for the elderly, even though such homes are already under construction in many parts of Germany, and some are already in operation (e.g., in the city of Diessen). This paradigm shift is already reducing the emphasis on pure nursing care, and it is directed toward greater independence and self-determination, even for those of a very advanced age and despite the need for nursing and other care.

A quantum leap in quality can be observed since the late 1990s in Germany with regard to the construction and organization of old people's homes. As an alternative to the conventional nursing home, with its high proportion of institutional structures resembling a hospital, where residents often felt neglected and staff are overworked, planners and development companies working on innovative projects are now placing more emphasis on a systematically decentralized organizational structure.

In adapting the French and Dutch examples to German conditions, the KDA developed the concept of home communities further, working jointly with the initiators and operators of various local projects. Home community designs qualify for considerable economic support, under the German federal government's model program for improving the lives of those in need of nursing care. This substantial financial support was provided by the Federal Ministry of Health. Moreover, some of the Ministers of Health from individual German states also support the home community concept, and it is the contributions at the state level that have given impetus to the further development and implementation of the "made in Germany" version of home communities.

HOME COMMUNITIES—WHERE IS THE DIFFERENCE?

As a general rule, there is a fairly clear separation in conventional nursing homes between the wards that contain the areas for sleeping and nursing and the living areas used for cooking and eating, typically located in a dining room with a central kitchen. By contrast, home communities simulate small, local, family-like residential structures. This means that a maximum number of 8 persons needing nursing care live here together in one household. Within a large apartment, each resident has a self-contained living/bedroom of his or her own, with its own small bathroom and toilet as well as a small entrance hall.

The core of the community area is a generously proportioned, cozily furnished live-in kitchen, fully equipped for a household of 8 persons, often with its own sheltered terrace or balcony. The social life of the household revolves around the live-in kitchen; the stimulating diversity of daily activities, with their smells, noises, conversations, and human companionship, it is hoped, will enliven the residents. They can take part, either actively or passively, in ordinary everyday activities, depending upon their abilities and preferences. The household is run in close proximity to the residents, and they can see, hear, and smell all that is occurring.

Everyday life, as well as the daily care and nursing work in this family-like community, is managed by a primary caregiver, a person to whom the residents can relate, also known as the day-to-day manager (usually a woman). She helps the residents, as needed, with their daily activities. She also serves as the housekeeper: she draws up the catering plan, organizes the shopping, prepares the meals, and does the washing. In addition, she is the contact person in the psychosocial sense, facilitating communication among the residents and arbitrating the disagreements that inevitably occur in any group living together. She also looks for and organizes contacts with relatives, friends, and neighbors, as well as with the physicians and nursing staff. The specialist nursing staff are brought in whenever the day-to-day manager considers this necessary and depending upon the residents' individual needs. A qualified nurse is on duty at night, which is typical in conventional nursing homes.

A concept totally oriented toward normality is designed to ensure that older people who need nursing care and who are mentally confused do not have to make do without a familiar environment and the feeling of being personally sheltered. The home community principle, therefore, is based upon the following criteria.

- To replace the institutional structure, it is necessary to abolish the central catering system.
- The architecture of the home community must be homey and of manageable size, since the quality of (home) life includes more than the quality of nursing care.
- The great need frail older people have for help and assistance is met by small, family-like groups with a primary caregiver in permanent attendance.
- The activities in a home community are designed to simulate a normal household. Nursing services are necessary, but they are kept unobtrusively in the background and are limited to the level of each resident's individual needs.
- Each home community is autonomous but can be managed in conjunction with others or through a service center.

The organizational principles can be summarized as follows:

- Decentralization
- Normalization
- Continuous presence of a primary caregiver (*Bezugsperson*)
- Flexible organization of nursing staff.

Home communities regard themselves as residential options, integrated into their neighborhoods, and they are generally available for older people needing nursing care. Because they offer special possibilities, such as the freedom of choice that residents have to retire to their own rooms or to seek contact with others, a stimulating milieu, and human proximity, they are also particularly suitable for older persons with dementia.

The residents of home communities do not basically differ from the residents of other nursing homes, neither with regard to age structure nor the frequency of required nursing care. Because of their legal status under the Homes Act and related legislation, as well as the nature of their activities and target groups, home communities are treated as registered residential nursing homes for the elderly and are financed by long-term care insurance whether organized singly or in conjunction with others. By contrast, various other *cohousing communities* for older people with high levels of care needs do not have such legal status in Germany. Those communities are often founded by personal initiative and operate primarily on an outpatient basis with the residents retaining their status as tenants. They organize nursing and other care either on their own, or with help from a third party or support group.

PHILOSOPHY AND OPERATING CONCEPT OF HOME COMMUNITIES

The philosophy of home communities places the individual human being at the heart of its concerns and endeavors. It does not rob the elderly person of his or her personality and does not disempower him or her by imposing excessively rationalized working procedures based upon urgent nursing necessities, or other caregiver concerns. Instead, it accepts the preferences and interests of the individual elderly person and takes these interests as the yardstick for programmatic actions. In this respect, the approach adopted by home communities is client centered and biography orientated. The aim of the design is to create a social and physical quality that takes as its ideal the resident's former living milieu. It also tries to promote well-being in what is after all the last stage in the resident's life without reducing the professional quality of care and nursing. The objective is to ensure that elderly people who can no longer cope on their own and are forced to move should be able to find a living situation with which they are familiar and comfortable. Thus, the philosophy of organization of home communities differs fundamentally from that of the conventional nursing home.

The organization of home communities, compared with that of conventional homes, is dominated by the all-embracing aim of decentralization. Starting with the architecture and the internal planning, the functional processes and the deployment of the staff involve "redistribution from centralized to decentralized functions" and, therefore, a democratization and upgrading of the role and responsibility of each individual employee. The domestic staff no longer work in central kitchens or laundries, far away from the residents—such facilities no longer exist. The staff now work in immediate proximity to the residents in each individual home community. At the same time, at least one employee is present at all times. Without incurring any additional costs, the residents encounter more of the staff, and the staff proximity results in greater direct assistance and attention, as well as increased supervision and guidance.

The design concept of the home community is intended to bring wide-ranging benefits to the residents. The faces of the staff members, it is hoped, will become increasingly familiar. Interpersonal relationships will be formed, resulting in feedback control circuits or direct error-monitoring systems among the residents, their relatives, and the staff. The continuous presence of an employee in the home community answers much of the greater need for feeling protected and secure among those receiving nursing care. All these services which ensure and increase quality can be provided by the home community even though their financing under conventional systems has always been considered to be highly problematic.

The KDA has calculated personnel costs on the assumption that a home community with 8 residents will require one attendant to be present during the day to handle all the domestic and quasi-nursing work. However, on-going practice and conclusions derived from practical experience in home communities will allow more precise estimates of parameters to determine optimum group size. It is also assumed that an attendant will be available every day between 8.00 A.M. and 10.00 P.M., including Sundays and public holidays; obviously residents need as much nursing on these days as on any other.

For the average home community with 8 residents, 3.25 attendants and 2.75 nursing staff must be provided to achieve the high standards described above, round the clock and all year long. Each home community will remain a relatively autonomous entity even if managed in collaboration with other communities or a services center. Such collaboration will tend to be the rule, in order to achieve benefits such as reduced administrative costs and more efficient night service. Considering parameters such as average annual salary and working hours set by collective wage agreements in Germany's western states (and taking the state of Hessen as a base for estimations), the personnel cost component of the nursing rates works out to DM 104.69 per day for care-level 1, DM 133.55 for level 2, and DM 152.42 for level 3. For comparison purposes, at the time of writing of this chapter, the DM equaled approximately $0.45.

The construction of home communities, which is based on the guideline costs and square-footage parameters of conventional nursing homes, is therefore no more expensive than other high-quality nursing homes. The home communities, however, offer much more in terms of attendant and nursing services.

CONCLUSIONS

It is clear that home communities offer elderly people needing high levels of care a secure home and a dignified way of life, without increasing financial burden. In this respect, home communities are able to improve the quality of life substantially, in a sustainable manner, especially for those elderly suffering from dementia. Such homes enjoy the added advantage of securing the jobs of the personnel. By directly involving their residents, home communities can make a major contribution to breaking down the patterns of institutionalized violence, which, sadly enough, continues to give rise to complaints about so many old people's homes in Germany.

If we are to respond to the challenge that has arisen partly from demographic trends and partly from the current qualitative shortcomings of old people's care, we will have to extend our imagination and creativity to develop and promote intermediate forms of care, in addition to the home communities model. We should also examine to what extent noninstitutional care efforts are already being networked, and how they should be networked in the future.

REFERENCES

Bundesministerium für Familie, Senioren, Frauen und Jugend (BMFSFJ) [Federal Ministry for Family Affairs, Senior Citizens, Women and Youth]. (Ed.). (1998). *Zweiter Altenbericht der Bundesregierung: Wohnen im Alter* [Second report on the situation of older people. Housing in old age]. Bonn, Germany: Eigenverlag.

Großjohann, K., & Stolarz, H. (1998). *Selbständiges Wohnen fördern* [The promotion of self-reliant housing]. Altenhilfe sollte Trennung von Normal- und Sonderwohnformen aufheben. *Pro Alter, 31*(2), 6–10.

Kitwood, T. (2000). *Demenz* [Dementia reconsidered]. Der personenzetrierte Ansatz im Umgang mit. verwirrten Menschen. Deutschsprachige Ausgabe hrsg. von Müller-Hergl, C., Bern, Switzerland: Hans Huber Verlag.

Kuratorium Deutsche Altershilfe (KDA) [German Foundation for the Care of Older People]. (2000a). *Hausgemeinschaften. Die 4. Generation des Altenpflegeheimbaus* [Home communities: The 4th generation of nursing home design]. Cologne, Germany: Bundesministerium für Gesundheit.

Kuratorium Deutsche Altershilfe (KDA) [German Foundation for the Care of Older People]. (2000b). *Wohnen in Gemeinschaft* [Communal living]. Dokumentation des deutsch-niederländischen Experten-Workshops am 20. und 21. Januar in Königswinter. KDA-Schriftenreihe "thema 156." Cologne, Germany: Kuratorium Deutsche Altershiffe.

CHAPTER 9

Linking Subjective Housing Needs to Objective Living Conditions Among Older Adults in Germany

Frank Oswald

T his chapter focuses on the link between housing needs and housing conditions from a psychological point of view and emphasizes the perceived housing situation of the older individual. Three examples of perceived housing in old age are considered, namely, housing satisfaction, the variety of meanings of home, and the reasons for moving from home to home. These aspects are regarded from the perspective of the complementary/congruence of well-being (Carp & Carp, 1984), especially the differentiation between basic or lower-order needs versus higher-order needs when emphasizing person-environment fit (see also Lawton, 1998). Empirical data from different studies were considered.

HOUSING CONDITIONS AND HOUSING NEEDS IN OLD AGE

Objective housing conditions subsume the observable physical and social framework of housing. They include the attributions of being supportive, stimulative, recreational, and familiar, as specified by the taxonomies of environmental attributes (Lawton, 1999) or design principles (Pynoos & Regnier, 1997; Regnier, 1997). Housing conditions can be optimized by making modifications to old facilities or building new homes that facilitate the maintenance of independent living. Housing conditions can also be changed through relocation. Elders can be confronted with their existing housing conditions, for instance, when they suffer a competence loss. Optimal housing can foster development in old age, when people, on the average, spend more of their time at home than younger age groups (Baltes, Maas, Wilms, & Borchelt, 1999; Küster, 1998). Even for dependent elders, supportive housing conditions would be a resource for maintaining, regaining, or enhancing the quality of life.

The subjective housing needs of older adults can be regarded as basic requirements or as sophisticated preferences of the individual. They can be analyzed from a theory-based perspective; for example, following the distinction of lower-order versus higher-order needs (Carp & Carp, 1984) or the taxonomies of environmental preferences (Kahana, 1982) and need domains, such as autonomy, efficacy, privacy, aesthetic experience, and learning (Lawton, 1987). In adapting the differentiation of lower-order and higher-order needs for housing, lower-order or basic needs in this domain are oriented toward maintaining autonomy with respect to necessary activities of daily living; higher-order housing needs reflect such development-oriented needs as privacy, comfort, familiarity, stimulation, or favored personal activities (Lawton, 1998). Basically one would assume that there is a variety of housing needs in different situations in old age, covering both basic and higher-order needs. Housing needs can be examined in terms of housing satisfaction as expressions of fit between basic needs and conditions, or in terms of hidden or less obvious needs, which are often defined by the general meaning of "home." In addition, changed or unfulfilled needs may motivate changes in housing and the decision to relocate. Housing needs can vary between members of different birth cohorts, over the life course, as well as in different cultures, regions, and situations. Loss of competence is often a mediating factor for changing needs in old age. Housing needs are related to a person's coping strategies, for example, to tolerate unmet or competing needs. Finally, the impact of psychological and sociostructural factors on housing, as well as the relation of housing needs to individual needs in other domains of life, are relevant to the process of aging. If housing conditions meet the occupant's needs, the home environment becomes a resource for maintaining or regaining autonomy and life quality. However, if housing conditions do not fit with individual needs, then the home environment may be perceived as unsatisfactory or may become dangerous for the person (due to loss of competence, for example), and the likelihood of transfer to an institution may increase.

Empirical data from various studies within the field of environmental gerontology are reported here to represent salient aspects of housing for elders in Germany. The chapter deals with 3 topics.

1. Living arrangements have been rapidly changing since reunification, particularly in the former East Germany. Data from a large survey and from a longitudinal study on adult development, including information on changing housing conditions in East and West Germany and its impact on housing satisfaction in a group of relatively healthy young-old adults, are presented. The focus of this part of the chapter is on the relation of housing conditions and housing satisfaction as an expression of fulfilled basic housing needs (Kahana, 1982). The question here is to determine what types of housing changes are related to increased housing satisfaction.

2. The majority of older adults wish to remain in place even when suffering from a loss of competence, and the growing number of home modifications and innovations will meet their need to stay put as long as possible. Data from a qualitative in-depth study on the meaning of home in a group of severely impaired older adults are presented. The focus of this section is on the broad scope of functional, behavioral, cognitive, emotional, and social housing needs, including the less obvious higher-order needs, in particular, those reflecting person-environment proactivity (Lawton, 1985) and place attachment (e.g., Rowles, 1983, 1994; Rubinstein, 1989, 1998; Rubinstein & Parmelee, 1992). Here the question is whether these needs become apparent when the meaning of home is assessed and whether such needs are also important in the context of home modifications.

3. Current projections show rapidly increasing numbers of older adults moving "from home to home" (Friedrich, 1995; Golant, 1998; Haas & Serow, 1993; Litwak & Longino, 1987). Data gathered from a telephone-based semistructured study on the reasons for moving in a group of financially secure older adults are presented. The focus of this section is on the content and kind of reasons for moving including both lower-order and higher-order needs (Carp & Carp, 1984). The question here is whether existing housing alternatives (e.g., assisted living) meet the whole scope of housing needs of older adults.

HOUSING SATISFACTION IN LIGHT OF CHANGING HOUSING CONDITIONS

Compared to the United States (see, for example, United States Census Bureau, 2000), data from Germany reveals that about 93% of older adults aged 65 years and older live independently in their communities (Bundesministerium für Familie, Senioren, Frauen und Jugend [BMFSFJ] [Federal Ministry for Family Affairs, Senior Citizens, Women and Youth], 2001). More than half of these approximately 9.6 million private households in Germany are single-person households, 43.1% are couple households, and 5.5% are households with more than 2 persons (Statistisches Bundesamt [StBA] [Federal Statistical Office of Germany], 2000a). A decade ago, German reunification provided the opportunity for a "natural experiment," in which older adults in the eastern and the western parts of the country with different experiences in housing and with different housing conditions could be compared. Data from a large survey ($N = 3,042$) showed that, in contrast to many other European countries, most persons in East and West Germany did not own their homes but lived in rented apartments (StBA, 2000b). After reunification, however, the number of owner-occupants increased in both East and West Germany. Basic indicators for the rapidly changing housing conditions in East Germany since reunification are presented in Table 9.1. Most strikingly, the percentage of persons over 65 years of age who live in modern apartments (apartments with a bathroom, inside toilet, and central heating) increased in West Germany from 74% (1988) to 94% (1998), and

TABLE 9.1 Changes and Stability in Objective Housing Conditions

	West			East		
Year of assessment	*1988*	*1993*	*1998*	*1990*	*1993*	*1998*
Housing tenure (owner)	47%	49%	62%	25%	30%	36%
Bathroom, toilet, central heating	74%	88%	94%	33%	41%	85%
More than 1 room per occupant	89%	91%	91%	75%	74%	81%
Satisfaction with home environment (0–10)[a]	8.8	8.6	8.9	7.2	7.4	8.1

Note: Data from a national survey study (the *Wohlfahrtssurvey*) 1988 (West), 1990 (East), 1993, 1998 ($N = 3,042$; StBA, 2000). Analyses cover persons 65 years and older living alone or with a partner in 1- or 2-person households.

[a]Self-evaluation rating on an 11-point scale; higher scores indicate higher satisfaction.

in East Germany from 33% (1990) to 85% (1998). Although older adults in East Germany have experienced great improvements in housing, housing standards nevertheless have generally remained higher in West Germany than in East Germany. The number of rooms per occupant serves as an indicator for greater comfort at home: in West Germany, the number of rooms per occupant remained stable, but it increased slightly in East Germany (see Table 9.1).

Other data analyses indicate that the young-old benefited especially from the improvements. In 1993 the proportion of substandard apartments (no bathroom or inside toilet) among the 60- to 65-year-olds amounted to 4% in West Germany and 18% in East Germany. Among persons 80 years and older, 7% in West Germany and 32% in East Germany lived in substandard apartments (Motel, Künemund, & Bode, 2000). Although there has been some equalization of housing conditions, there are still differences between East and West Germany today. The differential increase in housing satisfaction, as an index of met basic housing needs, seems to be related to objective improvements. While slight improvement in housing conditions is associated with stable subjective evaluations of housing satisfaction in West Germany, the huge improvements in housing since reunification in East Germany have been accompanied by a substantial increase in housing satisfaction. By and large, objective housing conditions have improved, especially in East Germany, where basic amenities were relatively scarce a decade ago. Housing satisfaction is also higher today in East Germany than it was in 1990.

We can assume, then, that physical improvements have led to a better fit between housing needs and housing conditions in general and, thus, to higher satisfaction (Carp & Carp, 1984; Kahana, 1982). Empirical evidence for that assumption on a more detailed level can be provided by data from the Interdisciplinary Longitudinal Study on Adult Development (ILSE). This study included 1,390 participants from 2 birth cohorts born between 1930 and 1932 and between 1950 and 1952 from urban areas in East and West Germany (time period between T1 and T2: $M = 4.1$ years). Standardized questionnaires and semistructured in-depth interviews, which included objective aspects of the living arrangement and the subjective evaluation of housing, were conducted (Oswald, Schmitt, Sperling, & Wahl, 2000). To assess the quality of the rating measures, the interviewers' ratings in selected parts of the interview were compared against a standard rating. All interviewers reached a minimum of 80% agreement with the standard rating. The average agreement with the standard rating for selected parts of the interview was 88%, and the average interrater correlation was $r = .946$. As expected, East German participants reported extremely high frequencies of relocation and reconstructions owing to the bad housing conditions before reunification in the former German Democratic Republic. One out of 4 participants moved in East Germany, whereas only about 1 out of 10 moved in West Germany. Reconstruction of the notorious Plattenbau apartment houses was especially widespread in East Germany (see Table 9.2).

In contrast to the welfare survey (StBA, 2000b), housing satisfaction in the ILSE study remained relatively stable between T1 and T2 in both West and East Germany. Focusing on data from the birth cohort between 1930 and 1932 only, housing satisfaction (self-evaluation rating from 1 = very low to 5 = very high) in West Germany was $M = 4.2$ ($SD = 0.8$) at T1 and $M = 4.2$ ($SD = 0.7$) at T2; in East Germany, it was $M = 4.0$ ($SD = 0.8$) at T1 and $M = 4.1$ ($SD = 0.7$) at T2. On the individual level, no significant relation was found with respect to the fit between standard of housing conditions and subjective evaluations in the West German area; in East Germany, the quality of housing conditions was more closely related to housing satisfaction at T1 ($r = .46$; $p < .001$) than at T2 ($r = .25$; $p < .01$). Thus, especially at T1 in East Germany, dissatisfaction with housing was highly related to bad housing conditions. After housing conditions were improved at T2, the relation was weaker, probably because the level of amenities is now higher and permits a certain level of satisfaction for all participants in East Germany, comparable to the participants in West Germany at T1 and T2. In other words, only those who must endure bad housing conditions perceive the misfit between basic housing needs and amenities, and this is reflected in low satisfaction ratings (Diener & Diener, 1998;

TABLE 9.2 Results from the ILSE Study on Types of Changes in Objective Housing Conditions

Types of changes (%)	West ($n = 223$)	East ($n = 226$)	W/E-Diff.[a]
Relocation	9.9	26.6	***
Reconstruction	23.3	57.6	***
Renovation, modification	50.7	59.4	ns
New amenities or furniture	31.4	60.3	***

Note: Data from the Interdisciplinary Longitudinal Study on Adult Development (ILSE), changes in housing conditions from T1 to T2 ($M = 4.1$ years), birth cohort 1930–1932. The study is supported by the German Federal Ministry of Family Affairs, Senior Citizens, Women and Youth (BMFSFJ) and the Baden-Württemberg Ministry of Science, Research and Art (MWK), grant Ref. 314-1722-102/16.
[a]$p < .001$.***

Weideman & Anderson, 1985). Beside correlative data, detailed analyses of different varieties of change in housing conditions and its relation to changes in satisfaction show that, in West Germany, "reconstruction" was slightly related to an increase in housing satisfaction ($r = .17$; $p < .01$). In contrast, in East Germany, only "relocation" was related to higher housing satisfaction ($r = .43$; $p < .001$). Participants who reported other or no changes had no statistically significant increase in satisfaction.

MEANING OF HOME IN LIGHT OF HOME MODIFICATIONS

Home modifications are a common practice among elders. They not only provide older adults with a basic standard of amenities but also allow elders with competence loss to remain independent as long as possible (e.g., Pynoos, 1995). A systematic analysis of 626 home modifications for older adults in Germany showed not only effectiveness in terms of maintaining daily activities, but also cost effectiveness (relative to paying for care insurance) (Niepel, 1999). A study conducted by the American Association of Retired Persons (AARP), *Fixing to Stay*, which included 2,000 persons 45 years of age and older, showed that many Americans modify their homes and make simple changes to make their homes easier to live in (American Association of Retired Persons [AARP], 2000). Another recent report showed the positive effects of educational and environmental modifications in a randomized controlled study of patients with dementia; for example, fewer declines in instrumental activities of daily living (Gitlin, Corcoran, Winter, Boyce, & Hauck, 2001). Nevertheless, better empirical evidence and a more differentiated approach, focusing on moderating effects and acceptance, are still needed. For example, Gilderbloom and Markham (1996) showed that respondents who had difficulties in daily activities nevertheless did not view housing modifications as being particularly helpful and rejected them, regardless of their cost. These respondents did not feel any need for adaptation. According to Wister (1989), older adults tend to maintain their present environment and initially try to adapt themselves psychologically to the environment instead of adapting the environment to compensate for disabilities. Personal attitudes and individual preferences have an impact on the adaptation process. Beside offering various home modifications, an individualization of the modifications is often requested (e.g., Connell & Sanford, 1997). Easy solutions do not fit complex or competing housing needs (e.g., access versus security or privacy versus stimulation). It is easy to assume that home modifications do meet everyday functional basic housing needs and related activities of daily living. However, we know very little about the role of other, nonfunctional, higher-order needs that are not related to essential daily activities, especially when suffering from loss of competence (Carp & Carp, 1984; Lawton, 1998).

To provide some data on the scope and frequency of various housing needs, data are presented from a study originally designed to explore the meaning of home. The results of this study may contribute to the understanding of the variety of housing needs. Data were drawn from qualitative, in-depth, semistructured interviews with 126 participants between the ages of 61 and 92 ($M = 76.4$ years). One-third of the participants were in good health, one-third suffered from severe mobility impairment, and one-third were blind. A docility hypothesis perspective would suggest that housing designed to meet basic needs to perform everyday activities in an accessible, safe, and supportive barrier-free environment is especially relevant for impaired elders (Lawton & Nahemow, 1973). From a complementary/congruence perspective (Carp & Carp, 1984), as well as from a proactivity-hypothesis perspective (Lawton, 1985), or from a place attachment and meaning of home perspective (Rowles, 1983, 1994; Rowles & Ravdal, 2002; Rubinstein, 1989; Rubinstein & Parmelee, 1992), however, housing needs are also related to higher-order cognitive or emotional aspects such as privacy, familiarity, and stimulation. Relevant individual statements were collected and categorized. By means of a multiphasic coding procedure, different meaning categories were established. Each statement was coded into categories with satisfying reliability (Cohen's Kappa: 0.77–0.83) (Oswald, 1998; Oswald & Wahl, 2001). About half of the statements on the subjective representation of housing did not pertain to functional aspects of housing amenities but, instead, reflected emotional, cognitive, and social bonding to the home environment. Different groups of participants revealed different patterns of meaning (see Figure 9.1).

As shown in Figure 9.1, physical aspects of housing (Type I, e.g., the experience of location, access, and furnishing) were significantly lower among the mobility impaired and again lower among the blind participants. Cognitive, especially biographical aspects (Type III, e.g., the experience of familiarity, insideness, and remembering in place), were significantly higher among the mobility impaired and even higher among the blind participants compared to the healthy participants. Behavioral (Type II, e.g., modifying, adapting to, or rearranging things at home) and social aspects (Type V, e.g., relation to the fellow lodgers, neighbors, or visitors) showed no significant

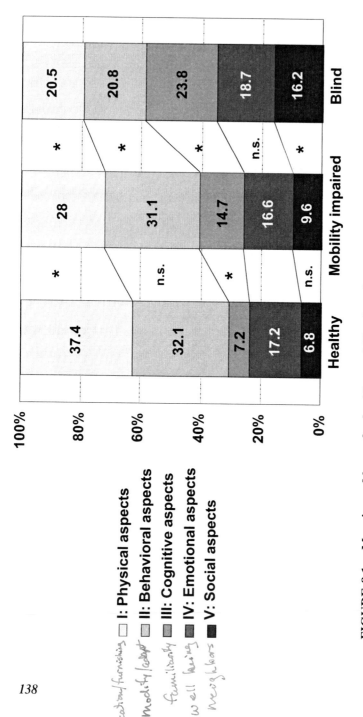

FIGURE 9.1. Meanings of home for healthy, mobility-impaired, and blind older adults.

Note: Evaluation of verbal transcripts and tapes, based on 1,804 statements of $N = 126$ subjects. Mean number of statements per person amounted to 14.3. Multivariate MANOVA procedure for 5 domains of place attachment was conducted to test differences between subgroups (Wilk's Lambda = .707; $F = 4.40$ (10,232); $p < .05 = *$; explained variance: 29.3%). To show differences in detail, univariate simple contrasts were computed for each category between healthy and mobility impaired, as well as between mobility impaired and blind subjects.

differences between healthy and mobility-impaired elderly. However, there were lower frequencies in the behavioral domain and higher frequencies in the social domain among the group of the blind participants compared to the mobility impaired. About the same proportion of statements reflected emotional aspects across all 3 groups of participants (Type IV, e.g., experience of satisfaction, well-being, and privacy).

In accordance with assumptions from the complementary/congruence model, proactivity theory, or the place-attachment perspective, the data reveal a variety of meanings of home among healthy as well as impaired elders, including both basic and higher-order housing needs. Moreover, one might assume that different patterns of meanings reflect ways of adaptation and coping with competence loss at home in old age in a compensatory (complementary) style. The 2 different kinds of competence losses lead to different meaning patterns emphasizing those aspects that are still available to the individual. Blind participants concentrated more on their social context and less on behavioral aspects; mobility-impaired elders showed a pattern of place attachment in the behavioral domain similar to healthy participants. Possibly mobility impairment has fewer effects on everyday behavior within the home environment, whereas blindness leads to compensation of discontinued behavior on a social level. Participants who are diminished in their ability to cope actively with the environment show high portions of meanings in the cognitive domain. Cognitive and emotional bonding may reflect higher-order needs for familiarity, privacy, or retreat in particular. Emotional bonding seems to be important in old age in general, regardless of health status. However, these are the very individuals for whom home modifications are planned, addressing explicit physical and behavioral aspects of housing. Higher-order needs may be less obvious for visitors than basic needs, and these are not easy to address with functional adaptations. Nevertheless, emotional and cognitive bonding to the home should not be regarded as liabilities (e.g., being attached to the way in which things are counteracts the efficacy of home modifications), but as advantages (e.g., familiar environmental supports orientation for the blind) when it comes to coping and to the process of proactively shaping the home environment to suit one's needs (Lawton, 1985).

REASONS FOR MOVING AND RELOCATING FROM HOME TO HOME

To age in place is a housing preference for many older adults. Data from the German *Alterssurvey* ($N = 4,034$) show that 70- to 85-year-old participants live on the average 31.6 years in the same apartment and 50.3 years in the same town. The percentage of persons living in the same apartment for more than 40 years is 28.4% in West Germany and 34.7% in East Germany (Motel et al., 2000). Besides home modifications, other forms of assisted living have been developed to meet the housing needs of elders, such as needs for security, safety, and autonomy. Purpose-built homes have been designed to provide a barrier-free environment combined with a multilevel set of accessible supportive services, allowing older individuals to enjoy autonomy at home as long as possible. A recently published German longitudinal study based on 173 older adults in 7 facilities (Saup, 2001) revealed, however, that persons who moved into these facilities had unrealistic expectations and were poorly informed about housing alternatives. The assessment took place before and after relocation. The participants had moved in order to circumvent certain risks that occur in old age, although many of them were already suffering from loss of competence when they moved in. The participants expected that they could stay put at their new home until death (70.8%), even when intensive care was required (92.4%), or if they started to exhibit mental deterioration (65%), which were unrealistic expectations. Most of them did not know about alternatives to assisted living facilities, such as home modification (88.9%) and counseling (83.6%). Thus, assisted living facilities did not seem to conform with the housing or moving needs of older adults.

From a broader perspective on moving in old age in general, extrapolation from a large survey in Germany (Socio-Economic Panel, SOEP) shows that about half of all older adults (55 years and older) will move at least once before age 75 (Heinze, Eichener, Naegele, Bucksteeg, & Schauerte, 1997). Linking again housing needs and conditions, the focus here is on the reasons for moves, reflecting changed or unfulfilled housing needs, possibly strong enough to lead to relocation and apparently related to basic needs for security, safety, and support in old age. Friedrich (1995) found 3 typical forms of moving incentives in Germany: to be "closer to the family," to have an "attractive home," and to "overcome bad housing conditions" (see also Serow, Friedrich, & Haas, 1996). The literature often mentions the differentiation between "push" and "pull" factors (Haas & Serow, 1993). Although this distinction is useful, in this study the content of motives (e.g., personal versus environmental) was examined. The very same reason for a move (e.g., housing amenities) can, in one case, have a push motive, and in another case, have a pull motive. In addition, a differentiation was made between lower-order or basic versus higher-order needs (Carp & Carp, 1984; Lawton, 1998).

To provide empirical evidence on the scope and frequency of move motives, reflecting unfulfilled or changed housing needs before a relocation decision, data on reasons for moving were obtained from a group of well-off older adults (N = 217, mean age = 70.7; range 60–89) who moved from home to home within a 3-year period (M = 1.9 years, SD = 0.9) before assessment. The study differentiates between content (person, physical environment, social environment, or societal) and level of need (basic needs, higher-order needs) motivations, with respect to relocation. Each single motive was characterized by 2 independent raters in a 4 × 2 disjunct category system with satisfying interrater reliability (Cohen's Kappa: 0.77 to 0.85) (Oswald, Wahl, & Gäng, 1999; Oswald, Schilling, Wahl, & Gäng, 2002). Results indicate that subjects had multiple reasons for moving, many of which addressed higher-order needs (see Figure 9.2).

Each participant mentioned about 4 different reasons for moving, com-

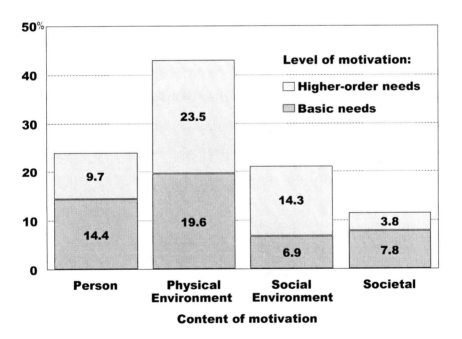

FIGURE 9.2.   Reasons for moving, cross-classified by level and content of motivation.

Note: The relative frequency of varying move motives is shown above. A total of 961 reasons for the move were coded from N = 217 participants, which represents a mean of 4.4 reasons for moving per person.

binations of the levels and categories shown in Figure 9.2. With respect to the content level of motives, physical environmental motives were most prevalent; for example, basic housing needs ("I found the apartment was too large to do my daily work") or as higher-order needs ("Because we're spending more and more time at home, we wanted to have a balcony and a view"). In the domain of social environmental motives, the differentiation between basic ("My daughter can do the shopping for me now, because she lives just around the corner") and higher-order needs ("I wanted to spend more time with my grandchildren") can also be shown. Links were found between basic needs and barrier reduction, as well as between social motives and proximity of family after the move. The main results were that there is not one single reason for moving, but a set of changed or unfulfilled housing needs leading to relocation. Although the participants in this study varied in their health status, they reported many higher-order level needs in the face of moving in old age.

CONCLUSION

The aim of this chapter was to present empirical data on the link between housing needs and housing conditions of older adults from a psychological perspective, particularly from a complementary/congruence perspective on person-environment fit (Carp & Carp, 1984; Lawton, 1998). Data from 3 studies demonstrated facets of the person-environment relation on the microlevel of the home environment in the face of salient aspects of housing in old age.

With respect to the first study, the focus was on housing satisfaction as the expression of fulfilled housing needs for basic amenities (especially in East Germany) after reunification. It was demonstrated that housing satisfaction as an expression of fulfilled needs is related to improvements in housing conditions for only some types of changes. With regard to application, these data may support the assumption that, first, housing satisfaction is especially sensitive for changes in housing conditions on the level of basic amenities and, second, distinct objective changes in housing conditions are related to an increase in housing satisfaction owing to the type of change, geographical location, former experience, and former level of amenities.

The second study emphasized cognitive and emotional aspects of place attachment as an expression of important but less obvious higher-order housing needs, especially for those individuals with loss of competence (e.g., in the context of home modifications). The data showed that housing needs cannot be reduced to functional aspects for those individuals who age in place and want to stay put, especially when suffering from loss of competence. These data revealed that there is definitely a need to sensitize planners and those responsible for home modifications to the whole scope of meanings of home—reflecting lower-order and higher-order housing needs—and to appreciate the less obvious aspects of place attachment, especially those that become salient when suffering from competence loss, such as the importance of familiarity.

The third study emphasized reasons for moving as expressions of changed or unfulfilled basic and higher-order housing needs, which has led to an increasing number of relocations "from home to home" among older adults. The study pointed out that the older adult who moves from home to home has other housing needs, in addition to the basic wish of remaining independent. With regard to application, one may emphasize the need to consider development-oriented move motives among older adults, only partially met by purpose-built housing alternatives like assisted living.

In sum, the data support the assumption that housing satisfaction alone is not sufficient to evaluate housing needs. As was assumed in the complementary/congruence model of well-being (Carp & Carp, 1984) and from other theoretical perspectives—for example, on proactivity and place attachment (Lawton, 1985; Rowles, 1983)—the data revealed further empirical evidence for a broad range of housing needs, including both lower-order or basic and higher-order needs. Various needs were observed; for instance, the home was associated with different personal meanings, and reasons for moving were likewise diverse. Whether or not older individuals suffer from loss of competence or prefer to stay put or to move, they express a broad range of housing needs instead of single requirements for support or assistance.

In further studies, these results must be related to needs in other domains of life, such as outdoor activities or health. Research on the global construct of housing satisfaction needs to be differentiated toward other aspects possibly more relevant for individual housing decisions or the question of which is the "right" house or apartment in old age. In addition, we need to learn more about how older adults cope with changing needs or how they negotiate between competing needs (e.g., to modify versus to maintain, to stay versus to move) as well as the process of decision making in detail. However, the data may encourage providers of purpose-built housing to reflect on changing housing needs of today's and tomorrow's elders and on the unknown impact of the housing market on forthcoming housing needs. The variety of housing needs in different circumstances of aging showed also that older adults need to be involved into the planning process, to be better informed about alternatives, and to be supported in anticipating and influencing their own future housing conditions.

REFERENCES

American Association of Retired Persons (AARP). (2000). *Fixing to stay: A national survey of housing and home modification issues.* Washington, DC: AARP.

Baltes, M. M., Maas, I., Wilms, H.-U., & Borchelt, M. (1999). Everyday competence in old and very old age: Theoretical considerations and empirical findings. In P. B. Baltes & K. U. Mayer (Eds.), *The Berlin Aging Study* (pp. 384–402). Cambridge: Cambridge University Press.

Bundesministerium für Familie, Senioren, Frauen und Jugend (BMFSFJ) [Federal Ministry for Family Affairs, Senior Citizens, Women and Youth]. (Ed.). (2001). *Dritter Altenbericht der Bundesregierung: Alter und Gesellschaft* [Third report on the situation of older people: Aging and society]. Bonn, Germany: Eigenverlag.

Carp, F. M., & Carp, A. (1984). A complementary/congruence model of well-being or mental health for the community elderly. In I. Altman, M. P. Lawton, & J. F. Wohlwill (Eds.), *Human behavior and environment*, Vol. 7, *Elderly people and the environment* (pp. 279–336). New York: Plenum Press.

Connell, B. R., & Sanford, J. A. (1997). Individualizing home modification recommendations to facilitate performance of routine activities. In S. Lanspery & J. Hyde (Eds.), *Staying put: Adapting the places instead of the people* (pp. 113–147). Amityville, NY: Baywood.

Diener, E., & Diener, S. (1998). Subjective well-being and age: An international analysis. *Annual Review of Gerontology and Geriatrics, 17,* 304–324.

Friedrich, K. (1995). *Altern in räumlicher Umwelt. Sozialräumliche Interaktionsmuster in Deutschland und in den USA* [Aging in the spatial context: Social-environmental patterns of interaction in Germany and the United States]. Darmstadt, Germany: Steinkopff.

Gilderbloom, J. I., & Markham, J. P. (1996). Housing modification needs of the disabled elderly: What really matters? *Environment & Behavior, 28,* 512–535.

Gitlin, L. N., Corcoran, M., Winter, L., Boyce, A., & Hauck, W. W. (2001). A randomized controlled trial of a home environmental intervention: Effect on efficacy and upset in caregivers and on daily function of persons with dementia. *The Gerontologist, 41* (1), 4–22.

Golant, S. M. (1998). Changing an older person's shelter and care setting: A model to explain personal and environmental outcomes. In R. J. Scheidt & P. G. Windley (Eds.), *Environment and aging theory: A focus on housing* (pp. 33–60). Westport, CT: Greenwod Press.

Haas, W. H., & Serow, W. J. (1993). Amenity retirement migration process: A model and preliminary evidence. *The Gerontologist, 33*(2), 212–220.

Heinze, R. G., Eichener, V., Naegele, G., Bucksteeg, M., & Schauerte, M. (1997). *Neue Wohnung auch im Alter* [New homes for the aged]. Darmstadt, Germany: Schader-Stiftung.

Kahana, E. (1982). A congruence model of person-environment interaction. In M. P. Lawton, P. G. Windley, & T. O. Byerts (Eds.), *Aging and the environment: Theoretical approaches* (pp. 97–121). New York: Springer.

Küster, C. (1998). Zeitverwendung und Wohnen im Alter [Use of time and housing in old age]. In Deutsches Zentrum für Altersfragen (Ed.), *Wohnbedürfnisse, Zeitverwendung und soziale Netzwerke älterer Menschen: Expertisenband 1 zum Zweiten Altenbericht der Bundesregierung* [Housing needs, use of time, and social networks of older adults]. Frankfurt, Germany: Campus.

Lawton, M. P. (1985). Housing and living environments of older people. In R. H. Binstock & E. Shanas (Eds.), *Handbook of aging and the social sciences* (2nd ed., pp. 450–478). New York: Van Nostrand Reinhold.

Lawton, M. P. (1987). Environment and the need satisfaction of the aging. In L. L. Carstensen & B. A. Edelstein (Eds.), *Handbook of clinical gerontology* (pp. 33–40). New York: Pergamon Press.

Lawton, M. P. (1998). Environment and aging: Theory revisited. In R. J. Scheidt & P. G. Windley (Eds.), *Environment and aging theory: A focus on housing* (pp. 1–32). Westport, CT: Greenwood Press.

Lawton, M. P. (1999). Environmental taxonomy: Generalizations from research with older adults. In S. L. Friedman & T. D. Wachs (Eds.), *Measuring environment across the life span* (pp. 91–124). Washington, DC: American Psychological Association.

Lawton, M. P., & Nahemow, L. (1973). Ecology and the aging process. In C. Eisdorfer & M. P. Lawton (Eds.), *The psychology of adult development and aging* (pp. 619–674). Washington, DC: American Psychological Association.

Litwak, E., & Longino, C. F., Jr. (1987). Migration patterns among the elderly: A developmental perspective. *The Gerontologist, 27*(3), 266–272.

Motel, A., Künemund, H., & Bode, C. (2000). Wohnen und Wohnumfeld älterer Menschen [Housing and living arrangements of older adults]. In M. Kohli & H. Künemund (Eds.), *Die zweite Lebenshälfte—Gesellschaftliche Lage und Partizipation im Spiegel des Alters-Survey* [The second half of life—Societal stage and participation in the light of the *Alters-Survey*] (pp. 124–175). Opladen, Germany: Leske & Budrich.

Niepel, T. (1999). *Wohnberatung: Erfolge, Wirkungsmechanismen und Qualitätssicherung* [Housing counceling: Sucess, mechanisms and quality assurance]. Bericht im Projekt "Wohnberatung für Bürgerinnen und Bürger in NRW" im Auftrag des Ministeriums für Arbeit, Soziales und Stadtentwicklung, Kultur und Sport des Landes Nordrhein-Westfalen und der Landesverbände der Pflegekassen NRW. Bielefeld, Germany: Universität Bielefeld.

Oswald, F. (1998). Erleben von Wohnalltag bei gesunden und gehbeeinträchtigten Älteren [How healthy versus mobility-impaired older adults perceive their home environments]. *Zeitschrift für Gerontologie und Geriatrie, 31*(4), 250–256.

Oswald, F., Schilling, O., Wahl, H.-W., & Gäng, K. (2002). Trouble in paradise? Reasons to relocate and objective environmental changes among well-off older adults. *Journal of Environmental Psychology, 22*(3), 273–288.

Oswald, F., Schmitt, M., Sperling, U., & Wahl, H.-W. (2000). Wohnen als Entwicklungskontext: Objektive Wohnbedingungen, Wohnzufriedenheit und Formen der Auseinandersetzung mit dem Wohnen in Ost- und Westdeutschland [Housing as environmental context: Housing conditions, housing satisfaction, and types of housing-related coping in East and West Germany]. In P. Martin, K. U. Ettrich, U. Lehr, D. Roether, M. Martin, & A. Fischer-Cyrulies (Eds.), *Aspekte der Entwicklung im mittleren und höheren Lebensalter: Ergebnisse der Interdisziplinären Längsschnittstudie des Erwachsenenalters (ILSE)* [Development in middle and late adulthood: Findings from the Interdisciplinary Longitudinal Study on Adult Development] (pp. 201–219). Darmstadt, Germany: Steinkopff.

Oswald, F., & Wahl, H.-W. (2001). Housing in old age: Conceptual remarks and empirical data on place attachment. *Bulletin on People-Environment Studies, 19,* 8–12.

Oswald, F., Wahl, H.-W., & Gäng, K. (1999). Umzug im Alter: Eine ökogerontologische Studie zum Wohnungswechsel privatwohnender älterer in Heidelberg [Relocation in old age: Results from an environmental gerontology study on moving from home to home in Heidelberg]. *Zeitschrift für Gerontopsychologie und psychiatrie, 12,* 1–19.

Pynoos, J. (1995). Home modifications. In G. L. Maddox (Ed.), *The encyclopedia of aging: A comprehensive resource in gerontology and geriatrics* (2nd ed., pp. 466–469). New York: Springer.

Pynoos, J., & Regnier, V. (1997). Design directives in home adaptation. In S. Lanspery & J. Hyde (Eds.), *Staying put: Adapting the places instead of the people* (pp. 41–54). Amityville, NY: Baywood.

Regnier, V. (1997). *Assisted living housing for the elderly: Design innovations from the United States and Europe.* New York: Van Nostrand.

Rowles, G. D. (1983). Geographical dimensions of social support in rural Appalachia. In G. D. Rowles & R. J. Ohta (Eds.), *Aging and milieu: Environmental perspectives on growing old* (pp. 111–129). New York: Academic Press.

Rowles, G. D. (1994). Evolving images of place in aging and "aging in place." In D. Shenk & W. A. Achenbaum (Eds.), *Changing perceptions of aging and the aged* (pp. 115–125). New York: Springer.

Rowles, G. D., & Ravdal, H. (2002). Aging, place, and meaning in the face of changing circumstances. In R. Weiss & S. Bass (Eds.), *Challenges of the third age: Meaning and purpose in later life* (pp. 81–114). New York: Oxford University Press.

Rubinstein, R. L. (1989). The home environments of older people: A description of the psychosocial processes linking person to place. *Journal of Gerontology: Social Sciences, 44,* 45–53.

Rubinstein, R. L. (1998). The phenomenology of housing for older people. In R. J. Scheidt & P. G. Windley (Eds.), *Environment and aging theory: A focus on housing* (pp. 1–31). Westport, CT: Greenwood Press.

Rubinstein, R. L., & Parmelee, P. A. (1992). Attachment to place and the representation of life course by the elderly. In I. Altman & S. M. Low (Eds.), *Human behavior and environment,* Vol. 12, *Place attachment* (pp. 139–163). New York: Plenum Press.

Saup, W. (2001). *Ältere Menschen im Betreuten Wohnen: Ergebnisse der Augsburger Längsschnittstudie* [Older adults in assisted living: Findings from the Augsburg Longitudinal Study]. Augsburg, Germany: Verlag für Gerontologie.

Serow, W. J., Friedrich, F., & Haas, W. H. (1996). Residential relocation and regional redistribution of the elderly in the USA and Germany. *Journal of Cross-Cultural Gerontolgy, 11,* 293–306.

Statistisches Bundesamt (StBA) [Federal Statistical Office of Germany]. (2000a). *Fachserie 1: Bevölkerung und Erwerbstätigkeit, Reihe 3: Haushalte und Familien. Ergebnisse des Mikrozensus* [Population and employment: Households and families: Findings from the microcensus]. Stuttgart, Germany: Metzler & Poeschel.

Statistisches Bundesamt (StBA) [Federal Bureau of Census]. (2000b). *Datenreport 2000: Ergebnisse des Wohlfahrtssurvey* [Data report 2000: Findings from the *Wohlfahrtssurvey*]. Stuttgart, Germany: Metzler & Poeschel.

United States Census Bureau. (2000). *The older population in the United States.* Current Population Reports, September 2000. Washington, DC: U.S. Census Bureau.

Weideman, S., & Anderson, J. R. (1985). A conceptual framework for residential satisfaction. In I. Altman & C. M. Werner (Eds.), *Human behavior and environment,* Vol. 8, *Home environments* (pp. 153–182). New York: Plenum Press.

Wister, A. W. (1989). Environmental adaptation by persons in their later life. *Research on Aging, 11,* 267–291.

CHAPTER 10

Home Technology, Smart Homes, and the Aging User

Sibylle Meyer and Heidrun Mollenkopf

M odern gerontologists agree that aging processes and outcomes depend not only on biological but also on contextual influences. In western industrial societies, this means that technology is becoming an ever more crucial "environment" for aging and the aged. Although differing by degree and geographical location, communication, mobility, housekeeping, and entertainment are no longer conceivable without technological support. The relevance of modern Information and Communication Technologies (ICT) and of smart home technologies for living arrangements has increased considerably in the past few years. Two principal developments will therefore be considered in this chapter. First, we show the extent to which older Germans use ICT devices based on findings from a representative survey conducted in Germany in 1999. Second, empirical data from the Berlin Institute for Social Research (BIS) are used to analyze the smart home technologies that aim to automate homes in order to facilitate activities of daily living.

OLDER GERMANS' USE OF INFORMATION AND COMMUNICATION TECHNOLOGIES

To answer the first question, we present data from a survey that is part of an interdisciplinary research project, funded by the German Research Foundation (Deutsche Forschungsgemeinschaft), at the Technical University of Berlin (see Mollenkopf, Meyer, Schulze, Wurm, & Friesdorf, 2000). The principal objective of this project, entitled "Everyday Technology for Senior Households," is to investigate the needs and problems of older men and women with respect to technological appliances in their domestic environments. It is also designed to take appropriate steps for optimizing existing devices and developing innovative products. The representative survey was conceived by a team of social scientists in cooperation with experts from the natural sciences, engineering, and design. The sample included 1,417 men and women aged 55 years and older, stratified by age (55–64 years, 65–74 years, and 75 years and older), gender (50% women, 50% men), and location (Eastern versus Western Germany) (Wurm, 2000). Potential participants were selected according to the ADM (Arbeitskreis Deutscher Marktforschungsinstitute e.V. [Association of German Market Research Agencies]) Master Sample System and interviewed by trained interviewers with a mean of 53 years of age. Each case was assigned an individual weight to correct for biases caused by sample stratification, so that the findings could be reliably generalized to the German population aged 55 years or older. The questionnaire assessed housing, housework, information and entertainment, communications and social relations, health care, safety and mobility in the home, and demographic information. Psychological scales and attitudes toward technology were also assessed because we assumed that both objective and subjective variables affect the presence and use of technology in the home. In particular, we included an instrument assessing future time perspective (Brandstädter & Wentura, 1994; Brandstädter, Wentura, & Schmitz, 1997): "Perceived Obsolescence" (e.g., the item: "I feel more and more unease with today's lifestyle") and "Affective Valence" (e.g., the item: "The future is full of hope for me"); subjective remaining lifetime (essentially: "How much longer do you think you will live?"), and external control beliefs (Baltes & Mayer, 1998). Furthermore, we included items related to technology: Positive attitudes toward ICT (e.g., "I always keep my ICT state-of-the art"); pragmatic attitudes toward ICT (e.g., "I only buy a new device if the old one is broken"), and finally "Technological Experience" ("I always had a lot to do with technology in my life"). In the following, our focus will be on ICT, since they have the potential of both supporting older people in their daily routines and meeting their needs for communication, stimulation, and entertainment.

The availability of a device in a person's household does not necessarily mean that it is actually used (for instance, the computer may belong to the daughter in the family). We therefore consider in the following only those technologies that are, in fact, used by the respondents. Figure 10.1 shows that 4 of the examined devices were currently available and used in more than two-thirds of the senior households. All of these—particularly televisions and radios—can therefore be called standard devices. A second group of devices was also relatively widespread, used by from one- to two-thirds of the older population. These include, for example, the video recorder, the CD player, and the cordless telephone. Those ICT devices that were used by less than one-third of the elderly people are the most modern devices, such as the computer, the Internet connection, and the cellular telephone.

Comparison by gender (Figure 10.2) shows that men used more ICT devices than women: men used an average of 7 devices; women, 6. The mean difference between these groups proved to be highly significant ($F = 49$; $p < .001$). The question is, however, whether this difference is of great importance in everyday life.

When comparing the 3 age groups (Figure 10.3), it was found that the youngest group used ICT equipment the most; the oldest age group used them the least. The striking modal value in the last-mentioned group was 4 devices, and the mean value was 5.6. Again, statistical comparisons revealed highly significant mean differences between the 3 age groups: in the 2 younger groups, there is a broad spectrum of persons who use ICT, but in the oldest group, the vast majority uses only few such devices.

Of course, we were also interested in the predictors of the availability and use of ICT equipment. To answer this question, we computed an ordinal logistic regression, including objective and subjective variables as potential predictors. As *objective predictors* we included gender, children ("Do you have children—yes or no?"), living circumstances ("Are you living alone or with someone?"), education, income, and age. As *subjective predictors* we included 2 subscales and a single-item measure from the instrument assessing future time perspective mentioned above, subjective remaining lifetime, external control beliefs, items related to positive and pragmatic attitudes toward ICT, and technological experience.

Among the objective variables, living together with a partner and/or having children were the strongest predictors of having and using ICT equipment. As expected, education, income, and age were found to be significant predictors too. Young, affluent, and well-educated respondents were more likely to use a larger number of modern ICT devices. Surprisingly, gender did not play a role in this respect. The most powerful positive subjective predictors of having and using modern IC technologies were positive attitudes toward ICT; conversely, pragmatic attitudes toward ICT and experienced obsolescence were negative predictors. External control beliefs,

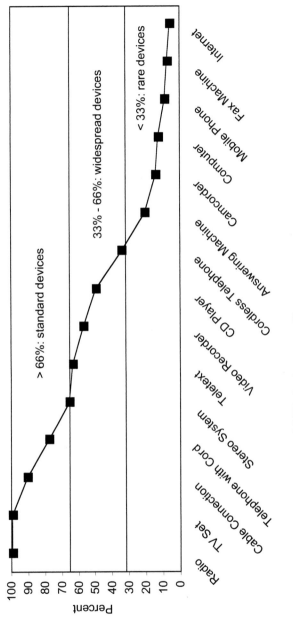

FIGURE 10.1. Presence and use of ICT devices overall.

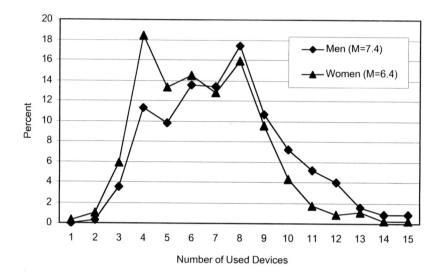

FIGURE 10.2.   Presence and use of ICT devices by gender.

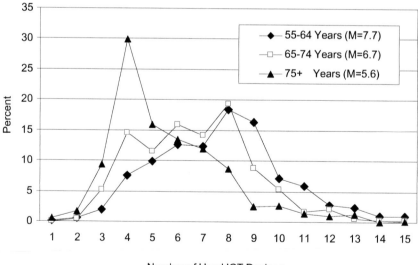

FIGURE 10.3.   Presence and use of ICT devices by age groups.

TABLE 10.1   **Predictors of Older Germans' Use of ICT (Logistic Regression Analyses; Model 2 = without nonsignificant predictors from Model 1)**

	Model 1		Model 2	
	Standard Odds Ratios	*99% C.I.*	*Standard Odds Ratios*	*99% C.I.*
Gender: 1 = male	1.239	0.883–1.740		
Children: 1 = yes	1.622	1.026–2.564	1.571	1.011–2.440
Living circumstances: 1 = married or with partner	2.596	1.853–3.637	2.792	2.049–3.804
Education: 1 = at least 10 years	1.981	1.428–2.750	1.981	1.447–2.712
Income: 1 = higher	1.858	1.368–2.524	1.754	1.306–2.354
Chronological age	0.607	0.500–0.735	0.592	0.508–0.690
Subjective remaining lifetime	1.091	0.904–1.317		
External control beliefs	1.038	0.872–1.235		
Technological experience	1.098	0.915–1.318		
Positive attitude toward ICT	1.454	1.233–1.714	1.495	1.284–1.740
Pragmatic attitude toward ICT	0.659	0.559–0.778	0.635	0.543–0.741
Experienced obsolescence	0.823	0.686–0.988	0.805	0.688–0.942
Difference in chi-square (likelihood ratio)	571.16		602.27	
Difference in degrees of freedom	12		8	
Pseudo R-Square	0.402		0.395	

C.I. = Confidence Interval.

subjective remaining lifetime, or technological experience did not contribute to predicting the amount of technology used (see Table 10.1).

These findings suggest that both the objective and subjective preconditions for actively shaping one's environment by means of ICT are not equally distributed among older persons. In view of these findings, one question remains: How do older people think and feel about technologies which automate homes, and what are the potentials and constraints of such technologies?

SMART HOME—A FUTURE PERSPECTIVE FOR OLDER PEOPLE?

Smart home, or "home automation," refers to safety and security issues, living comfort, and technologies which via internal computer networking allow one to control several home appliances. In addition, external networking technologies in the field of information and communication can offer the "aging user" a great variety of potential services, including telemedicine, telecare, teleshopping, video on demand, home consulting via monitor, and education or entertainment services. These technological developments can be valuable for the elderly in future living arrangements.

To date, the Berlin Institute for Social Research (BIS) has completed 3 in-depth studies on the acceptance of smart home technologies in individual households. At 3 points—1997, 1999, and most recently in 2001—representatives of individual households were surveyed on their views and desires with respect to intelligent technology. Each investigation covered the latest technological advances. Research results are based on the use of diverse data collection methods: qualitative individual interviews (Smart Home I, 1997) (Meyer, Schulze, & Müller, 1997), standardized oral surveys (Smart Home II, 1999), and standardized written surveys (Smart Home III, 2001) (Meyer & Schulze, 2001; Meyer, Schulze, Helten, & Fischer, 2001). The objective of the empirical smart home studies was to collect data on customer needs for smart home applications and the acceptance of smart home products. In the most recent consumer survey of October 2001, we looked at the general level of knowledge about the smart home, as well as consumer acceptance of networked systems. Our central concern here was to understand which smart home features are most acceptable to consumers, and which are seen to be less relevant. More differentiated analyses were then conducted to target particular consumer groups. Data from standardized questionnaires from 423 individuals were evaluated. The questionnaire was based on the BIS concept of technology acceptance, including variables such as "attitude toward technology," "usage patterns," and "purchase patterns" (Meyer et al., 2001). The sample was drawn from the BIS-ICT sample, which includes 1,200 persons; the questionnaire was sent to 700 persons in this sample; and those who participated were aged 16 to 83 years. The smart home survey 2001 focused on knowledge of smart technologies, attitudes toward smart technologies, attitudes toward new technologies in general, and areas in which the usage of smart technologies is preferred. The findings were analyzed for different groups (by age, gender, education, income, real estate, and level of technology acceptance in general).

When asked about concepts such as "Smart Home" or "Intelligent Living," most people first thought of everyday conveniences or objects that simplify daily chores (88%). Even if the exact nature of such conveniences remains vague, the respondents already seemed to have an image of the smart home as providing practical help with everyday living. Convenience is closely followed by more specific ideas such as "increasing security" (73%), "greater household comfort" (72%), "expanding information and communication" (67%), and "memory aid" (67%). By comparison, respondents had fewer expectations that a smart home could "save energy" (60%) or "make life at home more fun or enjoyable" (56%).

The reason why fewer people expect a smart home to make life at home more fun is that the smart home concept is seen as a rational means of completing functional household tasks. Games and entertainment play a subordinate role in this view. However, even though the smart home is primarily linked with functional tasks, it is important to note that over half the people surveyed believed that a smart home would also increase the overall level of fun or enjoyment at home.

The overall evaluation of the smart home was positive. Among the study participants, there was clearly more agreement with positive features such as "offers assistance" (81%) and "increases comfort" (80%) than with negative features such as "takes away personal control" (12%) or "creates anxiety" (8%). Three-quarters of the persons surveyed are of the opinion that the smart home "keeps things under close watch" (76%). Keeping one's own home under close watch can, for security reasons, be felt as positive, but also as negative because of possible restrictions to personal freedom and autonomy. Fun and enjoyment, as well as cost-saving, rank lower than other features in judgments of the smart home.

Of all the areas in everyday life where technical assistance through smart home technology is applicable, security clearly ranks first. This issue is followed by the areas of organizing everyday life/housework, information and communication, mobility, health, and education. Those surveyed showed a similar pattern of interest in these areas of application. They expressed very little interest in leisure/entertainment and child care. This may be due to the fact that the respondents could not imagine how smart home technology might be applied to leisure and child-care activities. Many persons judge social contact to be highly important in caring for and raising children and therefore resist its replacement by technology.

Energy-saving and security functions are regarded as being particularly attractive and rank as the most desirable of all the functions listed. These functions include lowering the thermostat when away from home and automatic heating regulation in response to outside temperatures. Security functions include checks when leaving the home, simulating movement when away from home, and information on the remote operation of appliances. Important social values such as "saving energy" and "increasing security" are considered highly desirable smart home functions. The creature comforts provided by smart home applications are less important or less desirable from the users' point of view. Compared to other functions, for example, few participants desire their bathtub to be filled automatically. In summary, the smart home has left a positive impression on the respondents, resulting largely from the hope that one can use this technology to help ease the chores of everyday life. At the same time, the results also show a certain gap between the views of what the smart home is and the desired attributes of smart home applications. The image of the smart home is primarily determined by comfort and overall convenience and help in everyday life, whereas the desires of potential users are directed first and foremost toward security and energy-saving functions.

Target-Group Analyses: Smart Homes for Younger People and Older Persons

When comparing the views of younger and older persons (aged 16 to 52 years and 53 to 83 years old; men/women 50:50) of the smart home, only small differences are found (see Figure 10.4). Older persons tend to expect more from this kind of technology than younger persons, which is rather surprising. Older people imagine that the smart home will simplify their everyday lives, improve and expand their access to information and communication resources, and make their home environments more fun.

The greatest difference between younger and older people concerns the range of information and communication possibilities. Here, younger people are less likely to see possible applications for smart homes. There is hardly any difference in how each age group views the smart home's potential in terms of increasing household comfort, reminding the resident to perform maintenance functions, and saving energy. The data also show that younger people are less likely to believe that smart homes could increase security and comfort and make home life more fun. Younger people are also more likely to say that this technology creates anxiety. Compared to older people in the study, younger people accord greater significance to the time-saving features of the smart home. Older people in the survey tend to believe that the smart home increases security and comfort and can make home life more fun. At the same time, however, they are more apprehensive that this technology could be too complicated.

Younger and older people differ very little in their responses with respect

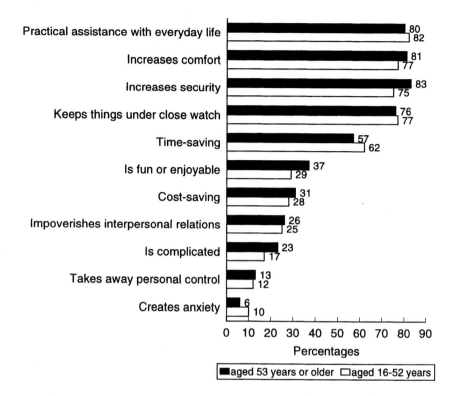

FIGURE 10.4. How the smart home is judged (by age groups).

to desired areas of smart home applications (see Figure 10.5). The greatest differences are their interests in technological assistance found in the areas of health and education. The desire for assistance in the health area is clearly stronger among older people. For older persons, technological assistance with health is just as important as help with housework and organizing everyday life. Security is the only area where the interests of older people in smart home applications outstrips that for health and household support. Older people also have a greater desire for smart home assistance in the area of education. Only small age differences were found in the organization of everyday living and housework, and in leisure and entertainment activities.

The ranking of functions according to preference is basically the same for both age groups; however, some slight differences can be observed. If one looks at the functions found interesting by all those surveyed, it becomes

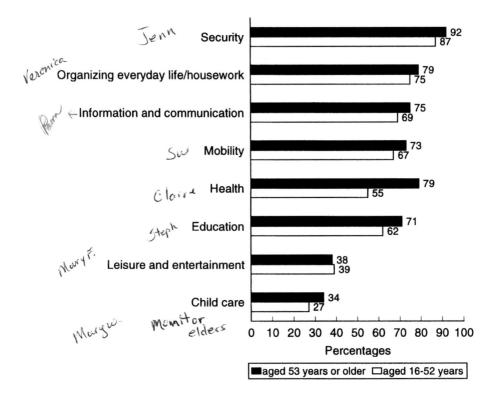

FIGURE 10.5.   Interesting areas of application (by age groups).

clear that older people are interested in a larger number of smart home applications (see Figure 10.6). In their households, older people desire more functional applications such as energy-saving functions and, above all, security functions, such as the simulation of movement to protect against break-ins and theft. On the other hand, older people do not really perceive comfort functions, such as automatically making coffee, checking what is inside the refrigerator while away, or filling the bathtub as making a significant difference in their everyday lives. Although we found that younger people primarily desire functional smart home applications, this age group is clearly more interested in comfort functions and technological games and pastimes (for example, automatically making coffee, checking the refrigerator while away). Security is somewhat less of a concern for the younger people surveyed.

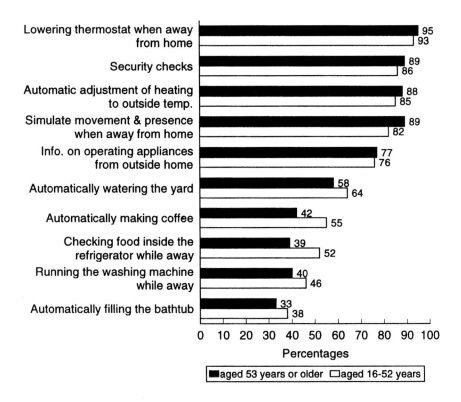

FIGURE 10.6.   Desired functions (by age groups).

CONCLUSIONS

All in all, older people have higher expectations of the smart home; they are more likely than younger people to assume that the smart home can improve their everyday lives. These expectations could be the result of a greater need for such assistance, but they might also arise from their relative inexperience with modern information and communication technology—a situation that might change with future cohorts of older people.

Older people place greater emphasis on the expected increase in security, while younger people are more fascinated with technological games and pastimes and tend to value the more time-saving aspects in the smart home. Health-related applications, too, play an important role for older people. Among the negative attributes attached to the smart home by older people is a fear that the technology will be too complicated. More younger people mention that the smart home creates anxiety. Younger persons tend to express greater acceptance of comfort-related functions, while older persons, for their part, are more interested in energy-saving and security functions.

On the basis of both studies, we can conclude that the everyday needs and requirements of older people must be considered more seriously in future research and development. Older people have high expectations regarding smart home applications, but they also feel that this technology could be too complicated for them. Even single ICT devices are troublesome for a large proportion of the elderly people, and their current use of modern technologies depends greatly on having a partner, education, and income.

Thus, if we believe that older individuals should equally be able to profit from new technologies, objective as well as subjective barriers will have to be minimized, but ICT and smart home technologies themselves must be optimized in a manner that does not create new barriers to the application of technologies designed to enhance the autonomy and social participation of older persons.

REFERENCES

Baltes, P. B., & Mayer, K. U. (1998). *The Berlin Aging Study.* Cambridge: Cambridge University Press.

Brandstädter, J., & Wentura, D. (1994). Veränderungen der Zeit- und Zukunftsperspektive im Übergang zum höheren Erwachsenenalter: Entwicklungspsychologische und differentielle Aspekte [Change in temporal and future perspective during the transition to later adulthood]. *Zeitschrift für Entwicklungspsychologie und Pädagogische Psychologie, 26,* 2–21.

Brandstädter, J., Wentura, D., & Schmitz, U. (1997). Veränderungen der Zeit- und Zukunftsperspektive im Übergang zum höheren Alter: Quer- und längsschnittliche Befunde [Change in temporal and future perspective during the transition to later adulthood: Cross-sectional and longitudinal findings]. *Zeitschrift für Psychologie, 205,* 377–395.

Meyer, S., & Schulze, E. (2001). *Vom Otto Normalverbraucher zur Smart Family? Akzeptanz und Anforderungen der Konsumenten 2000* [From Joe Consumer to a smart family? Consumer acceptance and expectations, 2000.] Der aktuelle Smart Home Survey des BIS-Berliner Institut für Sozialforschung. Berlin: BIS.

Meyer, S., Schulze, E., Helten, F., & Fischer, B. (2001). *Vernetztes Wohnen: Die Informatisierung des Alltagslebens* [Networked living: The digitalization of everyday life]. Berlin: Edition Sigma.

Meyer, S., Schulze, E., & Müller, P. (1997). *Das intelligente Haus—Selbständige Lebensführung im Alter. Möglichkeiten und Grenzen vernetzter Technik im Haushalt alter Menschen* [The intelligent home—leading an independent life in old age: The potential and limits of networking technology in the households of older persons]. Frankfurt, Germany: Campus.

Mollenkopf, H., Meyer, S., Schulze, E., Wurm, S., & Friesdorf, W. (2000). Technik im Haushalt zur Unterstützung einer selbstbestimmten Lebensführung im Alter—Das Forschungsprojekt "sentha" und erste Ergebnisse des Sozialwissenschaftlichen Teilprojekts [Technology to help older people maintain an independent household]. *Zeitschrift für Gerontologie und Geriatrie, 33*, 155–168.

Wurm, S. (2000). *Technik und Alltag von Senioren* [Technology and the everyday life of seniors]. Unveröffentlichter Arbeitsbericht zu den Ergebnissen der sentha-Repräsentativerhebung. [Unpublished Report.]

CHAPTER 11

Creating Places for People with Dementia: An Action Research Perspective

Gerald D. Weisman

The past three decades represent a period of substantial advance in our understanding of therapeutic environments for people with dementia and how we might most effectively create such settings. New facilities which break with tradition have been constructed, significant findings have been reported, and there are important lessons to be learned. It is essential, however, to recognize at the outset that these findings and lessons relate to *process* as much as they do to *substance*. Without fresh approaches to their planning, programming, and design—specifically a rethinking of the relationship between research and design application—these projects, and the substantive understanding they have yielded, may not have come to pass.

To underscore this relationship between substance and process, my review of substantive findings will be placed within a framework focused on a process of social and environmental change, specifically the *action research model* first advanced by social psychologist Kurt Lewin more than 50 years ago (Lewin, 1946), which is perhaps less well known than his "field theory" approach to social science. Lewin included only one article explicitly focused on action research (Lewin, 1946) in his 1948 and 1951 edited volumes; other papers by Lewin, especially those concerning effecting social change (e.g., Lewin, 1947)—while they do not make explicit reference to action research—do raise related issues. More recently, there is renewed interest in the potential contribution of Lewin's work to environmental gerontology; however, the focus once again is field theory, with action research conspicuous by its absence (Parmalee, 1998).

Most critical to understanding his model of action research is Lewin's rethinking of the traditional relationship between research and practice. Rather than viewing research as "basic" science—to be conducted without concern for eventual application—Lewin considered the two as intertwined. Indeed, Lewin argued, it was often essential to act on a social system, to first understand and then to change it. "The research needed for social practice," Lewin suggested, "is a type of action-research, a comparative research on the conditions and effects of various forms of social action." "Research that produces nothing but books," he argued, "will not suffice" (Lewin, 1946, reprinted in Lewin, 1997, p. 146).

It is not the intention of this chapter to suggest that the innovative dementia care projects of recent decades emerged out of an explicit and conscious adaptation of Lewin's model of action research. However, with the benefit of hindsight, I believe one can reasonably argue that much of this work is congruent with it and provides a useful illustration of Lewin's vision. Based upon a review and synthesis of Lewin's writing, this chapter is organized around 5 necessary and interrelated conditions for effecting social and environmental change: (1) unfreezing the situation, (2) decision making as a spiral of steps and group decision making, (3) a systemic perspective, (4) linking general and local knowledge, and (5) the triangle of action, research, and training. The following review and analysis of the most significant dementia care projects of recent decades in terms of these 5 conditions will hopefully provide lessons about both process and substance—application as well as research—and remind us of the essential relationship between the two.

UNFREEZING THE SITUATION

Before one can initiate the process of social and environmental change, it is often necessary to "unfreeze the situation" . . . in spite of the application of a force, the level of the social process will not change because of some type of "inner resistance" to change. To overcome this inner resistance, an additional force seems to be required, a force sufficient to "break the habit" and "unfreeze the situation." (Lewin, 1947, reprinted in Lewin, 1997, p. 330)

In the case of long-term care facilities—nursing homes—in the United States, the "habit to be broken" was all too clear. The "medical model"— the creation and operation of nursing homes as "miniature hospitals"— gained dominance in the United States in the 1960s—a response to the shortcomings of an earlier generation of small-scale board and care facilities. The medical model focused on quality of care, often to the exclusion of quality of life. Like acute-care hospitals, nursing homes were organized around 40 to 60 patient nursing units, with double-occupancy rooms arrayed along both sides of long corridors. Large nursing stations were found at the intersections of these corridors, and lighting, materials, and furnishings all conveyed an institutional character. There was precious little that was home-like about the nursing home.

As is the case with other place types (cf., Weisman, Chaudhury, & Moore, 2000), such medical-model nursing homes comprised a set of essential features—organizational, architectural, and experiential—which reflected and reinforced societal understanding of what long-term care settings for the elderly ought to be. While there were some early efforts at reform—the work of Lorraine Hiatt (1991) and Joseph Koncelik (1976), in particular— efforts to unfreeze the situation faltered for several decades. It was only in the early 1980s that a "thaw" began, bringing with it a reconsideration of the essential nature of the nursing home. This thaw, or unfreezing, I would suggest, was a direct response to rapidly rising public and professional awareness and concern regarding Alzheimer's disease and the psychological, social, and economic costs it was beginning to exact in American society. The National Institute of Medicine endeavored to broaden the goals of the nursing home, moving beyond quality of care to quality of life. The traditional medical model was increasingly replaced by a "social model" focusing on the resident as a whole person, not simply a set of symptoms (Johnson & Grant, 1985).

A Succession of Model Projects

As part of the effort to grapple with the implications of Alzheimer's disease, a succession of model or demonstration dementia-care facilities was developed in the United States. These projects endeavored consciously to rethink the essential nature of the nursing home—organizationally, socially, and architecturally—and each was meant to be a test bed for the evaluation of new approaches to long-term care. These projects have been critical in the unfreezing of our understanding of the nursing home and in creating an openness to new kinds of environments for dementia care (Weisman, 1997).

The first of these demonstration projects, fittingly, was the vision of Powell Lawton at the Philadelphia Geriatric Center (Lawton, Fulcomer, & Kleban, 1984). The Weiss Institute broke new ground architecturally by eliminating the traditional double-loaded corridor; resident rooms were instead arrayed around a large activity area. It was hoped that making activities visible to residents as they exited their rooms would encourage participation and minimize the cognitive demands of finding one's way to nonvisible destinations. Dorothy Coons's Wesley Hall project in Chelsea, Michigan, endeavored to create a small-scale (11-resident) dementia-care setting within the context of a large, institutional nursing home; her evaluation study suggested that some of the "problem behaviors" associated with dementia may be mitigated through thoughtful design of the organizational and architectural environment, as well as a careful consideration of the relation between the two (Coons, 1991). Key features of Wesley Hall included re-creation of familiar spaces (e.g., living room as opposed to day room), single-occupancy resident rooms, absence of staff uniforms, and opportunities to engage in familiar tasks.

The Kennebec Valley Alzheimer's Care Center in Gardiner, Maine, was consciously planned and designed to be a national model (Faunce & Brunette, 1986). The Corinne Dolan Center in Chardon, Ohio, remains one of the most imageable of these demonstration projects. Visually complex, clearly noninstitutional in appearance, the Dolan Center follows the open-plan pattern of the Weiss Institute, but it houses 24 residents instead of 40. Widely publicized in the popular press, as well as in care-provider publications, the Dolan Center clearly served as an agent for change (Namazi et al., 1991). While equally imageable, Woodside Place in Pittsburgh, Pennsylvania, took a different, more domestic approach. Thirty-six residents were accommodated in 3 households, each with familiar living, dining, and kitchen spaces in a small-scale pitched-roof structure (Sliverman et al., 1995). Finally, the Bader Center in Milwaukee, Wisconsin, like the Dolan Center, consists of 2 households of 12 residents each, with flexible connections between them. Dining and social areas have distinctive views to a busy street or to Lake Michigan (Kovach, Weisman, Chaudhury, & Calkins, 1997).

Each of these projects, I would submit, demonstrates the powerful role of "places" in effecting social and environmental change (Weisman et al., 2000). Each project endeavored to rethink the nature of long-term care—from organizational philosophy, to job descriptions, to the kind of clothing worn by staff, and to the physical setting within which the care was provided. Each endeavored to deal with dementia care systemically and allowed others—including both care providers and designers—to see that nursing homes could become something other than that which society had traditionally defined them to be. By serving as innovative and compelling examples, each place served as an agent of change by unfreezing our attitudes and preconceptions. This thaw in attitudes is reflected in multiple ways, including the downsizing of nursing homes through the early 1990s (from 300 or 400 residents to facilities half that size) and the invention and introduction of new place types such as dementia day care (Moore, Geboy, Weisman, & Mlizeva, 2001) and assisted living facilities (Regnier, 1994).

SPIRAL OF STEPS AND GROUP DECISION MAKING

The next condition for effecting social and environmental change includes 2 facets, both of which focus on the process by which "action" decisions are made.

> Rational social management . . . proceeds in a spiral of steps each of which is composed of a circle of planning, action, and fact finding about the results of this action . . . there is a great difference in asking for a decision after a lecture or after a discussion. Since discussion involves active participation of the audience and a chance to express motivations corresponding to different alternatives, the audience might be more ready to "make up its mind." (Lewin, 1946, reprinted in Lewin, 1997, p. 146)

Such a spiral process has been proposed for the planning, programming, and design of environments for older persons (Windley & Weisman, 1977) as well as for environmental design research more broadly (Zeisel, 1981). Indeed, each of the demonstration projects highlighted in the previous section emerged out of an extended, participatory planning process. Planning of the Weiss Institute extended over 6 years, as did Woodside Place, while the Dolan Center required 4; each process included research conferences and the explicit articulation of a project philosophy which, in subsequent decision-making cycles, guided the articulation of goals and design principles.

Equally important, none of these demonstration projects ended after construction and occupancy. Each was also the subject of summative evaluation, with results fed forward to subsequent decision making. This is most notable in the case of Woodside Place, the basic pattern of which has now gone through 3 generations of replication and modification in Edmonton, Alberta, Canada (Milke, 1996). Here again, research results have been quite widely disseminated in the professional press and, in some cases, the popular press as well.

A SYSTEMIC PERSPECTIVE

Lewin's action research perspective departed from more traditional notions of science, with its focus on experimental treatment of a very limited set of variables. By contrast, Lewin's conceptualization of action research was predicated on a more holistic approach, encompassing social systems at multiple scales. In describing his efforts to improve intergroup relations—a particular focus of his work—Lewin argued for a *systemic perspective* cutting across multiple levels of social aggregation.

> It (i.e., social relations) deals with the small social body of a family, a club or a friendship group, with the larger social body of a school or school system, with neighborhoods and with social bodies of the size of a community, of a state, a nation, and with international problems. (Lewin, 1946, reprinted in Lewin, 1997, p. 144)

Just such a systemic perspective has been fundamental to much of the most important research conducted in environmental gerontology in recent decades. The conceptual models which guided the research of Rudolf Moos and Powell Lawton and their colleagues have built upon a multilevel, systemic perspective. Moos's model includes organizational, demographic, social, and architectural dimensions (Moos, 1981); Lawton encompasses personal, group, suprapersonal, social, and physical dimensions of environment (Lawton, 1986).

This systemic perspective, along with the work of Lawton and Moos, has shaped the conceptual framework employed for the development, in *Holding on to Home* (Cohen & Weisman, 1991), of planning and design guidelines for dementia-care environments. Following Lawton and Moos, *Holding on to Home* identifies social, organizational, and architectural dimensions of the environment. Reflective of the spiral of steps proposed by Lewin, decision making is conceptualized at multiple levels, in terms of successive sets of decisions ranging from broad planning principles, to general attributes of place experience, to overall building organization, and finally to guidelines for specific rooms and activity spaces. The conceptual link between the nature and needs of people with dementia and the planning and design of residential environments are what we characterized as "therapeutic goals," hypothesized as supportive of effective dementia care. Such therapeutic goals include ensuring residents' and staff privacy, supporting positive social interaction, and maximizing orientation with respect to space, time, and social occasion.

GENERAL AND LOCAL KNOWLEDGE

Therapeutic goals of the sort just described, as well as the planning and design guidelines developed in *Holding on to Home*, might best be viewed as broad hypotheses or notions of best practice—distilled from our review of the relevant literature—regarding what ought to make a difference in environments for people with dementia. At the same time, these guidelines were never viewed as universally applicable, in the way that traditional models of positivist science were directed toward the formulation of ultimately generalizable principles. These guidelines were meant to be precisely that— broad principles the application of which must be tempered by circumstances specific to individual dementia-care settings. Again, with the benefit of hindsight, I would suggest a relationship to another precondition for social and environmental change reflected in Lewin's writing: a focus on the importance of *local* as well as *general* knowledge.

> Lawfulness in social as in physical science means an "as if" relation, a linkage between hypothetical conditions and hypothetical effects. These laws do not tell us what conditions exist locally, at a given place at a given time . . . the laws don't do the job of diagnosis which has to be done locally. (Lewin, 1946, reprinted in Lewin, 1997, p. 145)

Thus an experienced physician, in making a diagnosis, utilizes familiarity with the individual patient and professional experience as well as research findings and broad theory. No one form of knowledge is sufficient by itself. In similar terms, an action research perspective requires the linking of broad principles (the general) with setting specific conditions (the local). Unlike more traditional models of science, where research is conducted first and then followed by application, within an action research perspective, research and application may proceed in parallel, or an innovative action may spur further theorizing and investigation.

A review of the research literature on the design of environments for

dementia care illustrates just such a bidirectional relationship between research and action, and between general and local knowledge. Day, Carreon,
and Stump (2000) make this very point in their excellent review of the
empirical literature on the therapeutic design of environments for people
with dementia. They note that guidance for the planning and design of such
environments is "frequently based upon the practical experience of designers
or facility administrators" while at other times "design guidance is research
based, applying findings from clinical research on dementia in the form of
design 'solutions' " (Day et al., 2000, p. 397).

Furthermore, the review by Day et al. (2000) provides substantial support
for many of the broad recommendations presented in the various design-for-
dementia guidebooks. Following the conceptual model of *Holding on to
Home*, Day et al. organize their review in terms of broad planning principles,
general attributes of place experience, building organization, and specific
rooms and activity spaces. They have found substantial support in the empirical literature for the most fundamental of the planning principles advanced by Cohen and Weisman, the clustering of residents in groups
substantially smaller than the traditional nursing unit of from 40 to 60. Various design guides have advanced the proposition that the presence of fewer
residents on a unit may reduce sensory and social overstimulation by lowering noise levels and encounters with others.

> This recommendation is supported by research findings . . . larger unit
> sizes are associated with increased intellectual deterioration and emotional
> disturbance. . . . Further, residents in larger units exhibit more frequent ter-
> ritorial conflicts, space invasions, and aggressiveness toward other resi-
> dents. . . . In contrast, people with dementia residing in smaller units
> experience less anxiety and depression and more mobility. (Day et al.,
> 2000, pp. 406–407)

This is perhaps the most significant of the findings from the design-for-
dementia literature: decisions regarding group size impact all subsequent
planning, programming, and design decisions. At the same time, it should
be noted that the literature offers "no consistent numbers . . . for what constitutes a 'large' or 'small' unit" (Day et al., 2000, p. 407). Again, we must
take general knowledge and apply it, as best we can, to local conditions.

The design guidance literature advances a variety of recommendations
regarding general attributes of the dementia-care environment. Considerable
emphasis is placed on the creation of less institutional settings through in-
clusion of domestic furnishings and personal artifacts, plants, pets, and other

natural elements. Again, Day et al. have found substantial support in the empirical literature.

> Noninstitutional environments . . . are associated with improved intellectual and emotional well-being, enhanced social interaction, reduced agitation, reduced trespassing and exit seeking, greater preference and pleasure, and improved functionality of older adults with dementia and other mental illnesses. (Day et al., 2000, p. 407)

Concerns regarding overstimulation, discussed above with respect to group rise, reemerge at the scale of attributes as well, with overly high levels of sensory and social input seen as disruptive. The use of partitions—to reduce both visual and auditory stimulation—were found to enhance residents' ability to attend to a task (Day et al., 2000, p. 408).

Finally, at the smallest scale of individual spaces, Day et al. found strong support for the recommendation, common within the design-for-dementia literature, to locate dining and kitchen activity areas within each dementia unit or "household." At the same time—reflective of the systemic character of dementia-care settings—perpetuation of "institutional staff practices (e.g., assigned seating, institutional food service)" continued to "provoke disruption and agitation in dining rooms with homelike design features" (Day et al., 2000, p. 411). This systemic perspective, coupled with the recognition that knowledge gained through action at the local level can inform more general understanding, reinforces the importance of lessons regarding process as well as substance.

THE TRIANGLE OF ACTION, RESEARCH, AND TRAINING

Having linked research and action in a manner quite different from that of traditional positivist science, Lewin took a next step and suggested that training is also an essential element in effecting social and environmental change.

> We should consider action, research, and training as a triangle. . . . The training of large numbers of social scientists who can handle scientific problems but are also equipped for the delicate task of building productive hard-hitting teams with practitioners is a prerequisite for progress in social science. (Lewin, 1946, reprinted in Lewin, 1997, p. 145)

As described in the discussion of the spiral of steps above, each of the model and demonstration projects developed in the United States emerged from an extended planning, programming, and design process. Having devoted substantial time and energy to educating themselves about critical issues in designing for dementia, each of these organizations endeavored to then share their knowledge through consultation with and training for other care providers. Equally important, the places they created—the Weiss Institute, Wesley Hall, and others—became important agents for social, organizational, and environmental change in their own right, as visitors came and saw new and different approaches to the conceptualization and provision of dementia care.

Recognizing this powerful role of "living" places as agents for social and environmental change, the national office of the Alzheimer's Association has funded the Institute on Aging and Environment at the University of Wisconsin-Milwaukee to sow the seeds of what we hope will be the next generation of model facilities. The first phase of our National Alzheimer's Design Assistance Project (NADAP) presented a general introduction to issues of design for dementia to planning and design teams from 40 care-provider organizations in all regions of the United States. A second phase of the NADAP project provides follow-up technical assistance to a subset of 10 facilities committed to advancing the state of the art of therapeutic environments for Alzheimer's care.

CONCLUSION

As suggested at the outset, the creation of environments for Alzheimer's care has been an arena of great activity and creativity over the past 30 years, marked by growth in both numbers of innovative, model facilities and careful research studies. There is now a substantial, and expanding, body of research; from just a half dozen studies conducted between 1981 and 1985, the number more than quadrupled from 1991 to 1995, with the expectation that research on design and dementia will continue to grow in the foreseeable future (Day et al., 2000). Equally important, there is also a growing number of model facilities, with care providers increasingly willing to develop environments which purposefully implement and evaluate innovative approaches to dementia care.

The findings and lessons to be derived from the body of work on dementia care environments seem to be substantial. They should not, however, be limited to those derived solely from the empirical research on environments for people with cognitive impairments. It is equally important that we keep in mind the innovative ways in which these model facilities were planned, programmed, and designed; the systemic way in which they were conceptualized; and the innovative ways in which they have been publicized. Nursing homes—like schools, office buildings, shopping centers, and other place types—are *social constructions*. We as a society collectively decide what such settings ought to be organizationally, architecturally, and experientially. Once reified in both regulations and standard practice, place types come to be taken for granted and grow exceedingly difficult to change; as described in the first section of this chapter, they become "frozen in place." It requires a fortuitous set of circumstances—such as those surrounding the design for dementia for the past 30 years—to bridge the all-too-common gap between research and design and to effect a meaningful social and environmental change.

REFERENCES

Cohen, U., & Weisman, G. (1991). *Holding on to home: Designing environments for people with dementia.* Baltimore, MD: Johns Hopkins University Press.

Coons, D. (1991). A model of residential living. In D. Coons (Ed.), *Specialized dementia care units* (pp. 36–54). Baltimore, MD: Johns Hopkins University Press.

Day, K., Carreon, D., & Stump, C. (2000). The therapeutic design of environments for people with dementia: A review of the empirical literature. *The Gerontologist, 40*(4), 397–416.

Faunce, I., & Brunette, M. (1986). The Alzheimer's project of Kennebec Valley: A national model. *American Journal of Alzheimer's Care, 1*(4), 8–13.

Hiatt, L. (1991). *Nursing home renovation: Designed for reform.* Boston: Butterworth.

Johnson, C., & Grant, L. (1985). *The nursing home in American society.* Baltimore, MD: Johns Hopkins University Press.

Koncelik, J. (1976). *Designing the open nursing home.* Stroudsburg, PA: Dowden, Hutchinson & Ross.

Kovach, C., Weisman, G., Chaudhury, H., & Calkins, M. (1997). Impacts of a therapeutic environment for dementia care. *American Journal of Alzheimer's Disease, 12*(3), 99–116.

Lawton, M. P. (1986). *Environment and aging.* Albany, NY: Center for the Study of Aging.

Lawton, M. P., Fulcomer, M., & Kleban, M. (1984). Architecture for the mentally impaired. *Environment & Behavior, 16*(6), 730–757.

Lewin, K. (1946). Action research and minority problems. *Journal of Social Issues, 1*, 34–46. Reprinted in K. Lewin, *Resolving social conflicts & field theory in social science.* Washington, DC: American Psychological Association.

Lewin, K. (1947). Frontiers in group dynamics. *Human Relations, 1*, 2–38. Reprinted in

K. Lewin, *Resolving social conflicts & field theory in social science.* Washington, DC: American Psychological Association.

Lewin, K. (1948). *Resolving social conflicts.* New York: Harper & Row.

Lewin, K. (1951). *Field theory in social science.* New York: Harper & Row.

Lewin, K. (1997). *Resolving social conflicts & field theory in social science.* Washington, DC: American Psychological Association.

Milke, D. (1996). *McConnell Place North post occupancy evaluation.* Edmonton, Alberta: Capital Care Group.

Moore, K. D., Geboy, L., Weisman, G., & Mlizeva, S. (2001). *Designing a better day: Planning and design guidelines for adult and dementia day care centers.* Milwaukee, WI: Institute on Aging & Environment, University of Wisconsin–Milwaukee.

Moos, R. (1981). The practical utility of environmental evaluation of sheltered care facilities. In R. Stough & A. Wandersman (Eds.), *Optimizing environments: Practice & policy* (pp. 7–21). Washington, DC: Environmental Design Research Association.

Namazi, K., Whitehouse, P., Rechlin, L., Calkins, M., Brabender, B., & Hevener, S. (1991). Environmental modifications in a specially designed unit for the care of patients with Alzheimer's disease: An overview and introduction. *American Journal of Alzheimer's Care and Related Disorders & Research, 6,* 3–9.

Parmalee, P. (1998). Theory and research on housing for the elderly: The legacy of Kurt Lewin. In R. Scheidt & P. Windley (Eds.), *Environment and aging theory: Focus on housing* (p. 161–185). Westport, CT: Greenwood Press.

Regnier, V. (1994). *Assisted living housing for the elderly: Design innovations from the United States and Europe.* New York: Van Nostrand Reinhold.

Sliverman, M., Ricci, R., Saxton, J., Ledowitz, S., McAllister, C., & Keane, C. (1995). *Woodside Place: The first three years of a residential Alzheimer's facility.* Pittsburgh, PA: Presbyterian Senior Care.

Weisman, G. (1997). Environments for older persons with cognitive impairments. In G. Moore & R. Marans (Eds.), *Advances in environment, behavior, and design,* Vol. 4, *Toward the integration of theory, methods, research, and utilisation* (pp. 315–346). New York: Plenum Press.

Weisman, G., Chaudhury, H., & Moore, K. D. (2000). Theory and practice of place: Toward an integrative model. In R. Rubinstein, M. Moss, & M. H. Kleban (Eds.), *The many dimensions of aging: Essays in honor of M. P. Lawton* (pp. 3–21). New York: Springer.

Windley, P., & Weisman, G. (1977). Social science and environmental design. *Journal of Architectural Education, 31*(1), 16–19.

Zeisel, J. (1981). *Inquiry by design.* Monterey, CA: Brooks/Cole.

PART IV

Aging Independently
"Outdoors": Mobility

CHAPTER 12

Impact of Transportation Systems on Mobility of Elderly Persons in Germany

Heidrun Mollenkopf

Mobility (the ability to move about) and transportation (the movement of people, goods, and news) have been key factors in the course of history in the emergence of modern states. They remain the prerequisite, engine, and outcome of economic development in modern societies. Mobility and transportation are essential factors in more than just developing and maintaining society at large. With today's increasing functional and spatial separation of the occupational and personal spheres of life—of commercial, residential, and leisure domains—all members of society find that mobility is not simply a basic human need for physical movement. Mobility has become an ever more important aspect of making it possible to conduct one's everyday life, maintain social relations, and participate in many kinds of activity outside one's own walls.

As a person ages, the importance of mobility increases. Grown children leave home, and retirement spells the end of occupational contacts and frees up a great amount of time and energy. Also one must cope with the loss of intimate relations and close friends. All these changes require increased mobility if the elderly person is to continue being part of society. Aging, of course, is also accompanied by an increased risk of physical disabilities, declining sensory abilities, and hence restriction of mobility. Mobility and the use of the transportation system, whether as a pedestrian or by means of personal or public transportation, therefore become major components in maintaining the quality of life in old age.

In this chapter, I will first identify some basic factors which shape mobility in Germany in general and among elderly people in particular. I will then, in the second part, present findings from 2 studies conducted in urban and rural areas of East and West Germany on the travel behavior of various groups of older people, and I will conclude with an analysis of the most salient problems and implications for problem-solving strategies to meet their mobility needs.

MOBILITY AND TRANSPORTATION IN GERMANY

As in most industrialized countries, increased motorization has primarily shaped transportation policy and planning since the 1950s. This orientation has led to massive projects for building new roads, upgrading old ones, and reducing the German railroad network. The German road network, disregarding metropolitan areas, extends over 231,000 kilometers, 5% of which are expressways. Germany has the largest net of expressways in the world after the United States. With 1 passenger car (including station wagons) for about every 2 inhabitants, the automobile has become the dominant means of transportation in Germany. Of the 49.6 million licensed motor vehicles in early 1998, about 41.7 million were passenger cars (including station wagons) accounting for 85% of all vehicles. Passenger cars made up 84% (755 billion person-kilometers) of all passenger travel [Statistisches Bundesamt (StBA) (Federal Statistical Office of Germany), 2000, pp. 350, 354]. The perpetual growth of traffic volume has resulted partly from economic development and trends toward mass tourism. It is due primarily, however, to changes in urban and regional structures, such as the establishment of industrial and commercial enterprises outside of residential areas and the functional separation between personal lives and work as well as between leisure and activities required to provide for one's daily needs. This division makes it necessary to bridge the widening gap between these functional areas (see, e.g., Flade, 1994).

The times have passed when the increasing density of passenger cars was regarded solely as an indicator of personal and macrosocial prosperity. Despite a growing awareness of the problems posed by motorized transportation, however, the automobile has lost little of its allure, and the density (more road users) and volume (more kilometers driven) of traffic have continued to grow in recent years. The number of routes walked or driven per inhabitant each day has scarcely changed, but the distances traveled have increased substantially (Brög, 1992a, 1992b). Whereas total passenger transport in Germany amounted to 854 billion person-kilometers in 1991, this figure had risen to 895 billion in 1997. Individual motorized and railroad transportation have risen from 83.6% to 84.3% and from 6.7% to 7.2% respectively, during this period. At the same time, local public transportation by means of trams, buses, and subways decreased from 9.8% to 8.5% of the total (StBA, 2000, p. 354).

The number of passenger cars in Germany will continue to rise in the coming years. This development is due in no small part to the growing number of car owners, especially women, among persons below 65 years of age. One could really speak of women "making up mobilization" in Germany. Since the regime shift in East Germany, traffic volume has expanded enormously in the new states as well. The east-west gap has almost leveled off in this regard, particularly among the younger age groups. However, the number of retiree households that own a car still varies greatly. For 2-person households in which both partners were 55 years old or older, the figures for Western Germany (81%) are clearly still higher than those for Eastern Germany (72%). Car ownership is especially low among elderly persons living alone. Among single-person households, the possession of a car is lower than average, and there are still considerable differences between Eastern and Western Germany. In Eastern Germany, only 18% and in Western Germany 29% of such households owned a car in 1998 (according to the German Socio-Economic Panel, 1998 survey; SOEP Group, 2001) (see Figure 12.1).

As was the case for Western Germany, the shift to private passenger transport coincided with cutbacks in public transport in Eastern Germany. The once dense network of retail shops is giving way to suburban supermarkets and downtown shopping centers. Hence, people living on the periphery of cities, and especially those in rural regions who do not have access to this type of shopping mall, find it ever more difficult to shop for their everyday needs at reasonable prices unless they have a car or can ride with someone else.

The number of accidents involving personal injuries, however, has remained relatively constant in the last 20 years despite the growing volume of traffic. The increase in the number of vehicles has been accompanied by measures to improve the safety of roads, including expansion of the road system, mandatory use of seat belts, and safety features in vehicles. Given the power and performance of motor vehicles, the risk of having an accident has clearly declined in Western Germany since the early 1970s. Whereas, in

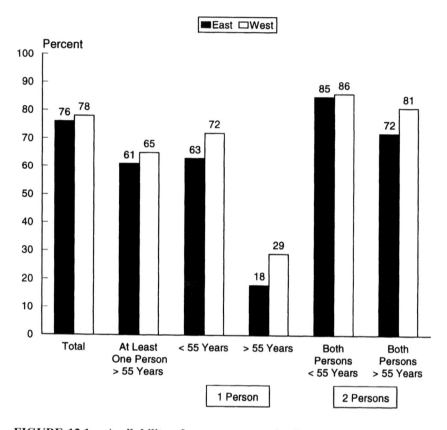

FIGURE 12.1. **Availability of passenger cars in Germany, 1996 (by age and type of households, in percentages).**
Database: SOEP (Socio-Economic Panel) 1998; own calculations.
Source: SOEP Group, 2001.

1970, more than 21,000 persons died in traffic accidents in East and West Germany combined, the number of people killed on German roads in 1998 was 7,792 [Bundesanstalt für Strassenwesen (BASt) (Federal Highway Research Institute), 1999; StBA, 2000]. In Eastern Germany, however, the number of accidents soared beginning in 1990 because of the rapid rise in the number of cars in that part of the country, the poor road conditions there, and drivers' overestimation of their own abilities. Since June 1990 the risk of being killed in a traffic accident has remained clearly higher in Eastern Germany than in the western part of the country. In Western Germany there are 91 traffic fatalities per 1 million inhabitants, whereas the figure in Eastern Germany is nearly twice as high (161 per 1 million; StBA, 2000, p. 359). On the average, 21 persons are killed every day on German roads. Elderly drivers do not have a disproportionately greater frequency of involvement in accidents than younger drivers. As a person ages, though, the risk of his or her having an accident grows in relation to driving performance (and hence in relation to the exposure to danger). Elderly persons are also very vulnerable as pedestrians. Very old pedestrians have a higher-than-average rate of injury or death in traffic accidents (see Chapter 14).

On the whole, then, the mobility conditions of aging women and men are not highly favorable. Outside the home, many environmental features further complicate the elderly person's ability to move about. Public buildings, the general service infrastructure, and even the immediate vicinity are often not readily accessible. In many cases, transportation facilities are deficient by modern standards or are absent altogether. The impact that the abrupt increase in personal means of transportation has on elderly people varies. On one hand, the greater availability of personal automobiles increases the mobility of elderly people; on the other hand, the growing volume of traffic also increases the potential hazards of such travel. Traffic congestion, particularly in urban centers, has reached an extent that may unsettle elderly people and keep them from venturing out. The question of whether and how external conditions and demands of the environment can be harmonized with individual needs and resources is the topic examined in the next section.

THE OUTDOOR MOBILITY OF OLDER PEOPLE IN URBAN AND RURAL AREAS OF EAST AND WEST GERMANY

Research on mobility has thus far been confined largely to observations of transportation behavior among various age groups—number of routes, distance traveled, choice of transport, and purposes of trips—or to problems and adjustment strategies among elderly drivers. It is generally not known, however, whether the reduced mobility behavior of elderly people has resulted from health problems or environmental obstacles. It is also not known to what extent, if any, there is a greater desire for mobility outside the home; and what specific causes may frustrate such a desire. Therefore, the international project entitled "Keeping the Elderly Mobile," the results of which will be presented in the following, focused on the needs, behaviors, and problems of older persons with regard to their mobility outside the home (Mollenkopf, Marcellini, & Ruoppila, 1998).

In the fall of 1995, data were collected on a sample of 804 persons, aged 55 years or older, in urban regions featuring different settlement and transport infrastructures in Eastern and Western Germany (Chemnitz and Mannheim). The samples were drawn from the obligatory city registers by a random sampling procedure and disproportionately stratified by gender and age (55–74 years and 75 years and older). The data collection was launched with standardized interviews, combined with a diary of mobility behavior in which the respondents recorded their movements over a 3-day period. A comparable survey was conducted in 1999 in rural areas in East and West Germany (East: Oberspreewald-Lausitz; West: Rhine-Hunsrück-Kreis), with a sample of 412 persons, again aged 55 years or older, collected in a random route procedure, and likewise stratified by gender and age.

In both studies, structured interviews focused on aspects of the objective environment such as housing and neighborhood conditions. The satisfaction of older adults with important components of everyday life like neighborhood and public transport, availability of facilities and services, mobility, and leisure time activities were considered, too. The objective of the research was to identify specific ways to facilitate the mobility of elderly people in order to help them participate in society and thereby maintain their quality of life in old age. In addition, the comparison between various urban and rural areas makes it possible to shed light on the way in which the mobility of elderly people is affected by different regional infrastructures.

Before describing and comparing the differences of objective and subjective mobility conditions in rural and urban settings in Eastern and Western Germany and the mobility patterns of older people, it should be noted that only the East-West differences allow a valid statistical comparison. The data for the rural-urban comparison were derived from different years, by a different sampling procedure; and the samples are of different sizes. Nevertheless, we can at least identify the most obvious differences between urban and rural areas.

With respect to the natural conditions of human aging, we found only minor East-West differences (see Table 12.1). Living alone is the common fate of the very old, and the ability to move about is also significantly related to age. Mobility is better in the younger age groups, but it is also better among the young-old in the rural areas. Correspondingly, older persons more often reported difficulties in reaching important contact persons and participating in fewer outdoor activities than younger persons. These restrictions

TABLE 12.1 Basic Individual Conditions of Mobility

Variable	55–74 years old						75 years and older					
	Rural (n = 221)			Urban (n = 412)			Rural (n = 191)			Urban (n = 392)		
(M, SD) or (%, n)	East	West	Differences	East	West	Differences	East	West	Differences	East	West	Differences
Living alone (%)	34	22	ns	23	26	ns	57	47	ns	52	45	ns
(Very) good ability to move about (%) (self assessed)	52	63	*	42	47	ns	32	33	ns	30	34	ns
Difficulties in reaching important persons (%)	15	11	ns	18	27	*	40	35	ns	41	36	ns
Outdoor leisure activities (0–13)[a]	4.0	6.2	***	3.3	4.6	***	2.4	3.9	***	2.3	3.3	***
Satisfaction with leisure activities (0–10)[b]	7.0	7.1	ns	7.1	7.5	ns	6.2	6.3	ns	6.6	6.7	ns

[a]Activities such as gardening; hiking; visiting a theater, concert, or movies; actively pursuing sports; and so on.
[b]Self-evaluation rating on an 11-point scale; higher scores indicate higher satisfaction.
*p < .05; **p < .01; ***p < .001.

183

find their expression in lower satisfaction with leisure activities in the older age group. Significant differences can be seen in pursuing outdoor leisure activities. Older persons in both rural and urban areas seem to be less active outdoors in Eastern than in Western Germany. Nevertheless, we found no significant differences between their respective levels of satisfaction.

With regard to basic neighborhood conditions (see Table 12.2), such as shopping facilities, health care, post offices, and banks, cities provided more shops and services than the rural areas in both Western and Eastern Germany. When it comes to comforts afforded by the neighborhoods, such as cultural facilities, public services, and senior or care centers, our data show that the East German rural and urban areas under investigation offer significantly fewer amenities than the corresponding areas in West Germany. As a consequence, there was lower satisfaction with services in the rural areas of East Germany. These results may be due to the better provision of public transportation services in the cities and the greater incidence of automobiles in the rural areas of Western Germany which make access to more distant facilities easier. As far as feelings of safety and security are concerned, our data show that older people feel safer and more secure in rural than in urban areas, and in the western rural area they feel significantly safer than in the eastern area under investigation. The same is true for the appraisal of the outdoor environment in general. People in the rural areas are much more satisfied with their neighborhoods than their contemporaries in the 2 cities.

With respect to basic technical conditions for mobility (see Table 12.3), we also found considerable differences between the rural and urban situations and between East and West Germany. In Germany as a whole, few members of the current generation of older persons—mainly of older women—possess a driver's license. In addition, the East-West gap still remains as far as the availability of personal automobiles is concerned. Therefore, the outdoor mobility of older individuals depends heavily on public transport systems. However, public transport is wanting and simply not an alternative in rural areas. As expected, satisfaction with public transport is low in rural areas. Satisfaction with mobility opportunities in general revealed itself to be lower only in the East German compared to the West German city. Unfortunately, our data cannot explain whether the repeatedly observed pattern of diverging environmental conditions accompanied by similar levels of satisfaction is caused by different expectations or by adapting to insufficient but unchangeable circumstances.

The differing individual and structural conditions are reflected by different patterns of mobility in cities and rural areas. During the 3 days documented

TABLE 12.2 Basic Neighborhood Conditions and Subjective Evaluations

Variable (M, SD) or (%, n)	55–74 years old						75 years and older					
	Rural (n = 221)			Urban (n = 412)			Rural (n = 191)			Urban (n = 392)		
	East	West	Differences	East	West	Differences	East	West	Differences	East	West	Differences
Basic neighborhood resources (0–8)[a]	5.3	5.6	ns	6.9	7.0	ns	5.7	6.1	ns	7.1	7.1	ns
Comforts afforded by neighborhood (0–12)[b]	6.5	7.4	*	4.3	7.6	***	6.2	8.0	***	4.6	7.3	***
Satisfaction with services (0–10)[c]	6.7	7.5	*	7.1	7.3	ns	7.0	8.3	**	7.3	7.5	ns
Feeling safe/secure (1–4)[d]	1.8	1.5	***	2.3	2.3	ns	1.9	1.6	**	2.4	2.4	ns
Satisfaction with outdoor environment (0–10)[c]	8.1	9.2	***	7.3	7.0	ns	8.3	9.1	**	7.6	7.7	ns

[a]Food store, other shopping facilities, pharmacy, doctor/health care center, bank, post office, bus stop, tram station.
[b]Hairdresser, foot care/physiotherapy, senior center, day nursing care, hospital, sports facilities, public services, cultural facilities, park/green areas, railway station, church, cemetery.
[c]Self-evaluation rating on an 11-point scale; higher scores indicate higher satisfaction.
[d]Self-evaluation rating on a 4-point scale (1 = very safe to 4 = very unsafe).
$*p < .05; **p < .01; ***p < .001.$

TABLE 12.3 Basic Technical Conditions of Mobility

Variable	55–74 years old						75 years and older					
	Rural (n = 221)			Urban (n = 412)			Rural (n = 191)			Urban (n = 392)		
(M, SD) or (%, n)	East	West	Differences	East	West	Differences	East	West	Differences	East	West	Differences
Actively driving a passenger car (%)	39	66	***	37	55	***	16	27	ns	12	32	***
Use of public transport (at least occasionally) (%)	42	44		88	82		48	37		74	77	
Satisfaction with public transport (0–10)[a]	5.5	5.7	ns	7.5	7.1	ns	5.8	6.4	ns	7.3	7.3	ns
Satisfaction with mobility (1–10)[a]	8.0	8.5	ns	7.7	8.2	*	6.9	7.2	ns	6.9	7.4	*

[a]Self-evaluation rating on an 11-point scale; higher scores indicate higher satisfaction.
*p < .05; ** p < .01; ***p < .001.

in the diaries, older men and women in Mannheim left their homes most often, that is for 3.6 trips (by our definition, a trip begins with leaving home and ends with returning home), whereas older people in Hunsrück were on the go the least often with 3 trips. The East German respondents took an average of 3.4 trips over 3 days. In the cities, an average trip, including trip-related activity, lasted 2 hours and 48 minutes whereas in the rural areas, trips were shorter (150 minutes in Hunsrück and 124 minutes in Lausitz).

Most elderly persons in both East and West Germany and in urban as well as rural areas cover the distances of their trips without any technical support: they walk (see Figure 12.2). Thus, their most common and most frequently used modes of transport are their own feet. The automobile is the most often used mode of transportation in the West German rural area (for 37% of the respondents) and city (for 30% of the respondents). About one-third of all trips are conducted by automobile, either as drivers or as passengers. In the East German areas, the automobile is used for fewer trips, in fact for about every fifth trip (city: 22%; rural area: 20%), which reflects the lower availability of automobiles in East Germany. The use of a bicycle of course depends largely on the geographical conditions of the different regions, and the low figures on the use of public transportation indicate the lack of such transport modes in rural areas.

DIFFICULTIES WITH IMPORTANT ASPECTS OF MOBILITY

More than half (54%) of the people 55 years old or older reported difficulties in at least 1 area that is important for leading their lives and taking part in society—making their way to friends and relatives, institutions that provide services, and recreational facilities. All in all, approximately one-fourth of the elderly persons in the 2 cities and just under 20% in the rural areas reported problems with 1 aspect of mobility or another. As expected, there were high correlations between difficulties and physical health and age. The predominant share of younger respondents experienced no hardships in reaching whatever destinations they wished to reach. The problems are concentrated among the very old and those who are physically limited in their mobility. Consequently, the problem reported most frequently by the elderly was the state of their health. Nonetheless, almost one-third of the respondents 80 years old or older were still able to reach important destinations without difficulty.

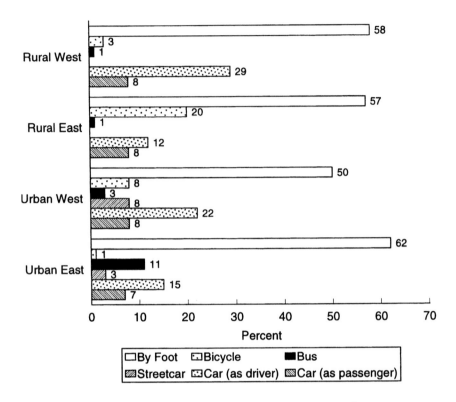

FIGURE 12.2.   Transport modes (rural and urban areas, in percentages).

Basis: Trips performed during 3 days.

Sources: Mollenkopf, Oswald, Schilling, & Wahl, 2001; participants' outdoor mobility diaries (1995) and rural mobility diaries (1999).

Other reasons for mobility limitations can be traced back to objective environmental conditions such as long distances, unfavorable bus or train connections, difficulties in using public transport, or the lack of opportunities for shopping and leisure activities in the near vicinity. There were also unexpected reasons. For example, social reasons, such as having no one to go with or the need to care for a family member, played a role. Older respondents in the rural areas specifically mentioned that high costs prevented them from meeting important relatives or friends. The diary entries, in which the respondents could describe their daily trips in detail, reveal yet another problem: many older men and women in the cities experienced certain public interactions as particularly disagreeable, for example hectic traffic, excessive bustle in the streets and shops, or inconsiderate traffic participants.

Although most elderly people have become accustomed to the conditions mentioned above and have adapted their own behaviors as pedestrians, bicyclists, or drivers, nearly one-fourth of elderly urbanites in Western Germany, as many as one-third in the Eastern German city, and almost 2 out of 10 in the rural areas feel helpless or disadvantaged in traffic. They agreed with such statements as, "As an elderly person you feel disadvantaged in today's traffic" and "Traffic is sometimes so busy that you don't dare to go out on the street" or "Nowadays I often feel helpless in traffic." Thus, it is no wonder that what elderly people desire most is more courtesy and respect from other road users. Safety also plays a major role for them: in traffic, on public squares, on the streets, and in underpasses. Users of public transport in our sample were primarily the ones who also called for technical improvements in buses and streetcars. More reasonably priced fares or taxi coupons were also felt by some to be necessary.

CONCLUSIONS

Taking the findings of the 2 studies described in this chapter into account, it becomes evident that keeping elderly persons mobile is not limited to technical or spatial improvements, but it is also a social and societal task because of 2 types of environmental obstacles to mobility. One is the prevailing spatial or technological context. Barriers of this sort are a serious hindrance particularly for persons whose motor and perceptual abilities are limited. On the whole, however, the difficulties arising from this domain have proved to be less serious than hitherto presumed. Of greater consequence are the restrictions stemming from a second problem area characterized by deficiencies in transportation as a field of social action. Impediments to the outdoor mobility of elderly people in this domain are caused by a lack of mutual consideration, the hectic pace and aggressive behavior of road users, and actual or feared hazards in public space and the vicinity of one's home. Thus, to make it easier for elderly people to move about outdoors and to ensure them the opportunities to remain full members of society despite their physical impairments, it is also necessary to improve social behavior. Such improvements must focus as much on transportation policy and sociopolitical measures as on appropriate urban and rural development planning.

Health-related constraints on mobility and adverse residential and infrastructure conditions can be compensated to some extent by good local transportation services, but, in view of the lack of alternatives currently available, the practical possibilities of the automobile comes closest to meeting the desires and mobility needs of the elderly. For that reason, it is likely that the proportion of automobile owners and users will continue to increase in future generations of elderly people. The elderly person's options for mobility may thereby increase, but the greater traffic density that results may also immediately reduce them again. Elderly people who do not have the alternative of using a personal automobile may come to suffer structural discrimination if important elements of the infrastructure, basic services, and recreation facilities continue to depend on personal transportation and remain concentrated either in city centers or in remote areas. Important services are often difficult to come by in rural regions and urban suburbs. Hence, sociopolitically and ecologically, it is becoming increasingly urgent for coordinated spatial, social, and transport planning (1) to create flexible, user-centered options for mobility that offer a genuine alternative to both the personal automobile and traditional local public transport services and (2) to provide for neighborhood facilities and services that respond to the needs and wishes of an aging population. For elderly people whose life space gradually but steadily contracts because of changes in their ability to deal with their environment, it is crucial that their neighborhoods contain readily accessible stores, medical services, appropriate public transport, and other facilities that will allow them to continue leading independent lives, maintain social contact, and take advantage of recreational activities. Such coordinated measures would both promote the integration of elderly people in the community and avoid ecologically undesirable transportation without reducing the action radius or excluding elders from the privileges and opportunities granted to all members of society. Environments that are structured and developed in such a manner would make a major contribution to enhancing the quality of life not only for elderly persons, but for those of any age.

REFERENCES

Brög, W. (1992a). Entwicklung der Mobilität unter veränderten Bedingungen der Bevölkerungs-, Siedlungs- und Verkehrsstruktur—Teil 1 [Developments in mobility under changing demographic, settlement, and traffic conditions—part 1]. *Verkehr und Technik, 1,* 3–8.

Brög, W. (1992b). Entwicklung der Mobilität unter veränderten Bedingungen der Bevölkerungs-, Siedlungs- und Verkehrsstruktur—Teil 2 [Developments in mobility under changing demographic, settlement, and traffic conditions—part 2]. *Verkehr und Technik, 2,* 57–62.

Bundesanstalt für Strassenwesen (BASt) [Federal Highway Research Institute] (Ed.). (1999). *Verkehrs- und Unfalldaten: Kurzzusammenstellung der Entwicklung in der Bundesrepublik Deutschland* [Road traffic and accident data: Brief overview, Germany]. Bergisch Gladbach, Germany: BASt.

Flade, A. (Ed.). (1994). *Mobilitätsverhalten: Bedingungen und Veränderungsmöglichkeiten aus umweltpsychologischer Sicht* [Travel behavior: Conditions and possibilities of change from an environmental psychology perspective]. Weinheim, Germany: Beltz, Psychologie Verlags Union.

Mollenkopf, H., Marcellini, F., & Ruoppila, I. (1998). The outdoor mobility of elderly people—a comparative study in three European countries. In J. Graafmans, V. Taipale, & N. Charness (Eds.), *Gerontechnology: A sustainable investment in the future* (pp. 204–211). Amsterdam: IOS Press.

Mollenkopf, H., Oswald, F., Schilling, O., & Wahl, H.-W. (2001). Aspekte außerhäuslicher Mobilität älterer Menschen in der Stadt und auf dem Land: Objektive Bedingungen und subjektive Bewertung [Aspects of older adults' outdoor mobility in cities and rural areas: Objective conditions and subjective evaluations]. *Sozialer Fortschritt, 50*(9–10), 214–220.

SOEP Group (2001). The German Socio-Economic Panel (GSOEP) after more than 15 years—Overview. In E. Holst, D. R. Lillard, & T. A. DiPrete (Eds.), Proceedings of the 2000 Fourth International Conference of German Socio-Economic Panel Study Users (GSOEP2000). *Vierteljahreshefte zur Wirtschaftsforschung* [Quarterly Journal of Economic Research], *70*(1), 7–14.

Statistisches Bundesamt (StBA) [Federal Statistical Office of Germany] (Ed.). (2000). *Datenreport 1999* [Data report 1999]. Bonn, Germany: Bundeszentrale für politische Bildung.

CHAPTER 13

The Safety of Older Drivers: The U.S. Perspective

Jane C. Stutts

In the United States, older adults rely heavily on the personal automobile for meeting their transportation needs. Although such travel provides convenient and flexible mobility, it is not without risks. As people age, declines in sensory, cognitive, and physical functioning can make them less safe drivers, as well as more vulnerable to injury once in a crash. This chapter provides a U.S. perspective on the safety of older drivers. It begins by offering contextual information on the importance of driving to the elderly, including data that can help to predict future travel and safety trends. This is followed by a series of viewpoints on the safety of older drivers and information about their crashes. Finally, the chapter briefly discusses the range of options available for achieving the dual goals of mobility and safety for the older adult population.

THE IMPORTANCE OF DRIVING TO THE ELDERLY

Americans have had a long and highly public love affair with the car. Ever since the first Model T Ford rolled off the assembly line in Detroit, Michigan, in 1908, Americans have increasingly turned to personal autos for meeting their transportation needs. According to Nationwide Personal Transportation Survey (NPTS) data, 92% of U.S. households in 1995 had at least 1 vehicle; 19% had 3 or more vehicles. Nine out of every 10 trips taken were by personal vehicle, and in 7 of 10 trips people drove themselves (Hu & Young, 1999).

As Americans age, they continue to rely on their autos, although less as drivers and more as passengers. Still, over two-thirds of the trips older Americans make are as drivers of their own vehicles. Even for those age 85 and above, more trips are made as car drivers than as car passengers. Walking, bicycling, and use of public transportation (buses, trains, taxis, and so on) account for only about 8% of the trips made by older Americans (European Conference of Ministers of Transportation [ECMT], 2000).

In the United States, mobility, or the ability to meet one's transportation needs outside the home, is largely dependent upon access to cars. Simply stated, those who have cars and who drive are more mobile than those who do not. An analysis of 1995 NPTS data shows that older drivers average almost twice as many trips per day as do older nondrivers.

There is no evidence that future cohorts of American elderly will be any less dependent on driving for meeting their transportation needs. If anything, trends are toward higher licensure rates and more miles traveled by personal vehicles, especially among women. Between the 1983 and 1995 NPTS surveys, a period of 13 years, the percentage of older adults licensed to drive increased dramatically, especially among women and among the oldest age categories of drivers. At the same time, virtually every measure of driving exposure also increased—and at a rate higher than that for younger drivers. For example, average daily vehicle trips per driver increased from 1.7 to 2.9, and average daily vehicle miles per driver increased from 9.8 to 19.6 (Hu & Young, 1999).

In short, older Americans are very dependent on personal auto travel for maintaining mobility, and this dependency appears to be growing rather than abating. Within this context, the safety of older drivers becomes an issue of paramount importance.

OLDER DRIVER SAFETY

How safe are older drivers? The answer to this question depends upon how *safety* is measured. There is no question that the various physiological changes associated with aging can reduce one's ability to operate a motor vehicle safely. As a group, older adults are more likely to have impaired vision and to experience cognitive impairments, including memory loss and problems with selective and divided attention. Their reaction time declines, and they lose muscle strength and joint flexibility. Older adults are also more likely to suffer from chronic medical conditions, such as heart disease, dementia, and diabetes, and to consume medications that can adversely affect their driving. The question, however, is how all of this translates into reduced driving performance and increased involvement in crashes.

The answer is not simple. When faced with medical problems and functional losses, many older adults choose not to drive, or to limit their driving to times and situations that lower their crash risk. It has already been noted how, as people age, they are more likely to ride as passengers in cars; they also accumulate fewer overall travel miles. Such self-regulation positively impacts safety. But still we hear about an older driver safety problem. What exactly is the nature of this problem?

The problem is not that older adults are involved in a greater number of crashes per licensed driver. The most recent available information from the United States shows that, on a licensed driver basis, even those age 85 and older are among the safest drivers on the road (see Figure 13.1). The average annual number of crashes in the United States is 68 per 1,000 licensed drivers, while the corresponding rate for drivers 65 and older is only 37 (Cerrelli, 1998). On a licensed driver basis, the greatest safety concern has always been with young novice drivers.

The picture changes somewhat when crash rates are calculated on the

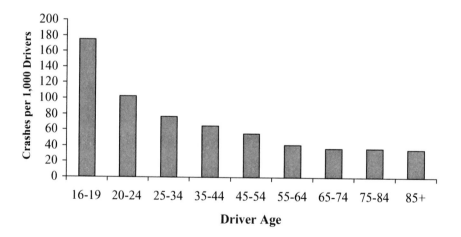

FIGURE 13.1. Annual crashes per 1,000 licensed drivers by age of driver.

Source: Cerrelli, 1998.

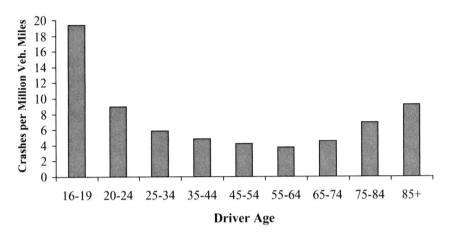

FIGURE 13.2.   Crashes per million vehicle miles traveled by age of driver.
Source: Cerrelli, 1998.

basis of miles traveled. Using this measure of exposure, older adults are at increased crash risk (see Figure 13.2). The increase is evident for 65- to 74-year-olds, but it becomes even more pronounced with age. Drivers age 85 and older have about the same (high) crash rate per mile driven as 20- to 24-year-olds. Still, they are much safer than 16- to 19-year-olds.

The real safety concern for the older driver arises when one also takes into consideration their increased likelihood of being injured or killed once in a crash. Compared to an overall fatality rate of 2.0 per 1,000 crashes, drivers ages 65 to 74 experience 3.2 fatalities per 1,000 crashes. For drivers ages 75 to 84, the rate is 5.3, and for drivers age 85 and above, it climbs to 8.6. If instead of measuring safety in terms of crashes per licensed driver and crashes per mile traveled, we measure it in terms of fatalities per licensed driver and fatalities per mile traveled, there is clearly cause for concern (see Figures 13.3 and 13.4). Both begin to increase by age 55, and the increase is especially dramatic for those age 85 and older.

A final measure of older driver safety, and one that is often employed by epidemiologists, is injury and fatality rates per 100,000 population. As can be seen in Figures 13.5 and 13.6, motor vehicle injury rates in the United States per 100,000 population decrease steadily with age; fatality rates, however, show the same characteristic U-shape curve demonstrated earlier. This

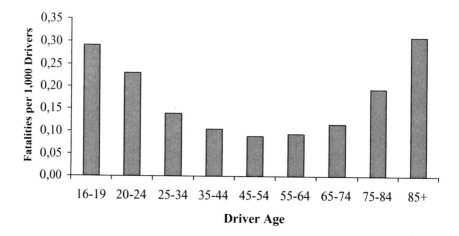

FIGURE 13.3. Driver fatalities per 1,000 licensed drivers by age of driver.

Source: Cerrelli, 1998.

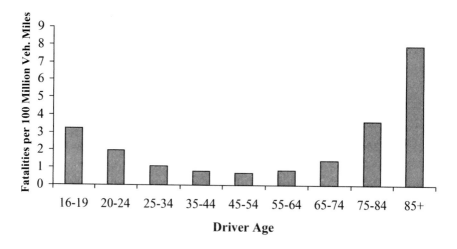

FIGURE 13.4. Driver fatalities per 100 million vehicle miles traveled by age of driver.

Source: Cerrelli, 1998.

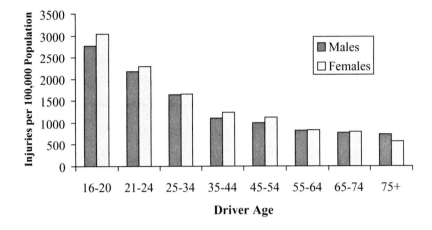

FIGURE 13.5. Motor vehicle crash injury rate per 100,000 population by driver age and sex.

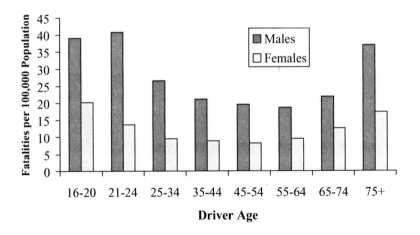

FIGURE 13.6. Motor vehicle crash fatality rate per 100,000 population by driver age and sex.

is especially true for males, who are more likely to retain their licenses into old age and who drive more miles.

Taken together, these results suggest that the safety problem confronting older adults is as much an issue of crash survivability as it is crash avoidance. Older adults who choose to continue to drive are both more likely to be in a crash, and more likely to be injured in that crash. The following section provides some insight into the specific situations that pose problems for older drivers.

SITUATIONS THAT CAUSE PROBLEMS FOR OLDER DRIVERS

Studies have shown that, compared to younger drivers, older drivers are more likely to be involved in crashes at intersections, and they are especially likely to be attempting a left-turn maneuver at an intersection (which, in the United States, is across traffic). Based on an analysis of North Carolina crash data, older drivers are also overrepresented in crashes involving right turns, U-turns, backing up, starting in the roadway, and parking or leaving a parked position (Reinfurt, Stewart, Stutts, & Rodgman, 2000). Although the crashes of older drivers tend to occur at lower speeds, they are more likely to involve side impacts, a factor which may contribute to their higher injury rates.

While much attention has been given to the higher frequency of intersection crashes for older drivers, less attention has been given to their considerably lower frequency of single vehicle, run-off-roadway crashes. Driving exposure may play an important role in both situations; in other words, older drivers are more likely to crash at intersections because a greater proportion of their driving takes place in cities and on local streets. At the same time, they may be less likely to run off the roadway because less of their driving is on rural, 2-lane roadways where these types of crashes typically occur.

Another approach to identifying situations that cause problems for older drivers is to examine violation, citation, and conviction data. For the North Carolina crash data referenced above, older drivers were more likely than younger drivers to be cited for the following violations in connection with their crashes: yield sign, stop sign, or traffic signal violations; improper lane changes; improper turns; improper backing; driving left of center; and other safe movement violations. They were also less likely than younger drivers to be cited for speeding, careless and reckless driving, and alcohol or drug use (Reinfurt et al., 2000).

Related to the above, one can also examine whether the older driver was at fault in crashes involving more than 1 vehicle. In North Carolina, police officers are not asked to assign fault when filling out a crash report form; however, fault can be inferred from the "violation indicated" data provided. Specifically, if 1 or more violations are indicated for 1 driver in a 2-vehicle crash, and none for the other driver, then the first driver is the at-fault driver in the crash. By using this approach, it was found that the likelihood of being at fault in a 2-vehicle crash increases with driver age: whereas only 30% of 45- to 54-year-old drivers were at fault in their crashes, nearly half of 65- to 74-year-olds and three-fourths of those 85 and older were at fault in their crashes. Similar results were found using national databases such as the Fatality Analysis Reporting System for fatal crashes and the General Estimates Systems for all police-reported crashes (Reinfurt et al., 2000).

Specific crash types where older drivers were increasingly likely to be found at fault in the North Carolina data included angle collisions (usually involving 2 vehicles passing through an intersection on perpendicular paths), left turn and right turn across traffic collisions, and slowing or stopping collisions (Reinfurt et al., 2000). The fact that all of these collision types typically occur at intersections suggests that intersections do indeed pose problems for older drivers, and that it is not just a matter of older drivers having more exposure to intersection situations. Slower information processing, reduced ability to divide attention between tasks, and slower reaction times could all play a part in older drivers' increased involvement in intersection crashes.

In summary, the safety of older drivers is a concern. Knowing the types of situations that cause problems for older drivers can help guide efforts to enable older adults to continue driving safely longer.

MEASURES TO IMPROVE OLDER DRIVER SAFETY AND MOBILITY

In the Transportation Research Board report, *Transportation in an Aging Society: A Decade of Experience* (Transportation Research Board [TRB], in press), a dominant theme is helping older adults continue to drive safely, longer. This is especially important in the United States, where mobility is so closely linked to owning and operating a car. Efforts to improve the safety of older drivers have generally fallen into 3 categories: driver regulation and education; roadway and environmental improvements; and vehicle improvements. In addition, improvements to the larger transportation system can help make it easier for older adults to choose other modes of travel without sacrificing mobility. Following is a brief overview of the types of activities occurring in the United States that will affect the safety, as well as the mobility, of our growing older population.

Driver Education and Licensing

One of the earliest responses of the highway safety research community to the recognition of an older driver safety problem was to try to find ways to identify the unsafe drivers so that they could be removed from the driving pool. In the United States we have continued our focus on identifying high-risk older drivers but within a broader context that includes driver education, training, and counseling. As noted above, the overall focus of these efforts is to assist older adults in continuing to drive as long as they safely can, and when driving is no longer possible, to help them identify alternative ways of meeting their transportation needs. Pilot programs have been implemented in both driver license office and community settings. In most cases, a tiered approach has been followed in which older adults are initially evaluated using a few carefully selected, brief screening tests; increasingly comprehensive assessments are used as needed. While some individual tests (e.g., useful field of view, trailmaking) have been shown to predict crash involvement in groups of older drivers, they lack the required sensitivity and specificity to be the basis for individual licensing decisions.

To address the particular concerns that arise from the increased incidence of Alzheimer's disease and other dementias with aging, some U.S. states (e.g., California and Pennsylvania) have increased efforts to involve physicians and other health professionals in reporting unsafe drivers. Currently, 14 U.S. states require physicians to report patients with potential driving impairments to licensing authorities; only the state of California, however, specifically requires physicians to report patients diagnosed with dementia (Staplin, Lococo, Stewart, & Decina, 1998). Other states (e.g., New York State) have worked to encourage greater involvement by family members in making driving decisions (LePore, 2000).

Apart from efforts to screen and identify high-risk older drivers, education programs have been developed to target the older driver. Examples include the 55 Alive, Mature Driver Program, offered by the American Association of Retired Persons (AARP), a national organization representing adults age 50 and above, and the Coaching the Mature Driver course offered by the National Safety Council. These courses, which generally last from 6 to 8 hours, are limited to classroom instruction. Although they are widely available through the private sector, only a small percentage of older adults participate in a given year. Recently, increased attention has also been given to the potential usefulness of on-road driving evaluations by certified driving instructors as a way of helping some older adults make more responsible decisions about continuing or stopping driving (Stutts, Wilkins, Reinfurt, Rodgman, & Causey, 2001; Wilkins, Stutts, & Schatz, 1999).

Some U.S. states require adults past a certain age to renew their licenses more frequently, or to pass additional vision tests; however, efforts to pass stricter age-based laws are generally viewed as discriminatory, and some would argue not cost effective. One of the few attempts made to evaluate the impact of differential licensing requirements in the United States found lower rates of fatal crash involvement for drivers age 70 and older in states with required vision testing at license renewal, compared to states without required vision testing (Levy, Vernick, & Howard, 1995).

Roadway and Environmental Improvements

The Federal Highway Administration, a part of the U.S. Department of Transportation, recently published an updated *Highway Design Handbook for Older Drivers and Pedestrians* (Staplin, Lococo, Byington, & Harkey, 2001a), along with a condensed report focusing on just the recommendations (Staplin, Lococo, Byington, & Harkey, 2001b). The handbook, directed toward state and local highway designers and traffic engineers, contains more than 100 recommendations selected on the basis of their potential for improving the safety of older drivers and their feasibility of implementation. Recommendations are given for increasing the visibility of the roadway at nighttime (through high-contrast edgelines, raised delineation markers, larger and brighter signs, roadway lighting, and so on); improving the safety of urban and suburban intersections (through improved geometric design elements and improved traffic control and signage); improving the safety of freeway ramps and merge zones (through better signage, improved acceleration lane geometrics, and so on); and improving pedestrian crossings. Since the cost of implementing the recommended changes across the board would be prohibitively expensive, users of the manual are encouraged to focus on implementing them in all new construction and in scheduled reconstruction or maintenance. In addition, specific recommendations should be considered for spot treatment of identified high-risk crash sites (Staplin et al., 2001a, 2001b).

Vehicle Improvements

In the past, vehicle (as well as roadway) design standards in the United States have been based on the attributes of young, healthy males. Fifty years ago, this might have been a reasonable characterization of the driving population, but it is not a true reflection today, and it will become less true over the coming decades. Automotive safety designers are recognizing the need to design for an aging, more diverse driver population which has reduced physical abilities and is more fragile. Vehicle improvements that can be especially beneficial to older drivers include smart airbags that adjust to the size and weight of the occupant, side airbag protection systems, mayday systems that automatically alert emergency medical personnel in the event of a crash, in-vehicle navigation systems (especially audio-based systems), and sensors to alert the driver to approaching traffic. Extensive progress has also been made in adapting or modifying vehicles to meet the needs of drivers with more extensive disabilities. Examples include hand controls for drivers unable to use their feet to operate the gas and brake pedals, left foot brakes, special mirrors, and adjustable seats that make it easier to get into and out of a car.

Transportation System Improvements

Improved driver education and regulation, roadways, and vehicles can all help older adults continue to drive safely longer. At some point, however, many older adults will need to stop driving. In order to continue to meet their transportation needs, they might need to be able to access alternative forms of transportation. Even if they are still capable of driving, older adults may want to use other forms of transportation in certain situations, (e.g., to travel at nighttime or when the weather makes driving hazardous). For these older adults, it is imperative that appropriate alternative transportation is available. Unfortunately, the United States lags far behind most European countries in providing public transportation that is accessible and attractive to the elderly population. As noted earlier, the elderly in the United States rarely use public transportation or taxis. While special *paratransit* services may be available to those disabled enough to qualify, they generally service only necessary destinations (for example, the doctor's office or pharmacy) and cannot begin to match the convenience and flexibility of driving. Private transportation programs like the Independent Transportation Network, which operates in Portland, Maine, are scarce (Freund, 2000).

One important form of alternative transportation that is often overlooked is walking. Walking is the second most frequent mode of transportation used by the elderly, accounting for about 6% of their travel trips (Hu & Young, 1999). Unfortunately, the same physical disabilities that can make driving hazardous for older adults also make it difficult for them to walk places. Approaches for improving conditions for walking were included in the Federal Highway Administration's updated *Highway Design Handbook* (Staplin et al., 2001a, 2001b).

In conclusion, older adults in the United States are highly dependent on personal automobiles for maintaining their mobility and independence. With increasing age, however, comes greater risk of injury and death from involvement in motor vehicle crashes. Efforts to improve the safety of older drivers through licensing, education, and roadway and vehicle modifications can help them continue to drive safely, longer. As an added bonus, many of these changes will reap safety benefits for other road users as well.

REFERENCES

Cerrelli, E. C. (1998). *Crash data and rates for age-sex groups of drivers, 1996.* Washington, DC: U.S. Department of Transportation, National Highway Traffic Safety Administration.

European Conference of Ministers of Transportation. (2000). *Transport and aging of the population.* Round Table 112. Paris, France: ECMT.

Freund, K. (2000). Independent transportation network: Alternative transportation for the elderly. *Transportation Research Board News, 206,* 3–12.

Hu, P., & Young, J. R. (1999). *Summary of travel trends: 1995 Nationwide Personal Transportation Survey.* Washington, DC: U.S. Department of Transportation, Federal Highway Administration.

LePore, P. R. (2000). *When you are concerned.* Albany: New York State Office for the Aging.

Levy, D. T., Vernick, J. S., & Howard, K. A. (1995). Relationship between driver's license renewal policies and fatal crashes involving drivers 70 years or older. *Journal of the American Medical Association, 274*(13), 1026–1030.

Reinfurt, D. W., Stewart, J. R., Stutts, J. C., & Rodgman, E. A. (2000). *Investigations of crashes and casualties associated with older drivers.* Chapel Hill: University of North Carolina Highway Safety Research Center.

Staplin, L., Lococo, K., Byington, S., & Harkey, D. (2001a). *Highway design handbook for older drivers and pedestrians.* Report No. FHWA-RD-01-103. Washington, DC: U.S. Department of Transportation, Federal Highway Administration.

Staplin, L., Lococo, K., Byington, S., & Harkey, D. (2001b). *Guidelines and recommendations to accommodate older drivers and pedestrians.* Report No. FHWA-RD-01-

105. Washington, DC: U.S. Department of Transportation, Federal Highway Administration.

Staplin, L., Lococo, K. H., Stewart, J., & Decina, L. E. (1998). *Safe mobility for older people notebook.* Report No. DTNH22-96-C-05140. Washington, DC: U.S. Department of Transportation, National Highway Traffic Safety Administration.

Stutts, J. C., Wilkins, J. W., Reinfurt, D. W., Rodgman, E. A., & Causey, S. V.-H. (2001). *The premature reduction and cessation of driving by older men and women.* Chapel Hill: University of North Carolina Highway Safety Research Center.

Transportation Research Board. (In press). *Transportation in an aging society: A decade of experience.* Washington, DC: The National Academies, Transportation Research Board.

Wilkins, J. W., Stutts, J. C., & Schatz, S. J. (1999). Premature reduction and cessation of driving: Preliminary study of women who choose not to drive or to drive infrequently. *Transportation Research Record 1693* (pp. 86–90). Washington, DC: Transportation Research Board.

CHAPTER 14

Safety and Accidents Among Older Drivers: The German Perspective

Bernhard Schlag

ACCIDENT INVOLVEMENT AND ACCIDENT CAUSATION

In the year 2000, there were nearly 13 million people in Germany aged 65 and over (out of a total population of 82 million). The absolute number and the proportionate share of elderly persons in the population continues to rise—but the number of elderly drivers is growing even faster. Cohorts are aging now for whom driving has always been part of their lives. It is therefore prudent to prepare for the future road safety problems that probably will be caused by older drivers—even if today's accident figures do not seem to be very dramatic (see Tables 14.1 and 14.2).

Traffic accident figures for the elderly are best described by the simple phrase: "fewer accidents, but higher risk of severe injuries." Until now the elderly have not been involved in traffic accidents overproportionally. When they do experience an accident, however, the consequences are often extremely severe. This is especially true for bicyclists, who account for about 20% of fatally injured older people, even though the elderly do not choose bicycling as part of their traffic participation as often as others. Over the past decade, the proportion of older automobile drivers injured in traffic has steadily grown. At present, the following trends in the frequency of accidents among elderly drivers can be observed.

TABLE 14.1   Killed and Injured Persons in Road Traffic in Germany (1999)

Age (years)	Killed	Injured	Killed	Injured	Population (Mil.)
	absolute number		*rate per 100,000 capita*		
Under 15	317	49,184	2.4	379	12,980
15–17	391	36,337	14.1	1,314	2,765
18–24	1,694	116,620	26.8	1,847	6,313
25–64	4,061	290,011	8.7	618	46,912
65+	1,306	36,747	10.0	281	13,067
Total	7,769	528,899	9.5	645	82,037

Source: Statistisches Bundesamt (Federal Statistical Office of Germany), 2000.

TABLE 14.2   Mode of Traffic Participation of Injured Persons Aged 65+ in Germany, 1999

Mode of traffic participation	Injured persons 1999			
	Fatally	*Severely*	*Minor*	*Total*
Car	563	4,201	13,459	18,223
Motorbike	30	526	764	1,310
Bicycle	257	2,692	4,953	7,902
Pedestrian	426	3,185	3,547	7,158
Bus/Other	30	426	1,688	2,154
Total	1,306	11,030	24,411	36,747

Source: Statistisches Bundesamt (Federal Statistical Office of Germany), 2000.

1. Until now the absolute number of elderly car drivers involved or injured in traffic accidents has been comparatively low in Germany.

2. The risk of being injured or killed in a traffic accident increases with age.

3. Elderly drivers involved in traffic accidents are more often cited by the police as being at fault for the accident (e.g., McGwin & Brown, 1999).

4. Proportionally to the number of members of their age group, elderly drivers are no more frequently involved in traffic accidents than middle-aged drivers.

5. The situation remains virtually unchanged if the number of persons holding a driver's licence or owning a car is considered: on an average, elderly motorists drive less than drivers in other age groups, thus reducing their accident exposure.

6. However, if reduction of driving is taken into account and the actual accident exposure is considered, either as a distance or a time parameter, the accident-performance ratio (injured drivers per 1 million kilometers driven) or accident-time ratio (injured drivers per 1 million hours of traffic participation) increases (Hautzinger, Tassaux-Becker, & Hamacher, 1996; Schlag, 1993).

Internationally there are marked differences in the extent of increased risk with age, as well as the age when the increased risk is assumed to begin. If the accident risk is related to exposure figures, it becomes clear that the risk increases slightly for drivers over 65 year of age and rises markedly for drivers over 75 years. This increase in risk at advanced ages has frequently been reported in American studies. Compared to Germany, there is a far greater proportion of active elderly drivers in the current U.S. population; there, the broad motorization of the entire population began a generation earlier. The accident risk for elderly pedestrians and—above all—the risk of fatal injuries begins to rise clearly at 65 years of age. Relative to their exposure, the accident risk for older bicycle riders in Germany also seems to be rather high.

Findings regarding the type of accidents characteristic of different age groups are more consistent: the "typical" accident for elderly drivers occurs at intersections and junctions—three-quarters of the accidents caused by elderly drivers occur there—due to failures to yield the right of way or other errors committed when changing direction (see Figure 14.1). These findings agree with U.S. reports. For example, Preusser, Williams, Ferguson, Ulmer, and Weinstein (1998) calculated the risk of fatal crash involvement for older drivers relative to drivers aged 40 to 49. Drivers aged 65 to 69 were 2.26 times and drivers aged 85 and over were 10.62 times at greater risk for multiple-vehicle involvements at intersections.

We analyzed a particular set of accident data, obtained from the Federation of German Insurance Companies, in regard to accident causation risks for different groups of drivers in different driving situations. The data com-

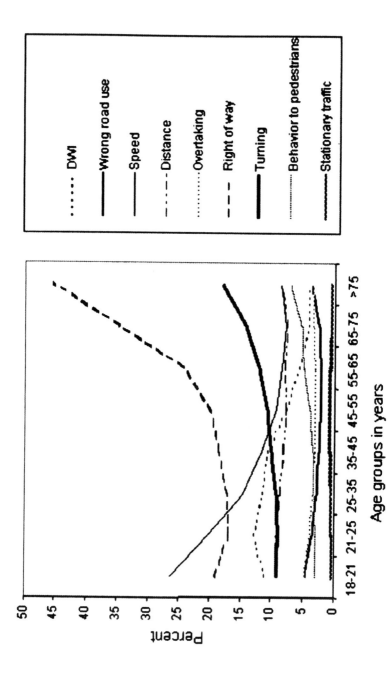

FIGURE 14.1. Car driver accident causation in Germany, 1997.

prised 16,007 2-car collisions in 1990 and 1991. We used a risk index based on the comparison of car drivers cited to be at fault by police and the other drivers involved in a given accident. The drivers cited to be at fault probably would have displayed some kind of erroneous behavior leading to the accident, whereas the other drivers might be considered as having been involved by chance, thus representing a sample of the total driving population (Schupp & Schlag, 1999; Stamatiadis & Deacon, 1997). This index indicates the risk of different groups of automobile drivers for causing a 2-car collision. The average value of this index across all groups is 1.

Table 14.3 shows the accident causation risk for 2-car collisions compared across different age groups. It should be pointed out that this index is limited to the type of accidents in which elderly drivers are overrepresented: 2-car collisions occurring primarily at junctions. The risk of being at fault for such accidents (because of their own mistakes or some type of faulty driving behavior) by far exceeds the risk of other age groups (2.15 times the average). On the other hand, drivers aged 65 and older were involved in only 2% of all 16,007 accidents analyzed. Given the currently low absolute accident involvement of elderly drivers combined with their rather high accident causation risk, increased future accident rates among the elderly might be anticipated in Germany.

Examining matters in greater depth, we analyzed the types of collisions most likely to be caused by elderly drivers (Büro für Kfz-Technik des Verbandes der Haftpflichtversicherer, Unfallversicherer, Autoversicherer und Rechtsschutzversicherer e.V., 1994). The 2-car collision types we distinguished are illustrated in Figure 14.2.

Side/front and rear end/front collisions are caused considerably more often by drivers aged 65 and older (and to a lesser extent also by persons aged 55 to 64 years). Problems in right turns and especially left turns at junctions, entering or exiting driveways, or in following seem to be associated with a wide range of age-related changes or failures to adapt to such changes (cf. Ellinghaus, Schlag, & Steinbrecher, 1990; Schlag, 1993, 2001). Differences in accident causation risks across age groups are highly significant for most of the investigated 2-car collisions (p < .001). On the other hand, the actual risks of young drivers are not represented adequately because of limiting the present analysis to 2-car accidents.

TABLE 14.3 Index of Accident Causation Risk for 2-Car Collisions

Age	At fault	Involved	Risk index
18–20	1,865 55.8% 11.7%	1,480 44.2% 9.73%	1.26
21–24	2,476 49.2% 15.5%	2,559 50.8% 16.0%	0.97
25–34	3,343 44.4% 20.9%	4,178 55.6% 26.2%	0.80
35–44	1,775 44.5% 11.1%	2,218 55.5% 13.9%	0.80
45–54	1,799 49.8% 11.3%	1,814 50.2% 11.4%	0.99
55–64	1,030 52.3% 6%	940 47.7% 6%	1.10
65+	797 68.3% 5%	370 31.7% 2%	2.15
Other	2,890 54.7% 18.5%	2,396 45.3% 15.2%	1.21
Total	(1) 15,975 50% 100%	(1) 15,955 50% 100%	1.00

Note: $\chi^2 = 383.21$; $df = 8$; $p < .001$.
Source: Author's own data calculations based on Federation of German Insurance Companies.

1. Collision type: Front/Front

1.1. Longitudinal axis of cars in a line without angle: 0.57

1.2. Longitudinal axis of cars parallel with lateral shift: 1.00

1.3. Longitudinal axis of cars angular with full overlay: 1.09

1.4. Longitudinal axis of cars angular without full overlay: 1.41

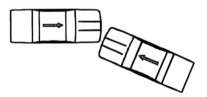

FIGURE 14.2. Collision types.

2. Collision type: Side/Front

2.1. Longitudinal axis of cars exact 90: 2.43

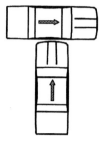

2.2. Longitudinal axis of cars angular: 2.65 (often)

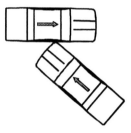

2.3. Longitudinal axis of cars angular but in the lateral forefront: 2.92 (often)

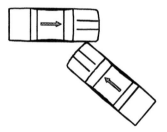

2.4. Longitudinal axis of cars angular but in the lateral rear area: 2.83

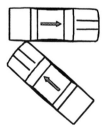

FIGURE 14.2. *(continued)*

3. Collision type: Rear end/Front

3.1. Longitudinal axis of cars in a line without angle: 1.50

3.2. Longitudinal axis of cars parallel with lateral shift: 2.10 (often)

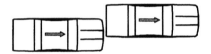

3.3. Longitudinal axis of cars angular with full overlay: 9.51 (seldom)

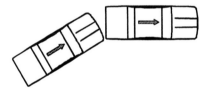

3.4. Longitudinal axis of cars angular without full overlay: 2.23

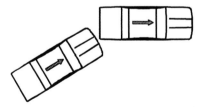

FIGURE 14.2. *(continued)*

LABORATORY AND DRIVING TESTS WITH ELDERLY DRIVERS

On behalf of the Federal Highway Research Institute, we conducted driving tests for 80 elderly drivers (60 to 82 years old), compared with a reference group of 30 middle-aged motorists (40 to 50 years), and we studied their relation to laboratory performance data and interviews.

Main Findings of Laboratory Tests

Significant performance differences were found between the age groups on laboratory tests, especially the tests involving vision and reaction speed:

1. In far and close visual acuity by daylight (measured by Tytmus-Vision-Tester), even when assisted by optical aids

2. In the visual acuity at twilight and in the dark, with and without glare (measured by Rodenstock-Nyktometer)

3. In objective and (upon questioning) subjective assessment of visual performance, a discrepancy which steadily increased with age

4. In the number of omissions in a traffic-related tachistoscopic test of perceptive faculty (TAVT-N), especially in failure to notice 2-wheeled vehicles and traffic signs (the reduced visual acuity of elderly people possibly has a negative influence on the perception of details in complex traffic situations in these kinds of perception tests)

5. In the amount of time required to perform tasks involving error and time variables, such as in a tracking experiment, and tests with the Wiener Determinations-Gerät (WDGT). (In the latter test, fewer stimuli were correctly dealt with by the elderly, more stimuli were answered with greater delay, and more were not responded to, but the number of completely erroneous reactions was no higher.)

Results such as these in laboratory tests are generally considered relevant to driving performance. Thus, the prognosis for elderly drivers on the whole, based on these findings, would be relatively discouraging. This point is all the more valid because the results of the interviews show that the elderly persons' perceptions of these changes are limited. In fact, most of the older study participants felt their psychophysical capacity to be virtually equal to that of middle-aged persons.

Main Findings of Driving Tests

We tested the hypothesis that elderly motorists compare unfavorably with middle-aged drivers in their driving behavior and that this is essentially due to deficiencies in the psychophysical domains of perception and reaction. The test was conducted with an instrumented car provided by the German Federal Highway Research Institute. We conducted a driving test lasting approximately 1 hour on a standard route of 35 kilometers in the Cologne area with the above-mentioned 110 test persons, 40 of whom were between 60 and 64 years, another 40 of whom were 65 years or older (up to 82 years) and, for comparison, 30 of whom were between 40 and 50 years (cf. Ellinghaus et al., 1990). The course included motorways, country roads, and, above all, city traffic with a total of 38 differently regulated junction situations, comprising various degrees of complexity.

The results of the laboratory tests (if they can be credited with high prognostic validity) gave rise to the hypothesis that driving behavior differs markedly between the age groups tested. We compared the 40 to 50 age group, the 60 to 69 age group, and the 70+ age group to test this hypothesis.

The fact is that differences in actual driving behavior between the age groups were small in the overwhelming majority of driving situations. This is true when the groups are compared on the basis of chronological age; but it is also the case when laboratory performances of the different age groups were examined in relation to driving parameters.

In individual situations, however, and for specific behavior parameters, we did obtain several interesting differences between elderly and middle-aged drivers.

The elderly drivers tended to drive more slowly on motorways in traffic of comparable density, and some elderly drivers had difficulties (more often than younger drivers) getting into the proper lane at complex motorway entrances. Elderly drivers often tried to enter the lane hesitantly, their attempts were interrupted, and the result was sometimes very late entry and hence risky merging into the traffic flow (see Figure 14.3).

On country roads, the elderly motorists, on the average, displayed a particularly uniform driving style with fewer accelerations and braking actions and with a tendency to drive more moderately.

City traffic normally allows less room for exhibiting individual driving

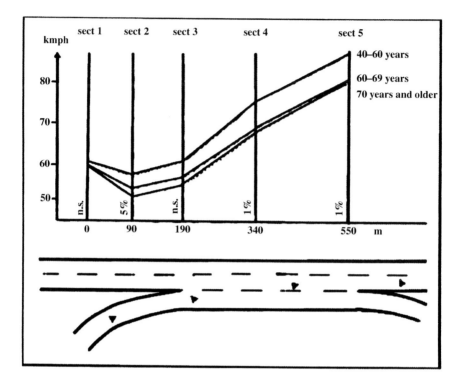

FIGURE 14.3.   Increase in speed when getting into lane at a motorway entrance.

Source: Calculations based on data from the Statistisches Bundesamt (Federal Statistical Office of Germany), 1998, pp. 294–300.

behavior. Hence, there were few (but rather critical) differences observed between the age groups in the inner-city sections. There was a markedly higher incidence of incorrect action among elderly motorists above all in two situations at junctions (see Table 14.4):

1. At junctions regulated by traffic lights, the elderly drivers (even though the number of driving tests was relatively low) ignored red lights more often, but driving through yellow lights was observed less frequently among the elderly.

2. Furthermore, they more often disregarded the right-before-left priority, and, similarly, more often failed to reduce their speed adequately at road-level railway crossings.

TABLE 14.4   Problematic Behavior of Elderly Drivers at Junctions

		All	40–50	60–69	70+	AV resp. χ^2
				Age		
Traffic line overrun,	*M*	2.8	2.8	2.8	2.9	*ns*
observed at least once	%	86.4	80.0	88.5	89.5	*ns*
Traffic light: red overrun,	*M*	0.1	0.0	0.0	0.2	**
observed at least once	%	5.4	0.0	0.0	21.1	*
Traffic light: yellow overrun,	*M*	1.0	1.5	0.9	0.7	*
observed at least once	%	64.5	90.0	55.7	52.6	*ns*
Stop: did not stop,	*M*	0.3	0.2	0.4	0.5	*ns*
observed at least once	%	29.1	16.7	32.8	36.8	*ns*
Right-before-left disregarded,	*M*	0.5	0.1	0.5	0.7	*
observed at least once	%	39.1	13.3	45.9	57.9	*

Note: *$p < .05$; **$p < .01$.
Source: author.

Unsafe behavior at junctions occurred increasingly from the age of 65 onward. On the whole, however, the elderly drivers showed a tendency to approach junctions more slowly; they had in most cases reduced their speed earlier and thus slowed down more smoothly.

DISCUSSION

If one compares and contrasts the driving behavior between elderly and middle-aged motorists, one must conclude that there are far more similarities than differences. Among the few age differences observed, some result in higher safety among elderly drivers, whereas others are extremely dangerous.

The relationships between chronological age, laboratory performance data, and parameters of driving behavior measured on the road were investigated further by means of analyses of variance and covariance and by multiple regression analyses. In the analyses of covariance, for example, the explanatory value of age and sex and of 5 test results (long-range vision and twilight vision without glare, omission errors in the tachistoscopic perception test, time needed in the tracking experiment, and the main result in the Wiener Determinations-Gerät) was examined individually as well as jointly for the different driving parameters. Among these variables, chronological age proved to be the relatively strongest factor but, alone, could not explain the observed cases of a different driving behavior among the elderly, especially in relation to speed (elderly drivers tending toward lower speeds) and reactions at difficult junctions (less satisfactory among the elderly), unless the influence of test performance data pertaining to age was filtered out. Chronological age thus represents a complex aggregation of influential parameters which might combine to yield a tentative predictor of driving behavior, but by itself, it is in no way of sufficient prognostic value.

The differences between middle-aged and elderly drivers in actual traffic situations turned out to be much less obvious than expected, especially in terms of the driving performance tests. On the other hand, these results correspond to the expectations and estimations of the elderly drivers themselves: they do not regard themselves as being very different from middle-aged drivers, and to the extent that they do perceive age-related changes, they mostly regard them as being irrelevant to their own driving safety.

How do we explain the fact that elderly drivers perform worse in the laboratory while in most cases their actual driving behavior does not compare unfavorably with that of middle-aged motorists? There are 3 possible explanations.

First, it should be noted that statistical comparisons have a leveling effect: even if the behavior of the least capable 5% or 10% of elderly motorists tested had often been conspicuous, this would become statistically relevant only in extreme situations. Precisely this was the case with the drivers running a red light, those ignoring right-before-left priority, and those reacting inadequately at railway crossings.

Second, it is also possible that the measurement of psychophysical performance exposes age differences more precisely than is possible to accomplish by conducting driving tests in road traffic. Average driving demands are usually met by the elderly with as much skill as by middle-aged motorists. Moreover, unsatisfactory psychophysical fitness as measured in the laboratory has perhaps only unpleasant consequences in extreme situations in real traffic. This leads to methodological difficulties: a strategy of testing the limits, intended to assess the potential flexibility of behavior, must obviously be confined to the laboratory; it is out of the question for road-based driving tests.

Third, it may in fact be true that the functions measured in the laboratory are less relevant to normal driving demands and in most cases can be compensated for by adequate adaptive ability. This possibility is supported by the results of additional factor analyses combining laboratory with driving data. When the complexity of the data was reduced, separate factors were obtained for the laboratory and driving test data.

REFERENCES

Büro für Kfz-Technik des Verbandes der Haftpflichtversicherer, Unfallversicherer, Autoversicherer und Rechtsschutzversicherer e.v. [Office for Motor Vehicle Technology of the Association of Third-Party Insurers, Accident Insurers, Car Insurers and Legal Costs Insurers] (Ed.). (1994). *Fahrzeugsicherheit 90—Analyse von PKW-Unfällen, Grundlagen für künftige Forschungsarbeiten* [Vehicle security 90—analysis of motor vehicle accidents, foundations for future research]. Munich, Germany: HUK-Verband.

Ellinghaus, D., Schlag, B., & Steinbrecher, J. (1990). Leistungsfähigkeit und Fahrverhalten älterer Kraftfahrer [Capabilities and driving behavior of elderly motorists]. *Unfall- und Sicherheitsforschung Straßenverkehr der Bundesanstalt für Straßenwesen, 80.* Bremerhaven, Germany: Wirtschaftsverlag NW.

Hautzinger, H., Tassaux-Becker, B., & Hamacher, R. (1996). Verkehrsunfallrisiko in Deutschland [Traffic accident risk in Germany]. *Berichte der Bundesanstalt für Straßenwesen, M 58.* Aachen, Germany: Maintz-Verlag.

McGwin, G., Jr., & Brown, D. B. (1999). Characteristics of traffic crashes among young, middle-aged, and older drivers. *Accident Analyses and Prevention, 31*(2), 181–198.

Preusser, D. F., Williams, A. F., Ferguson, S. A., Ulmer, R. G., & Weinstein, H. B. (1998). Fatal crash risk for older drivers at intersections. *Accident Analysis and Prevention, 30*(2), 151–159.

Schlag, B. (1993). Elderly drivers in Germany. *Accident Analysis and Prevention, 25*(1), 47–55.

Schlag, B. (1996). Fahrverhaltensbeobachtungen bei jüngeren und älteren Kraftfahrern [Behavior behind the wheel: Observations of younger and older motorists]. *Verkehrswachtforum, 2.* Meckenheim, Germany: Deutsche Verkehrswacht.

Schlag, B. (2001). Ältere Menschen im Pkw unterwegs [Elderly people behind the wheel]. In A. Flade, M. Limbourg, & B. Schlag (Eds.), *Mobilität älterer Menschen* (pp. 85–98). Opladen, Germany: Leske & Budrich.

Schupp, A., & Schlag, B. (1999). Das Risiko, einen Unfall zu verursachen: Analysen für Männer und Frauen, für Beifahrerkonstellationen und Altersgruppen [The risk of accident causation: Analyses for men and women, for passenger constellations and age groups]. In B. Schlag (Ed.), *Empirische Verkehrspsychologie* (pp. 111–132). Lengerich, Berlin: Pabst Science Publications.

Stamatiadis, N., & Deacon, J. A. (1997). Quasi-induced exposure: Methodology and insight. *Accident Analyses and Prevention, 29*(1), 37–52.

Statistisches Bundesamt (Ed.). (1998). Jahresbericht Verkehr [Annual report traffic]. In *Fachserie 8, Reihe 7, Verkehrsunfälle 1997.* Stuttgart, Germany: Metzler-Poeschel.

Statistisches Bundesamt (Ed.). (2000). Jahresbericht Verkehr [Annual report traffic]. In *Fachserie 8, Reihe 7, Verkehrsunfälle 1999.* Stuttgart, Germany: Metzler-Poeschel.

CHAPTER 15

Self-Initiated Compensations Among Older Drivers

Georg Rudinger and Elke Jansen

T his chapter begins with some initial ideas about aging and mobility in the context of safety and security. We illustrate how compensation is defined and operationalized in the survey and follow with a short summary of the empirical results obtained on the associations between the compensation styles of elderly drivers and mobility-related traits, attitudes, and lifestyles. Finally, some suggestions for intervention strategies are offered.

AGING AND MOBILITY: SAFETY AND SECURITY

Various studies have shown that enjoying an active physical life, as well as an active social life, improves successful aging (e.g., Baltes & Lang, 1997; Rowe, 1996; Rudinger & Thomae, 1990). The maintenance of mobility has been widely acknowledged to be essential for the elderly to continue living an active life [e.g., Bundesministerium für Familie, Senioren, Frauen und Jugend (BMFSFJ) (Federal Ministry for Family Affairs, Senior Citizens, Women and Youth), 2001; see also Gonda, 1982]. Mobility, however, has a price. The public discussion about the safety and security of the elderly as participants in modern traffic systems is characterized by some basic but rather undifferentiated assumptions: due to increasing age-related deficits in physical, sensory, and cognitive domains, older participants in the traffic system are assumed to bear a massive risk potential for themselves and the system. Statistics illustrate that elderly road participants are more prone to serious injury than middle-aged persons, and they bear the same risk of injury as the very young traffic participants. They also die more frequently as a result of these accidents (e.g., Mäder, 1999). Furthermore, there are age-related deficits in physical, sensory, and cognitive domains (e.g., Brouwer & Ponds, 1994; Craik & Jennings, 1992; Klein, 1991; McDowd & Birren, 1990). Accidents instigated by older car drivers are often attributed to these very deficits: limitations of the visual field or difficulties in estimating speed and distance (e.g., Cremer, Snel, & Brouwer, 1990). However, age developments are very individual, which implies that old age itself does not inevitably bring about these deficits. It is possible to counteract loss in driving (perceptual-motor) skill, and compensatory mechanisms and self-initiated processes can overcome or at least reduce some of them (e.g., Marsiske, Lang, Baltes, & Baltes, 1995).

In the context of automobile mobility, compensation for age-related deficits can be achieved by adapting the environment to the needs and abilities of elderly drivers (e.g., Charness & Bosman, 1995) or by changing driving habits. The elderly driver can perform special modes of driving or make intelligent traffic or travel choices (e.g., Chaloupka, 1994; Hakamies-Blomqvist, 1993), such as driving more slowly, choosing shorter distances, driving during the day, and driving under less stressful weather conditions. Results from the AEMEÏS research project show that the majority of older drivers make mindful use of compensatory mechanisms based on such meta-cognitive skills (Jansen, 2001).[1] Nevertheless, some elderly appear neither able nor willing to adjust to their deficits, nor do they even recognize their possible impact on driving competence.

COMPENSATION OF AGE-RELATED DEFICITS AMONG ELDERLY DRIVERS

One fundamental research topic of AEMEÏS was to identify factors or conditions among the elderly which lead to this kind of improper and risky traffic behavior (i.e., not adjusting one's driving habits). Another dominant theme was to explore the factors that might help the elderly to adjust to the objective deficits in driving performance or trepidation about driving in general. Answers to these questions could then be used to enhance traffic safety among the elderly through intervention strategies.

In the AEMEÏS survey, a sample of more than 2,000 (N = 2,032) individuals, aged from 55 to 94 years, was interviewed very generally on the subjects of mobility needs, mobility attitudes, and mobility behavior. Additionally, 1,259 elderly people, still actively driving, were interviewed regarding compensatory mechanisms.[2] One limitation of large survey-studies must be kept in mind: research in this context depends upon self-reports. The level of correspondence of subjective and objective data thus depends on the (selective) awareness of the people questioned, including their degree of self-disclosure and their tendency to answer according to social acceptance.

DEFINITION AND OPERATIONALIZATION OF COMPENSATION IN A SURVEY STUDY

An enormous variety of definitions of *compensation* can be found in current scientific discussions and psychological papers (e.g., Dixon & Bäckman, 1995; Marsiske et al., 1995). The first of these overviews presents a definition of compensation which summarizes the main trends in literature, whereby compensation is defined as a "process of overcoming losses or deficits" (Dixon and Bäckman, 1995, p. 6). In the context of mobility and driving behavior among the elderly, health deficits can be regarded as very important personal risk factors which might lead to a mismatch between driving skills and environmental demands. Deteriorated health is the most frequently indicated reason for the elderly to stop driving (e.g., Hakamies-Blomqvist & Wahlström, 1998; see also Jansen, 2001). Considering this, within the research work of AEMEÏS, we explored various health complaints of elderly drivers, especially physical, sensory, and cognitive problems which are of relevance for driving tasks; for example, fatigue, lack of concentration, and slow reaction times.[3]

According to Dixon and Bäckman (1995), overcoming losses is managed through "one of several recognizable mechanisms" (p. 6). Compensation mechanisms entail investing more time or effort in tasks, developing new skills, altering goals, or developing new targets. Independent of particular compensation mechanisms, compensation will always lead to "a change in the behavioral profile" (p. 8). Studies about traffic psychology point out 2 different levels of behavioral changes in the context of age-related deficits: (1) the avoidance of difficult driving conditions and (2) a change of driving style which aims at reducing the mental load of the driving task (see Hakamies-Blomqvist, 1993).

In AEMEÏS, changes in driving behavior were detected when self-reports of current driving behavior were contrasted with self-reports of previous driving behavior at the age of 45. Both levels of changes were assessed in the survey: the alteration in driving style (for example, "more defensive than at the age of 45") as well as the avoidance of typically risky driving situations (for example, crossing dangerous crossroads, driving in the twilight, or driving during rush hour). We then extracted compensation patterns in a 3-step process: first, behavioral changes (avoidance and alteration) were detected; then traffic-related personal indicators—for example, exposure—and special conditions, like health deficits, were taken into account; and finally, 4 compensation patterns were developed.

The first step was to describe different types of elderly drivers based on the 2 classes or levels of behavioral changes: avoidance of risky situations and alteration of driving style. As illustrated in Table 15.1, this conceptual differentiation did not prove helpful in determining whether the behavioral patterns observed represented compensational efforts or not.

To be able to classify a change in driving habits as compensatory behavior, the reasons for such a change need to be defined. Therefore, in a second step, we examined whether the respondent perceived a need for compensatory behavior.

For the 4 groups of elderly drivers, subjective reports of health complaints and restrictions were used in order to assess the need to compensate. Indicators relevant to mobility (e.g., occupational changes and the alteration in exposure) were used to assess compensatory alterations in driving behavior. When, for example, the exposure—in our case, the number of driven kilometers per year—decreases, the experience of critical driving situations will automatically decline as well. However, this does not necessarily entail conscious avoidance of critical traffic situations or the use of an additional safety measure as a means of functional compensation.

As illustrated in Figure 15.1, in a third and last step, 4 types of compen-

TABLE 15.1 Avoidance and Alteration

		Alteration	
		+	−
Avoidance	+	Group 1	Group 2
	−	Group 3	Group 4

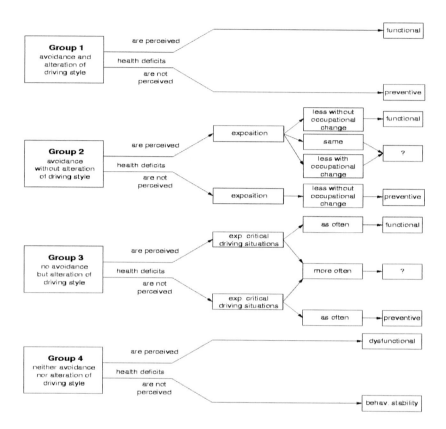

FIGURE 15.1.   Compensatory patterns.

sation patterns were identified: functional, dysfunctional, preventive behavior, and behavioral stability.

A part of Group 1, in which difficult driving situations were avoided and defensive driving was displayed, showed *functional* compensation, because they were aware of health deficits. Two other patterns appeared functional as well:

1. Elderly people with health-related deficits belonging to Group 2, who avoided risky situations, were considered to compensate *functionally*, if their exposure reduced *without* occupational changes.

2. Members of Group 3 with health-related deficits compensated *functionally* if their driving style changed toward a more defensive one without an increase of critical driving situations at the same time.

The same 3 patterns were called *preventive* if no health deficits were perceived (i.e., if compensation was not perceived to be necessary). If no alteration in driving behavior concerning difficult situations and driving style was displayed (Group 4), even though a health deficit had been recognized, the behavior pattern was termed *dysfunctional*. Finally, if no health deficits were perceived and the usual driving behavior was maintained, the respondent was said to exhibit *behavioral stability*. Unfortunately, some patterns could not be classified as clear forms of compensation. For example, some elderly with health-related deficits belonging to Group 3 changed their driving style toward a more defensive one, yet they also experienced an increase in difficult driving situations. Thus, it was not possible to say whether the alteration of driving style led to a gain of safety in the sense of functional compensation.

EMPIRICAL RESULTS

The 4 compensation types were *distributed* in the AEMEÏS survey as shown in Figure 15.2.

Functional compensation (awareness of deficits and subsequent behavioral adjustment in the direction of risk reduction) constituted 23.5%; dysfunctional compensation (awareness of deficits, however, no behavioral adjustment in the direction of risk reduction), 5.5%; preventive behavior (no deficits, but nevertheless behavioral adjustment in the direction of risk re-

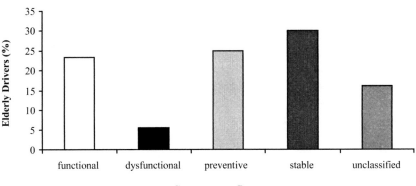

FIGURE 15.2. Distribution of compensatory patterns among elderly drivers (AEMEÏS), *n* = 1.259.

duction), 25%; and behavioral stability (no deficits and no risk reduction), 30% of all cases observed. Unfortunately, 16% of the cases could not be classified.

In order to validate our classification scheme, we examined whether there was an association between compensation patterns and involvement in traffic accidents. Concerning accident involvement during the last 2 years, the 4 compensation groups hardly differed. This, however, changes when the person causing the accident was taken into account (see Figure 15.3).

A comparison of the dysfunctional and functional compensators ($n = 364$ of 1,259 elderly drivers) showed that functional compensators were clearly more often involved in accidents without actually having made mistakes. In general, it is interesting to note that the dysfunctionally compensating drivers are more often considered fully at fault in the accidents they were involved in—not only compared to the functional compensating drivers, but to all the other drivers in the sample.

In this context, it was particularly interesting that the dysfunctional group of drivers chiefly comprised younger males (aged 54 to 64 years). Other mobility studies have shown that, among younger car drivers, young males—aged 18 to 24 years—take the greatest risks (e.g., Schulze, 1991). Hence, it seems to be a relative phenomenon: with an older reference population, the youngest males still show the largest risk potential.

A more detailed look at the compensation types reveals differences in the attitude profile of dysfunctionally and functionally compensating elderly (see Figure 15.4).

The 2 dimensions on the left side of the graph (risk taking/sensation seeking) measure disregard for safety, whereas the 2 dimensions on the right (risk perception/insight) measure concern about one's safety. Differences were observed in various traffic-related attitudes, such as risk taking (in the sense of positive attitudes toward fast driving), sensation seeking, risk perception, and insight into health-related reductions in driving skill. The *functionally* compensating elderly score more favorably in all fields, whereas the *dysfunctionally compensating* show more sensation seeking and less sensitive risk perceptions, a stronger risk-taking disposition, and less insight into their reduced driving skills. Furthermore they are, as we have already seen, more often wholly at fault when they are involved in traffic accidents.

As shown in Figure 15.5, dysfunctional elderly drivers also show overconfidence in their driving skills. They tend to judge their own driving competence to be significantly better than do the functionally compensating drivers, who regard themselves as worse drivers.

This kind of self-assurance, as well as a stronger risk-taking disposition,

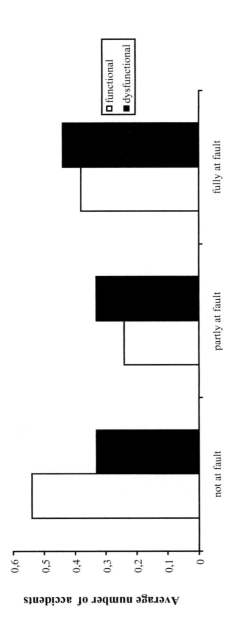

Accident Involvement

FIGURE 15.3. Compensatory patterns and accident involvement among elderly drivers (AEMEÏS), $n = 364$.

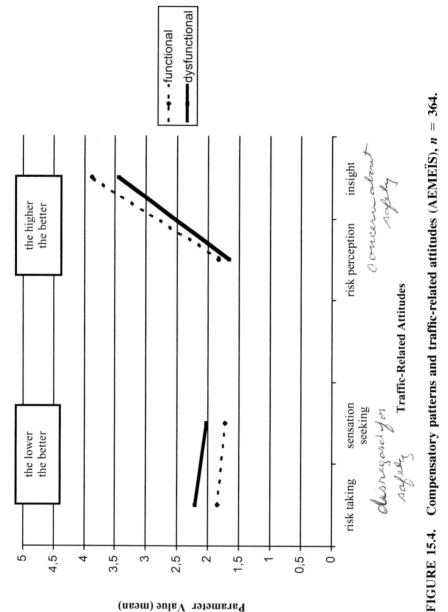

FIGURE 15.4. Compensatory patterns and traffic-related attitudes (AEMEÏS), $n = 364$.

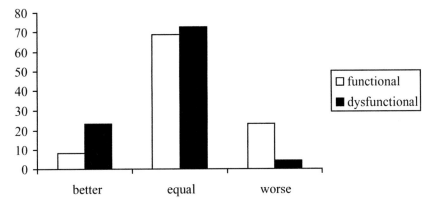

FIGURE 15.5. **Compensatory patterns and self-assessment as drivers in social comparison (AEMEÏS),** *n* = **364.**

are found not only among dysfunctionally compensating elderly drivers, but also among younger male drivers (e.g., Rudinger & Holte, 1996). This might be one possible explanation for the mentioned "pattern" of young, male, risk takers at the beginning and at the end of their active driving lives, since subjective safety and overconfidence are the actual sources of negligence, risk taking, and endangerment.

The research project AEMEÏS also examined to what extent driving behavior reflects individual lifestyles. Figure 15.6 shows the 5 lifestyles that were found among the elderly in the survey and their distribution among the dysfunctionally and functionally compensating types. These lifestyle types reflect different preferences regarding leisure time activities and living arrangements.

The largest differences between the 2 compensation types were found among dysfunctional compensators, who prefer an excitement-seeking lifestyle, and functional compensators, who adopt a widely interested, moderate lifestyle. The ones who seek excitement show great interest in activities concerning cars and in social activities, and they prefer exciting and thrilling television entertainment. The representatives of the other group show many interests and take part in a variety of activities but do so in moderation.

The results regarding risk potential and security among elderly drivers can be summarized as follows: fortunately, only about 5% to 6% of the

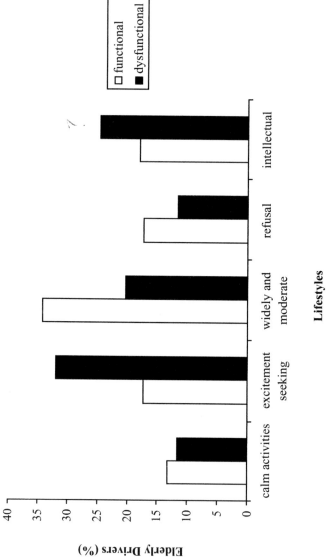

FIGURE 15.6. Compensatory patterns and lifestyles (AEMEÏS), $n = 364$.

elderly drivers showed a deficit in the ability or willingness to recognize the possible impact of age-associated losses in health on their driving skills. These drivers did not try to compensate for their deficits, either by avoiding critical driving situations or by choosing a defensive driving style. The results of AEMEÏS show that most elderly drivers in a self-regulating system are able to initiate compensation processes in order to take part in road traffic as drivers. Most elderly drivers on German roads compensate for their subjective deficits functionally, act preventively, or show behavioral stability, which seem to be adequate responses to the potential losses in driving skill that occur with age.

SUGGESTIONS FOR INTERVENTION STRATEGIES

In the present examination of safety in the whole traffic system—from the perspective of auto mobility—we focused on the subsystem of elderly car drivers as a risk potential. The findings have shown, however, that only a minority of elderly drivers compensate dysfunctionally. In fact, only some of the younger, mainly male elderly drivers are probable risk takers or, more aptly, "risk givers." In the context of person-centered interventions, it might be rather difficult to reach this group, since they typically believe that they are good or excellent drivers and do not recognize any necessity to change. In order to motivate them to take part in a training program, car insurance companies might consider offering a financial stimulus, based upon the higher insurance rates associated with frequent involvement in at-fault accidents. The goal of such intervention strategies should be to increase awareness of the behavioral consequences of progressive health deficits and demonstrate the benefits of a functionally compensating driving style, which include stress relief and safety. The implementation of these goals requires theoretical concepts as well as practical lessons, such as a simulation of complex driving situations, which should be discussed afterwards. Hence, to promote the integration of an adequate driving style in everyday driving, intervention strategies should not be limited to a single workshop.

The results of the survey indicate—in contrast to statements heard in the current German debate—that there is no need for the introduction of a general driving skill test procedure (by means of legal regulation) when a certain age is reached, since other factors, including state of health, lifestyle, and self-image, actually influence and determine driving skills. The results of AEMEÏS demonstrate that elderly people are capable of self-initiated compensation in order to take an active part in road traffic as car drivers. They should be permitted to do so as long as it actually enriches individual life and makes sense regarding the traffic system in total.

NOTES

1. This chapter presents the results from the research project AEMEÏS, recently accomplished at the University of Bonn (Jansen, 2001). AEMEÏS is an abbreviation for the German title *Ältere Menschen im Strassenverkehr* (The Elderly in the Traffic System). The study was conducted on behalf of the German Federal Highway Research Institute.

2. In our survey we took representative samples from the old and new *Bundesländer* (German states) regarding age and sex. Older female drivers were, however, considered over proportionally to safeguard a statistical review of specific research questions.

3. Specific scales to assess clinical phenomena like dementia were not administered in the survey.

REFERENCES

Baltes, P. B., & Lang, F. R. (1997). Everyday functioning and successful aging: The impact of resources. *Psychology and Aging, 12*(3), 433–443.

Brouwer, W. H., & Ponds, R. W. (1994). Driving competence in older persons. *Disability and Rehabilitation, 16*(3), 149–161.

Bundesministerium für Familie, Senioren, Frauen und Jugend (BMFSFJ) [Federal Ministry for Family Affairs, Senior Citizens, Women and Youth] (Ed.). (2001). *Dritter Altenbericht der Bundesregierung: Alter und Gesellschaft* [Third report on the situation of older people: Aging and society]. Available at http://www.bmfsfj.de/top/sonstige/Aktuelles/ix4748_27124.htm.

Chaloupka, C. (1994). Was hat es mit der Veränderung der Leistungsfähigkeit älterer Verkehrsteilnehmer wirklich auf sich? [What does the change in performance of older traffic participants actually imply?]. In U. Tränkle (Ed.), *Autofahren im Alter* [Car driving in old age] (pp. 321–334). Bonn, Germany Deutscher Psychologen-Verlag.

Charness, N., & Bosman, E. A. (1995). Compensation through environmental modification. In R. A. Dixon & L. Bäckman (Eds.), *Compensating for psychological deficits and declines* (pp. 147–167). Hillsdale, NJ: Lawrence Erlbaum Associates.

Craik, F. I. M., & Jennings, J. M. (1992). Human memory. In F. I. M. Craik & T. A. Salthouse (Eds.), *The handbook of aging and cognition* (pp. 51–110). Hillsdale, NJ: Lawrence Erlbaum Associates.

Cremer, R., Snel, J., & Brouwer, W. H. (1990). Age-related differences in timing of position and velocity identification. *Accident Analysis & Prevention, 22*, 467–474.

Dixon, R. A., & Bäckman, L. (1995). Concepts of compensation: Integrated, differentiated, and janus-faced. In R. A. Dixon & L. Bäckman (Eds.), *Compensating for psychological deficits and declines* (pp. 3–19). Hillsdale, NJ: Lawrence Erlbaum Associates.

Gonda, J. (1982). Transportation, perceived control, and well-being in the elderly. *Specialized Transportation Planning and Practice, 1,* 61–72.

Hakamies-Blomqvist, L. (1993). Compensation in older drivers reflected in their fatal accidents. *Accident Analysis and Prevention, 26*(1), 107–112.

Hakamies-Blomqvist, L., & Wahlström, B. (1998). Why do older drivers give up driving? *Accident Analysis and Prevention, 30*(3), 305–312.

Jansen, E. (2001). Ältere Menschen im künftigen Sicherheitssystem Straße/Fahrzeug/ Mensch [Elderly people in a future traffic system]. *Schriftenreihe der Bundesanstalt für Straßenwesen (BASt): Mensch und Sicherheit (Heft M 134)*. Bremerhaven: Wirtschaftsverlag NW.

Klein, R. (1991). Age-related eye-disease, visual impairment, and driving in the elderly. *Human Factors, 33,* 521–526.

Mäder, H. (1999). *Fahrradunfälle von Senioren im Jahr 1998* [Bicycle accidents of senior road users in 1998]. Unveröffentlichter Bericht der Bundesanstalt für Straßenwesen [Unpublished report of the German Federal Highway Research Institute].

Marsiske, M., Lang, F. B., Baltes, P. B., & Baltes, M. M. (1995). Selective optimization with compensation: Life-span perspectives on successful human development. In R. A. Dixon & L. Bäckman (Eds.), *Compensating for psychological deficits and declines: Managing losses and promoting gains* (pp. 35–79). Mahwah, NJ: Lawrence Erlbaum Associates.

McDowd, J. M., & Birren, J. E. (1990). Aging and attentional processes. In J. E. Birren & K. W. Schaie (Eds.), *The handbook of the psychology of aging* (3rd ed., pp. 222–233). San Diego, CA: Academic Press.

Rowe, R. W. (1996). Truly, you're as young as you feel. Interview in the *International Herald Tribune*, February 29.

Rudinger, G., & Holte, H. (1996). Subjektive Risikobewertung junger Fahrer [Subjective risk evaluation of younger car drivers]. In BASt (Ed.), *Junge Fahrer und Fahrerinnen* [Young drivers] (pp. 90–95). Referate der Ersten Interdisziplinären Fachkonferenz vom 12. bis 14. Dezember 1994 in Köln [Lectures of the first interdisciplinary conference in Cologne, 12–14 December 1994]. Bericht der Bundesanstalt für Straßenwesen. Mensch und Sicherheit. [Report of the German Federal Highway Research Institute: Man and security]. Heft M 52. Bremerhaven, Bergisch Gladbach, Germany: Wirtschaftsverlag NW.

Rudinger, G., & Thomae, H. (1990). The Bonn Longitudinal Study of Aging: Coping, life adjustment, and life satisfaction. In P. B. Baltes & M. M. Baltes (Eds.), *Successful aging: Perspectives from behavioral science* (pp. 265–295). Cambridge: Cambridge University Press.

Schulze, H. (1991). Risikoverhalten jugendlicher Verkehrsteilnehmer [Risk behavior of adolescent traffic participants]. In E. Lang & K. Arnold (Eds.), *Der Mensch im Straßenverkehr* [Man in road traffic] (pp. 202–213). Stuttgart, Germany: Ferdinant-Enke-Verlag.

CHAPTER 16

Macrointerventions: Roads, Transportation Systems, Traffic Calming, and Vehicle Design

Paul P. Jovanis

Older traveler mobility is directly influenced by a person's ability to utilize transportation services efficiently and safely. The goal of this chapter is to develop an appreciation for the process of transportation engineering design and the implications of several elements of the transportation system for elderly mobility. Beginning with the example of road design, engineering design is reviewed with an emphasis on the tools applied and the need for standardization through guidelines and policies. Several examples are then provided of proposed road design changes to accommodate older drivers and pedestrians better and more safely.

Although the chapter concentrates on road systems and design, 3 additional topics are discussed. Intelligent transportation systems (ITS) are discussed from the context of potential system services and capabilities that offer as yet unrealized benefits for older travelers. Traffic calming is discussed from the perspective of potential problems that it may raise to older traveler mobility. Finally, there is a discussion of likely changes in vehicle design that will benefit older drivers in particular. The chapter concludes with a summary of the most important issues for older traveler mobility.

ROAD DESIGN AND OPERATIONS

The design of road transportation systems has a long history. A basic premise of highway engineering design is that a driver is less likely to make an error and have a crash or other unintended event if the driver can expect to find similar designs and similar traffic control devices in similar traffic and environmental conditions. Engineers thus seek uniformity in design and operations by satisfying this "driver expectancy." Support for uniformity in design and operation is accomplished by using a variety of standards, policies, and guidelines, such as those listed below along with the responsible agency.

Design

- *A Policy on Geometric Design of Streets and Highways*, 1994, American Association of State Highway and Transportation Officials (AASHTO)
- *Intersection Channelization Design Guide*, 1985, National Cooperative Highway Research Program (NCHRP)

Operations

- *Traffic Engineering Handbook*, 1999, Institute of Transportation Engineers (ITE)
- *Manual of Uniform Traffic Control Devices for Streets and Highways*, 2000, Federal Highway Administration (FHWA)
- *Highway Capacity Manual*, 2000, Transportation Research Board (TRB)
- *Roadway Lighting Handbook*, 1984, Federal Highway Administration (FHWA).

It is important to note that many different agencies and committees are responsible for design and operations. For example, the *Manual of Uniform Traffic Control Devices* (Federal Highway Administration, 2000a) is a national guide that is overseen by a committee of practitioners, which vote on all changes to the manual. Any change in signs, signaling, or pavement markings to accommodate older travelers must be approved by the national committee before it is approved by any of the 50 individual states in the United States. This can be a laborious process, even for just a few changes. Wholesale changes in any of these design guides to accommodate older drivers will take years, even decades, for formal adoption.

One positive indicator of change and recognition of older travelers, however, is a series of design guides that have been published to provide substantive guidance concerning the needs of older travelers. The first, the *Older Driver Highway Design Handbook*, was published by the Federal Highway Administration in 1997. This document contains a thorough review of issues pertaining to older drivers and highway design, and it is supplemented with a briefer, supporting handbook (*Highway Design Handbook for Older Drivers and Pedestrians: Recommendations and Guidelines*, 1998), which was updated in 2000 (Federal Highway Administration, 2000b).

The new design guide provides updated, substantive recommendations as well as a process guideline to assist engineers in addressing the special needs of the older traveler. The process guidelines ask the engineer or analyst to divide the road network into *elements* or roadway sections of uniform consistency. For example, travel between 2 rural towns would be analyzed as occurring along a series of elements that would include straight road segments, curves, intersections, and, perhaps, a railroad-highway grade crossing. The analyst would have to complete the following 3-step procedure for each element: problem identification, identification of candidate applications, and implementation decision.

The problem identification phase is illustrated as step 1 in Figure 16.1. The analyst must first assess if there is a crash problem at the site or if there have been any complaints concerning operations. Next, the analyst is asked if there is a problem at the site, based upon engineering judgment. Next, the analyst is asked to consider whether the element lies along a path that is known to be frequented by elderly travelers. Finally, the analyst considers whether the census tract near the element contains a significant percentage of older travelers. This approach, known as a "safety audit," recognizes the need to pool data and information from nontransportation sources, such as health and human services agencies and department of aging. The fact that a safety audit approach is used is highly commendable as it represents the state of the art in site accident analyses.

In the second step, the analyst identifies candidate treatments or applications at the sites, describes differences from current practice, and summarizes benefits of the treatment. In the third and last step, the analyst indicates whether additional approvals are needed, whether there are additional costs, and whether the treatment is necessary.

Note that the process is a piecemeal one, containing many individual analyses of a road section by dividing it into many sections. Further, problems associated with safe elderly mobility are treated as the exception, rather than the rule. Additional justification is needed to support implementation, rather than treating the older driver need as a *basic* user with mobility needs that should be met. Despite these shortcomings, the process is scientifically valid, and it represents a substantial advance over previous efforts made in the United States.

In addition to the process guidelines, the design elements discussed in the guide include intersections, interchanges, road curvature and passing zones, construction/work zones, and highway–rail grade crossings. An example of special design considerations for older travelers at intersections is illustrated in Figure 16.2. This figure represents a plan view of an intersection of a 4-lane divided highway and a 2-lane minor road controlled by a stop sign. Older drivers have been documented to have problems guiding their vehicles safely through such intersections for 2 specific maneuvers: left turns from the major road and left turns from the minor road.

Major road left turns are problematic because of the older driver's difficulty in accurately assessing the position and the closing rate of vehicles approaching in the opposite direction. Measures illustrated in the figure to deal with this problem include the following:

1. Large signs, lettering, and high levels of retroreflectivity on signs to increase their conspicuity at night
2. A raised median and high-contrast raised pavement markings to alert the older driver as to their position on the roadway and within the lane (to facilitate the positioning of the vehicle in the center of the left turn lane, improving the driver's sight distance along the opposing vehicle approach)
3. Designing the left turn lanes to be "offset"—located so that the opposing left turn lanes are not directly in front of each other, but positioned to the right several feet as facing the lane. This facilitates left-turning driver in seeing around the opposing left-turning vehicle (when it is there), providing a much clearer and unobstructed view of opposing traffic. While this improvement benefits all drivers, research (Staplin, Harkey, Lococo, & Tarawneh, 1997) has shown that older drivers will benefit differentially from this engineering improvement.

Another example in the area of traffic-control devices is illustrated in Figure 16.3. This figure illustrates a recommended alternative for addressing the problem of older drivers being improperly positioned (wrong lane) sufficiently in advance of major exits from freeways. The recommended sign seeks to address older drivers' problems in the ability to localize most rel-

Implementation Worksheet for *Highway Design Handbook for Older Drivers and Pedestrians*

Project Title/ID: _____   Person Completing Worksheet: _____   Date: _____

Step 1: Problem Identification

Q1. Is there a demonstrated crash problem with older drivers or pedestrians, or has any aspect of design or operations at the project location been associated with complaints to local, municipal, or county-level officials from older road users?

| NO ___ |
| YES ___ |

Source(s):   Date of Contact   Source(s):   Date of Contact:

_____   _____   _____   _____

Q2. Are you aware of potential safety problem at this location, either through personal observation or agency documentation, applying you own engineering judgment?

| NO ___ |
| YES ___ |

Source(s):   Date of Contact   Source(s):   Date of Contact:

_____   _____   _____   _____

Q3. Is this project located on a direct link to a travel origin or destination for which, in the judgment of local planning/zoning authorities or other local officials, older persons constitute a significant proportion of current users?

| NO ___ |
| YES ___ |

Source(s):   Date of Contact   Source(s):   Date of Contact:

_____   _____   _____   _____

Q4. Is the project located in a census tract or zip code designation which has experienced an increase in the proportion of (non-institutionalized) residents aged 65 and older, for the most recent period in which the population was sampled?

| NO ___ |
| YES ___ |

Source(s):   Date of Contact   Source(s):   Date of Contact:

_____   _____   _____   _____

Step 2: Identification of Candidate Handbook Applications

Identify design elements for which a recommendation exists in the *Handbook* and the applicable recommendations. Then, (a) describe differences between the recommendation and standard practice, and (b) list benefits expected to result from implementing the *Handbook*.

Design Elements Addressed by *Handbook* Recommendations	Applicable *Handbook* Recommendations	Differs from Existing State or Local Practice?		If YES	
		NO	YES	Explain Difference	Identify Expected Benefits

Step 3: Implementation Decision

List each recommendation identified as a candidate for implementation. Document wh ether additional approval is needed, and whether increased costs or other special considerations may impact implementation. Then decide whether it is or is not necessary to implement each candidate. Check YES or NO, and add your initials to record your judgment. Add supplemental comments as deemed appropriate.

Candidate Handbook Recommendation	Implementation Considerations			Necessary to Implement?
	Added Costs?	Added Approvals?	Other	
				NO _____ Initials____________ YES _____ Comments:
				NO _____ Initials____________ YES _____ Comments:

FIGURE 16.1. Implementation worksheets for *Highway Design Handbook for Older Drivers and Pedestrians*.

Source: Federal Highway Administration, 2000b.

The diagram presented below illustrates the countermeasures as described
above in *Handbook* Recommendations E(4a)–(4f).

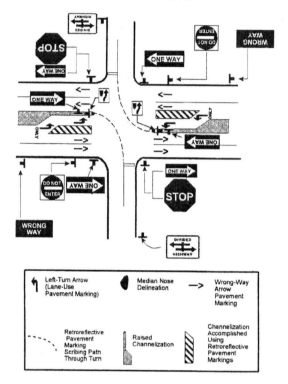

Recommended signing and delineation treatments for intersections with
medians 9-m (30-ft) wide or wider, and medians with channelized left-
turn lanes, to reduce the potential for wrong-way movements for drivers
turning left from the minor roadway.

**FIGURE 16.2.   Example of special design considerations for older
travelers at intersections.**
Source: Federal Highway Administration, 2000b, p. 22.

evant stimuli, the ability to switch rapidly between multiple targets, reductions in working memory, and reductions in processing speed. The objective
is to allow more time for the older driver to identify the proper lane
and safely maneuver the vehicle into that lane with increased situational
awareness.

Important progress has also been made in initiating an awareness of user

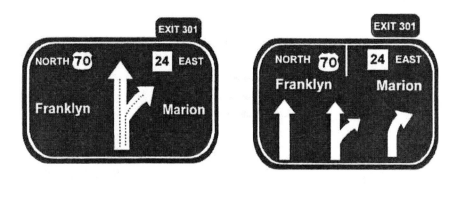

Existing *MUTCD* format   Recommended Alternative

FIGURE 16.3. Example regarding traffic-control devices.
Note: MUTCD means *Manual of Uniform Traffic Control Devices.*

limitations within the procedures contained in the U.S. *Highway Capacity Manual*, the guide for traffic engineers and, increasingly, planners, in their assessment of transportation system performance [Transportation Research Board (TRB), 2000]. Researchers at Penn State University have led an effort to consider the *perceptions* of users in the assessment of the quality of service provided by transportation facilities (Pecheux, Pietrucha, & Jovanis, 2001).

Why is this important to older travelers? The answer is that this line of research could lead to a fuller recognition by engineers of the benefits that the transportation system provides to older travelers. The *Highway Capacity Manual*, in many cases, is the standard used by analysts; therefore, it directly influences the infrastructure in areas such as the number of lanes, traffic signal timing, and freeway improvements at ramps and interchanges. Consideration of user perceptions of service quality thus provides an opportunity to design a traffic system matched to the perceptions of older travelers.

The TRB committee's midyear meeting in July 2001 featured, for the first time, a session on user perception of transportation system performance. While there is much research yet to be conducted in this area, there is significant interest by both researchers and practitioners. As an element of future research, it is important for this fundamental engineering tool to continue to recognize the needs of the user, including the older traveler.

INTELLIGENT TRANSPORTATION SYSTEMS

Intelligent transportation systems (ITS) are electronic systems that seek to improve the efficiency and safety of transportation systems by enhancing operator control, improving traffic detection and control, and providing information to influence traveler decisions. One of the most commonly used and deployed systems are advanced traveler information systems (ATIS), which seek to provide the traveler with the location, type, and severity of congestion or incidents. There have been several thoughtful discussions of the potential risks posed by ITS systems that are improperly designed for elderly drivers and travelers (e.g., Hanowski & Dingus, 2000; Henderson & Suen, 2000). Much of the discussion concerning traveler information has focused on in-vehicle route guidance and the challenges of designing an effective and safe driver interface.

Discussions about crash risk miss the point concerning an opportunity for traveler information systems to *enhance* safety through more effective routing of elderly drivers. With intelligent or adaptive route guidance, routes that avoid or eliminate high-risk situations can be selected for the elderly (e.g., left turns against opposing flow, the need for gap acceptance maneuvers, high-speed facilities). In addition to providing the quickest route, the system could generate one or more "safe" routes that can be based on drivers' preferences (according to their own self-stated criteria) or preferred routes gleaned from actual choices. The system could also include recommendations for avoiding late night driving (i.e., advising on time of day of travel) and specific highways. By providing the information before the trip, the challenges of multitasking while driving can be avoided.

Detailed studies of route choice behavior have revealed a range of motivations and factors influencing route choice other than minimizing time or distance, including selection of safe routes. These more qualitative aspects of route choice were explored in a series of surveys made in Southern California (Abdel-Aty, Kitamura, & Jovanis 1995a, 1995b; Abdel-Aty, Kitamura, Jovanis, Reddy, & Vaughn, 1995). One of the principal findings of the studies was the importance of travel time variability in route choice: many travelers sought to avoid routes with uncertain, or highly variable, travel times. In fact, a stated preference experiment revealed that travelers would trade one minute of time saved for each minute in travel time variability avoided. These experiments and surveys provide a basis to explore and develop services that are specifically targeted to the older driver, and aimed at enhancing safety through choice of specific routes, because they reveal that traveler route choice is complex, involving many factors other than minimizing time.

There is recent additional evidence of the importance of reliable trip timing. A recent study conducted in Washington, D.C., identified reliability and trip timing benefits of ATIS (Wunderlich, Hardy, Larkin, & Shah, 2001). The studies used a "simulated yoked driver" approach to assess benefits of following traveler information advice under uncertain travel times. Typical field assessments find that travelers *perceive* time savings, but attempts to measure them in the field have found few savings. These new studies indicate that *time management* benefits are substantially greater than pure time savings. Travelers with information are better able to cope with uncertainty and can predict their arrival at a destination more precisely. This has particular relevance for older drivers who can use such information to plan and execute trips better for health care or other means of basic support, without substantial schedule buffering (e.g., arriving 15 minutes early so you are not 10 minutes late).

There have also been some attempts, through advanced public transit systems (APTS), to improve the performance of flexible route transit, which serves the elderly in many urban and rural markets. Rather than focus on improved customer service, however, the tests have often sought to use technology to manage, and occasionally punish, drivers. New technologies are emerging for precision docking of buses; these are likely to focus on convenience benefits to users.

In summary, advanced traveler information systems offer substantial potential advantages to elderly travelers, but much of the potential is unrealized. Systems could identify safer routes by specifically avoiding routings that take older drivers through high-risk locations for them.

TRAFFIC CALMING

European and Asian engineers are significantly more advanced in the use of traffic-calming techniques than their U.S. counterparts. In most cases, the calming measures are undertaken to reduce speed of auto traffic as well as to provide reduced access to city and town centers through road restrictions and parking management. The aim is to increase use of public transit, bikes, and walking as modes of transportation.

Of these alternative modes, public transit is the most viable option for large numbers of older travelers, but traffic calming creates potential problems for this group of users. Traffic calming may increase the walking distance between auto parking and transit service, as part of a plan to reduce auto dependence by creating disincentives for auto use. This creates increased difficulty for an older traveler undertaking a linked trip in which the auto is used to access longer distance transit travel. Further, movement of parking to greater distances from town centers can reduce the access of older pedestrians to these destinations, again because of the parking policies. While handicapped spaces are provided, they are typically few in number and are not intended to serve a large population of travelers. In the United States, traffic calming would be instituted as part of an open transportation planning process in which older travelers may be heard. While any implementation would involve tradeoffs in design (e.g., number of parking spaces and their location), it seems imperative that community support groups and individual elderly people themselves be alert for potential implementation of calming plans.

The conclusion is, therefore, that traffic calming should be carefully examined, as it may not deliver the benefits intended for older travelers.

VEHICLE DESIGN

A number of vehicle-based technologies are beginning to be deployed which may improve auto traveler safety by reducing the risk of an accident involvement and reducing the severity of crash outcomes. Crash reductions are sought through vehicle-based adaptive cruise control and collision-avoidance systems. These systems use a variety of sensors and associated software to sense the presence of vehicles in the proximity of the instrumented vehicle (straight ahead if adaptive cruise control or in several directions if collision avoidance). The adaptive cruise control system will then automatically adjust the speed of the instrumented vehicle through electronic downshifting of the transmission, electronic application of brakes, or both. Collision avoidance will include some type of warning to the driver of an impending collision, although the modalities of the most effective warnings are still under development.

Focus group–based explorations of preferences for collision-avoidance system warning messages showed strong differences between older and younger drivers (Jovanis, Campbell, Klaver, & Chen, 1997). Older drivers preferred text messages that focused on describing the action that they should take to avoid the crash, while younger drivers preferred icons and other diagrammatic information that described the nature of the impending crash, but were not prescriptive of the type of action to be taken. The conclusion is that both collision-avoidance and adaptive cruise control systems, while not targeted at older drivers, may need a level of customization to meet older driver needs and preferences in order to be effective.

Auto manufacturers are also about to deploy a series of adaptive and advanced air bags which will withstand side collisions and offer additional support for the head and neck during a crash. Along with "smart" air bags, which have variable deployment speeds based on inputs from seat-based and speed sensors, these systems offer the promise of reduced injury severity, given a crash. There is no question that these enhanced systems offer the potential to reduce the severity of occupant injury, particularly for the more susceptible older drivers and passengers.

SUMMARY

In summary, the implementation of new road design guidelines and standards are complex and likely to take several years. While significant research has been conducted concerning older driver issues, the deployment of new design and operational practices are made difficult by the multitude of committees and institutions involved in the decision making. Design change implementation is thus likely to be fragmented, and progress is likely to be slow. Unfortunately, design for older drivers continues to be viewed by many as the exception rather than the norm. As a consequence, older drivers are likely to find themselves unable to use the road design features and traffic control devices with full effectiveness. The consequences are, at a minimum, low-quality, stressful travel and possibly travel with a higher risk of a collision, with requisite implications for morbidity and mortality. Recent research by the team at Penn State has resulted in a new awareness of the importance of user perception of transportation system performance which offers the potential to directly address the capabilities and limitations of older travelers in traffic operational decisions.

ITS traveler information systems will help travelers deal better with travel uncertainty. This benefit is generally overlooked, particularly so for older travelers. Customized guidance systems, which could recognize the driving preferences of the elderly, have not yet been deployed, limiting their mobility and their ability to manage their personal time and travel effectively. While having indirect influences on safety, there are strong implications for an older traveler's ability to deal with schedule uncertainties, an issue of almost daily life for those with frequent visits to medical and other service facilities.

Traffic calming may be helpful to achieve environmental goals, but access to transit and economic activities may be restricted for older travelers with walking limitations and thus may not support older traveler needs. There is a possibility for a reduction, rather than an increase, in mobility with narrowly prescribed traffic calming. Evolving vehicle technologies offer the potential to reduce injury, given a crash. Systems are more likely to be accepted if they include features that are targeted to older driver preferences and recognize their physical and cognitive limitations. There is evidence that the automotive industry is responding to this challenge.

Older drivers are likely to face continued mobility challenges. While considerable progress has been made in road design standards, intelligent transportation system services, traffic-calming measures, and vehicle design, a great deal more is possible. Hopefully, progress will accelerate in learning about the travel needs of older drivers and in developing policies that encourage implementation of actions to support mobility and enhance safety.

REFERENCES

Abdel-Aty, M. A., Kitamura, R., & Jovanis, P. P. (1995a). Investigating the effect of travel time variability on route choice using repeated-measurement state preference data. In Transportation Research Board (Ed.), *Transportation Research Record 1493* (pp. 39–45). Washington, DC: Transportation Research Board.

Abdel-Aty, M. A., Kitamura, R., & Jovanis, P. P. (1995b). Exploring route choice behavior using GIS-based alternative routes and hypothetical travel time information input. In Transportation Research Board (Ed.), *Transportation Research Record 1493* (pp. 74–80). Washington, DC: Transportation Research Board.

Abdel-Aty, M. A., Kitamura, R., Jovanis, P. P., Reddy, P. D., & Vaughn, K. M. (1995). A new approach to route choice data collection: Multi-phase, CATI panel surveys using a geographical information system database. In Transportation Research Board (Ed.), *Transportation Research Record 1493* (pp. 159–169). Washington, DC: Transportation Research Board.

American Association of State Highway and Transportation Officials (AASHTO). (1994). *A policy on geometric design of highways and streets.* Washington, DC: AASHTO.

Federal Highway Administration. (2000a). *Manual of uniform traffic control devices for streets and highways.* Washington, DC: Federal Highway Administration.

Federal Highway Administration. (2000b). *Highway design handbook for older drivers and pedestrians: Recommendations and guidelines.* FHWA-RD-01-051. Washington, DC: Federal Highway Administration.

Hanowski, R. J., & Dingus, T. A. (2000). Will intelligent transportation systems improve older driver mobility? In K. W. Schaie & M. Pietrucha (Eds.), *Mobility and transportation in the elderly* (pp. 279–298). New York: Springer.

Henderson, S., & Suen, S. L. (2000). ITS: A two-edged sword for older drivers? *Proceedings of Transportation Research Board Annual Meeting, January 9–13, 2000* [CD-ROM]. Washington, DC: Transportation Research Board.

Jovanis, P. P., Campbell, J., Klaver, K., & Chen, W. H. (1997). Driver preferences for visual and auditory collision warning alerts. *Proceedings of the Fourth ITS International Congress, Berlin, October 1997* [CD-ROM]. Washington, DC: U.S. Department of Transportation.

Pecheux, K., Pietrucha, M., & Jovanis, P. P. (2001). User perception of level of service at signalized intersections. *Proceedings of the Transportation Research Board Annual Meeting, Washington, D.C., 2001,* [CD-ROM].

Staplin, L., Harkey, D., Lococo, K., & Tarawneh, M. (1997). *Intersection geometric design and operational guide for older drivers and pedestrians, Vol. 1: Final report.* FHWA-RD-96-132. Washington, DC: Federal Highway Administration.

Transportation Research Board (TRB). (2000). *Highway capacity manual.* TRB special report 209. Washington, DC: Transportation Research Board.

Wunderlich, K. E., Hardy, M. H., Larkin, J. J., & Shah, V. P. (2001). *On-time reliability impacts of advanced traveler information services (ATIS): Washington, D.C. Case Study.* McLean, VA: Mitretek Systems.

CHAPTER 17

Microinterventions: Assistive Devices, Telematics, and Person-Environment Interactions

Berthold Färber

THE VISION

The ultimate vision of researchers and automobile engineers is a car that drives automatically, with multisensor environment detection using cameras, and infrared and radar sensors. An information processing unit will compare the preprocessed data with a knowledge base. Actuators will perform steering (lateral control), as well as acceleration and braking (longitudinal control). The driver's only task will be to program the destination and to press the start button. These cars could be ideal transportation means for older drivers, solving most of their perception and action problems. Furthermore, many of the technical devices to enhance the mobility of the older driver, explained below, would become superfluous. It is a long way, however, from research laboratories to everyday traffic. Although the first prototypes have been able to achieve speeds of 110 kilometers per hour (Dickmanns, 2000), mass production is not yet in sight.

THE CURRENT SITUATION

If one asks leading automobile companies and engineers the question, "What are you doing specifically for older drivers?," the standard answer seems to be, "Our products are so user friendly that older persons are able to use them without any problems. We don't feel that it's necessary to design specific cars or devices for older people." It is readily admitted that sports cars in particular are not the perfect transportation means for an elderly user group because of the seat position, driving comfort, and problems in getting into and out of the car. However, most manufacturers carry models other than sports cars.

If one asks marketing people from the automobile industry the same question and, if they answer honestly, they will admit that devices specifically designed for older people are hard to sell. The terms "older" and "handicapped" often evoke negative associations and are unattractive from a marketing point of view. The dilemma for car manufacturers is that they are aware of the specific needs of mature drivers, but their product must avoid the image of being a "grandparent's car." As a consequence, specific designs for older drivers are quite rare.

Given the long and unclear time period for the production of automatic driving cars and the dearth of cars specifically designed for older drivers, one must consider which assistive devices—probably not specifically designed for this user group—currently exist or will be available in the near future.

Relatively simple assistive devices, such as physical entry aids (see Figure 17.1), can be integrated without problem in each and every car. In addition to these add-on systems, a variety of electronic devices are available or will be available in the coming years. These systems differ in at least 2 aspects from simple add-on systems: they are not specifically designed for older people, and they must be integrated into the car and the car-driver interface. An example of such a system, an emergency system, can be seen in Figure 17.2. If a driver experiences a heart attack, or any other problem, he or she can push a button, and the system automatically reports the location of the car and calls for rescue personnel. Even if older drivers never activate the system, it provides them with a feeling of safety.

Electronic driver-assistance systems are partly onboard systems, which means that they do not require any infrastructure; however, they may also need a connection to a provider or to satellites. The first category is generally defined as driver-assistance systems, the second as telematic systems, but this terminology is not universally accepted.

Although many systems are not specifically designed for older people, I wish to analyze the existing systems or those that will soon become available with respect to their presumed effect for an elderly user group. The analysis is provided with respect to the 3 widely accepted levels of car operation:

FIGURE 17.1. Physical entry aid distributed by SENIO.
Note: *drehbar* means turnable.

FIGURE 17.2. Add-on emergency system.

the handling and control level, the maneuvering level, and the planning and navigation level (Rasmussen, 1986).

DRIVER-ASSISTANCE SYSTEMS AT THE CONTROL LEVEL OF DRIVING

The control level of car operation covers all actions for longitudinal and lateral control (i.e., steering, braking, accelerating, and gear changing). The standard configurations for most modern European cars include several assistance systems to improve the driver's performance at this level of driving. An Anti-Block System (ABS) prevents the blocking of the wheels under difficult surface conditions, thus guaranteeing the steerability of the car. Another helpful electronic device developed in recent years came about in response to the "elk test," a specific driving maneuver, first performed by a Swedish motor journalist to test the driving stability of the A-Mercedes. The test presumes that an elk is crossing the road, and the driver reacts with a specific steering maneuver to avoid hitting the animal. The test with the A-Mercedes resulted in a crash, and car manufacturers and suppliers made every effort to develop and produce an electronic device that guarantees the stability of the car under these difficult driving conditions. Thanks to the elk test, the Electronic Stability Program (ESP) was developed, and it is today available in many European cars as a standard feature, or at least as an affordable extra. Finally, Electronic Traction Control (ETC) prevents the slipping of the wheels on slippery roads.

Driving through a curve is a combination of an open-loop and a closed-loop behavior. In the open-loop part, the driver chooses the principal steering angle, while in the closed-loop part, he or she fine-tunes the procedure by compensating and correcting steering wheel movements. Lane maintenance assistants—still under development—will assist the driver with closed-loop steering behavior. The driver needs only initiate the curve-driving maneuver; the rest is done by an automated system. The presumed gain of such an assistance system is to relieve the driver from a permanent monitoring and controlling task requiring extensive visual and cognitive resources.

There is an ongoing discussion among traffic safety experts about the positive effects of the above systems with respect to risk compensation. Risk homeostasis theory, formulated by Wilde (1982), states that progress in safety caused by technological development (like ABS or ESP) is compensated for by increased risky behavior of the drivers. One group observed

taxi drivers and found support for this theory for the ABS system (Aschenbrenner, Bichl, & Wurm, 1988). Unfortunately, to date no study has concentrated specifically on older drivers. However, it can be hypothesized that
older drivers are less likely to compensate for the safety gain of assistance
systems at the control level than younger or middle-aged persons. If this is
true, then all these systems will ease the driving task for older drivers, giving
them greater capacity for maneuvering and planning tasks and enhancing
their mobility and safety.

ASSISTANCE SYSTEMS AT THE MANEUVERING LEVEL OF DRIVING

The maneuvering level comprises all actions in which a driver needs to
coordinate his or her behavior with that of other traffic participants. Traffic
can be regarded as a complex and interrelated system. It is known from
system dynamics that the stability of a system is directly related to the
dynamics and the variability of the parameters involved; in other words,
younger drivers often complain about older ones because "they drive slowly
and hesitantly." From the older driver's point of view, the younger ones drive
too fast and sometimes too aggressively. Is it possible, then, that assistance
systems at the maneuvering level can help harmonize driving behavior to
improve safety? Systems that are now on the market or that will soon be
available include braking assistants, autonomous cruise control, parking assistants, and enhanced-vision systems.

Braking Assistants

Older drivers have increased reaction times. They compensate for this deficit
by adopting a more defensive driving style, by maintaining greater distances
from leading vehicles, and by driving at slower speeds. However, traffic as
a complex system with a great diversity of participants (children, pedestrians,
young and competitive drivers, and so on) offers many unforeseen situations
as implicit parameters. Hence, defensive driving can mitigate problems but
will not eliminate them.

   However, the principal problem of older persons as traffic participants is
not increased reaction time, but rather, increased decision time. Decision
time describes the interval from the detection of an obstacle until the braking

maneuver attains maximal deceleration. Older and defensive drivers tend to hesitate too long before they adapt their braking behavior. They do not use the maximal deceleration power of their cars. Braking assistants measure the initial speed of brake pedal movement and calculate the intention of the driver from this parameter. If the driver starts the braking maneuver quickly because an unforeseen danger appears, the brake assistant decelerates with maximal power. To be clear, a brake assistant is not an automatic brake designed to initiate the braking maneuver to prevent an accident. The brake assistant is activated only by the driver and is designed to perform only the closed-loop part of the braking maneuver—it reduces decision and brake adaptation intervals.

Although we do not have a great deal of information about the long-term effects of braking assistants or precise reports from older persons who use braking assistants, it is reasonable to suppose that such systems will reduce visual and mental workload and will help older drivers.

Autonomous Cruise Control

Autonomous cruise control (ACC) systems regulate the desired speed as well as the distance to leading vehicles. The aim of these systems is to assist the driver with respect to the longitudinal maneuvering task. It is important to indicate that ACC is not a collision-avoidance device. Due to technical and legal constraints, ACC systems are limited by several restrictions: they cannot react to stationary objects, they cannot perform a hazardous braking maneuver, and they do not work at a speed of less than 5 kilometers per hour. As a consequence, the driver must monitor the situation and must be prepared to take over responsibility and vehicle control in hazardous and unforeseen driving situations. The gain in comparison to the conventional cruise control systems is mainly in driver comfort. Because the system includes both speed and distance regulation, it can cope better with high-traffic density and varying speeds of other cars. People who use the system for smooth and relaxed driving report a relief of stress and workload.

A further improvement of the ACC will be the "stop-and-go" ACC. This system will be able to accelerate from a dead stop to a restricted speed, decelerate to a dead stop, and react to nonmoving objects. Stop-and-go traffic is a stressful, high-load situation for everyone, irrespective of age. If older persons are to participate in everyday traffic to preserve full mobility, they will frequently experience stop-and-go situations. With a stop-and-go assistant, these situations could be converted from a high-stress to an almost recreational situation.

Parking Assistants

One of the dilemmas involved in maintaining the mobility of the elderly is the choice between taking public transport, combined with park-and-ride facilities, or using city parking lots. Public transport is rarely adapted to the needs of older persons. Centrally located parking facilities—especially in Europe—are extremely narrow, and many people are anxious when using them. Parking assistants with acoustical or optical information have clear benefits for older drivers with physical mobility problems. With parking assistants, they can use a personal means of transportation and master even difficult parking and maneuvering situations.

Vision-Enhancement Systems

Reduced vision at night is one of the most serious problems for older drivers. An important aspect is increased glare sensibility, caused by age-related changes in the lens of the human eye, as well as increased adaptation time. Many attempts have been made to improve night vision: polarized light, ultraviolet light, infrared light, and curve light. Simple solutions for curve light, which couple the steering wheel with the headlights (realized by Citroën in the 1970s), proved to be unsatisfactory. The driver had no preview— the curve was illuminated only when the driver turned the steering wheel, when he or she was already in the curve. Modern curve lights use a global positioning system (GPS), digital maps, and the driving speed to illuminate the curve in a predictive manner (see Figure 17.3).

ASSISTANCE SYSTEMS AT THE NAVIGATION LEVEL OF DRIVING

With increasing age, people avoid driving in new and unknown areas. Their behavior is triggered by their own observation that orientation in unfamiliar areas requires greater attention, which means resource use which competes with other requirements, for example, for the maneuvering task. Persons

FIGURE 17.3.   Intelligent curve light.
Source: BMW press photo.

driving in unknown or unfamiliar areas create problems for traffic safety (see Popp, 1988). Engels and Dellen (1989) coined the expression "foreigners' risk" to describe the fact that strangers are more often involved in accidents than local citizens given the same risk exposure time. Only older persons, however, seem to be aware of this problem. While younger and middle-aged drivers ignore the higher risk, older drivers realize it and restrict themselves to well-known surroundings. Navigation systems now offered in each car category could relieve orientation problems and thus be helpful in increasing the mobility of older persons.

From the above, the reader might gain the impression that, even if we are still far away from our vision of autonomous driving, we are indeed on the way to a golden future of mobility of older persons. But are we really? To be honest, the answer is more negative than positive. What then are the problems? The inherent problems of driver-assistance systems can be divided into 3 groups: divided attention, the user interface (displays and controls), and the complexity of menus.

Divided Attention

Many studies demonstrate the problems of older persons in dividing their attention between several tasks. However, Somberg and Salthouse (1982) argue that older people are not principally weaker in their ability to divide their attention. Instead, reduced information-processing speed is responsible for the age effects observed in divided-attention tasks. If one would take this fact into account and create experimental tasks requiring lower information-processing speed, the effect would disappear. Even if this argument is valid, it is irrelevant for everyday traffic. The information flow and thus the required information-processing speed is determined largely by others than the driver himself.

The question is then: do assistive devices and telematic systems overload older drivers in their ability to divide their attention between several tasks? We investigated this question some time ago with respect to auditory information systems. In principle, auditory information systems can relieve a driver's visual load. As shown in Table 17.1, however, listening to voice warnings also reduces the detection of peripheral signals. In other words, due to a limited information-processing capacity, the driver's angle of vision is reduced when listening to a voice warning.

The data show no significant increase in reaction time for the different age groups (i.e., no significant reduction in the ability to divide attention). Of course, the oldest age group included in the study was only 50- to 64-years old. However, another interesting and well-known finding from aging research can be observed in the data: an increasing variance within the group of older drivers. Some of the subjects are perfectly able to divide their attention between car driving and voice warnings; others are not.

The simple answer to the question of the effect of assistive devices for older drivers is therefore as follows: Assistive devices that directly influence

TABLE 17.1 Reaction Times (ms) on Peripheral Signals with and Without Speech Information

Condition	Age	18–29	30–49	50–64
With speech information	$\bar{x}$	1,604	1,621	1,654
	s	265	266	359
Without speech information	$\bar{x}$	1,458	1,397	1,480
	s	175	203	170

the automobile, needing no monitoring or input, and therefore no divided attention between traffic and in-car systems, enhance the mobility of older drivers. Typical examples of such devices are the "3-letter systems" (ABS, ESP, ETC, and so on). These systems—mostly acting at the control level of driving—are beneficial for older individuals as well as for young and inexperienced drivers. The specific gain for older drivers is, besides the enhancement of objective safety, the increase of subjective safety, which can be assumed to have a positive influence on mobility.

Systems improving the functionality of already existing aids, such as improved headlights, also provide a gain in the safety and mobility of older drivers. However, systems offering additional information—mostly visual displays or monitors—or systems requiring permanent monitoring by the driver, cause problems because they require divided attention.

User Interface

Automobile engineers have an insoluble dilemma between, on one hand, the restricted space available in the interior of the car and, on the other hand, the increasing number of systems required by displays and controls. A viable compromise necessitates either the minimization of controls and displays or the creation of multifunctional display and control units. Given that the ability for adaptation and accommodation declines as a function of age, smaller controls and ever smaller and smaller icons on displays are clearly suboptimal. Thus, several other attempts have been undertaken to optimize user interface in cars. Even if the rationale for these attempts was not the older driver, one can analyze to what extent older drivers profit from new technological or human factors approaches. Technology developed in recent years offers new ways of information presentation. Audio and tactile information presentation, as well as head-up displays, promise the reduction of visual distraction from the road. Speech command systems could enable drivers to interact with their cars in a natural manner.

Auditory warnings such as "your oil pressure is too low" or auditory information for route guidance ("turn left at next intersection," "switch to the right lane," etc.) can of course relieve visual load. The limits of application are twofold. First, warnings that indicate driver error can be embarrassing from the driver's point of view. For example, the warning "your battery power is low" simply calls the driver's attention to a problem with the car, while the message "please release your handbrake" indicates faulty driving behavior. Drivers, irrespective of their age, feel shown up by that kind of warning, especially when they have passengers in the car. The second problem concerns the annoyance that arises from frequent auditory information. Many drivers feel bothered by the permanent audio information of their navigation system when driving through a town. The application area for auditory information is therefore limited. For older drivers, a further limitation exists: the reduced ability to cope with low or negative signal-to-noise ratios. While young and middle-aged persons are able to understand speech information even at a negative signal-to-noise ratio (i.e., the relation between speech loudness and surrounding noise), this ability declines with increasing age. For conventional middle-class cars, the volume of acoustic warning or information had to be quite high in order to be understandable at higher speeds.

Head-up displays (HUDs), first developed for aircrafts, are among the research activities of every car manufacturer, but they still are not available in standard models. What are the reasons for it, and where are potential benefits for older drivers? The theoretical gain for older drivers is obvious. The virtual picture of a head-up display is located about 5 meters in front of the car; that means, no accommodation for reading this information is necessary. Because the accommodation power declines as a function of age, older drivers in particular should profit from HUD technology; however, HUDs encounter 2 kinds of problems: Man-Machine Interface (MMI) problems and technological problems. The main MMI problem is the masking of relevant objects on the road by HUD information. Attempts have been made to solve this problem by employing translucent images. Translucent images, however, have low contrast and poor visibility in bright sunlight. Another MMI problem is the control of the information currently displayed. In conventional displays, the driver decides the instant and kind of information he or she wants by a glance to the dashboard (which, of course, distracts the driver momentarily from traffic). On a HUD, not all information currently available on the dashboard can be shown without masking the road scenery. This presents the engineer with a quandary: what should be presented on the HUD, and how can the display be changed from instant to instant in accordance with the driver's needs? Until now, information on HUDs has been restricted to the speedometer (an instrument of minor relevance) and navigation information.

Besides these MMI problems, severe technological constraints still exist. For the generation of a virtual image, a so-called combiner is necessary. The combiner is integrated in the windshield as a grey or green disk. The driver's view is permanently disrupted at the transition from the combiner to the normal windscreen. Technological solutions like windscreens with changing thickness do not function well in bright sunlight.

In light of these difficulties, the current approach to generate a user-friendly interface in cars is the development of multifunctional displays and controls, where different functions can be displayed and controlled in a single control unit, using a menu structure.

Multifunctional Systems and the Complexity of Menus

A simple experiment highlights the nearly insoluble difficulties for the engineer and designer. Because user manuals often consist of 250 or more pages, most users, irrespective of age, try to learn a system by trial and error. Most users expect the system to be "intuitive"; that is, the system ought to be usable with a minimum of written instruction. The designer must therefore employ different user models and simultaneously combine as many functions as possible in one system with a minimum of controls and maximum display size. Two different approaches are shown in Figures 17.4 and 17.5.

The layout of the multifunctional system in Figure 17.4 uses specific hard

FIGURE 17.4. Multifunctional driver information system—COMAND.

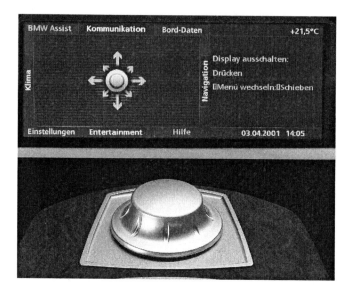

FIGURE 17.5.   Multifunctional driver information system with haptic feedback iDrive.

keys for the main menu selection (telephone, navigation CD, etc.) and a round control knob (down left) for selection within the submenus. The idea behind this design philosophy is fast and direct access to main functions (radio, telephone, etc.) and extensive possibilities within each functional group. Even if the design idea is good in principle, there is a gap between the designer model and the user model for many, especially for older drivers. An example prototypical of the problems and solutions facing us is shown in Figure 17.4.

To turn on the radio from the console displayed in Figure 17.4, the user must push the FM/AM button, not the ON button. The ON button is reserved for the entire system, and the radio is only a subsystem. Consequently, the ON button will activate the radio if the whole system is in the OFF position and if the radio was the last active system used before the whole system was switched off. If the FM/AM button is pushed again, the radio changes the frequency band from FM to AM. If a user has understood the difference between a conventional stand-alone radio and this integrated system, where the radio is only one of many subsystems, he or she will be able to adopt the logic to his or her mental models. Older drivers, however, often report problems with this changed logic and are therefore happy when they succeed in using basic functions. Other problems arise when handling the navigation system. Navigation systems can enhance the mobility of older drivers, but the programming is by no means a trivial task. At current technology levels, larger towns can be selected from a list, but smaller towns and streets need direct alphabetical input obtained by turning and pushing a control knob, a task which demands some degree of dexterity, and which is difficult for many, not only for older persons. The next generation of multifunctional systems (see Figure 17.5) considered this problem and provided differentiated haptic feedback at different levels of input. Even if this technical solution was not specifically designed for older drivers, they will profit from it.

CONCLUSIONS

Technical aids in the automobile, which are currently available or will become available in the next few years, will contribute to the maintenance of mobility of older drivers. Even if these technological developments are not specifically oriented toward older drivers, older drivers will benefit from these innovations. The development should increasingly take into account the following.

1. The real user's needs, especially those of older drivers; in other words, innovations should be user centered rather than driven by technology.
2. Be adaptive with respect to the user interface. Different user groups (the young, technology enthusiasts, the older) require different user interfaces. Since the group of older drivers is a growing and economically powerful group, it should be given recognition by engineers and designers.

REFERENCES

Aschenbrenner, M., Bichl, B., & Wurm, G. (1988). *Einfluss der Risikokompensation auf die Wirkung von Verkehrssicherheitsmaßnahmen am Beispiel ABS* [The influence of risk homeostasis on traffic safety measures exemplified with ABS]. Berichte der Bundesanstalt für Straßenwesen. Schriftenreihe Unfall- und Sicherheitsforschung, Heft 63, Bergisch-Gladbach, Germany.

Dickmanns, E. D. (2000). Vehicles capable of dynamic vision. In *Proceedings of the 15th*

International Joint Conference on Artificial Intelligence (IJCAI-97), Nagoya, Japan (Vol. 2, pp. 1577–1592). San Francisco: Morgan Kaufmann Publishers.

Engels, K., & Dellen, R. G. (1989). Der Einfluss von Suchfahrten auf das Unfallverursachungsrisiko [The influence of disorientation on accident risk]. *Zeitschrift für Verkehrssicherheit, 35*(3), 93–100.

Popp, M. M. (1988). Orientierungsprobleme von Kraftfahrern in fremden Städten: Subjektive Einschätzungen und objektive Beobachtungen [Orientation problems of drivers in foreign cities: Subjective evaluation and objective observations]. In M. Kastner (Ed.), *Fortschritte der Verkehrspsychologie '87* (pp. 385–394). Cologne, Germany: TÜV Rheinland.

Rasmussen, J. (1986). *Information processing and human-machine interaction: An approach to cognitive engineering.* New York: North-Holland.

Somberg, B. L., & Salthouse, T. A. (1982). Divided attention abilities in young and old adults. *Journal of Experimental Psychology: Human Perception and Performance, 8,* 651–663.

Wilde, G. J. S. (1982). Incentive systems for accident-free and violation-free driving in the general population. *Ergonomics, 25*(10), 879–890.

CHAPTER 18

Programmatic Interventions with the Older Driver: A Conceptual Framework

Sherry L. Willis

This chapter focuses on the dilemma facing the older driver in Western society. The concerns are perhaps most acute in North America given the singular dependence on the auto for many aspects of daily living. The private auto remains the primary mode of transportation in the United States, with persons over age 65 making more than 90% of their trips by private vehicle (American Association of Retired Persons [AARP], 1999). Many elderly people in the United States live in suburban areas where automobile transportation is the only choice. In 1983 a little over half of the adults aged 65 and older were licensed drivers; now over three-quarters of this age group are licensed drivers. A recent survey conducted in the United States found that almost three-quarters of people over the age of 75 still drive (AARP, 1997). Alarm has been expressed over emerging demographics suggesting the increasing magnitude of the problem in the near future as the baby boomers in the United States and in Europe approach old age and particularly old-old age (AARP, 1999; Schlag, 1993).

There is widespread recognition that major societal efforts to intervene into this phenomenon are required. Much debate is centered on intervening at the person versus environmental level (Schaie & Pietrucha, 2000). Government agencies are spending considerable effort on developing new, more appropriate tools for assessing older drivers—often with little thought about what interventions are appropriate and feasible with older adults, who are identified as having deficiencies when assessed with these new assessment tools. There is agreement that broad programmatic intervention efforts are needed; however, most current intervention efforts (e.g., share-a-ride programs) are quite small in scale and are designed for specific limited geographical areas (Freund, 2000).

In this chapter, a heuristic known as the lifespan intervention cube is presented to foster consideration of intervention efforts from a broad programmatic perspective. Programmatic interventions are seen as multidimensional such that a number of dimensions must be considered in combination when planning and evaluating intervention efforts. The intervention cube also serves as a schema for examining the scope of current intervention programs and for identifying missing niches within current intervention efforts.

LIFESPAN DRIVING INTERVENTION CUBE

The driving intervention cube is shown in Figure 18.1. It is adapted from a model proposed by Brim and Phillips (1988). The cube indicates that at least 3 broad dimensions must be considered in conceptualizing programmatic interventions: age, target of the intervention, and domain of intervention.

Age at Intervention

The age dimension focuses on the chronological age of the person or group targeted for the intervention. Intervention into driving is regarded as a lifespan phenomenon (Baltes & Danish, 1980). The age of the target may range from adolescence to old age. We have also included the category of nondriver, which is more likely to represent old-old adults but may be a status at any chronological age. Although the focus here is on the older adult driver, a life-span perspective of intervention is required for several reasons. First, driving skills and attitudes are typically developed early in life, and the older driver's performance and judgments represent the accumulation of experiences over the entire adult life course (Evans, 1991). Second, similar services and venues may be relevant for interventions with drivers of different ages; therefore, a life-span perspective is useful.

In many driving interventions, the *level of functioning* of the target person

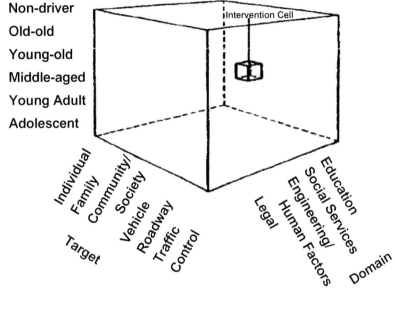

FIGURE 18.1. Intervention cube with intervention cell.

or group may be a more appropriate indicator than chronological age per se (Fozard, 2000; Staplin, 2000). For example, a recent national survey conducted in the United States, which focused on elderly people over age 75, found that 73% of elders over the age of 75 still reported some driving activity: 89% of the males and 64% of the females (AARP, 1997). Given that such a large percentage of old-old continue to drive in the United States, functional age, rather than chronological age, becomes increasingly important to consider, given the wide individual differences in functional competence within the old-old. When such a perspective is taken, this dimension represents functional age with respect to driving. Functional driving age may take into account such factors as cognitive skills related to driving, sensory limitations, mobility, and support systems (Fozard, 2000). Functional limitations, such as hearing and visual impairment, have been found to be important predictors of when older adults curtail their driving (Ball & Owsley, 2000; Schlag, 1993). Functional competence, rather than chronological age, is also important in cases of cognitive impairment. In the United States only 4% of those diagnosed with Alzheimer's disease are believed to continue to drive; however, these drivers are 2 to 4 times more likely to be in an accident than nondemented elders.

Whether age is considered chronologically or functionally depends in part on the domain of the intervention. For example, many legal approaches to intervention are based solely or primarily on chronological age—age of eligibility to drive and age at which specific criteria for renewal of licenses are imposed. Likewise, many social programs have chronological age eligibility criteria for certain services.

Target of Intervention

The second dimension of the cube focuses on the target of the intervention. The target of intervention may be at the individual or group level or at the environmental level. Interventions targeted at the individual or group level extend from the individual, to family and friends, to communities and society (Smyer & Gatz, 1987). In terms of the driving environment, the vehicle, the roadway, and the traffic control system can be targets of intervention (Hanowski & Dingus, 2000).

Interventions Targeted at Individual or Group

Individual-level interventions typically focus on the psychological and physical health and economic or social functioning of the person (Smyer & Gatz, 1987). A key assumption of individual-level interventions is that they are targeted primarily at the person, with little or no attempt to intervene into his or her primary social or physical context. In contrast, intervention at the level of family and friends focuses on the primary social context of the individual. Some community psychologists maintain that a family system perspective is needed for responding to the individual's mobility needs and concerns; focusing solely on the individual outside of the social context may limit the scope or durability of the intervention (Gesten & Jason, 1987). Community- and society-level interventions have as their desired outcomes improved functioning at the community or societal level. Community-level interventions would include van services, share-a-ride, and educational efforts to increase use of mass transportation options (Freund, 2000; Sterns & Sterns, 2000). Societal-level interventions include both citizen-initiated programs (e.g., MADD, or Mothers against Drunk Driving) and government-initiated efforts, such as the public information campaigns on using seat belts. Societal-level intervention may also involve social policy initiatives or the enactment of laws and regulations.

Interventions Targeted at the Driving Environment

The driving environment includes the vehicle, the roadway, and traffic-control systems (Hanowski & Dingus, 2000). Vehicle-related interventions include devices, such as air bags, antilock braking, and obstacle-detection systems (Swigart, 2000). Interventions into the roadway include traffic sign-age and markings, reflective pavement markings, traffic lanes, shoulder rum-ble strips, and left lane markings (Jovanis, 2000). These types of in-terventions are effective for all age groups. They are, however, particularly useful for elderly drivers with sensory deficits or in complex driving situa-tions requiring divided attention or multitasking, skills known to decline with age.

The distinction between targeting the individual driver versus groups of drivers for intervention is also relevant for intervention into the driving en-vironment. Vehicle-related interventions are focused on the individual driver, while roadway and traffic-control system interventions are targeted at large groups of drivers at the community or societal level. A recent, national U.S. study found that at least 30% of older drivers reported feeling uncomfortable with specific physical design aspects of roadways or traffic situations that they routinely encountered (AARP, 1997). Over one-third reported changing their driving patterns to avoid certain roadway or traffic situations. Over 50% of older drivers reported avoiding night driving and avoiding rush-hour traffic.

Domain of Intervention

The third dimension of the driving intervention cube is concerned with the domain or mechanism of the intervention. Five broad intervention ap-proaches are suggested: education, social services, engineering and human factors, the legal system, and economic subsidies.

Education

Educational programs have been one of the most common approaches to driving interventions. Educational interventions range from training on specific cognitive skills related to driving, to educational programs targeted at specific groups such as 55 Alive (AARP, 1999), to broad public service informationals alerting drivers to keep a certain distance from the car in front or to use seat belts.

Education-based driving interventions for older adults are generally provided by 3 sources: by nonprofit organizations or the private sector, by state driver education programs, and through self-assessment materials. Most educational interventions have focused on disseminating information; far fewer programs have focused on actual training of a specific skill or driving ability (Ball & Owsley, 2000). The AARP 55 Alive/Mature Driving Program is completed by 640,000 older drivers annually (AARP, 1999). A major incentive for attending driving renewal programs is that 34 states and the District of Columbia have laws that require insurance premium discounts or reductions in infraction points for older people who take an approved driving course such as 55 Alive (AARP, 1999).

Social Services

A second intervention approach has focused on the provision of services either to all citizens or to targeted groups, particularly groups of a certain age. Many of the traditional social services for the elderly have been targeted at elders making the transition from driving to not driving or to the frail elderly needing special assistance with transportation. These services include van services and share-a-ride systems (Freund, 2000; Sterns & Sterns, 2000). Also included are special incentives (fee reductions) for the use of public transportation and devices such as wheelchair lifts to aid in the use of public transportation.

While these types of interventions have traditionally been provided by community or governmental systems, the business or for-profit sector is becoming increasingly involved. Social or governmental agencies are either contracting with the for-profit sector to provide these services, or business is providing alternatives to the increasingly limited options provided by social services. Similarly, business is also moving into educational interventions related to driving.

Public transit has been recently touted as an option for elderly in the United States (see Burkhardt, 2000, for an alternative position). However, in the United States public transit accounts for only 3% of all trips taken by those aged 65 and over. Over 85% of nondrivers report that they do not use public transportation, citing lack of availability, inconvenience, and physical problems in usage. In a recent survey, 55% of nondrivers reported that a bus stop was farther than they could walk; however, 32% of the nondrivers who could not walk to an existing bus stop said that they would be able to walk if a bus stop were within 5 blocks of their residence (AARP, 1997). The types of social services described above are often more popular and accepted by elders than public transportation for several reasons. First, they are often planned and targeted to the specific needs and preferences of elders in a particular cultural or geographical setting. Second, they often enhance or maintain the personal freedom and control of the elder. For example, van services are provided to medical and shopping facilities of relevance to elders, rather than a transportation route of interest to the general public. The elder maintains control over timing of transportation and with whom he or she shares transit activities.

Engineering and Human Factors

Instead of targeting the individual, most engineering and human factors interventions are focused on the vehicle or roadway (Hanowski & Dingus, 2000). The focus is on altering or intervening into the physical driving environment. These types of interventions are sometimes presented as requiring little initiative or effort on the part of the individual; however, as these interventions become more cognitively complex, the competence of the individual using them is becoming increasingly important (Willis, 2000). For example, navigational systems in cars require that the individual be cognitively able to program and then to interpret the information provided by the instrumentation.

Legal System

The legal system intervenes by regulating all phases of the driving experience—determining who is allowed to drive, when and where one is allowed to drive, one's conduct while driving, and under what conditions one's driving privileges can be restricted or revoked (U.S. Roads-TranSafety, 1997). Two types of legal actions are directly relevant to older drivers: graduated licensing laws and age-based licensing laws (Insurance Institute for Highway Safety, 2001).

1. Graduated licensing laws have been enacted by approximately one-third of the states in the United States. These laws enable the state to identify driving conditions under which a particular driver's privileges might be restricted, and then to issue a graduated license that restricts the person from driving under those unsafe conditions. Holders of graduated licenses can be

licensed to drive only under specific conditions relating, for example, to time of day, destination, or type of vehicle.

2. Age-based licensing laws vary from state to state, but they often involve what is known as accelerated renewals (Insurance Institute for Highway Safety, 2001). These renewals require that above a certain chronological age individuals renew their licenses more frequently than younger drivers. In addition, some states require special testing or personal appearances at the time of license renewal for older drivers. Accelerated renewal and testing may create a disincentive for older drivers to attempt to renew their licenses. At this time, there has been limited research to determine whether age-based requirements result in removing unsafe older drivers or in simply reducing the number of older drivers whether they are safe drivers or not (AARP, 1999; U.S. Roads-TranSafety, 1997).

The particular intervention approach chosen often reflects basic assumptions regarding the primary causes of particular driving problems. These assumptions are often not explicitly stated. For example, many driving education programs, such as 55 Alive, are based on the largely untested assumption that lack of information regarding driving underlies the poor driving performance of elders. The instructional format for these educational interventions, furthermore, is based on the assumption that the needed information can be provided in a lecture format in a group setting. In a related manner, the legal system often appears to be operating under the assumption that punishment (financial, revoking license) of certain driving behaviors (e.g., speeding) is the most effective intervention to modify that behavior.

Economic subsidies are another possible intervention domain, but they are not included in the current cube. Such subsidies are implicit in many of the social and environmental interventions described above. There may be economic programs to provide battery-powered wheelchairs to individuals with physical or financial limitations. Alternatively, economic subsidies may be available for communities to acquire specially fitted vans for use by elders with mobility limitations.

DRIVING INTERVENTIONS: COMBINING DIMENSIONS OF THE CUBE

A particular driving intervention represents a combination of the above 3 dimensions of the cube. An intervention is typically focused on a certain age group. The target of the intervention can range from particular individuals to all drivers in a community, or may target the vehicle or roadway. In addition, a particular intervention involves a certain intervention approach, such as education, provision of services, or a legal action. By examining the portion of the intervention cube enclosed by a particular intervention, we gain a better understanding of the extent to which interventions are programmatic in nature (Brim & Phillips, 1988). Interventions that cover all age groups of drivers versus those targeted at a particular age group can be examined. Considering various parts of the cube indicates how different approaches to interventions intersect with certain targets of intervention.

Cells, Plugs, and Bars

The smallest unit of intervention would be an *intervention cell*, focusing on one specific age group (e.g., old-old), one target of intervention (e.g., individual), and one domain of intervention (e.g., legal). An intervention representing only one cell in the cube is quite narrow or focused on the impact of the intervention. By mapping various existing programs or interventions onto the cube, different shapes appear—plugs, bars, slices, blocks, and single cells. The shapes of the intervention units reflect how broad the age group or target is for the intervention, as well as what mechanism for intervening is most likely to be employed in relation to a particular driving concern or problem (Brim & Phillips, 1988). Different societies or countries may have very different shaped intervention units to deal with the same driving problem or concern. Also the shape of intervention units for the same driving problem may change over time. We will illustrate these issues with a few prototypical types of driving interventions.

Intervention Cell

One example of an intervention cell is age-based licensing laws (see Figure 18.1 above). Some states in the United States have special assessment and renewal procedures for drivers above a certain age. The intervention is focused on a particular, narrow age group (the old). The legal system is the domain or mechanism by which the intervention is administered. The target of the intervention is at the level of the state, indicated in the intervention cube as at the community or societal level. Such a narrowly targeted intervention would be represented by an intervention cell.

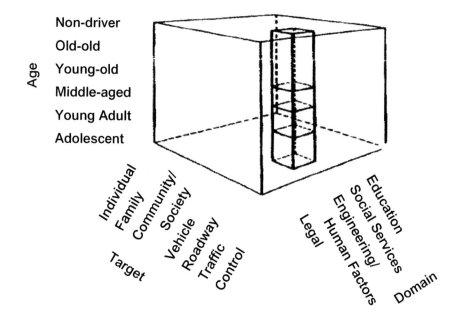

FIGURE 18.2.   Intervention plug.

Intervention Plug

An example of an intervention plug is driving in hazardous weather conditions (see Figure 18.2). Many of the recent interventions dealing with driving during dangerous weather conditions have involved engineering and human factor efforts (domain). These have focused on interventions in the vehicle and on the roadway (target). These intervention efforts typically have not been specifically focused on a particular age group, but have been standard features of vehicles or roadways that affect drivers of all ages. This type of intervention would thus represent a plug, extending across all ages, with the target of intervention being the vehicle or roadway and the intervention approach based on engineering or human factors.

Another example of a plug-shaped intervention is seat belt usage, illustrated by educational interventions targeted at the community or societal level. These include public service educational initiatives to encourage seat belt usage or to keep a certain distance from the proceeding car while driving. These educational interventions, targeted at all age groups, are focused at the community or societal level.

Broken Bars

We can alternatively think of combinations of interventions that are targeted at a special population group, such as the elderly (see Figure 18.3). These represent broken bars within the intervention cube. For example, some interventions focusing on the young-old and old-old involve services at both the individual and community levels. These may include education, social service, and legal approaches to intervention. For example, services focusing on elderly with driving limitations might include driver education, alternative transportation services (social services), and legal restrictions on time of day driving is permitted.

It should be noted that all the interventions and domains discussed above have been shown to be effective with respect to certain needs of the older driver. Interventions are often more effective when multiple intervention domains or targets are included. This multidimensional approach to interventions is best illustrated in the intervention plugs and broken bars discussed above. The multidimensional approach takes into account that the needs of

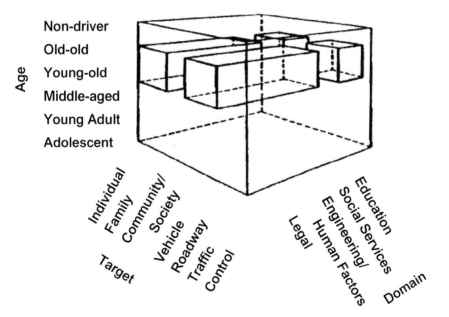

FIGURE 18.3.   Broken bars.

the elderly are often complex, and they are best dealt with by interventions involving both the individual and the setting (physical or social) in which the individual functions. For example, interventions into the sensory problem of glare encountered by many elderly may include corrective lenses in glasses that reduce glare, but also traffic lights and roadway surfaces that reduce glare. Likewise, intervening into the social context in which the elder lives may be more effective than intervening solely with the individual. Share-a-ride programs pair the transportation needs of one elder with the economic or social incentives of another member of the community.

CONSIDERATIONS RELATED TO THE POINT OF INTERVENTION

A number of additional issues related to programmatic driving interventions merit further discussion.

Target of Intervention: Active or Passive

The dimensions of the cube related to target and domain may be reconceptualized in terms of the extent to which the intervention represents a continuum from active to passive decision making (Evans, 1991). Active versus passive interventions are conceptualized in terms of the number of decision makers and the extent to which the intervention reflects volitional actions at the level of the individual. Targeting the intervention at the level of the individual suggests a form of intervention that involves volitional acts on the part of many decision makers—the most *active* form of intervention. Interventions targeted at the individual, such as driver education or seat belt usage, require many decision makers making volitional acts to implement the intervention.

In contrast, targeting interventions at the level of the vehicle or roadway typically involves interventions in which there are fewer decision makers and may require fewer volitional acts on the part of the individual—thus characterized as a more *passive* form of intervention. Passive interventions involving the vehicle or roadway include air bags and antilock braking in vehicles, as well as roadway designs, which are imposed on all drivers.

Voluntary versus Involuntary

A related dichotomy is voluntary, individually based interventions versus involuntary, legislative-based interventions. Voluntary individual-based interventions may be of 2 types. First, voluntary interventions may take the form of self-regulation (Dobbs, 2000; Evans, 1991). Three forms of self-regulation include compensation, avoidance, and cessation. For example, an individual may decide to self-regulate his or her driving behavior by avoiding driving while drinking, or ceasing night driving, or compensating for possible deficits by involving a copilot. The second form of voluntary, individual-based interventions focuses on educational efforts, such as 55 Alive.

Evans (1991) has suggested that one of the limitations to interventions based on self-regulation comes from individual drivers not being able to identify major driving risks from their own direct driving experience. There is often a sparsity of useful personal feedback available to the driver to use in making a judgment regarding self-regulation. Given the low incidence of serious auto crashes, the individual driver has little information on which of his or her driving behaviors might double or triple the likelihood of being involved in a serious crash. The role of limited feedback on self-regulation is particularly relevant for the older adult. Older adults have fewer accidents than members of other age groups, but they are more likely to experience serious injuries when a serious accident occurs.

It has been argued that passive or involuntary interventions with few decision makers are likely to have the most widespread effects on road safety. It is asserted that such interventions may be much more efficient to implement in the society as a whole. There are, however, limitations on the types of driving problems that can be easily resolved by using solely passive interventions. For example, there are limitations to passive interventions for driving situations that require complex decision making, such as safely executing a left-hand turn. It may be argued that, as the complexity of the driving situation increases, the difficulty will increase in devising a completely passive, nonvolitional intervention to deal with the situation. Some form of conscious action on the part of the driver often will be needed.

Timing of the Intervention: Primary, Secondary, or Tertiary

A key issue in prevention intervention research has focused on the timing of the intervention (Smyer & Gatz, 1987). *Primary* prevention is defined as that occurring before the problem arises. In terms of driving interventions, this would include crash-avoidance interventions. *Secondary* prevention occurs after the initial identification of the problem but before serious harm has arisen. Secondary prevention efforts, which involve prompt treatment of identified problems, may be particularly important in terms of intervention efforts with the elderly. These types of interventions might be initiated after a fender bender in which no one was injured, after a driving assessment, or after a "near miss." Although secondary interventions are often implemented at a different stage in the problem, many of the interventions may be similar to those included as primary interventions. *Tertiary* interventions occur after the problem has progressed to a more critical stage. In terms of driving, this would include crash-protection interventions, or withdrawal of driving privileges after an accident.

A complete model of driving interventions must consider the range of interventions from those to avoid crashes (primary prevention) to interventions to protect during a crash (tertiary intervention). Most interventions focus on primary prevention or crash avoidance (Evans, 1991); however, a number of the engineering and human factors approaches targeted at the vehicle, in particular, are aimed at protection during a crash. These include air bags, seat belt restraints, and special materials (shatterproof glass, padded dash boards) to reduce the likelihood of an injury as a result of a crash. Many of these interventions, aimed at protecting during a crash, can be labeled as passive, rather than active.

Interventions focused on crash avoidance include both passive and active interventions. Many of the same types of intervention may be involved in primary-prevention and secondary-prevention efforts. Active crash-avoidance interventions include education, possible use of copiloting, and driving restrictions for time of day or certain types of roadways. Passive crash-avoidance interventions include road construction and vehicle equipment, such as obstacle-detector systems and antilock braking. Although crash-avoidance interventions are more frequent and have been given greater attention, they are often much more difficult to evaluate. Part of the difficulty in evaluating crash-avoidance interventions is in documenting and counting the incidents of crash avoidance. Active crash-avoidance interventions are particularly difficult to evaluate. In contrast, crash-protective interventions, implemented during a crash, and particularly those which are passive, are considered the easiest to evaluate.

Research shows that public attitudes toward interventions are influenced by evidence demonstrating an identifiable survivor or beneficiary of an intervention (Evans, 1991). It has been much easier to document survivors or beneficiaries of crash-protective interventions, particularly of the passive type, than beneficiaries of crash-avoidance interventions. This characteristic of public attitudes toward interventions may contribute to the difficulty in obtaining public support for and adherence to certain types of crash-avoidance interventions.

SUMMARY

In this chapter we have discussed issues related to programmatic interventions with the older driver. We have argued that programmatic interventions must be conceptualized as multidimensional. We have presented an intervention cube as one schema for thinking about programmatic interventions into driving. The 3 dimensions of the cube include the age group, the target of the intervention (individual, community, vehicle, or roadway), and the domain or mechanism for administering the intervention. Common intervention mechanisms include education, provision of services, human factors and engineering, and legal actions.

Each intervention mechanism is based on assumptions that are rarely articulated fully; for example, educational interventions assume that the driver's deficit is due to a lack of knowledge. Current educational interventions focus on dissemination of factual information with much less focus on developing skills and enhancing actual driving performance. Legal-based interventions often assume that chronological age rather than functional age is an appropriate criterion for determining the group to be the target of the intervention (Fozard, 2000).

By considering various existing interventions with respect to the intervention cube, we can begin to determine what types of programmatic interventions represent certain cells, plugs, or blocks of the entire cube. We suggest the cube has heuristic value for examining what aspects of the cube characterize existing interventions and what future interventions might be needed to involve other dimensions of the cube.

REFERENCES

American Association of Retired Persons (AARP). (1997). *Community transportation survey.* Washington, DC: AARP.

American Association of Retired Persons (AARP). (1999). *Older drivers.* Washington, DC: Public Policy Institute, AARP.

Ball, K., & Owsley, C. (2000). Increasing mobility and reducing accidents of older drivers. In K. W. Schaie & M. Pietrucha (Eds.), *Mobility and transportation in the elderly* (pp. 213–250). New York: Springer.

Baltes, P. B., & Danish, S. J. (1980). Intervention in life-span development and aging: Issues and concepts. In R. R. Turner & H. W. Reese (Eds.), *Life-span developmental psychology: Intervention* (pp. 49–78). New York: Academic Press.

Brim, O. G., Jr., & Phillips, D. A. (1988). The life-span intervention cube. In E. M. Hetherington & R. M. Lerner (Eds.), *Child development in life-span perspective* (pp. 277–299). Hillsdale, NJ: Lawrence Erlbaum Associates.

Burkhardt, J. E. (2000). Limitations of mass transportation and individual vehicle systems for older persons. In K. W. Schaie & M. Pietrucha (Eds.), *Mobility and transportation in the elderly* (pp. 97–124). New York: Springer.

Dobbs, A. R. (2000). Commentary: The role of concordance between perceived and real competence for mobility outcomes. In K. W. Schaie & M. Pietrucha (Eds.), *Mobility and transportation in the elderly* (pp. 251–268). New York: Springer.

Evans, L. (1991). *Traffic safety and the driver.* New York: Van Nostrand Reinhold.

Fozard, J. L. (2000). Sensory and cognitive changes with age. In K. W. Schaie & M. Pietrucha (Eds.), *Mobility and transportation in the elderly* (pp. 1–44). New York: Springer.

Freund, K. (2000). Commentary: Into the transportation future. In K. W. Schaie & M. Pietrucha (Eds.), *Mobility and transportation in the elderly* (pp. 145–156). New York: Springer.

Gesten, E. L., & Jason, L. A. (1987). Social and community interventions. *Annual Review of Psychology, 38,* 427–460.

Hanowski, R. J., & Dingus, T. A. (2000). Will intelligent transportation systems improve older driver mobility? In K. W. Schaie & M. Pietrucha (Eds.), *Mobility and transportation in the elderly* (pp. 279–298). New York: Springer.

Insurance Institute for Highway Safety. (2001). *U.S. driver licensing renewal procedures for older drivers.* Arlington, VA: Insurance Institute for Highway Safety.

Jovanis, P. P. (2000). Commentary: Intelligent transportation systems and the older traveler: Prospects for mobility. In K. W. Schaie & M. Pietrucha (Eds.), *Mobility and transportation in the elderly* (pp. 315–322). New York: Springer.

Schaie, K. W., & Pietrucha, M. (Eds.). (2000). *Mobility and transportation in the elderly.* New York: Springer.

Schlag, B. (1993). Elderly drivers in Germany—fitness and driving behavior. *Accident Analyses & Prevention, 25,* 47–55.

Smyer, M. A., & Gatz, M. (1987). Intervention research approaches. *Research on Aging, 8,* 536–558.

Staplin, L. (2000). Commentary: Countering mobility losses due to functional impairments in normally aging individuals: Applying Fozard's framework to everyday driving situations. In K. W. Schaie & M. Pietrucha (Eds.), *Mobility and transportation in the elderly* (pp. 63–70). New York: Springer.

Sterns, H. L., & Sterns, R. (2000). Commentary: Social structures and processes in public and private transportation. In K. W. Schaie & M. Pietrucha (Eds.), *Mobility and transportation in the elderly* (pp. 125–144). New York: Springer.

Swigart, T. F. (2000). Commentary: Intelligent transportation systems and the older driver: An auto industry perspective. In K. W. Schaie & M. Pietrucha (Eds.), *Mobility and transportation in the elderly* (pp. 299–314). New York: Springer.

U.S. Roads-TranSafety. (March, 1997). Licensing older drivers: Part 1. *Road Management and Engineering Journal.* Available at www.USRoads.com/journals/rej/9703/re970302.htm.

Willis, S. L. (2000). Commentary: Driving competence: The person × environment fit. In K. W. Schaie & M. Pietrucha (Eds.), *Mobility and transportation in the elderly* (pp. 269–278). New York: Springer.

PART V

Future Perspectives of Aging Independently: Combining Perspectives of Aging Inside and Outside the Home

Future Developments in Living Environments for Older People in the United States and Germany

Hans-Werner Wahl and Laura N. Gitlin

This chapter examines the future of living environments for older people with particular emphasis on American and German perspectives. A central issue is to identify those elements that may have considerable impact on future living environments such as competencies, attitudes, behaviors, and health (at the individual level) as well as aspects of the formal/informal care and prevention system (at the societal level). It is important to acknowledge individual and societal factors that are subject to ongoing change and thus deserve special deliberation with respect to future predictions. We will examine how aging in place might change in the future and how future living environments will support healthy aging and aging with chronic conditions.

Our gaze into the crystal ball to predict the future of living environments is based on several important assumptions. First, in order to predict the future, it is best to start with the current situation of older people's living environments. Because this issue has already been treated in earlier chapters of this book, we are brief in this regard, summarizing only those points that are of particular relevance to the future of living environments in the United States and Germany. We trace the historical development of living environments for the elderly and describe what needs of the elderly have yet to be met. Second, we describe critical societal trends and factors that we believe will shape present and future living environments of older people in the United States and Germany.

Based on these considerations, we make a set of concrete predictions regarding future living environments of older people in both the United States and Germany in the near future—over the next 15 to 20 years. Furthermore, we examine the implications of these predictions for the meaning of aging in place, health, illness, and disability, and the participatory style of forthcoming elders both for the United States and Germany. It is important to emphasize that extrapolations into the future necessarily tend to be based on generalized trends (e.g., broad cohort dynamics) which reduce and simplify to some extent the existing heterogeneity and pluralism of the aging population.

CURRENT LIVING ENVIRONMENTS OF ELDERS IN THE UNITED STATES AND GERMANY: BASIC POTENTIAL AND CONSTRAINTS SHAPING THE FUTURE OF LIVING ENVIRONMENTS

We begin with a brief examination of the early days of environmental gerontology in the 1950s and 1960s, represented in works by Kleemeier (1959), Carp (1966), Rosow (1967), and Lawton and Simon (1968). Characteristic of this research on the living environments of elders was the emphasis placed on those still living in their "normal" private homes, those living in nursing homes, and factors contributing to relocation (typically to the nursing home). This research consistently showed that the private-home environment was the preferred living arrangement and setting for aging for most elders at that time. At that time, older adults were, in a sense, prepared to relocate to an institution even in their young-old age in anticipation of severe decline as well as the (perceived) need of their family for safety and optimal care for the "just in case" scenario. Moreover, at that time, dementia was not the most important reason for relocation to an institution. In contrast to Germany, the residential pattern for older people became more complex in the United States in the early 1960s: A third alternative to housing, retirement communities, such as the continuing care retirement communities, and specialized housing projects, such as the now-famous Victoria Plaza in San Antonio, Texas (Carp, 1966) emerged in some regions.

Since then, living environments have changed considerably, and many more options are now available to older people in terms of private or quasi-private home settings. In general, housing quality has significantly improved since the 1950s in both the United States and Germany, and elders have clearly profited from these improvements. Consequently, most elders today live in the best housing ever available to older people. The risk of a forced and involuntary surrender of the home environment has been significantly reduced, particularly as a result of the development of ambulatory and home health care services and rehabilitation programs intended to support an elder's capability to remain at home. In Germany, the introduction of a long-term care insurance system covering home-care services in 1995, and expanded in 1996 to cover institutional care expenses as well, has strengthened the trend considerably (Schneekloth & Müller, 2000). According to the scheme, every person in the labor force pays into the system, thereby gaining the right to receive payment for formal and informal care in the case of severe disability. Furthermore, in the past, homes in neither the United States nor in Germany were a target (as they are today) for a wide range of home health care services and home modification strategies [Bundesministerium für Familie, Senioren, Frauen und Jugend (BMFSFJ) (Federal Ministry for Family Affairs, Senior Citizens, Women and Youth), 2001; Pynoos & Regnier, 1991]. These strategies are designed to reduce person-environment misfits, specifically those following the occurrence of a chronic health condition or an acute episode leading to disability (e.g., stroke, hip fracture). In addition, many new housing alternatives for the elderly have filled the gap between traditional private housing and institutional living. For example, many variations of assisted living facilities have emerged, and living arrangements including different generations or disabled people, home-owner communities, and other forms of living communities have become much more frequent in both countries (BMFSFJ, 2001; National Center for Assisted Living, 1998; Regnier, 1994; see also Chapter 7 in this volume).

Moreover, a rather dramatic shift in the "world of institutions" for the elderly has taken place: There has been a jump in both the age of the residents and their level of impairment in both Germany and the United States. In Germany, the average resident living in an institution is over 80 years of age; in the United States, the average age is 80 for females and 75 years for males. Moreover, in the United States, only about 13.5% of the persons living in nursing homes are between the ages of 65 and 74; 50% of the residents are 85 and older. Similar trends can be observed in Germany.

Besides the sharp rise of the oldest-old, the increased number of persons with dementia, which is currently estimated to be over 50% of all elders in nursing homes in both countries (BMFSFJ, 2001; National Center on Health Statistics, 2000; Schneekloth & Müller, 2000; Weyerer & Schäufele, 1999), has led to quite a dramatic change in the composition of the nursing home population. Accordingly, beginning in the late 1980s, institutions have become more specialized as evidenced by the development of special care units and similar institutional settings that serve older persons with dementia (e.g., Day, Carreon, & Stump, 2000).

Table 19.1 provides data on the current living situation of older people in the United States and Germany. There is a striking difference between these countries with regard to home ownership, which is much higher in the United States (BMFSFJ, 1998, 2001; U.S. Census Bureau, 1997): 79% of older people in the United States live in their own homes versus 48% of older people in Germany. There is, however, a need for further differentiation of this general trend in each country. In the United States, the rate of home ownership among Hispanic and African American elders is clearly lower compared to that of white elders. In Germany, the rate of home ownership is lower in elders residing in the so-called new states in the East compared to the old states in the West (30% versus 53%) (BMFSFJ, 1998). This is also true for the subpopulation of elderly migrants, most of whom come from Turkey (23%) (Dietzel-Papakyriakou & Olbermann, 1998). It is important to note that in both countries, only a small portion of the older population currently lives in substandard housing, defined as apartments or houses with inadequate plumbing (without an indoor toilet or bathing facility), inadequate heating, extreme disrepair, lack of electricity, or extreme infestation. However, here again, a differential pattern emerges: Those in substandard housing tend to be the old-old (75+), older women, minorities, elderly migrants, and the rural elderly in both the United States and Germany (e.g., BMFSFJ, 1998, 2001; Hermanson & Citro, 1999; Kendig & Pynoos, 1996). In Germany, substandard housing among elders is still more prevalent in the new eastern states compared to the old western states, although much improvement has been achieved since 1990 in the former (BMFSFJ, 2001; Kohli & Künemund, 2000).

Also shown in Table 19.1 is the percentage of older people living in a variety of forms of assisted living. This tends to be somewhat higher in the United States (between 2.4% to 4.8% versus 1.6% in Germany). Assisted living, a relatively new living choice for older people, is the fastest growing type of senior housing in the United States and Germany (Kopetz et al.,

TABLE 19.1 Basic Characteristics of Housing in the United States and Germany

Type of housing	Estimated number in the United States (65+)	Estimated number in Germany (65+)	Source material
Homeowners	79% (16.5 mil.) Hispanics: 66% African Americans: 65% White: 81%	48% (about 5.6 mil.) West: 53% East: 30% Elderly immigrants: 23%	U.S. Census Bureau, 1997; BMFSFJ, 1998
Renters	21% (4.4 mil.)	52% (about 6 mil.)	
Substandard housing	About 8%	West: 6% East: 15%	Kendig & Pynoos, 1996; Statistisches Bundesamt, 2000
Assisted living facilities (including *Betreutes Wohnen* in Germany)	2.4% to 4.8% (500,000 to 1 mil.)	1.6% (200,000)	National Center for Assisted Living, 1998; BMFSFJ, 2001
Nursing homes (including special care units in the United States)	4.3% (1.47 mil.)	5.3% (655,000)	National Center on Health Statistics, 2000; Schneekloth & Müller, 2000

2000; Saup, 2001). In Germany, the term "assisted living" (*Betreutes Wohnen* or the less frequently used term, *Service Wohnen*) covers a broad range of living facilities, the common denominators of which are a (mostly) barrier-free apartment (normally including an alarm system) and a graded system of care from none or low to very intensive. Various organizational forms, such as affiliations with nursing homes, apartment complexes with their own care provision unit, and apartments or clusters of apartments served by the community home-care providers, can be found (see also Chapter 8 in this volume). In the United States, the definition of assisted living varies from state to state; however, it is usually defined as a residential setting that provides or coordinates personal care services, 24-hour supervision, and social and health-related activities (see also Chapter 7 in this volume). In the United States there are approximately 25,000 to 30,000 assisted living facilities which target primarily physically frail older people who need assistance. Although originally conceptualized for the physically frail elder, a growing number of assisted living residents have dementia or a memory impairment so that now many facilities offer specialized dementia care services. The growth of assisted living reflects the strong desire of older people to age in place or in a living arrangement that affords the emotional, social, and physical comforts of home. While assisted living is generally affordable for only those with a high income, some states provide Medicaid waivers to low-income households to help offset the financial costs of the services provided (National Center for Assisted Living, 1998).

Available data suggest that only a very small number of people 65 years and older live in nursing homes: 1.47 million (4.3%) of the U.S. population and 5.3% of the German population (Schneekloth & Müller, 2000). Noteworthy, however, is that in the United States, as well as in Germany, the percentage increases dramatically with age. In the United States, for example, the age increases from 1.1% for persons 65 to 74 years of age to 4.5% for persons 75 to 84 years of age to 19% for persons who are 85 years of age or older (National Center on Health Statistics, 2000). A similar trend exists in Germany. Only rough estimations are available regarding other living arrangements in the United States (such as continuing care retirement communities and boarding homes; see Chapter 7 in this volume for details) and Germany (such as housing community projects and housing projects with a mixed-generation approach; an estimated 1,000 of these units have been reported) (BMFSFJ, 1998).

In summary, although some differences exist between the United States and Germany, the current context from which to consider future living environments of elders appears to be rather comparable along several important points. First, the private home is still clearly the preferred setting of today's elders in both countries. However, it is important to note differential ownership patterns between and within both countries based on socioeconomic status as well as racial and ethnic identity. Second, the potential for older adults in the United States and Germany to remain at home as long as possible has, for a variety of reasons, never been stronger. Chief among these is the greater availability of home health care programs, home modification programs, and, in Germany, a new long-term care insurance system that was introduced in the 1990s. Furthermore, for both countries, there is less substandard housing than ever before, although differentiation according to age, sex, minority status, and macro setting (urban-rural) still points to unmet needs. Third, the range of options in terms of different housing as well as institutional settings has never been broader, thus offering today's elders in both countries a wide range of living arrangement options. Nonetheless, living arrangements beyond the "normal" private household are still the exception in both countries. Fourth, although there are numerous alternatives to nursing home relocation, the possibility of living in an institution is imminent for certain subgroups of elders in Germany and the United States, including those suffering from severe dementia or other chronic conditions involving unpredictable basic medical care needs. The decision for nursing home placement is strongly influenced by social factors such as the availability of informal support, which has worsened as a result of an increase in single households and the younger generation's proclivity to settle in places far from home.

FACTORS SHAPING THE PRESENT AND FUTURE LIVING ENVIRONMENTS OF OLDER PEOPLE

A consideration of the future of living environments for older people must account for general trends that have broad acceptance in the gerontological community as to their impact on the future situation of older people. One important trend is reflected in what is now frequently referred to as the baby boomer generation, that is, those born roughly between the close of World War II and 1960, a significant portion of whom will approach retirement age in the forthcoming 10 to 20 years. To take the example of the United States, the first wave of 3.2 million baby boomers turned 55 in 2001, and approximately 17 million will turn 55+ within the next 5 years. Currently, there are close to 34 million persons 65 years or older living in the United

States, representing 13% of all Americans. This number is expected to grow to 69 million, which will represent 20% of all Americans by 2030, and then to almost 80 million by 2050. This is in contrast to an expected population increase of only 7% for those under 65 years of age (Federal Interagency Forum on Aging Related Statistics, 2000). In addition, an ensemble of demographic trends will play a particularly critical role in shaping the future of aging. The first trend is that the proportion of elders within the total population will further increase as noted above for the United States and similarly in Germany. It is predicted that about one-third of the German population will be 60 and older in 2050 (Deutscher Bundestag, 1998). Second, the oldest-old (in most industrialized countries) will continue to be the fastest growing population segment. Third, older people from minority groups in both countries will increase significantly. The number (or proportion) of mentally disabled older persons will also increase significantly in Germany in the near future for the first time with respect to those born after World War II (BMFSFJ, 2001). Fourth, the trend in the aging population toward *singularization* will be clearly evident in the forthcoming 15 to 20 years because of the long-term effects of current high divorce rates and childless marriages (among other factors). Fifth, a general decline in the availability of informal caregivers, for a variety of reasons (such as increased geographic mobility, growing level of labor force participation of women, growing physical distance of family members forced by the job market, and perhaps also new cultural values regarding the obligation and provision of informal care), is another expected trend in both countries.

General Trends

Against this background of demographic changes, Silverstone (1996) formulated several major trends regarding the psychosocial profile of tomorrow's older people, the baby boomer generation. With respect to societal impact, future groups of elders will probably have, simply by their sheer size, more political influence, and this will be enforced by the dissemination of more positive images of old age. Elders will also be enormously diverse with regard to cultural background, competencies, attitudes, and societal expectations. Conversely, aging baby boomers will also share some critical common characteristics. They will be far better educated than the elders of today. Their aspiration to live as active, integrated members of society will strengthen their standing while the "silver market" they represent will support their rise in importance within society. For example, the market force they represent will influence the development of universal products, variation in physical environments, and the integration of technological tools into "normal" aspects of everyday life in the later years. Independence will thus represent the top priority for future elders who, we project, will be motivated to use any means necessary to achieve that goal. Moreover, the vast majority of elders will have the economic resources to obtain their goals. Furthermore, older people will be far more confident about their age and societal status than today's elders are; that is, self-confidence as older consumers with equal rights within the society will be very strong. Older people, owing to their number and wealth as a group, will greatly influence the market and product growth.

Regarding health and functioning, future elders will be far better off than those of today. Also, we speculate that there will be a much stronger sense of having control of one's health or being one's own agent of self-care. The role of prevention in maintaining one's health and activity will be more widely understood, and steps will be taken to ensure one's continued physical well-being. Furthermore, healthy activities such as sports will be more accessible to elders and considered a normal part of daily life. The occurrence of illness will be understood predominantly in functional terms, which will also mean that there will be a strong expectation that everything possible should be done to reduce functional losses or to regain functioning in daily life. By and large, these expected developments will be channeled into a new cultural understanding of health in the second half of life, one that relates health and independent daily functioning to biological as well as psychosocial and contextual influences and the potential of intervention, rehabilitation, and improvements.

A differential view is needed, however, with respect to the expected significant increase in the oldest-old. The positive health and functioning scenarios will apply chiefly to future elders in their *third age*, that is, those roughly between 60 and 80 years, who, on the average, will exhibit a high level of competence in activities of daily living, leisure, and social functioning as well as physical and mental health. This potential trend, however, is far less clear for those in their *fourth age*, that is, those beyond 80 to 85 years of age. This group is characterized today by a sharp decline in daily functioning and health status as well as a sharp increase in disability and the need for sheltered environments (for the distinction between the third and fourth ages, see Baltes & Smith, 1999).

Additional Trends Directly Linked to Future Living Environments

United States

Since health and living arrangements are inextricably linked, foremost in considering future living environments is an understanding of the current and projected health status of an aging population. Most older people in the United States today are living longer and better than previous cohorts, and they rate their health as good or excellent. Nevertheless, although the prevalence of disability among the older population has declined, the absolute size of the physically disabled older population is increasing (Manton, Corder, & Stallard, 1997). The number of elderly at risk of disability is expected to increase as a function of the aging population, particularly as the baby boomer generation reaches retirement age, and with the unprecedented growth of the oldest-old.

Physical disability is the primary threat to the ability to remain at home and age in place among older people. It represents a major adverse outcome of aging and age-related chronic and debilitating conditions, such as stroke, arthritis, diabetes, osteoporosis, memory impairment, depressive symptoms, or heart disease. Furthermore, disability is associated with activity limitations, particularly a diminished capacity to perform self-care and instrumental tasks that compromise the ability to remain at home (Fried & Guralnik, 1997; Guralnik & Simonsick, 1993). The proportion of older adults with one or more functional limitations increases with age. An estimated 35% of adults 65 years of age and over, and 62% of those 85 and over, living at home report difficulty with one or more activities of daily living. Additionally, these difficulties are more prevalent among elders who are low-income, minority group members (Diehl, 1998). Thus, those most vulnerable to functional difficulties are the oldest-old, women, minority group members, and low-income elders (older people with limited resources who may not be able to take full advantage of the multiple housing options existing now and in the future).

Functional difficulties are associated with the need for increased personal assistance, the chief factor contributing to the decision to move from a private home to that of a family member or a residential facility. The need for personal assistance with everyday activities increases with age; 50% of persons 85 and older in the United States are estimated to require help with basic self-care activities such as bathing, getting around inside the home, preparing meals, and shopping (Federal Interagency Forum on Aging Related Statistics, 2000). Thus, although many elderly live alone in good health, as a group, they face increasing dependency, and this is especially the case for the fastest growing segment of the elderly population, the oldest-old (85+).

Recent trends in home modification and environmental redesign suggest that, with increasing dependency, older people are willing to adapt their homes. National representative surveys in the United States (LaPlante, Hendershot, & Moss, 1992; Manton et al., 1997; Norburn et al., 1995) show a trend toward greater use of assistive devices and environmental accommodations and a subsequent decline in the use of personal assistance by functionally impaired older adults. The ability of older people to stay put at home rests on the availability of informal supports and supportive services such as home-care and home-modification services.

Other trends linked to the future of living environments are the current market forces driving the changes in health care delivery. These trends include the rise of new technologies that contribute to early discharge and the future possibility of treating a vast array of conditions (e.g., cancer, heart, stroke) in the home as opposed to the hospital, increased medical and societal focus on prevention and lifestyle adjustment to maintain health and functioning, a focus from individual treatment to understanding population-based needs, and increased delivery of services in community settings, such as adult day care, congregate meals, and medical care in senior centers or apartment buildings. An important development is the emerging paradigm shift in medical care from an acute to a chronic care perspective reflecting the core health difficulties of an aging population. This shift from the treatment of fixed disease states to a focus on the functional consequences of complex syndromes necessitates comprehensive and coordinated geriatric care including the consideration of the living arrangement and its role as a barrier to or supporter of the aging person. Thus, the role of the home for assessment, treatment, and outcome will be even more central to a functional geriatric perspective in the future.

Germany

With regard to long-term care needs, it is especially worth mentioning that an estimated 1,261,000 Germans living in private households currently report profound basic care needs, and about 79% of these persons are more than 60 years old (Schneekloth & Müller, 2000). Substantial increases are expected until the year 2020 as a result of the increase of the oldest-old, up to well over 2 million, when considering both those with long-term care needs served in the home-care and institutional settings (BMFSFJ, 2001). There appears to be a clear expectation (and consensus) on the individual and societal level that persons with long-term care needs should be cared for in a private-home environment. This raises the question of how normal homes can become the center of the care system and best provide support to elders with disability. As has already been mentioned, the introduction of a long-term care insurance system in the home health care domain in Germany in 1995 has contributed to the (perceived and real) possibility for older people to remain at home even with chronic conditions and pronounced disabilities (Schneekloth, & Müller, 2000). In addition, the increasing availability of reimbursable home-modification opportunities all across Germany (with, however, some variation according to regions or states) has further contributed to this possibility (BMFSFJ, 2001).

Another strong trend in Germany is the development of alternative private home environments with institutionalized support structures for the "just in case" scenerio (in particular, *Betreutes Wohnen*). There is a growing acceptance within the aging population of changing one's place of aging, although only a small (but growing) portion of the elderly has already decided to relocate to these new living facilities. An issue of some debate in Germany is bewilderment concerning financial issues as well as doubt concerning the housing and care quality of these living environments (BMFSFJ, 1998, 2001). A current trend among the German elderly population is to frame the issue of housing as an important component of the silver market, that is, as a consumer article that should be tested and provide proven quality for one's hard-earned cash. This trend is strongly supported by consumer organizations (such as *Stiftung Warentest*, the German equivalent of *Consumer Reports* in the United States), and it is becoming more pronounced with respect to the quality of care provided in institutions. Conversely, it is also fair to say that the preferences and satisfaction of elders as consumers of living environments are becoming a strong market force in designing living environments for older people in their full variety. That is, elders and their family members are increasingly being viewed as consumers of living environments who have the market power to exercise choice, rather than blithely to accept what is doled out to them. As such, it is expected that consumer preference and satisfaction will increasingly take precedence in designing both home and institutional arrangements.

Another significant trend that influences the future role of living environments for older people is an attitudinal change in the health and care delivery system in Germany. Preventive efforts, even in very old persons, are now strongly encouraged, and chronic illnesses are mainly framed in terms of their functional consequences. This emphasis is also supported by the basic premise underlying the care assurance system. Thus, rehabilitation, which is understood as a multidisciplinary and multiprofessional enterprise to help people regain as much autonomous functioning as possible in old age, is increasingly becoming as important, if not more so, than acute treatment. This paradigm shift, which also exists in the United States, clearly strengthens the role of private living environments in old age, but it also extends its role as a critical contextual component of rehabilitative efforts.

Finally, the impact of new technologies on living environments is also worth consideration. For example, the Internet is already providing a mechanism by which elders with disability or those who are socially isolated can keep contact with the "world" and, in this way, remain integrated in society. Internet use provides a way in which to learn about preventive health measures or strategies for managing functional losses (e.g., online ordering of products or medication). The introduction of high-technology assistive devices (e.g., systems to compensate for severe vision or hearing loss), as well as the use of intelligent housing systems (see also Chapter 10 in this volume), has the potential to offer to the private-home environment important features that lend support, compensation, and surveillance. Such features were not possible before, were available only in institutional settings, or required the direct involvement of caregivers in the households of older people. Technology thus provides the most powerful innovation that will change the "culture" of living environments for older people and their ability to overcome potential needs and constraints.

FUTURE LIVING ENVIRONMENTS OF OLDER PEOPLE: PREDICTIONS AND IMPACT ON FUTURE AGING

What implications do the general population trends, as well as the particular developments in the United States and Germany described above, have for future living environments? We propose 3 sets of predictions: the primacy of home, the assisted living model, and a more general view of new homes for "new agers."

Our first prediction is that the primacy of the private-home environment will not only persist, but will be even more significant for elders in the future. Older people of tomorrow (that is, the baby boomers of today) will, more so than today's elderly, come to regard the private-home environment as the central place for aging. Aging at home will be a cultural expectation; the home will become the normal place to be at the end of one's life. The primacy of home will be strengthened for the elderly with physical and cognitive limitations as new intervention research validates home-based medical and social care strategies (see Gitlin, Corcoran, Winter, Boyce, & Hauck, 2001). Also, current experimentation with financial packaging and types of bundled home-care services will yield economically feasible life care plans, although the extent to which all elders will have access to such benefits is perhaps suspect. Private-home environments will become the central location for the delivery of a wide range of long-term care services including hospice, caregiving, rehabilitation, and acute care. The primacy of home in this regard will be further reinforced by the general trend toward early hospital discharge. There has even been discussion on the potential replacement of hospitals with the home-hospital, a concept initially developed in England and currently being tested in the United States (Fried, Van Doorn, Tinetti, & Drickamer, 1998; Leff & Burton, 1998; Leff et al., 1999).

Our second prediction is that the quantity, quality, and variety of assisted living models will change quite dramatically in the future (see also Chapter 7 in this volume). The design of new "homes" for elders will integrate basic elements of a "normal" home environment with customized care and treatment options. This will lead to a range of highly acceptable new living environmental forms which will be viewed by tomorrow's older people as "reasonable" and "normal" alternatives to moving into a more sheltered environment. Due to the current variation of assisted living models and the expected growth of this industry in the near future, however, the readiness to move will touch significantly more elders in the future than today. Readiness to move will reflect not only the motivation to compensate effectively for disability consequences, but also simply to enhance life quality and wellness in the later years in general. The assisted living model will provide the future elderly with an alternative living environment, and it will become one of the preferred ways of dealing with the transition from the third to the fourth age, one of the major challenges of aging. Obviously, the importance of assisted living models will be further underscored by the forthcoming decline in informal caregivers and trends toward singularization, which will have a stronger impact on older men in the future (e.g., BMFSFJ, 2001). Probably, most of these developments in housing will be based on for-profit initiatives and will thus also become a major driving force in the silver market and eventually even in the larger consumer market.

A third prediction, which we refer to as "new" homes for "new" aging, is meant to cut across the different domains of living environments of future elders and, as such, is a more general prediction. For one, retrofitting private homes as well as planning for and building new flexible housing to achieve barrier-free environments will become much more common than today. This will be accomplished with the use of the full scope of technological tools and will be viewed as a normal aspect of everyday life. The referral to the home setting as a major base for prevention and rehabilitation will become much greater in the future as well. Second, the highly diverse aging population of tomorrow will be better served in terms of an increasing scope of nontraditional home alternatives, as well as an increased specialization of nursing facilities and assisted living facilities aimed to serve different subgroups of very sick elderly (see also our second prediction). Alternately, families may themselves seek flexible housing arrangements to accommodate a frail, elderly family member. Future elders will seek housing options that will support and maintain socialization, stimulation, and opportunities for self-realization or enhanced life quality. This new future is already evident in the development of senior living communities near university campuses, the increase in the number of older people relocating to traditional college towns, and the baby boomers moving to remote areas of the United States known for their geographical beauty. This development might also be interpreted as an enlargement of the consumer market of the future that must better address the specific needs of a variety of subgroups among the older population. It might even represent a major innovation in the ongoing development of the consumer market in general.

Impact of Predictions in Terms of Future Day-to-Day Aging

Let us first address here expected changes regarding the cultural notion of aging in place. With this issue, we reflect upon one essential of the "good life" in old age (Lawton, 1983), the *maintenance* function of the physical and spatial environment (see Lawton, 1989). It is clear to us that private-home environments will remain and even enhance their maintenance function to support continuity across the later life phase. The *stimulation* function of living environments will become more important and more significant, and their *support* function will be taken very much for granted compared to the housing of today's elders. We can expect that the notion of aging in place will further change its meaning in the future as a result of the capacity of future elders for extensive outdoor mobility. Furthermore, the natural use of new technologies and communication media will probably facilitate independence, leisure engagement, and social involvement. It may obviate concerns regarding the specific location of one's home (e.g., in terms of a central city versus remote location) or its physical connection to the outdoor world (e.g., in terms of public transport). Finally, older people of tomorrow will have a richer scope of living arrangement alternatives compared to today's elders, and this will probably contribute to a broader, more flexible understanding of what is meant by aging in place and its value for the good life in old age. In turn, this will contribute to the development of a positive culture of old age, its diversity and heterogeneity. Living environments will thus have a more important role in the aging process and will become a significant part of the cultural expression of quality of life in our societies in general.

Due to a much more comprehensive understanding of health in functional terms, living environments will gain a more significant role in the future for health prevention and the maintaining and regaining of functioning in the later years. An even more pronounced (and perhaps provocative) version of this argument is that loss of competencies will be less constraining for tomorrow's elders as a result of well-adapted physical and technical environments. One might even expect that the notion of competence loss typically associated with old age will lose its negative connotation in the future as a result of the powerful role that technology and purpose-built environments will naturally play in compensating for functional limitations. This might become particularly critical for the forthcoming oldest-old in terms of what has been described as "declining the decline" (Baltes & Smith, 1999, p. 159). In other words, technological support and environmental design are important cultural means of attenuating the decline experienced most keenly among the oldest-old.

Finally, the planner-user gap frequently observed in the creation of today's living environments for older people deserves particular attention (see also Chapter 9 in this volume). What is the future of elders' participation in developing their own living environments and the associated challenges for community and political agendas? We expect that it will become an absolute essential in the future to involve elders more in the planning processes for the development of all kinds of living environments including institutions. The models and possibilities to do so will be diverse (including the Internet and other communication technologies). In any case, we speculate that elders of the future will want an active, participatory role and will not tolerate having their environmental needs defined by designers, architects, and urban planners (among others). As a consequence, this will probably lead in the long run to further optimization with respect to person-environment fits for a variety of groups of older people, from the very competent to the very fragile. However, this also implies that new challenges will present themselves in the professional field to develop different ways of creating adequate living environments for elders in the future. Designers and architects, as well as community agencies, will have to muster goodwill and creativity to achieve this goal effectively in the future.

German-American Similarities and Differences

In summary, it is our belief that there are more similarities than differences between the United States and Germany with regard to the future of living environments. Thus, we would assume that our major predictions and their impact on the lives of future elders do not need major qualifications in terms of country-specific issues. We believe that the primacy of the private-home environment will persist and that an ongoing diversification in living environment options will be the major trajectory in both countries. Also, a consumer perspective will increasingly take over as a driving market force for arranging or rearranging living environments in old age. This, in turn, will positively impact upon the development of the consumer market. The growing role of living environments (including its ongoing technological "rearmament") in the context of healthy aging and its major compensation potential after the occurrence of chronic conditions is quite comparable between the United States and Germany as well.

Among the distinctions between the United States and Germany regarding future environments for older people are structural differences in the health and care provision system and the role of racial and ethnic diversity. In particular, the long-term care insurance system introduced in Germany in 1995, built on the notion of a *Solidargemeinschaft* (solidarity community), enables the elderly with severe care needs to remain at home, but it has no counterpart yet in the United States. Furthermore, the sharp difference in home ownership will probably have a differential impact on the readiness of German and U.S. elders to leave their "normal" home environments. This might, however, be counterbalanced by a stronger cultural tendency in the United States to move to a different place after retirement. Moreover, in the United States, those with limited socioeconomic resources, older women, minorities, rural aging elders, and the oldest-old may remain at a distinct disadvantage with regard to their ability to take advantage of the varied living options of the future. Hopefully this may be tempered by the current recognition of the urgency to develop low-cost alternatives for this core group of elders. Finally, the United States offers a wider range of different living environment options than Germany, owing to regional, climate-related, and perhaps also cultural specifics. Prototypical examples are retirement communities and sun cities in the United States.

CONCLUSION

Although we expect no dramatic shifts in living environments for older people in the forthcoming 15 to 20 years, critical alterations in person-environment systems on the micro- (individual) and macro- (societal) levels will make a significant difference in housing quality and the ability to age in place compared to today. These incremental improvements will be driven by, among other factors, specific cohort dynamics of the baby boomers, by the expected paradigm shift in the medical and geriatric system (toward a function-oriented view), and most important, by new technologies in the home environment including smart homes and computer surveillance capabilities.

Private homes will maintain and even enhance their primacy in old age. The expansion of the variety of living environment options, as well as a trend toward in-depth specialization, will further enhance person-environment fits for the great variety of elderly of tomorrow. We speculate that this will hold true for the entire array of living arrangements; that is, from private-home environments to assisted living facilities and institutions. Hence, living environments will become more important and their role will expand to include the full gamut of maintenance, stimulation, and support functions that can be provided by the environment. Lawton's (1983) vision of the potential for a good life in old age, including good environments as a major component, will come closer to reality through these developments.

REFERENCES

Baltes, P. B., & Smith, J. (1999). Multilevel and systemic analyses of old age: Theoretical and empirical evidence for a fourth age. In V. L. Bengtson & K. W. Schaie (Eds.), *Handbook of theories of aging* (pp. 153–173). New York: Springer.

Bundesministerium für Familie, Senioren, Frauen und Jugend (BMFSFJ) [Federal Ministry for Family Affairs, Senior Citizens, Women and Youth] (Ed.). (1998). *Zweiter Altenbericht der Bundesregierung: Wohnen im Alter* [Second report on the situation of older people: Live in age]. Bonn, Germany: Eigenverlag.

Bundesministerium für Familie, Senioren, Frauen und Jugend (BMFSFJ) [Federal Ministry for Family Affairs, Senior Citizens, Women and Youth] (Ed.). (2001). *Dritter Altenbericht der Bundesregierung: Alter und Gesellschaft* [Third report on the situation of older people: Aging and society]. Bonn, Germany: Eigenverlag.

Carp, F. M. (1966). *A future for the aged.* Austin: University of Texas Press.

Day, K., Carreon, D., & Stump, C. (2000). The therapeutic design of environments for people with dementia: A review of the empirical research. *The Gerontologist, 40*(4), 397–416.

Deutscher Bundestag (1998). *Demographischer Wandel: Zweiter Zwischenbericht der Enquete-Kommission "Demographischer Wandel."* [Demographic transition: Second report of the German Parliament Commission "Demographic Transition"]. Bonn, Germany: Universitäts-Buchdruckerei.

Diehl, M. (1998). Everyday competence in later life: Current status and future directions. *The Gerontologist, 38,* 422–433.

Dietzel-Papakyriakou, M., & Olbermann, E. (1998). Wohnsituation älterer Migranten in Deutschland [Living arrangements of older migrants in Germany]. In Deutsches Zentrum für Altersfragen (DZA) [German Center of Gerontology] (Ed.), *Wohnverhältnisse älterer Migranten* [Living arrangements of older migrants] (pp. 9–25). Frankfurt, Germany: Campus.

Federal Interagency Forum on Aging Related Statistics. (2000). *Older Americans 2000: Key indicators of well-being.* Available at www.agingstats.gov/chartbook2000.

Fried, L. P., & Guralnik, J. M. (1997). Disability in older adults: Evidence regarding significance, etiology, and risk. *Journal of the American Geriatrics Society, 45,* 92–100.

Fried, T. R., Van Doorn, C., Tinetti, M. E., & Drickamer, M. A. (1998). Older persons' preferences for site of treatment in acute illness. *Journal of General Internal Medicine, 13,* 522–527.

Gitlin, L. N., Corcoran, M., Winter, L., Boyce, A., & Hauck, W. (2001). A randomized, controlled trial of a home environmental intervention: Effect on efficacy and upset in caregivers and on daily function of persons with dementia. *The Gerontologist, 41,* 4–14.

Guralnik, J. M., & Simonsick, E. M. (1993). Physical disability in older Americans. *Journal of Gerontology, 48,* 3–10.

Hermanson, S., & Citro, J. (1999). *Progress in the housing of older persons: A chartbook.* Washington, DC: American Association for Retired Persons.

Kendig, H., & Pynoos, J. (1996). Housing. In J. E. Birren (Ed.), *Encyclopedia of gerontology* (Vol. 1, pp. 703–713). San Diego, CA: Academic Press.

Kleemeier, R. W. (1959). Behavior and the organization of the bodily and external environment. In J. E. Birren (Ed.), *Handbook of aging and the individual* (pp. 400–451). Chicago: University of Chicago Press.

Kohli, M., & Künemund, H. (Eds.). (2000). *Die zweite Lebenshälfte: Ergebnisse des Alters-Surveys* [The second half of life: Results of the *Alters-Survey*]. Leverkusen, Germany: Leske-Budrich.

Kopetz, S., Steele, C. D., Brandt, J., Baker, A., Kronberg, M., Galik, E., Steinberg, M., Warren, A., & Lyketsos, C. G. (2000). Characteristics and outcomes of dementia residents in an assisted living facility. *International Journal of Geriatric Psychiatry, 15,* 586–593.

LaPlante, M. P., Hendershot, G. E., & Moss, A. J. (1992). *Assistive technology devices and home accessibility features: Prevalence, payment and trends.* Advance Data No. 217. Hyattsville, MD: U.S. Department of Health and Human Services.

Lawton, M. P. (1983). Environment and other determinants of well-being in older people. *The Gerontologist, 23,* 349–357.

Lawton, M. P. (1989). Three functions of the residential environment. In L. A. Pastalan & M. E. Cowart (Eds.), *Lifestyles and housing of older adults: The Florida experience* (pp. 35–50). New York: Haworth.

Lawton, M. P., & Simon, B. B. (1968). The ecology of social relationships in housing for the elderly. *The Gerontologist, 8,* 108–115.

Leff, B., & Burton, J. R. (1998). Future directions: Alternative approaches to traditional hospital care-home hospital. *Clinics in Geriatric Medicine, 14,* 851–856.

Leff, B., Burton, L., Guido, S., Greenough, W. B., Steinwachs, D., & Burton, J. R. (1999). Home hospital program: A pilot study. *Journal of the American Geriatrics Society, 47,* 697–702.

Manton, K., Corder, L., & Stallard, E. (1997). Chronic disability trends in elderly United States populations: 1982–1994. *Proceedings of the National Academy of Sciences, 94,* 2593–2598.

National Center for Assisted Living. American Health Care Association. (1998). *The assisted living sourcebook.* Washington, DC.

National Center on Health Statistics. (March 1, 2000). *An overview of nursing home facilities: Data from the 1997 National Nursing Home Survey.* Advance Data No. 311.

Norburn, J. E. K., Bernard, S. L., Konrad, T. R., Woomert, A., DeFriese, G. H., Kalsbeek, W. D., Koch, G. G., & Ory, M. G. (1995). Self-care and assistance from others in coping with functional status limitations among a national sample of older adults. *Journal of Gerontology: Social Sciences, 50B,* S101–S109.

Pynoos, J., & Regnier, V. (1991). Improving residential environments for the frail elderly: Bridging the gap between theory and application. In J. Birren, J. Lubben, J. Rowe, & D. Deutchman (Eds.), *The concept and measurement of quality of life in the frail elderly.* New York: Academic Press.

Regnier, V. (1994). *Assisted living housing for the elderly: Design innovations from the United States and Europe.* New York: Van Nostrand Reinhold.

Rosow, I. (1967). *Social integration of the aged.* New York: Free Press.

Saup, W. (2001). *Ältere Menschen im Betreuten Wohnen: Ergebnisse der Augsburger Längsschnittstudie Band 1* [Older people in assistive living facilities: Findings of the Augsburg Longitudinal Study]. Augsburg, Germany: Verlag für Gerontologie.

Schneekloth, U., & Müller, U. (2000). *Wirkungen der Pflegeversicherung* [Impact of the long-term care insurance system], Vol. 127, *Schriftenreihe des Bundesministeriums für Gesundheit.* Baden-Baden, Germany: Nomos Verlagsgesellschaft.

Silverstone, B. (1996). Older people of tomorrow: A psychosocial profile. *The Gerontologist, 36,* 27–32.

Statistisches Bundesamt (StBA) [Federal Statistical Office of Germany]. (2000). *Datenreport 1999: Zahlen und Fakten über die Bundesrepublik Deutschland* [Data report 1999: Figures and facts about the Federal Republic of Germany]. Bonn, Germany: Bundeszentrale für Politische Bildung.

U.S. Census Bureau. (1997). *American housing survey.* Washington DC: U.S. Government Printing Office.

Weyerer, S., & Schäufele, M. (1999). Epidemiologie körperlicher und psychischer Beeinträchtigungen im Alter [Epidemiology of somatic and psychic impairments in old age]. In A. Zimber & S. Weyerer (Eds.), *Arbeitsbelastung in der Altenpflege* [Job burden in working with older people] (pp. 3–23). Göttingen, Germany: Hogrefe.

CHAPTER 20

Future Developments in Mobility for Older Citizens: The View of an American Scholar

Patricia F. Waller

T he Western world is aging. This enormous shift in age distribution has been well documented, but the broader implications of that shift have only begun to be explored. Attention has usually focused on identifying the growing need for goods and services so that the elderly can live full and satisfying lives, a worthy and laudatory goal. However, allocation of resources does not occur in a vacuum. In a world of limited resources, those devoted to meeting the needs of the elderly must come at the expense of meeting other needs. Because of the sheer size of the older population, their voice is more likely to be heard than voices expressing competing concerns. Yet the ultimate health and survival of a society require that there be balance in how limited resources are distributed, and the needs of the elderly must be considered in light of the larger context of the political and social environment.

DIMENSIONS OF THE DEMOGRAPHIC SHIFT

Fertility rates, that is, the average number of children born per woman, in the developed nations have fallen below replacement levels (see Figure 20.1),

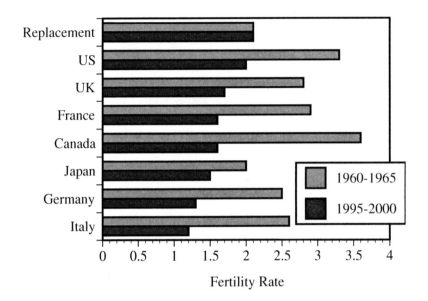

FIGURE 20.1. Fertility rates for developed countries, 1960–1995, 1995–2000.

Source: Center for Strategic and International Studies (CSIS) & Watson Wyatt Worldwide (WWW), 2000, p. 3.

with many nations far below replacement (Center for Strategic and International Studies [CSIS] & Watson Wyatt Worldwide [WWW], 2000). The United States would be in worse shape were it not for immigration.

In the United States, Florida has the highest proportion of older citizens, approaching 1 in 5 persons. By 2025, 39 of the 50 states will be like Florida is today (Research and Policy Committee of the Committee for Economic Development, 1999). Elsewhere this effect will be realized even earlier. Italy will have reached this level as of 2003, with Japan and Germany close behind, by 2005 and 2006, respectively. France and Britain are on track to reach this level by 2016, and Canada by 2023 (Peterson, 1999).

Global life expectancy has grown more in the last 50 years than in the previous 5,000 years. Unitl the Industrial Revolution, those aged 65 and older accounted for no more than 2% to 3% of the population. Today they account for 14% of the population in the developed world, and by 2030 they will make up 25% and more in some countries (Peterson, 1999).

CHANGING FINANCIAL PICTURE

Most older people in the United States collect Social Security payments (Purcell, 2000). Similar programs to support the elderly operate throughout the developed world and have enabled most older people to live in dignity. However, because of programs like Social Security and Medicare, the percent of gross domestic product committed to pensions and health benefits is growing, as seen in Figure 20.2 (CSIS & WWW, 2000).

Unless there are drastic changes, such as major reductions in pension benefits or significant increases in taxes, public pension deficits are projected to consume the net national savings of the developed world, as shown in Figure 20.3 (CSIS & WWW, 2000).

The increased longevity of the elderly is markedly diminishing the proportion of the life spectrum that is spent in the paid labor force. The latter must provide for the young end of the age continuum as well as for the elderly, plus those in between who, for whatever reason, are not able to

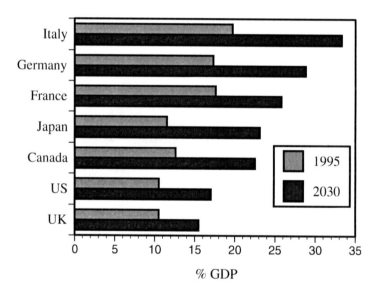

FIGURE 20.2.   Percent of GDP committed to pensions and health benefits in developed countries, 1995–2030.

Source: Center for Strategic and International Studies (CSIS) & Watson Wyatt Worldwide (WWW), 2000, p. 8.

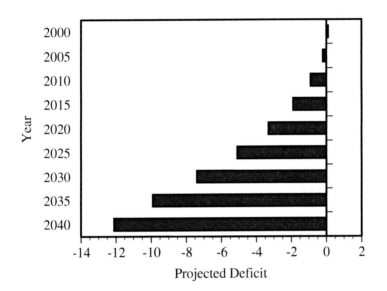

FIGURE 20.3. **Change from 1995 in the combined G-7 budget balance attributable to projected public pension deficits, as a percentage of G-7 GDP, 2000–2040.**
Source: Center for Strategic and International Studies (CSIS) & Watson Wyatt Worldwide (WWW), 2000, p. 10.

support themselves. Since the ratio of taxpayers to pensioners is dropping precipitously, fewer and fewer taxpayers are supporting more and more older citizens (CSIS & WWW, 2000; see Figure 20.4).

In the United States, since 1959, the proportion of all age groups living below the poverty level has dropped significantly. Even more striking, however, is the shift that has occurred for the oldest group. Until the early 1970s, the elderly had by far the highest proportion of people living in poverty. As shown in Figure 20.5, the elderly now have the lowest poverty levels (Dalaker & Proctor, 2000; Thurow, 1996). With these changes has come a marked reversal in spending power. In the 1960s, the average 70-year-old spent only 60% as much as the average 30-year-old. By 1996, that 70-year-old was spending 20% more (Thurow, 1996). This shift in wealth is unprecedented in recorded history.

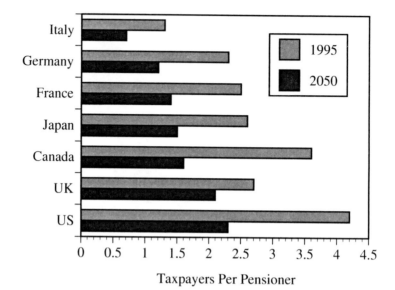

FIGURE 20.4.   Ratio of contributors to retired pensioners in the public pension system, 1995–2050.
Source: Center for Strategic and International Studies (CSIS) & Watson Wyatt Worldwide (WWW), 2000, p. 7.

IMPACTS OF CHANGES IN AGE AND WEALTH

What are the implications of these changes in the age distribution of the population and the corresponding shifts in wealth? In the United States today, the largest group living in poverty is children age 5 and under (Dalaker & Proctor, 2000). The government spends 9 times more on the elderly (those who vote) than on the young (those who do not vote). Yet it is the young who need investments if our economies are to succeed in the future. How will these young people be able to earn enough to carry the increasing tax burden created by the growing elderly population?

In the United States, the elderly are transferring wealth to their children and grandchildren at an unprecedented rate, but this intergenerational generosity does not extend to younger people in general. In some states in the United States, retirement communities, built especially for the elderly and excluding children and young people, are exempt from school taxes. In most states, the elderly have repeatedly refused to increase support for the schools. In 1993, in one town in Michigan with a large retirement population, the

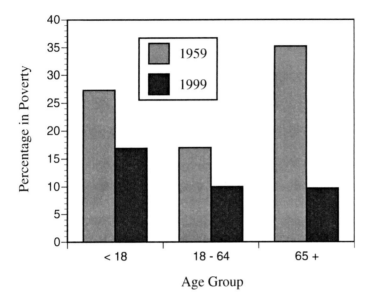

FIGURE 20.5.   Proportion of population living in poverty, by age group, 1959–1999.
Source: Dalaker & Proctor, 2000, p. B-7.

school funding was raided to pay for snow plowing during an exceptionally harsh winter; however, the voters refused to replace the school funds, and the schools had to close down several months early (Thurow, 1996).

TRANSPORTATION IMPLICATIONS

How does transportation relate to these large shifts in demographics? Societal resources are limited and are not sufficient to meet all needs, however legitimate they may be. Resources will become even less adequate as the population continues to age and the ratio of workers to pensioners decreases. Consequently, transportation systems cannot function for older persons only. The allocation of resources must include the elderly but not be limited to their use. Systems must provide universal design, enabling use by older people as well as others.

What is needed goes beyond simply providing universal design of vehicles, terminals, bus stops, and walkways, or even routing and scheduling of transit. There is an immediate need for transportation professionals to reach out to others in the community to explore societal needs and opportunities that can be met by older citizens (Waller, 1998). One example concerns greater participation of older people in the labor force, an option that is increasingly attractive to those seeking workers.

In the United States, a recent study found that a significant proportion of older people who are not working are willing and able to work (see Figure 20.6). These proportions represent between 5 million and 6 million people who would welcome the opportunity to continue working, at least on a part-time basis (Research and Policy Committee of the Committee for Economic Development, 1999). The transportation community should participate with others to redesign work opportunities, including retraining opportunities, more flexible working hours, part-time work opportunities, modification of the work environment to facilitate older worker performance, and user-friendly transportation to get people back and forth to training and work. Of particular importance, for everyone but especially for the elderly, is that transportation facilities be viewed as safe. In the United States, older people are concerned about personal safety when using public transportation.

There are other ways for older citizens to become more integrated into

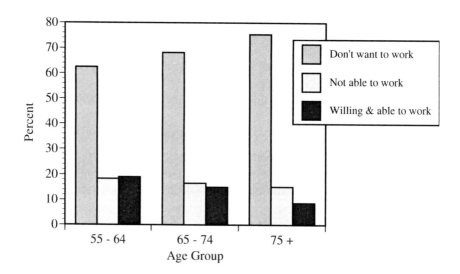

FIGURE 20.6.   Proportion of U.S. nonworking elderly by work preference.

Source: Research and Policy Committee of the Committee for Economic Development, 1999, Table 1, p. 13.

the larger society, as well as ways to make opportunities for participation more attractive to older people. A growing need for volunteers could be better met by older participants if transportation were available. It is in this arena that the transportation community needs to be a strong participant.

CONCLUSIONS

In summary, global aging in the developed world is creating a crisis. Much discussion of transportation and mobility for older citizens fails to consider the larger context in which transportation must be provided. In light of the changing demographics, including the increase in both numbers and proportions of elderly, as well as the increase in longevity, we will be faced with hard choices to make in the overall allocation of societal resources. Greater consideration must be given to those people who cannot speak for themselves: young children.

Given the political power of the older generations, policy makers will be pressured to ignore realities and perhaps to make choices that have devastating consequences for the longer-term viability of Western society. To the extent possible, transportation programs to improve the lives of older citizens must be considered in light of how they might advantage the rest of the age spectrum as well.

Society will increasingly need the contributions and involvement of older citizens. For many, transportation issues will be a barrier to that participation. While transportation issues are not the only problem in achieving greater involvement, more often than not they are a part of the solution. User-friendly transportation systems can assist increased integration of older citizens into the larger economy and society.

As our society ages and the elderly acquire increasing power in both numbers and influence, there is a saying that captures the spirit of what is needed: Old people planting trees they'll never sit under.

We need to be creating transportation and mobility systems that facilitate and encourage more old people to plant the trees they'll never sit under.

REFERENCES

Center for Strategic and International Studies (CSIS) & Watson Wyatt Worldwide (WWW). (2000). *Global aging: The challenge of the new millennium.* Catalog No. W-315. Washington, DC: Center for Strategic and International Studies.

Dalaker, J., & Proctor, B. D. (2000). *Poverty in the United States: 1999.* U.S. Census Bureau, Current Population Reports, Series P60-210. Washington, DC: U.S. Government Printing Office.

Peterson, P. G. (1999). Gray dawn: The global aging crisis. *Foreign Affairs,* January/February, 42–55.

Purcell, P. J. (2000). Older workers: Employment and retirement trends. *Monthly Labor Review,* October, 19–30.

Research and Policy Committee of the Committee for Economic Development. (1999). *New opportunities for older workers.* HD6280.P76. New York: Committee for Economic Development.

Thurow, L. C. (1996). *The future of capitalism.* New York: William Morrow.

Waller, P. F. (1998). Transportation to meet societal needs. *ITS Quarterly,* 6(1), 5–11.

CHAPTER 21

Future Developments of Mobility in the Elderly: A German Traffic Psychologist's Perspective

Günter Kroj

Technological progress as well as demographic and cultural changes are having a hitherto unimagined effect on our lifestyle and behavior patterns; they are opening up new worlds of experience to us, and the speed of change is constantly increasing in our era. As the models within our society change, the self and outside images of the different generations also change, as do ways of perceiving and communicating with each other. As the needs and habits of the elderly change, so necessarily does their mobility (Rudinger, Jansen, Jung, & Kahmann, 1999).

The changed needs, habits, and modes of behavior among the elderly and the way in which society deals with them have been the subject of numerous new studies, which have in part yielded contradictory results. Studies investigating communication between the generations, day-to-day traffic encounters, and use of modern communication among the elderly are of particular significance here. These studies indicate that the elderly will claim more political influence in the medium and long term, a higher social profile, and greater social recognition (Jansen, 2001).

The increased desire of today's elders for staying mobile as long as possible not only is fostered by industry and commerce, but also is associated with a wider range of opportunities for mental stimulation and cultural activity. In view of the struggle for ever-scarcer resources for all generations, however, it is not clear where the aging societies of highly civilized Western countries will set social and political limits, or how they will be able to accept these limits in the face of economic and ecological constraints. Finding socially harmonized strategies for the integration of the elderly with their particular individual mobility requirements presents a task of increasing political significance (Becker et al., 2001).

OPPORTUNITIES AND LIMITS

Let us begin our discussion of these issues by first reviewing the results of an international conference on questions concerned with the opportunities and limits of older adults' outdoor mobility, which took place in May 2000 in Cologne, Germany, under the auspices of the Federal Highway Research Institute, the German Road Safety Council, and the Ministry of Transport, Building, and Housing together with the European Union [Bundesanstalt für Strassenwesen (BASt) (Federal Highway Research Institute), 2000]. The following conclusions were drawn from this conference:

- The widely held recognition that elderly people do not form a homogeneous group is also true with respect to their outdoor mobility. Older adults are characterized by a very pronounced variety in terms of mobility-related expectations and lifestyles.

- Elderly persons are the experts as far as their everyday life and everyday mobility are concerned. They must therefore be more closely involved in the development, introduction, and implementation of road safety measures and traffic technologies.

- Elderly persons have an interest in learning and further training. This interest also applies to technological progress and modern developments in road safety work.

- The positive evaluation of and attitudes toward old age which are developing at present must be grasped and taken advantage of through new road safety work models.

- In order to increase road safety—not only for the elderly—a greater orientation toward the unprotected and weaker participants in road traffic is recommended. This particularly involves decreasing the speed of traffic in residential areas.

- The mobility habits which are acquired during one's lifetime are largely retained in old age. This means that mobility for elderly people should be retained and encouraged by means both of technology and training opportunities.
- Safe participation in road traffic results from a lifelong learning process. The maintenance of independence, as well as the retention and encouragement of skill and mobility, plays a particularly important role for older individuals in this connection. The use of local public transport should be encouraged by making it as user friendly as possible.
- Technological systems can compensate for the loss of driving skill and enhance travel planning, thus contributing to accident reduction.
- When implementing road safety measures, varying types of communication should be selected which are suited to the different life situations and lifestyles of older adults, taking new media particularly into consideration (BASt, 2001).

The foregoing considerations are based on the following precept which is widely accepted in Europe: societal integration of elders should take precedence over exclusion. Measures which allow older people to participate actively in social life and in traffic and encourage their mobility are given priority. Measures to eliminate certain individuals or to limit participation in traffic should be taken only when it is not otherwise possible to ensure safety. Preventing elderly individuals from accidents and encouraging their mobility are thus somewhat at odds with one another. In trying to solve this dilemma, it might be useful to differentiate between elders in the *third* and *fourth* ages, as well as between older people of today and future generations of elders, to design better tailored programs for participation of those who are actively mobile and those who need to cope with their diminished mobility. The basic message from the Cologne conference (BASt, 2000), as well as from a project group held at the Federal Highway Research Institute (BASt, 2001), is that society needs the elderly to be mobile; if the elders are mobile, they can give a lot to society. This message leads to the following conclusion: If negative selection mechanisms are used as sparingly as possible, trust in the competence of elderly people as well as active support for maintaining their mobility will result.

Mollenkopf (2000) presented a more fundamental way of viewing future developments and their resulting problems. Based on changes in social structure and lifestyles, she concluded,

In the future there will be more elderly people and more elderly people who live alone. These people will have different experiences, opportunities and different expectations as regards their mobility and participation in road traffic than the elderly of today. However, based on the technical possibilities which are available to them in all areas of daily life, it is an open question as to whether they will stay at home more or go out more— both would be possible. (Mollenkopf, 2000, p. 140)

Particularly important in this line of argumentation is that the elderly need quite new abilities and skills in order to use the available technology. It might well be that this will lead to the experience of new inadequacies and new discrimination tendencies in old age. An ever-widening gap between the technically educated and the technically inexperienced means that many elderly persons will be able to use all the technical possibilities that are open to them in an optimal manner, but others will have to do without. Although the proportion of nonusers may become smaller over time, their problems must not be ignored (Mollenkopf, 2000, p. 140). This is particularly true of older road users who are not able to cope with the increasing intensity and speed of traffic and who are not able, for whatever reason, to use the new traffic and vehicle systems. The situation becomes particularly precarious when public and private services are increasingly directed toward mobile car drivers and Internet users, as then there is the danger that a considerable proportion of the elderly will be excluded from important areas of society. This would be a fatal consequence of social and technical change (Mollenkopf, 2000, p. 141).

A study conducted by various gerontological research institutions in Germany examined traffic development, traffic prognoses, and such other factors as personal attitudes and lifestyles affecting the influence of traffic on mobility. An interdisciplinary workshop, which discussed the influence of demographics, industry and commerce, politics, society, traffic development, town and regional planning, and individual development on mobility, was convened to create a questionnaire to be used by a larger group of experts (Rudinger et al., 1999). A scenario for the safety of the elderly in the German traffic system in the year 2010 was then described (Jansen, 2001).

The conclusion drawn from this research was that, because of a widening gap in income, there will be increasing social and financial polarization of the population. This could cause difficulties with regard to the safety of the elderly in traffic. For example, the older and socially disadvantaged might be excluded from society, owing to differences between the t-rich (technically rich) and the t-poor (technically poor) road users and an increase in antisocial behavior with regard to traffic interaction between the generations. A positive effect on the safety of elderly road users in the long term may be caused by changes which will already begin within the next 10 years. If older people in the future are able to make extensive use of new information and communications technologies in connection with their mobility and specific new services (e.g., teleshopping), this might lead to less need for actual movement. Whether such services are used by the elderly depends upon whether the services are affordable and user friendly. Also, age-related increases in resources (expertise, traffic experience, dealing with loss of ability, compensation techniques) can improve subjective feelings of safety and decision-making behavior among the mobile elders.

One should consider here as well the argument that, because of the expected stagnation in the funding of local public transport and target group–oriented safety programs, some experts hold the view that the opportunities for increasing safety for elderly road users are in jeopardy (Jansen, 2001). Similarly, due to the continuing deficits of local public transport and the railways and the same tight financial constraints, it is likely that little consideration will be paid to the interests of older people when matters relating to traffic are being planned and implemented. This will mean that safe forms of mobility for the elders, which are also viable in the long term from an ecological point of view, will not be given due attention. However, this estimate of the present situation appears somewhat pessimistic, given the increasing wealth of our society. Interestingly, experts in the field do not expect that the safety of elderly people will be reduced because of the mere fact that there will be more older drivers on German roads. On the contrary, it is assumed that there could be an increase in safety because of the increase in the number of female drivers, a group which is generally characterized by a higher ability to compensate for any problems and a more defensive driving style (Jansen, 2001).

Based on the large number of changes and the continuation of traditions and tendencies which affect traffic safety, a reasonable overall expectation is that there will be a slight reduction in safety for older road users in the near and far future, particularly against the background of the stagnation in funding of traffic safety programs. Against this background, a project group which combines the Federal Highway Research Institute with the leading German safety organizations has proposed a series of pilot projects aimed to further road safety for elderly people (Becker et al., 2001). Some of the ideas deduced from this research are described in the following paragraphs.

CONCEPTS FOR MOBILITY AND TRAFFIC SAFETY FOR ELDERLY PEOPLE

While some elders are skilled and experienced and have become internationally mobile on a more or less flexible basis, others are largely limited to local mobility. Technical developments, here in particular the increase in traffic flow and information about current traffic conditions, confronts a heterogeneous target group of elderly people and accentuates the differences between them even further. The organizers of a website for seniors report that the elderly often use the Internet to gain information about traffic and ways of optimizing their mobility (www.senior.web.uni-bonn.de). However, at the same time, many of the elderly are worried about whether they will be able to traverse an intersection on foot. Large interpersonal differences in economic resources and state of health after retirement are other reasons why elderly people have varying expectations regarding mobility.

The challenge of integrating all elderly persons into traffic remains. Because of the increase in traffic volume itself, elders face higher demands on their competence, orientation, and speed of decision making. Use of information and communications technology will become a significant factor here. Consequently, in a pilot study of mobility and elderly people, we intend to carry out trials on a combination of broad dissemination of information and individual information programs within a limited geographical and time framework in 2 communities over 2 years. The Federal Highway Research Institute will promote scientific support and evaluation of the project (Becker et al., 2001). The central aim of the measures is related to the prevention of road accidents. In view of the challenges presented by modern motorized road traffic and the difficulty of integrating elderly people into it, however, a further aim of the measures is simultaneously to maintain their mobility. Following a socially balanced strategy, particularly elderly men and women who feel insecure and who require help and those who are handicapped or ill should not be excluded from the development processes in relation to the group of more active elders. Encouraging mobility among elderly people should not be undertaken at the expense of ecological considerations; rather, use should be made of sustainable variants.

In more detail, measures are proposed in the following 4 areas. Measures for broadly targeted dissemination of information to elderly road users are intended to make them aware of particular potential sources of danger and should offer recommendations regarding behavior (by communication agencies, informational campaigns, magazines, newspapers, weekly supplements, radio programs, brochures with a local focus, CD-ROM, and video). Forms of individual communication are, above all, directed to strengthening individual skills so as to lessen traffic risk. For the other road users who interact with elderly persons, a broadly targeted information campaign is proposed, aimed at creating understanding and consideration between the generations in road traffic situations. Measures for the prevention of traffic accidents are aimed at using all the available forces, including the different local organizations, in order to support safe participation in traffic for elderly individuals.

With regard to informational campaigns, one must check whether the target group is being reached by the form of address used. In particular, the aim is to determine what combinations of media and individual address achieve the greatest effect with regard to the target group. One must also check whether the publicity succeeds in drawing the attention of the elderly to the messages and convincing them of their importance. Trials are initially aimed at establishing what offerings are actually taken up by the elderly. This means that the elderly participating in the program will be asked explicitly if they find the measures attractive and acceptable. Finally, it must be established whether the interventions have an effect on the actual behavior of road users. With regard to the measures aimed at other road users who interact with the elderly, one must examine to what extent the younger generation can be persuaded to afford the elderly persons more consideration on the road. Structural improvements to the traffic system for the benefit of elderly persons must also be assessed; ideally, the system should motivate the elders to protect themselves in traffic, and a task force, created by regional institutions, might be created to monitor progress in this regard.

The model project is fundamentally influenced by the concept of "social marketing." The main question is how the services (measures) which are created can be marketed effectively in order to reach the intended target group. It is therefore necessary to deal with the question of how the targets of the 4 main aims of the program can best be reached. If the model proves successful, the measures which have been tried and proven could be put to use in other regions as early as 2003 [Bundesministerium für Verkehr, Bauen und Wohnen (BMVBW) (Federal Ministry of Traffic, Construction and Housing), 2001].

THE GENERATIONS MEETING IN TRAFFIC

The interventions outlined above address the motivation and behavior of traffic participants, based on their personal experiences of traffic situations.

Although much attention has been focused on the heterogeneity of elderly people in traffic, one cannot generally state that they are incompetent participants in the system. It is also the case that social exclusion of the older adults must be avoided in the thought and behavior patterns of the other road users. This means that an aim of the traffic safety work is to create an attitude of consideration and understanding toward the elders on the part of the young.

Thus, exploring the meeting of the generations in traffic situations is another objective of the series of the pilot studies mentioned above. One issue to be investigated is whether there actually is a conflict between the slower elderly and the faster young people in the road traffic situation. What seems to be clear is that some elderly people feel insecure because of the more intense and complex traffic situation which has developed. It is also known that younger people can have a critical attitude toward some elders and vice versa. However, few signs of conflict—for example, aggression between young and old—appear to be present in current traffic situations. The most promising perspective thus is that young and old have their special difficulties to overcome in the traffic situation, and they need to take care of each other in this social event. The use of traffic information can make the generations aware of each other and bring differences and common factors into focus. Training can as well include common activities for young and older people and, by this means, further the dialogue between different generations from young to middle and late adulthood. Moreover, one should not underestimate the mutual support between the different generations and between elderly people themselves. There are good reasons for both: intergenerational forms of meetings, on the one hand, and opportunities for the older individuals to consider their own traffic habits in an interchange with their contemporaries, on the other.

REFERENCES

Becker, S., Berger, R., Dumbs, M., Emsbach, M., Erlemeier, N., Kaiser, H. J., & Six, U. (2001). *Perspektiven der Verkehrssicherheitsarbeit mit Senioren* [Perspectives of traffic safety work with senior citizens]. Report M 131, Reports of the Federal Highway Research Institute. Bergisch Gladbach, Germany: BASt.

Bundesanstalt für Strassenwesen (BASt) [Federal Highway Research Institute]. (2000). Deutscher Verkehrssicherheitsrat e.V.; Bundesministerium für Verkehr, Bau- und Wohnungswesen, Kommission der Europäischen Union. *Internationale Konferenz: Mehr Verkehrssicherheit für Senioren* [More road safety for senior citizens]. Köln,

2.–4.05.2000. Report M 123, Reports of the Federal Highway Research Institute. Bergisch Gladbach, Germany: BASt.

Bundesanstalt für Strassenwesen (BASt) [Federal Highway Research Institute]. (2001). *Mehr Verkehrssicherheit für Senioren* [More road safety for senior citizens]. Bergisch Gladbach, Wissenschaftliche Informationen der Bundesanstalt für Strassenwesen, info 2/01. Bergisch Gladbach, Germany: BASt.

Bundesministerium für Verkehr, Bauen und Wohnen (BMVBW) [Federal Ministry of Traffic, Construction and Housing]. (2001). *Programme for more safety in road traffic*. Berlin: BMVBM.

Jansen, E. (2001). Ältere Menschen im künftigen Sicherheitssystem Straße/Fahrzeug/ Mensch [Elderly people in a future traffic system]. *Schriftenreihe der Bundesanstalt für Straßenwesen (BASt): Mensch und Sicherheit (Heft M 134)*. Bremerhaven: Wirtschaftsverlag NW.

Mollenkopf, H. (2000). Elderly motorists in a changing society. In *Berichte der Bundesanstalt für Strassenwesen* [More road safety for senior citizens]. Report M 123. Reports of the Federal Highway Research Institute. Bergisch Gladbach, Germany: BASt, pp. 136–141.

Rudinger, G., Jansen, E., Jung, C., & Kahmann, V. (1999). *Expertentagung im Auftrag der Bundesanstalt für Straßenwesen: Seniorenworkshop des Psychologischen Institutes der Universität Bonn*. Bonn, 4. Mai 1999 [Expert meeting: Senior citizens workshop organized by the Psychological Institute of the University of Bonn. Bonn, May 4, 1999].

CHAPTER 22

Living Environments and Mobility in Old Age in Germany and the United States: Integrative Thoughts on Aging Independently

Neil Charness

To meet the challenge of summarizing this rich set of chapters dealing with living environments and mobility, I will rely on 2 themes: person-environment (P-E) fit and person-community integration. One can ask about P-E fit for both places and for the mobility systems that enable us to traverse from place to place. Further, both environments and mobility systems can help or hinder the degree of person-community integration. I will reexamine some of the ideas expressed already in the chapters of this volume within these 2 themes.

Living environments and mobility at first glance seem to be disparate topics; however, they represent 2 sides of the same coin dealing with time and space use. Let me start with a personal example that highlights some important changes over the last century in Germany or the United States. On a typical weekday, I leave my home by walking into the garage, getting into my air-conditioned automobile, and driving about 15 to 20 minutes (traveling about 4.5 miles in moderate to heavy traffic) from my home to the parking lot across the street from my office. Once I arrive at work, I spend the majority of my time in my office, classrooms, and meeting rooms and a small amount of time walking between rooms in the buildings I work in and walking outdoors between buildings on my campus. I spend, perhaps, 20 minutes of outdoors time in total. After the return commute at the end of the day to my home, unless I work in my yard or take an exercise walk outside, I spend the remaining hours in my air-conditioned home. My time spent in the natural environment versus the artificial environments that our culture has assembled is probably completely reversed from that experienced by the earliest human beings living on the plains of Africa. The intensification of time in artificial environments and the minimization of time in natural ones has probably been radical even in comparison with that experienced by my grandparents and great-grandparents. The roughly 9 miles of road that I traverse by car in 30 minutes would take perhaps 3 hours of travel time by foot in my city environment and perhaps twice as long in an environment where there were no roads.

The tools for mobility that have been assembled in the past 100 years (mainly publicly funded roads and industry-assembled automobiles) serve the basic functions of our society very well indeed and are responsible in no small part for the wealth that has been created in modern industrialized societies. The artificial living environments we typically inhabit have also increased in functionality, if not in esthetics. A sign of the increased wealth in American (and probably in German) society is the decline in housing overcrowding (defined as more than 1 person per room) from 20% in 1940 to less than 5% in 1990 (U.S. Census Bureau, 2000a). The rooms we lived in 60 years ago were also a lot smaller than the rooms we inhabit today (as was abundantly clear from a visit that I made a decade ago to the home in which I grew up as a child). The time and energy people are willing to expend in maintaining a home is a testament to the human desire to create highly personalized artificial environments (see Chapter 6 in this volume).

Two issues of person-environment fit and person-community integration underpin the twin themes of this volume: living environments and mobility. One assumption is that, by designing better living environments, we can enhance the person-environment fit and hence satisfaction with the environment for older adults. A major reason why people value mobility is that it affords them the opportunity to connect with distant others and maintain a sense of belonging and integration within an extended (in space) community—one that more often now than ever before in history includes physically distant family and friends. Of all the inventions in the past few hundred years, the telephone has probably contributed the most (greatest percentage of the population as users) to bridging physical distance, although the automobile and airplane have contributed enormously too. So too has the very recent invention of e-mail which is so successful a bridging agent for current users of the Internet. Internet users are less often older adults (Newburger, 2001), and use varies enormously by country; for example, Internet use approaches 60% in Sweden but only about 10% in Greece (U.S. Department of Commerce, 2002).

The ability of technological advances to bridge space and time was made fully evident to me when I was unable to fly as planned on September 11, 2001, to the International Conference on Technology and Aging in Toronto, Canada, from Tallahassee, Florida, owing to the grounding of all aircraft in North American airspace. With the help of a telephone line link to the presentation room and by sending PowerPoint presentations ahead so the conference organizer could project them, my symposium peers and I were able to deliver our papers and answer questions from the distant audience. Communications efficiency and effectiveness (e.g., Charness, Park, & Sabel, 2001) is another important piece of the puzzle that constitutes well-being in old age.

Both of the themes treated in this volume can be viewed as contributing to a curious paradox. We want to design living environments that will be attractive and supportive. We also want to design transportation systems that are effective and efficient enough to lure people away from their attractive, supportive dwellings. The most cogent reason, though, for considering these topics together is that good design requires considering the constraints in each system. Even an apparently well-engineered home in the suburbs of a city can become a liability for someone who can no longer drive and might have to depend on others for transportation to a distant physician's office or to a shopping area. Having freeways to link distant parts of a city may be an unnecessary luxury if people are living in communities that provide primary services within walking distance from homes and apartments.

It may seem obvious, but it is worth examining why we are concerned with living environments and mobility for older adults. One reason is the perception that, particularly for our older citizens, neither living environments nor mobility are optimally designed. A second reason is the implicit belief that if we could redesign these systems we would significantly improve the well-being of seniors. We might assume both that there are acceptable ways to measure well-being and that we could determine whether a change in design would improve some aspect of daily functioning. To the skeptic, both assumptions are open to question. Furthermore, determining the most cost-effective way in which to achieve improvements is a topic well worth exploring. It appears that there are 2 main choices. Societies can adopt the plan of guaranteeing adequate income to seniors (and/or their caregivers) so that they can choose how to allocate their resources to improve functioning. If adequate income cannot be guaranteed and social safety nets must be fashioned, the scientific community will probably have to provide some metrics for how public resources should be spent across competing alternatives such as housing and transportation. As some comparisons of differences in approach between Germany and the United States make clear, there are very different social philosophies in play about the desirability of government intervention in the lives of its citizens.

PERSON-ENVIRONMENT FIT

Among the themes common to the chapters dealing with P-E fit are the interactive and transactional nature of the relationship, compensation processes to accommodate age-related changes, and the need for better data and theory, as well as some suggested frameworks.

The late Powell Lawton was probably most responsible for drawing our attention to the concept of P-E fit as it applies to aging (e.g., Lawton, 1977). P-E fit refers to the ability of a person to cope with his or her physical and psychological environments. As personal resources diminish owing to age-related declines in perceptual, cognitive, and psychomotor capabilities, environments that were initially in balance may become too demanding. The need to broaden P-E fit to consider people as part of the equation leads me to the consideration of person-community integration. Person-community integration refers to how integrated people feel within their social environments. As mobility declines normatively with age, the ability to communicate effectively with important social partners may become impaired. Also, as cohorts advance in age, they lose significant social partners.

To the extent that societies choose to intervene in the lives of their citizens, they need to do so in a way that respects personal goals and enhances the probability of their accomplishment. Part of that process should work toward improving the opportunity to access a social community as people advance in age.

One of the challenges for intervention is that there is enormous diversity in macroenvironments on our planet. Extreme heat and cold tax human thermoregulation ability, particularly that of older adults. As a result, humans actively manipulate their local microenvironments in order to survive. They do so by clothing themselves appropriately—dressing being one of the so-called activities of daily living (ADLs)—and finding and building appropriate dwellings.

One of the disappointments in the excellent set of chapters that have been assembled in this volume is that we have seen no models, few theories, and a liberal dose of loose frameworks. We have seen some interesting data, though mainly survey results. We are not yet in a mature science phase where we have models or theories that make predictions useful to service providers and designers—that is a good goal to strive toward. Ideally, we would like guidelines that would enable us to make intelligent choices among design alternatives. What is the optimal size for congregate housing dwellings for older adults at different levels of ability? Would subsidized taxi service or public transportation using specialized vehicles such as "wheeltrans" be better for older adults with mobility impairments? How long should traffic lights be set on green to allow older pedestrians to cross streets safely? The current state is a normal state of affairs for phenomena as rich and complex as living environments and mobility. Also, design has been and likely always will be more of an art than a science because of contextual constraints; that is, design guidelines may depend on unique features of the populations and places. For instance, issuing a guideline that the walking distance from public transit stops to target buildings should be no more than 0.5 kilometers could work for older adults in the flat terrain of Kansas but might not work well for those who must walk uphill in a mountainside village in Bavaria. There is a need to consider broad frameworks for living environments and mobility despite the difficulty in applying them to concrete situations.

Theoretical Issues in P-E Fit

In Chapter 1, Wahl provides a fine example of such an encompassing framework for considering living environments and their role in aging. Among Wahl's central points are that environments, seen broadly as encompassing physical and social aspects, can maintain, stimulate, and support competence and optimal aging. Also, there are important differences between private and institutional settings for competence enhancement. Important values are privacy, being at home, and socializing. We need to pay closer attention to measurement issues, the oldest-old, nonurban settings, new technologies, and the contextual aspect of aging. We also need to consider pluralism in theory development in this area.

I wonder whether, if we had better measurement and better data, it would be enough to ensure that we could improve the lives of older adults. How would such knowledge address potential political barriers to progress such as housing regulations? Some of these points are addressed in Chapters 8 and 11.

In Chapter 2, Schaie provides a thought-provoking rationale for why mobility is important for older adults and is not likely to be easily obviated by technology. The following reasons are given:

- Reduction of personal isolation
- Cultural and recreational activities
- Full choice of goods and services
- Access to health care and personal services
- Access to financial and personal consultants
- Worship and spiritual opportunities.

A critical reason for mobility support is psychological, namely, preserving individual choice. Old age is usually a time of diminishing resources, including physical, psychological, and financial ones. Maintaining choice is undoubtedly helpful to psychological well-being (e.g., Langer & Rodin, 1976), and its role in the well-being of older adults living in the community is probably underappreciated.

Most of Schaie's reasons for mobility fit the social needs of people. Others fit our instrumental needs as biological organisms. If we have to make a choice, based on financial considerations, we probably could rank order these from ADLs, such as feeding which requires grocery shopping, to instrumental activities of daily living (IADLs), such as banking which requires access to people outside the home, to social activities of daily living (SADLs) which require access to other people for social interaction to take place. The last activity fits with the notion of person-community integration.

In Chapter 3, Fozard provides some important contexts for P-E fit, focusing on the person side of the equation. According to Fozard, there are 3 dimensions of physical aging: structural, control, and information. These refer to what in information-processing system terms (e.g., Newell & Simon, 1972) concern the effector system, the decision-making system, and the receptor system. He points out the different classes of intervention for physical aging:

• Person: training, lifestyle options
• Environmental intervention: fit person, stimulate
• Combination: most common intervention.

One point is worth reiterating, namely, the role of prevention. Many of the infirmities of old age might be delayed, Fozard argues, if people acted proactively to maintain better fitness levels and avoided situations that might accelerate age-related loss in function, such as exposure to noise.

I would go beyond the injunction to avoid harm and argue that we should consider training for compensating for loss in function. Our society currently invests most of its resources in educating the young for a lifetime of work. As lives have lengthened, we probably need to consider, for the first time in history, education and training for old age. A crude example might be training for alternative input device use with computer systems. Using a mouse in the preferred hand for many years might be expected to lead to repetitive strain injuries. If we trained ourselves to use the mouse in each hand, we could either delay the onset of such injuries, or prepare for the case when disease (e.g., stroke) or injury disables the preferred hand by being immediately ready to use the other with high efficiency. Hopefully, better technology will help us avoid repetitive strain injuries, for instance by allowing us to substitute voice commands for manual ones.

Fozard reminds us of the goals and tools of human factors research: optimizing the productivity, safety, and comfort of the user by redesigning tools and environments and by training the user. This synthesis speaks mostly to issues of person-environment fit.

In Chapter 4, Kruse broadens the perspective of person-environment fit by attempting to address both individual and environmental measurement components. Kruse notes at the beginning the utility of viewing aging from different perspectives such as neuropsychological and cognitive. He points to the usefulness of considering the concept of subsidiarity, negotiating the maximal degree of independence between people and institutional settings, and using state intervention as a last resort, a perspective that fits particularly well in the current U.S. zeitgeist of individual reliance.

In his empirical work, Kruse shows the necessity of considering both environmental factors and psychosocial factors in predicting various dimensions of self-concept, including the notion of resilience. One intriguing finding that he presents is the lack of relation between objective and subjective evaluations for housing satisfaction. (Similar results are mentioned by Oswald in Chapter 9.) This finding leads to the sobering conclusion that measuring only the environment provides an incomplete picture of what older adults perceive to be important in their world. Though we have moved away from the trend of ascribing behavior to within subject characteristics and moved more toward attributing activities to environmental determinants (e.g., Vicente & Wang, 1998), we need to keep a balance by including both sets of variables in our prediction equations.

In Chapter 5, Gitlin provides a wonderful testimonial to the influential contributions of Powell Lawton. Aside from pioneering empirical work in developing many of the measurement scales used in gerontological science, Lawton developed compelling theoretical frameworks, none more impressive, perhaps, than that for P-E fit. Gitlin's chapter emphasizes the interactional nature of person-environment transactions. It conceptualizes P-E as a process and intervention as requiring attention to the multidimensional nature of this transaction. Some cogent examples are provided of such intervention strategies for people with Alzheimer's disease (e.g., the REACH project, a multisite, multitreatment randomized trial that deserves careful attention). Perhaps the most fitting tribute we can provide to commemorate Lawton's lifelong labor is to "get on with the work." We need to flesh out better measurement tools for assessing environments in order to understand their impact in supporting or inhibiting older adults as they strive to reach their goals and live the "good life."

For an environmental view of how to approach the "good life," Rowles and Watkins, in Chapter 6, poetically address the twin issues of person-environment fit and person-community integration with a "spaces into places" approach to the roles of history, habit, heart, and hearth. I was reminded of the old saying, "Science teaches us about life, but Art teaches us how to live." An important implication of this chapter is that we should not ignore a person's unique history when we draw up design plans in an attempt to make them feel at home in a new dwelling. Such intuitions about the role of implicit memory have experimental support. Studies demonstrate its preservation even in dementia (Sainsbury & Coristine, 1986). People with dementia who were unable to pick out relatives from strangers by using direct recognition could still "recognize" family members emotionally in terms of the choice of whom they might want to spend time with from among a set of photographs containing family members and strangers. Much hard work lies ahead if we are to operationalize these constructs and demonstrate that we can indeed improve the quality of life of older adults by designing dwellings that can serve as true home environments.

Pragmatic Issues in P-E Fit

As Regnier points out early in Chapter 7, nearly 15% of the older population (age 65+) in the United States live in some form of purpose-built housing, though only 5% dwell in traditional nursing homes. Hence 85% live in facilities built for the general population. Given the well-known changes in human abilities with increased age and the exponential increase in disability past the age of 65, it is obvious that there is going to be a significant need for adaptation and retrofitting of existing housing stock as the baby boom generation moves into old age.

Regnier notes the recent shift in categories of purpose-built housing that now include a more varied mix than ever before, including assisted living dwellings, one of the fastest growing forms of housing for the elderly in the United States. One reason that builders in the United States have shifted from traditional nursing home construction to assisted living construction is that it is far less regulated. Thus, there is a greater opportunity to experiment with more creative designs than would be the case with construction limited by more restrictive regulations. A side effect of this trend is the shift toward smaller numbers of units per dwelling and more upscale units. Furthermore, because of low staffing associated with assisted living dwellings (to cut costs and increase profitability over the more regulated nursing home dwelling), there is a greater need to have families involved in the support process. This has both good and bad side effects. Smaller, less institutional-looking environments are likely to encourage family participation to a greater extent than the more clinical-looking nursing homes. Such a side effect is welcome in helping to provide person-community integration. However, as people age and become more impaired and if they are physically distant from family members, they are less likely to remain in assisted living environments, unless technological innovations such as desktop videoconferencing take hold.

The bottom line is that those with more resources are likely to do well with this shift in building trends in the United States. Possibly, as more spaces are freed up in the less attractive environments, waiting lists could conceivably shrink there too. There may well be a "trickle down" effect that results in "a rising tide lifting all ships," to mix a few metaphors. If you are in the upper income level when you reach old age and become frail, your choices of housing environments are definitely improving in the United States. We need to consider mechanisms that will extend such choices to the rest of the aging population.

As the demographics cited by Großjohann at the beginning of Chapter 8 indicate, there is a great need to improve housing options for the frail elderly in Germany, particularly for the cohorts of age 80 years and above, and perhaps surprisingly, for those who dwell in what was once called West Germany. What form this housing should take is only now under active consideration, and the attempt to create "home communities" is especially praiseworthy. It helps to move toward the "spaces into places" philosophy espoused by Rowles and Watkins in Chapter 6. These new initiatives also offer promise for integrating housing into the surrounding community and providing outreach to the community. Part of making a house a home involves its location and degree of integration with the wider surrounding community.

In Chapter 11, Weisman notes that Kurt Lewin's approach to research, particularly his notion of "action research," still has considerable merit. Although Lewin was concerned primarily with social psychology, the idea of prodding complex systems in the real world to try to understand their dynamics is one that underlies much of the field of human factors. So-called field studies play an important role in fulfilling this Lewinian imperative. Weisman speculates on the efficacy of early efforts to "unfreeze" the medical model approach to caring for people with dementia, arguing that demonstration projects such as the one at the Weiss Institute in Philadelphia and others elsewhere were instrumental in supporting change. Although this seems plausible, it seems unlikely to be a full explanation. Recall that design features of many of today's automobiles probably appeared decades ago in so-called concept cars, futuristic automobiles on display at Detroit automobile exhibits. Having a model is necessary but not sufficient to explain adoption. A more sanguine explanation is that North American society became sufficiently affluent in the past 20 or so years to support these more expensive buildings and services. A December 2001 American Association of Retired Persons (AARP) study estimated the monthly cost of private-pay nursing home care at ~$4,500, or more than $50,000 annually (AARP, 2001). This figure is nearly double the $28,000 median income level in 2000 for households of people aged 65+ (U.S. Census Bureau, 2000c).

Diffusion seems to move from well-to-do early adopters to the masses, as evidenced by the rapid growth in the adoption of the digital computer in the past 20 years. A visit to most publicly funded nursing home facilities (or inner-city schools) in the United States today will show that progress in low-resource sectors has been quite unimpressive. Patience is a virtue when trying to engineer change. Even successes take a long time to diffuse. My favorite example is the time for widespread diffusion of the facsimile (fax) machine. Alexander Bain patented the concept in 1843.

Most illuminating was Weisman's discussion of the decision process underlying the creation of model projects. He reminds us how long it takes to put together a new project: between 4 and 6 years. Also, he wisely counsels obtaining feedback from ongoing projects before replicating them. A fundamental principle for successful learning is the need for feedback. Yet, how many readers have had an architect knock on their door to ask what is going right and what is going wrong in their current dwelling? It seems to happen all the time in the highly competitive restaurant industry (when your server stops by shortly after delivering your food to ask how it tastes). In the case of dementia care, though, that feedback mechanism might be quite complex, requiring polling of residents, staff, and family caregivers responsible for residents. In summarizing the extant literature on what are effective designs, Weisman advances the guideline of using smaller units in order to avoid overstimulating conditions. What is a good number? That may depend on local conditions.

How to assess the impact of local living environments is the main contribution by Oswald in Chapter 9. Perhaps the most salient finding is the surprisingly weak link between physical and psychological attributes of housing. Citing data from a longitudinal study on aging, Oswald indicates that there are modest relationships between housing satisfaction and housing attributes, with relocation to better housing positively related to current satisfaction levels, particularly for those in the former East Germany. When surveying those with disabilities and impairments, Oswald notes that changes in housing might even be unwelcome, which probably illustrates the wisdom in the old saying, "Better the devil you know than the devil you don't." These results point to the multidimensional nature of housing. It suits many different wants and needs, and what appear to be good interventions may sometimes lead to unintended consequences. The relocation study he mentions points to the need to consider person-community integration, particularly the desire to strengthen family ties.

Some have argued that modern technology may provide a means to bridge the gaps existing between living environments and mobility systems for older adults, particularly for those with mobility impairments that make both public and private transportation systems difficult to use. Rather than bringing the person to the service, modern technology (e.g., the Internet) can help bring the service to the person.

Meyer and Mollenkopf review several surveys in Chapter 10 that point to attitudes and personal characteristics that may affect the diffusion of smart home technology. Not surprisingly, as is the case in North America, technology use shows age-related declines for the number of owned devices, as well as a male preference for more devices. Such relationships are moderated by several factors. For instance, living situation (2 heads are better than 1 in solving problems with modern devices?), education (better self-efficacy about learning ability?), and income (more resources lead to more purchases?) make independent contributions to increased technology use. Having children in the household also leads to greater technology use. (Do you need more technology to manage them, or are they the vectors for technology adoption?) Some attitudinal predictors were also found. Nonetheless, there is no real option to turn off the flow of technology, so we need to consider what older people want.

A second survey showed that security is a major interest of older adults. In North America there is an expression, "Your home is your castle." As history teaches us, castles were built first and foremost as security systems, ways of defending territories against marauding armies. As the state of many of the castles in Europe underscore (e.g., Schloss Heidelberg), a fixed defense eventually falls to a determined offense. (Even the caves in Afghanistan are no exception.) Hence, smart defense is something that everyone prizes today. Interestingly, younger adults are more sanguine about what smart homes might do for them. Given the relative instability of many computer operating systems (think of the Windows operating system before the year 2000), and the lack of experience of older adults with such systems, it is not that surprising to find a difference in expectations between young and old. A safe prediction is that tomorrow's older adult will be more realistic than today's about the likely impact of technology in the home.

I take a few exceptions with the predictions made in Chapter 19 by Wahl and Gitlin in relation to housing in the future (next 20–25 years) for Germany and the United States. It is safe to assume that housing will change slowly unless major disasters affect a large proportion of the existing housing stock. Housing stock and housing occupancy should be differentiated. Americans are reputed to relocate more frequently than the citizens of any other country. The U.S. Census Bureau (2000b) reports that 40% of renter households had moved in the prior 15 months before a decennial census and 10% of owner households had moved. The notion of establishing a familial home, one that is passed down from generation to generation, is quite foreign in the United States. Hence, the twin issues of retrofitting existing homes and relocating to new accommodations loom large for upcoming cohorts of baby boomers. It appears often to be the transition from single living to married life (or changes in childbearing status) that trigger initial home buying in the United States. Thus, designers and builders usually focus on appealing to young consumers. My hope is that designers and architects will pay greater heed to the life expectancy of homes for owners who may age in place and to the probability that a home will need to be functional for older adults as well as for younger ones.

MOBILITY ISSUES

For the most part, the emphasis in the chapters on mobility is on the automobile-driving environment. It is not surprising to see such emphasis, given the growing importance over the past 50 years of the personal automobile for mobility in both Germany and the United States. Of course, the growth in kilometers driven over time in both countries has also been accompanied by a growth in crashes; fortunately, however, improvements in transportation systems have resulted in declines in crashes per kilometer driven in both countries (e.g., see Evans, 1991). The challenge is to find ways to maintain or increase safety and to mitigate the losses in personal mobility when people must give up driving owing to physical or mental impairments associated with increased age.

Germany is "Americanizing" in its use of the private automobile, although older adults still make the majority of their trips by foot. Such pedestrian shopping contrasts enormously with that for North American seniors. As Stutts observes in Chapter 13, more than 90% of the trips made by older adults in the United States are taken in automobiles. In Chapter 12, Mollenkopf notes that older cohorts (particularly Easterners and women) are becoming drivers, and for many older adults (rural dwellers) the auto provides the key to independent living and access to shopping and health care. However, as Mollenkopf points out, perceptions of older adults are that the transportation environment is quite unfriendly to use. She concludes that there is a need to create flexible, user-centered options for outdoor mobility and to provide more neighborhood facilities and services.

Such research suggests the need to modify both the driving environment and the living environment. Encouraging civility in driver, cyclist, and pedestrian populations could be an interesting challenge. An even bigger challenge is providing incentives to commercial and service sectors to relocate facilities to make them more accessible to local populations. Perhaps technology can be used to make the services come to the user (e.g., telemedicine, Web-based shopping). On the other hand, perhaps there will also be a need to support relocation opportunities for older adults as they become frailer in order to enable them to move from rural to urban settings.

As Stutts points out, Americans love their cars and have increased their driving over the years. Older adults have far fewer crashes than other age groups, because they drive less, but they die more frequently in crashes, pointing to physical frailty as a risk in crashes. Crash types for seniors point to cognitive process and attention problems and slowing in response time. Given demographic trends, baby boomer cohorts represent a major challenge in the years ahead for traffic safety. Road safety has increased for all drivers over the past 20 years, but we may need to maintain these trends with training and design changes. Finding effective interventions is currently an important research area, but time is not on our side given the rapidly approaching wave of older baby boom drivers.

In Chapter 14, Schlag indicates that, aside from pedestrian and bicyclist crashes, German statistics about crashes resemble American data. As usual, young adults are responsible for most of the deaths and injuries incurred on the road, but when an older driver is involved in a multivehicle crash he or she is much more likely to be deemed at fault. On-road tests reveal useful data about age trends in driving behaviors, underlining the perceptual/cognitive/psychomotor problems of older drivers: lane change and red light infractions. However, as others have observed, the degree of relationship between various laboratory psychophysical test measures and driving performance (on road tests) is low. Although some recent attention-capacity tests, such as useful field of view (Owsley, Ball, Sloane, Roenker, & Bruni, 1991), have shown moderate predictive power for crash occurrence, we are fortunate that crashes occur relatively infrequently for most drivers. However, the high risk of injury for cyclists and pedestrians points to the dilemma of license loss by seniors. They may be less safe when forced to use other forms of mobility such as travel by foot and bicycle. Is that a fair tradeoff to consider against the increased risk to themselves and others if they continue to drive?

Rudinger and Jansen note in Chapter 15 that although some older drivers recognize changing capabilities and adapt (the so-called functional ones), others do not (dysfunctional) though they do not account for a large percentage of older drivers (~6%).

Although crash rates do not vary much among the driver groups, the dysfunctional drivers have more at-fault crashes. Furthermore, such drivers were also classified as living more risk-taking lifestyles generally. Such studies suggest that targeted interventions may be warranted for so-called high-risk older drivers. However, more research may be needed to determine whether there are behavioral concomitants for dysfunctional drivers in terms of actual driving performance. Such drivers suffer from what the cognitive literature terms poor calibration or metacognition; that is, they do not accurately perceive the gap between their abilities and environmental demands, and they fail to modulate their behavior accordingly. Some interesting questions arise. Should we screen drivers for what appear to be personality traits such as risk taking? Given that so-called dysfunctional drivers did not experience higher crash rates than those in other categories, it would be difficult to argue for this action. Is poor calibration a warning sign of dementia?

Willis, in Chapter 18, argues that we need to consider a broader framework for driving intervention by using such dimensions as age, target of the intervention, and the domain of the intervention. After proposing age as a factor, Willis notes that chronological age may be inferior to functional capacity as a way of categorizing potential targets for intervention. That is indeed a wise choice.

In my home state of Florida, it is political anathema to propose age as a distinguishing characteristic in driver licensing legislation, at least for older drivers. It is not, however, heretical to propose entitling people to expanded social benefits based on age. At the risk of complicating things, I would add another important dimension to Willis's framework: financial. What are the costs and benefits of intervening in the sphere of mobility? Evaluating the effectiveness of an intervention eventually comes down to establishing cost effectiveness. Which intervention leads to the greatest increase in safety: better training of drivers or better construction of road systems? Which leads to the greatest increase in comfortable mobility: better personal vehicle design or better public transit systems? With political leaders ever mindful of the balance between taxing and spending, the research community has an important role to play in promoting better decisions about resource allocation.

In Chapter 21, Kroj notes the potential problems of having an even more diverse older population in the future, particularly from the perspective of technology awareness. There are gaps in knowledge and attitudes between current generations of older and younger adults, and these may widen over time. A good example might be found in the current studies of age and technology use in the United States by the Department of Labor. Whereas about 50% of households owned a computer in the year 2000, and over 40% had Internet access, for those age 65+ the figures drop to less than 30% and less than 15%, respectively (Newburger, 2001). How to prevent a "mobility divide" from widening between young adults and older adults is going to be of increasing importance as baby boom generations reach old age.

In Chapter 20, Waller advises us of a larger context for mobility (and housing environments), namely that of intergenerational conflict. As she points out, in the United States there has been a remarkable shift in public subsidies for seniors, probably at the expense of children. To fill in the picture, though, it is worth noting that the increase in poor circumstances for children probably results in large measure from the increase in single-parent families headed by women. Ironically, what we may be observing is a transfer of resources from younger to older women. Waller makes a salient observation about the necessity of providing better transportation options for older adults who want to continue participating in the paid labor force. I would argue that the solution to the Social Security problem—how a diminishing population of future workers can support the forthcoming increased population of baby boomers—is in inducing longer-living adults to be longer-working adults. Whether this will be solved with transportation improvements or technologies such as telecommuting remains to be seen. It is far less expensive to transport information via streams of electrons and photons than via vehicles filled with biological entities composed of electrons and their very costly-to-transport protons and neutrons.

MOBILITY DESIGN AND REDESIGN

Among the points that Jovanis raises in his review of engineering aspects of road design in Chapter 16 is the importance of what to optimize. He gives the example of using in-vehicle guidance systems to select routes for drivers. Normally, such systems find the shortest route between 2 points. Instead, perhaps conditioned by who the driver is, they could be programmed to find the least hazardous route between 2 points. Routes that avoid left turns, for instance, could minimize a major risk for crashes by older drivers. (My mother recently experienced a failure in the power steering system in her car that made left turns extremely demanding physically. She had to solve the problem of picking a route from the shopping center to her home that maximized the use of right turns.) Routes that take into account start time and amount of daylight available could minimize night driving.

Similarly, there is a need to consider optimizing safety and comfort differently for younger and older adults. As an example, Jovanis notes the trend to restrict automobiles from city centers, particularly in Europe, to provide safer pedestrian shopping experiences. One problem that arises, though, is that such restrictions force people to park farther from their intended destination. This may seriously inconvenience those with mobility impairments, predominantly very old adults. Similarly, he notes that age-related differences in preferences for display characteristics might dictate that different collision-avoidance system interfaces be presented to younger versus older drivers.

In Chapter 17, Färber outlines some issues for redesigning the automobile from the perspective of using technology to compensate for weaknesses in people's abilities to drive induced by aging processes. One of the main challenges of redesigning the automobile for older driver capabilities is overcoming perceptions of designers about ease of use, and not using designs that put the old and the disabled together for fear of stigmatizing the product. Färber lists and describes a variety of cutting-edge technologies: vision systems, transfer systems, emergency systems, brake assistant systems, cruise control, stop-and-go assistants, parking assistants, and curve lighting with GPS. (He also makes a powerful case for usability testing with his description of a quite unintuitive music system.) All of these technologies are expected to improve the performance of drivers, particularly under adverse circumstances such as poor weather and night driving. As a bonus, such assistive devices for cars can be expected to compensate for age-related negative changes in vision, hearing, reaction time, and attention.

Some critical questions are not well addressed in this developing field of automotive technology. Can these systems show both improved safety and comfort compared to current systems? According to Charness and Bosman,

> There is an interesting ethical dilemma facing designers. Should they succeed in making the driving environment more comfortable for older drivers, whose risk of accident on a per-mileage basis is higher than that of middle-age drivers, more older drivers will be killed and injured as they are encouraged to drive greater distances. (1992, p. 529).

Another critical question lies in the acceptability of these systems to older adults and to adults in general. Will consumers trust them? Without adequate usability testing to ensure effectiveness, the answer may be no (Kantowitz, Hanowski, & Kantowitz, 1997). Furthermore, are such technologies equally beneficial to older adults and younger adults? Preliminary investigations suggest that the answer is not straightforward (Dingus et al., 1997a, 1997b) and depends on what the alternatives are. You may well be safer dividing attention between the road and a GPS navigation system than between the road and a traditional paper map.

CONCLUDING REMARKS

I feel rather safe in arguing that more research that evaluates the impact of the living environment and mobility systems is needed in both Germany and the United States. Concepts such as person-environment fit and person-community integration require better operational definitions with an eye toward evaluating their consequences. What exactly should we be optimizing? There are many candidates: life satisfaction, housing satisfaction, mobility satisfaction, and social interaction. Cost effectiveness is of critical importance to consider given the current costs for constructing and staffing both living environments and transportation systems.

How do we handle competing interests among generations given competing demands for resources? In the time between the conference held in Heidelberg in the spring of 2001, which led to this volume, and the formulation of this chapter at the end of 2001, the world economy had sunk into a recession, and in my home state of Florida we had just finished putting in place current-year budget cuts where rancorous arguments arose between proponents of child care and elder care.

Some of the challenges for living environments and mobility exist at the system level; that is, mobility options can constrain the location of housing or commercial buildings as well as their design. Building new subdivisions in suburban locations often strains old transportation systems and eventually leads to the creation of new ones.

Significant attention is needed in order to make wise societal investments before the wave of baby boom cohorts washes up on the shores of old age. Scientific study is our best bet in the long run, but in the meanwhile, we need to consider establishing a database of "best practices" for design and make it available to a wider audience of potential consumers. As this volume indicates, there are robust data sets on living environments and mobility systems in both Germany and the United States which can be used to guide better policy formation. If such knowledge is diffused effectively, the resulting improvements in housing and transportation systems could play a critical role in enhancing both person-environment fit and person-community integration.

NOTE

Preparation of this chapter was supported in part by a grant from the National Institute on Aging, NIA 1 PO1 AG17211-03, for project CREATE (Center for Research and Education on Aging and Technology Enhancement).

REFERENCES

American Association of Retired Persons (AARP). (2001). Most Americans unprepared for long-term care costs. Available from http://www.aarp.org/press/2001/nr121101. html.

Charness, N., & Bosman, E. A. (1992). Age and human factors. In F. I. M. Craik & T. A. Salthouse (Eds.), *The handbook of aging and cognition* (pp. 495–551). Hillsdale, NJ: Erlbaum.

Charness, N., Park, D. C., & Sabel, B. A. (Eds.) (2001). *Communication, technology and aging: Opportunities and challenges for the future.* New York: Springer.

Dingus, T. A., Hulse, M. C., Mollenhauer, M. A., Fleischman, R. N., McGehee, D. V., & Manakkal, N. (1997a). Effects of age, system experience, and navigation technique on driving with an Advanced Traveler Information System. *Human Factors, 39,* 177–199.

Dingus, T. A., McGehee, D. V., Manakkal, N., Jhans, S. K., Carney, C., & Hankey, J. M. (1997b). Human factors field evaluation of automotive headway maintenance/collision warning devices. *Human Factors, 39,* 216–229.

Evans, L. (1991). *Traffic safety and the driver.* New York: Van Nostrand Reinhold.

Kantowitz, B. H., Hanowski, R. J., & Kantowitz, S. C. (1997). Driver acceptance of unreliable traffic information in familiar and unfamiliar settings. *Human Factors, 39,* 164–176.

Langer, E. J., & Rodin, J. (1976). The effects of choice and enhanced personal responsibility for the aged: A field experiment in an institutional setting. *Journal of Personality and Social Psychology, 34,* 191–198.

Lawton, M. P. (1977). The impact of the environment on aging and behavior. In J. E. Birren & K. W. Schaie (Eds.), *Handbook of the psychology of aging* (pp. 276–301). New York: Van Nostrand Reinhold.

Newburger, E. (2001). Home computers and Internet use in the United States: August 2000. Available from http://www.census.gov/prod/2001pubs/p23-207.pdf.

Newell, A., & Simon, H. A. (1972). *Human problem solving.* Englewood Cliffs, NJ: Prentice-Hall.

Owsley, C., Ball, K., Sloane, M. E., Roenker, D. L., & Bruni, J. R. (1991). Visual/cognitive correlates of vehicle accidents in older drivers. *Psychology and Aging, 6,* 403–415.

Sainsbury, R. S., & Coristine, M. (1986). Affective discrimination in moderately to severely demented patients. *Canadian Journal on Aging, 5,* 99–104.

U.S. Census Bureau (2000a). Historical census of housing tables crowding. Available from http://www.census.gov/hhes/www/housing/census/historic/crowding.html. Accessed March 3, 2002.

U.S. Census Bureau (2000b). Historical census of housing tables recent movers. Available from http://www.census.gov/hhes/www/housing/census/historic/movers.html. Accessed March 3, 2002.

U.S. Census Bureau. (2000c). Income 2000. Available from http://www.census.gov/hhes/income/income00/inctab1.html.

U.S. Department of Commerce. (2002). A nation online: How Americans are expanding their use of the Internet. Available from http://www.ntia.doc.gov/ntiahome/dn/nationonline_020502.pdf.

Vicente, K. J., & Wang, J. H. (1998). An ecological theory of expertise effects in memory recall. *Psychological Review, 105,* 33–57.

Appendix: Complete List of Participants of the Conference "Aging in the Community: Living Arrangements and Mobility," Held in Heidelberg, Germany, April 4–6, 2001

Abeles, Ronald P., Ph.D.
Associate Director for the Behavioral and
  Social Research/National Institutes of
  Health
Gateway Building, Rm. 2C234
7201 Wisconsin Ave., MSC 9205
Bethesda, MD 20892-9205
USA
AbelesR@OD.NIH.GOV

**Aner, Kirsten, Dipl. agr./Dipl.
  Soz.päd.**
Universität-Gesamthochschule Kassel
Arnold-Bode-Str. 10
34109 Kassel
Germany
aner@uni-kassel.de

Bondar, Albina, Ph.D.
Max Planck Institute for Human
  Development and Education
Lentzeallee 94
14195 Berlin
Germany
bondar@mpib-berlin-mpg.de

Breimesser, Fritz, Dipl.-Ing.
Siemens AG ZFE T IF H
Postfach 3220
91050 Erlangen
Germany
fritz.breimesser@erls.siemens.de

Burkhardt, Jon, Ph.D.
WESTAT Senior Study Director
1650 Research Blvd, RP 4010
Rockville, Maryland 20850
USA
burkhaj@Westat.com

Carder, Paula C., Ph.D.
Oregon Health Sciences University
Kaiser Center for Health Research
3800 N. Interstate
Portland, OR, 97227-1110
USA
paula.c.carder@kpchr.org

Charness, Neil, Ph.D.
Professor, Florida State University
Psychology Department
Tallahassee, FL 32306-1270
USA
charness@psy.fsu.edu

Chaudhury, Habib, Ph.D.
University of Wisconsin-Milwaukee
School of Architecture & Urban
Planning
5004 Betty Jean Way
Columbia, MO 65203
USA
chaudhury@missouri.edu

Engeln, Arnd, Dr.
Technische Universität Dresden Fakultät
für Verkehrswissenschaften
Mommsenstr. 13
01069 Dresden
Germany
arndengeln@hotmail.com

Fachinger, Beate, Dr.
Bundesministerium für Familien,
Senioren, Frauen und Jugend
Postfach 12 06 09
53048 Bonn
Germany

Färber, Berthold, Prof. Dr.
Universität BW München Institut für
Arbeitswissenschaft
Werner-Heisenberg-Weg 39
85625 Neubiberg
Germany
berthold.faerber@unibw-muenchen.de

Fozard, James L., Ph.D.
President, Florida Gerontological
Research and Training Services
2980 Tangerine Terrace
Palm Harbor, FL 34684-3940
USA
fozsingr@gte.net

Freund, Katherine
President and Executive Director,
Independent Transportation Network
309 Cumberland Avenue
Portland, ME 04101
USA
kfreund@itninc.org

Gitlin, Laura N., Ph.D.
Thomas Jefferson University
Community and Homecare Research
Division
130 S. 9th Street, Suite 513
Philadelphia, PA 19107
USA
Laura.Gitlin@mail.tju.edu

Großjohann, Klaus
Managing Director, Kuratorium Deutsche
Altershilfe
An der Pauluskirche 3
50677 Köln
Germany
Josefina.Amir@kda.de

Grünendahl, Martin, Prof. Dr.
Dipl.-Gerontol., Westsächsische
Hochschule Zwickau (FH)
FB Gesundheits- und
Pflegewissenschaften
08066 Zwickau
Germany
martin.gruenendahl@fh-zwickau.de

Heeg, Sibylle, Dipl.-Ing.
Universität Stuttgart Institut für
    öffentliche Bauten und Entwerfen
Keplerstr. 11
70174 Stuttgart
Germany
sheeg@gmx.de

Jansen, Elke, Dr.
Universität Bonn Projekt FRAME, ZEM
Römerstr. 164
53117 Bonn
Germany
Elke.Jansen@uni-bonn.de

Jovanis, Paul P., Ph.D.
Professor, Pennsylvania State University
    Department Head, Civil and
    Environmental Engineering
212 Sackett Building
University Park, PA 16802-1408
USA
ppj2@psu.edu

Kalavar, Jyotsna, Ph.D.
Penn State University
New Kensington Human Development &
    Family Studies
3550 Seventh Street Road
New Kensington, PA 15069
USA
jmk18@psu.edu

Khoschlessan, Darius, Dr.
Senio Heidelberg
Bergheimer Straße 19
69115 Heidelberg
Germany
khoschlessan@senio.de

Kroj, Günter, Dr.
Bundesanstalt für Straßenwesen
Postfach 10 01 50
51401 Bergisch Gladbach
Germany
kroj@bast.de

Kruse, Andreas, Prof. Dr.
Ruprecht-Karls-Universität Heidelberg
Institut für Gerontologie
Bergheimer Str. 20
69115 Heidelberg
Germany
Andreas.Kruse@urz.uni-heidelberg.de

Küting, Hans. J., Dr.
DaimlerChrysler AG HPC: G 202
70546 Stuttgart
Germany
hansjosef.kueting@DaimlerChrysler.com

Meyer, Sibylle, Dr.
Berliner Institut für Sozialforschung (BIS)
Ansbacher Str. 5
10787 Berlin
Germany
s.meyer@bis-berlin.com

Mollenkopf, Heidrun, Dr.
Deutsches Zentrum für Alternsforschung
    an der Universität Heidelberg
Bergheimer Straße 20
69115 Heidelberg
Germany
Mollenkopf@dzfa.uni-heidelberg.de

Oswald, Frank, Dr.
Deutsches Zentrum für Alternsforschung
    an der Universität Heidelberg
Bergheimer Straße 20
69115 Heidelberg
Germany
Oswald@dzfa.uni-heidelberg.de

Rapp, Michael, MD
Max Planck Institute for Human
    Development and Education
Lentzeallee 94
14195 Berlin
Germany
rapp@mpib-berlin.mpg.de

Regnier, Victor, FAIA, Ph.D.
Professor, University of Southern
    California
Andrus Gerontology Center
10610 Lindbrook Drive
Los Angeles, CA 90024
USA
regnier@rcf-fs.usc.edu

Rowles, Graham D., Ph.D.
University of Kentucky
Sanders-Brown Institute of Gerontology
Lexington, KY 40536-0230
USA
growl@uky.edu

Rudinger, Georg, Prof. Dr.
Psychologisches Institut der Universität
    Bonn
Römerstr. 164
53117 Bonn
Germany
rudinger@uni-bonn.de

Schaie, K. Warner, Ph.D.
Evan Pugh Professor of Human
    Development and Psychology
Director, Gerontology Center
Pennsylvania State University
135 E. Nittany Avenue
405 Marion Place
State College, PA 16801-5363
USA
kws@psu.edu

Schlag, Bernhard, Prof. Dr.
Technische Universität Dresden Fakultät
    für Verkehrswissenschaften "Friedrich
    List"—Verkehrspsychologie
Hettnerstr. 1
01062 Dresden
Germany
schlag@rcs.urz.tu-dresden.de

Stahl, Sidney, M., Ph.D.
National Institute on Aging/National
    Institutes of Health Behavioral and
    Social Research Program
Gateway Building # 533
7201 Wisconsin Ave.
Bethesda, MD 20892-9205
USA
Sidney_Stahl@nih.gov

**Steinhagen-Thiessen, Elisabeth, Prof.
Dr. med.**
EGZB—Ev. Geriatriezentrum Berlin
    Campus Virchow Klinikum der
    Humboldt Universität Berlin
Reinickendorfer Str. 61
13347 Berlin
Germany
elisabeth.steinhagen-thiessen@charite.de

Stutts, Jane C., Ph.D.
University of North Carolina
Highway Safety Research Center
CB# 3430
Chapel Hill, NC 27599-3430
USA
jane_stutts@unc.edu

Wahl, Hans-Werner, Prof. Dr.
Deutsches Zentrum für Alternsforschung
    an der Universität Heidelberg
Bergheimer Straße 20
69115 Heidelberg
Germany
Wahl@dzfa.uni-heidelberg.de

Waller, Patricia F., Ph.D.
Professor, University of Michigan
    Transportation Research Institute
1779 Crawford Dairy Road
Chapel Hill, NC 27516
USA
pwaller@umich.edu

Weisman, Gerald D., Ph.D.
Professor, School of Architecture and
    Urban Planning
University of Wisconsin
P.O. Box 413
Milwaukee, WI 53201
USA
Gweisman@csd.uwm.edu

Willis, Sherry L., Ph.D.
Professor, Pennsylvania State University
Department of Human Development and
    Family Studies
135 E. Nittany Avenue, Suite 405
State College, PA 16801
USA
slw@psu.edu

Zaccai, Gianfranco
Design Continuum Inc.
1220 Washington Street
West Newton, MA 02465-2147
USA
ffridlund@dcontinuum.com

Index

ABS. *See* Anti-Block Systems (ABS)
Accessibility in public infrastructure, 181, 187–189, 190
Access to services, 184, 325
Action research, 162–163, 167, 168, 170–171, 329
Activities
  participation in, 20, 22, 25
  physical, 22, 67–68, 105, 115
Activities of daily living. *See* ADLs
Adaptations
  behavioral, 65
  environmental, 36–37, 90–91
  process of, 136–137
Adaptive devices, 31, 70
Adjustment strategies, 92
ADLs (activities of daily living)
  difficulties with, 101
  help with, 32–33, 111–112, 290–291
  in the home, 55–56, 137
  maintaining competence in, 136, 323–324, 325
Advanced public transit systems (APTS), 243
Advanced traveler information systems (ATIS), 242. *See also* Route guidance; Technology
AEMEÏS research project, 221–222, 225–226
Age-related declines, 34, 41
Age-targeted communities, 106–107

Aging
  demographic shift, 302–304
  gains and losses from, 52–53
  patterns of, 51–52, 289, 313
  perception of, 53
  physical, 31–32, 33–34, 325
  successful, 220
  theory of, 6–7, 64
Aging in place
  effect of competence on, 142–143
  enhancing, 73, 110–111, 132, 295–296
  as a goal, 66–67, 82, 139–140, 294, 331–332
  and living environments, 281, 282
Air bags, 245
Alzheimer's disease
  care for, 9, 11, 102–103, 327
  and driving, 200, 265–266
  economic costs of, 164
  and memory, 83
  See also Dementia
Anti-Block Systems (ABS), 251–252, 257
Artifacts
  importance of, 84–86, 91, 169–170
  transference of, 92–93
Assisted housing, 119–120. *See also* Assisted living
Assisted living
  cost of, 286
  expectations for, 140
  generally, 101–103